"Norman Geisler has always been a 'trail-blazer' for people who want to speak out about their faith, and *Creation and the Courts* blazes a trail into the truth of creation vs. evolution. Through his firsthand personal experience in the 'Scopes II' trial and his exhaustive research into other similar trials, Geisler will draw you into the world of our legal system, better preparing you to address issues of creation and evolution."

—Josh D. McDowell,
author and speaker

"As both an eyewitness in the courtroom and a highly respected scholar in the classroom, Norman Geisler provides a unique perspective to one of the most critical discussions of our time. From the *Scopes* trial to the recent *Dover* case, Geisler summarizes and counters the often unexamined assumptions left in their wake. This is an invaluable resource on the subject, and I enthusiastically recommend it."

—Ravi Zacharias,
author and speaker

The concept of "intelligent design is being debated by jurists and scientists as well as the media all across America. Dr. Norman Geisler's *Creation and the Courts* adds to those discussions the important perspective of a philosopher, theologian, and biblical scholar. Of all the superb monographs written by Geisler, this one may be the most important. Every pastor and theologian should read this volume this year."

—Paige Patterson,
President, Southwestern Baptist Theological Seminary

"Norman Geisler has provided a compilation and commentary on the issue of evolution, public education, and the courts that will serve as an important resource for decades to come. Dr. Geisler convincingly shows that much of the debate over this issue is a jurisprudential mess resulting from philosophically confused though well-meaning scientists and jurists. He offers just the sort of clarity this debate requires."

—Francis J. Beckwith,
Associate Professor of Church-State Studies, Baylor University,
and author of *Law, Darwinism, and Public Education*

Creation & the Courts

Creation & the Courts

Eighty Years of Conflict
in the Classroom and the Courtroom

With Never Before Published Testimony from the "Scopes II" Trial

Norman L. Geisler

CROSSWAY BOOKS

A PUBLISHING MINISTRY OF
GOOD NEWS PUBLISHERS
WHEATON, ILLINOIS

Cover design: Josh Dennis
Cover art: Courtesy of Bridgeman Art Library; typewriter illustration, iStock Photos
First printing 2007

Printed in the United States of America

Library of Congress Cataloging-in-Publication Data

Geisler, Norman L.
   Creation and the courts : eighty years of conflict in the classroom and the court-
room : with never before published testimony from the "Scopes II" Trial / Norman L.
Geisler.
      p. cm.
   Includes bibliographical references and index.
   ISBN-13: 978-1-58134-836-1 (tpb)
   ISBN-10: 1-58134-836-3
   1. Creationism—Study and teaching—Law and legislation—United States. 2.
Evolution—Study and teaching—Law and legislation—United States. 3. Religion in
public schools—United States. I. Title.

KF4208.5.S34G45 2007
344.73'0796—dc22

                                     2006032679

SH 17 16 15 14 13 12 11 10 09 08 07
12 11 10 9 8 7 6 5 4 3 2 1

Contents

Foreword

Duane T. Gish[1]

N|o one is better prepared than Dr. Norman Geisler to write an account of the Arkansas creation/evolution trial of 1981. Geisler was not only present during the trial; he was the lead witness for the creationist side and one of its most brilliant witnesses. His testimony, in my view (I was present during the entire trial), effectively demolished the most important thrust of the case by the ACLU. Unfortunately, in my opinion, no testimony, and no effort by any team of lawyers, no matter how brilliant, could have won the case for the creationist side. Judge Overton accepted the ACLU mind-set that anything that hints of God, even scientific evidence for creation, must be barred from public schools. Secular humanism will be our official state-sanctioned religion, if Judge Overton's decision is allowed to stand.

Geisler's account of the trial (see chapter 3) is carefully and thoroughly documented. His description of the actual course of the trial is interesting, and his critique of Judge Overton's official decision is incisive,

---

1. Dr. Gish, a leading scientist defender of creation, was present for the entire 1981 "Scopes II" trial in Arkansas. He was an expert advisor to the defense and is a noted author and debater on behalf of scientific creationism. With only minor editing, this is the foreword he wrote for *The Creator in the Courtroom* (Norman L. Geisler with A. F. Brooke II and Mark J. Keough [Milford, Mich.: Mott Media, 1982]).

thorough, and accurate. Geisler's account is in refreshing contrast to the usually (though not always) distorted and biased accounts that appeared in the mass media and a relief from the sophistry that appeared in so many scientific journals. No eyewitness account can be accurate in all details, but I can certainly recommend this book's fair and thorough account of the famous 1981 Arkansas creation/evolution trial.

Preface

Wayne Frair[1]

Geisler on the Stand

In *McLean v. Arkansas Board of Education* (1982) the court considered an Arkansas statute that required balanced teaching of *both* evolution and creation when the subject of origins was discussed. After a two-week trial, December 7–17, 1981, the court ruled on January 5, 1982 that the statute was unconstitutional because it essentially would promote a biblical religious view. This Arkansas statute was a forerunner of the subsequent one in the state of Louisiana.

The December 1981 trial effectively was a travesty of justice, as is made clear in the only book by a person who was there for the entire trial (Norman Geisler, *The Creator in the Courtroom,* 1982). The federal court judge, William Overton, was from the start biased against the defense.

I personally arrived in the courtroom on Friday, December 11, the final of five days of testimony by the plaintiffs, who were represented

---

1. Dr. Frair was present at the Arkansas *McLean* trial (1981–1982). He was an expert witness who spoke in favor of teaching both evolution and creation. Dr. Frair is a longtime science teacher, author, member of the prestigious American Association for the Advancement of Science, and a world-renowned expert on turtles.

by the American Civil Liberties Union (ACLU). The first witness for
the defense, Dr. Geisler, was on the witness stand in the afternoon of
December 11. At that time I was sitting next to Dr. Duane Gish, who
was known as a leading creationist and an unexcelled debater in the
modern creationist movement.[2] Geisler's presentation was superb (see
chapter 4), and at its end Gish was absolutely exuberant (see foreword).
In no uncertain words he declared to me that Geisler successfully had
demolished every one of the arguments presented by ACLU witnesses
during their preceding five days of testimony.

Then in the cross-examination (see appendix 4), ACLU lawyer
Anthony Siano began to mock Dr. Geisler based not on his court
testimony but rather on some comments dealing with spaceships that
Geisler had made in a pretrial deposition. Geisler tried in vain to be
straightforward and honest as the cunning lawyer goaded him with
superfluous mockery—a pitiful miscarriage of justice that was not
opposed by Judge Overton.

My Testimony

On the following Monday I had the opportunity to be on the witness stand for about one and a half hours. Coverage of my testimony is
given in chapter 7 of *The Creator in the Courtroom*. I said that Arkansas
was "on the very cutting edge of an educational movement" that would
improve the quality of U.S. education. Without hesitation I added that if
Charles Darwin were alive today he would be a creationist. I backed up
that statement with quotations from L. S. Berg, A. H. Clark, H. Nilsson,
G. A. Kerkut, and S. Lovtrup. These date back to the 1920s.

The final material I used was from the famous British paleontologist
Colin Patterson, who had spoken about a month earlier (November 5,
1981) in New York City at the American Museum of Natural History
(AMNH). Patterson had expressed strong feelings against evolution,
and I quoted from his talk. The ACLU lawyer objected, but fortunately

2. See Marvin L. Lubenow, *From Fish to Gish* (San Diego, Calif.: Creation-Life, 1983).

Judge Overton overruled because I had been there for that AMNH presentation.

I felt that my testimony would have a positive impact for truth in opposition to what had been heard from the plaintiffs and their witnesses. They all had been coached thoroughly to stress two issues. These were (1) there is no science supporting a creation position, and (2) creation is religion, which should not be intruded into science. They said this repeatedly, even though the Arkansas law at issue in the trial prohibited religious instruction and clearly defines "creation science" as "the scientific evidences for creation and inferences from these scientific evidences."

Newspapers and magazines across the country thrived on articles about the trial—some very fair and others misleading (see appendices 1 and 2). A generally quite accurate newspaper coverage of the whole trial was written by reporter Cal Beisner and appeared in the weekly *Pea Ridge (Arkansas) County Times,* Wednesday, December 30, 1981. One very biased and inaccurate report was written by Roger Lewin and was published in the January 8, 1982 issue of *Science,*[3] arguably the world's leading weekly publication of scientific information. A major portion of the report was a gross misrepresentation of my testimony. After reading Lewin's article I wrote a letter to the magazine, from which I quote:

> Roger Lewin's treatment (*Science* 215:142) . . . of the Little Rock creation trial falls somewhat short of the quality of reporting I would consider the readers of *Science* should expect. . . .
>
> My presentation until cross-examination emphasized scientific data; and among other things I endeavored to make clear that from literature dating back into the 1920's and up to the present time there is a body of information published by respected scientists who have theorized and speculated in ways more consistent with a creation model than a macroevolutionary model. A Russian book, *Nomogenesis or Evolution Determined by Law* by Leo S. Berg (original edition 1922), was republished by Massachusetts Institute of Technology Press in 1969. The [foreword] to the recent edition was written by Theodosius Dob-

---

3. Roger Lewin, "Where Is the Science in Creation Science?" *Science* 215 (January 8, 1982): 141-146.

zhansky, who described Berg as "one of the outstanding intellects among
Russian scientists" and further that "the depth as well as the amplitude
of his scholarship were remarkable." (p. xi) In this 477-page book Berg
demonstrates that living things have developed polyphyletically.

There have been other scientific (and "non-religious") writings including [British] Kerkut's *Implications of Evolution,* Pergamon Press, 1960,
which have cast doubt upon a monophyletic model. I quoted from this
book at the trial because much of what Kerkut says currently is very
pertinent. For instance:

> Most students become acquainted with many of the current con-
> cepts in biology whilst still at school and at an age when most
> people are, on the whole, uncritical. Then when they come to
> study the subject in more detail they have in their minds several
> half-truths and misconceptions which tend to prevent them from
> coming to a fresh appraisal of the situation. In addition, with a
> uniform pattern of education most students tend to have the same
> sort of educational background and so in conversation and discus-
> sion they accept common fallacies and agree on matters based on
> these fallacies.
>
> It would seem a good principle to encourage the study of "sci-
> entific heresies." There is always the danger that a reader might be
> seduced by one of these heresies but the danger is neither as great
> nor as serious as the danger of having scientists brought up in a
> type of mental strait-jacket or of taking them so quickly through
> a subject that they have no time to analyze and digest the material
> they have "studied." A careful perusal of the heresies will also in-
> dicate the facts in favour of the currently accepted doctrines, and
> if the evidence against a theory is overwhelming and if there is no
> other satisfactory theory to take its place we shall just have to say
> that we do not yet know the answer.
>
> There is a theory which states that many living animals can be
> observed over the course of time to undergo changes so that new
> species are formed. This can be called the "Special Theory of Evo-
> lution" and can be demonstrated in certain cases by experiments.
> On the other hand there is the theory that all the living forms in
> the world have arisen from a single source which itself came from
> an inorganic form. This theory can be called the "General Theory

of Evolution" and the evidence that supports it is not sufficiently strong to allow us to consider it as anything more than a working hypothesis. It is not clear whether the changes that bring about speciation are of the same nature as those that brought about the development of new phyla. The answer will be found by future experimental work and not by dogmatic assertions that the General Theory of Evolution must be correct because there is nothing else that will satisfactorily take its place. (156–157).

It certainly is true that there are differences of opinion among creationists as there are among evolutionists, but both creation and evolution models can be presented in a broad sense within biology classes without this being a "religious" exercise. Neither evolutionists nor creationists need be paranoid regarding this issue, but we should realize that in our country we enjoy freedom *of* religion, not freedom *from* religion.

The causes of science education will not be served well by name-calling and misrepresentation or distortion of the ideas being presented by those with whom we disagree. It is true that most scientists today believe that macroevolution is a well-established concept; however, for improving scholarship and understanding, especially those promoting only macroevolution probably will profit from perceptively heeding what responsible creationists are trying to say.

The editors of *Science* did not print any portion of my letter or even acknowledge having received it. Their published write-up of my testimony at the Arkansas trial was so inaccurate that I wondered if the author, Roger Lewin, even was in the courtroom when I gave testimony.

I had written the letter to *Science* rather quickly and soon realized that there was a lot more I could have said; so I composed the following to present a more accurate account of what I actually had said during the trial:

I have been researching in biochemical taxonomy of reptiles since 1960, and did discuss some of my research from the witness stand. This write-up mentions three books which were earlier ones referred to; however I also quoted from a 1960 book, a 1969 book and other literature reaching into the 70's. These authors basically did not just have some misgivings about some aspects of evolutionary theory, they had serious objections.

My own studies on erythrocyte size indicated that an evolutionary progression is anything but obvious from the facts. Blood cells have not become smaller as animals have climbed the evolutionary tree because the largest cells are found among amphibians and some birds have larger cells than some fish.

With regard to the matter of my stating that considerable progress has been made in past decades, this is completely obvious. In my cross-examination ACLU lawyer Bruce Ennis mentioned in a somewhat casual way several fields of endeavor; and he said: "Haven't we made progress in these?" The answer was obviously, "Yes;" and I was not thinking of myself in an adversarial relationship to the lawyer at this point. I recognize now that I should have showed how in these fields the evidence has pointed more toward a creationist position than a macroevolutionary one. For instance, genetic drift. Genetic drift does not help in understanding macroevolution. It is one of their problems, because it runs counter to what would be anticipated on the basis of natural selection. . . . So what to me was an extremely minor concession to this lawyer has been made to look as though it were a big concession on my part.

During my testimony I indeed stressed the "limited change model"; and I referred to the natural groups which are found in nature. Act 590 used the term "kinds". This concept, by the way, is not a new one because it was commonly held 150 years ago. In fact, a recent book (Pitman, Michael. *Adam And Evolution.* Grand Rapids, MI: Baker Book House: 1984) presents nature as consisting of archetypes, which was the term used more than a century ago.

The question about the number of these "kinds" is a very good one. At present we do not know. I would estimate perhaps somewhere in the vicinity of 8,000. It is not easy to be concrete regarding "kinds" any more than it is for systematists to give a definition of any of the taxonomic categories other than species. One cannot readily define an order except in relation to class and family; and I tried to make this clear to the court. Our taxonomic schemes are human inventions; they are not rigid, but they are practical. A scientist who understands taxonomy is not deeply concerned about having precise definitions for his categories. The same holds for the "kinds" concept.

As a matter of fact, I did define "kind" in terms of reproduction, which is at least a partially acceptable definition. If organisms can reproduce hybrids, they may be considered to belong to the same kind. (See Lester, Lane P., Bohlin, Raymond G. *The Natural Limits to Biological Change.* Grand Rapids. MI: Zondervan Publishing House, 1984.) My current opinion, which was established after my research reported in 1985 (Frair, Wayne. "Biochemical evidence for the origin and dispersion of turtles." *Proceedings of the 11th Bible-Science Association National Conference;* 1985 August 14-16; Cleveland, OH. Harley Hotel: 97-105; and Frair, Wayne. "The enigmatic plateless river turtle, Carettochelys, in serological survey." *J. Herpetology.* 19(4):515–523: 1985), is that turtles represent a single kind. . . .

Next, the matter of the "ancestry" for man and apes. Lawyer Ennis referred to a quotation in our book from theologian Leupold; and he tried to make it look as though I had said this. I did not say it; and even though I may have agreed with the statement, I indicated to the court that I was there to talk about scientific matters and not my own personal beliefs about the Bible and what it says.

Lastly, with regard to the matter of faith, it certainly is true that faith is involved whether a person holds to an evolution or a creation position. Often the distinction is not made clearly between the faith commitment to a belief in supernaturalism or naturalism. One takes either of these two positions; one also takes the position either that there was an abrupt appearance of unrelated groups in nature or that all types of organisms are related in a single tree (see Frair, Wayne. Biochemical evidence for the origin and dispersion of turtles.) . . .

It is my hope that future scholars will obtain a copy of the trial transcript; but if this is not possible, at least my opinion regarding some of these matters now should be clearer.

Transcript Blockage

Because of other commitments, I did not try seriously to obtain a transcript of my trial testimony until the summer of 1998. I contacted the attorney general, who referred me to the Federal District Court Clerk's Office in Little Rock. He called me saying that the records had been transported to Fort Worth, Texas. But my efforts to learn how to locate the records there were unsuccessful.

My next step was to contact a very capable and experienced lawyer. After considerable effort, she reported a level of frustration similar to my own. I then suspended my efforts to obtain the transcripts, pending further time and resources for following through with other possible options.

Even though I and other defense witnesses so far have not been able to obtain copies of our defense testimonies, Dr. Geisler has subsequently obtained his, which is presented in this book (see chapter 4 and appendix 4). I not only listened to his oral testimony as it was given at the trial but also heard all the other nine defense testimonies, each of which produced valuable information supporting Act 590.

But it was Geisler's penetrating presentation that exposed the fallacies of the plaintiffs' underlying philosophical positions. His trial testimony, now published in this book, stands as a monument of powerful and persuasive logic. This material had an important historical impact, but now that it is in print many years later, it will serve to enlighten and encourage many of us who still are facing similar challenges today.

Acknowledgments

I wish to express deep appreciation to my wife, Barbara, my assistants Christina Woodside and Lanny Wilson, and to my friend Doug Van Gordon for their valuable help in the preparation of this manuscript.

Introduction

Creation versus evolution is in the news again. In fact, it has never left the news since the *Scopes* trial of 1925. It has only gone through mountain peaks and valleys.[1] The most important of these "peaks," as far as the courts are concerned, include the following decisions.[2]

The *Scopes* Trial (1925)

The case of *State of Tennessee v. John Thomas Scopes* is one of the most famous trials in American history. The issue was whether or not it was constitutional to teach evolution instead of the biblical account of creation in public schools. The law in question read: "It shall be unlawful for any teacher . . . to teach any theory that denies the story of Divine Creation of man as taught in the Bible, and to teach instead that man

---

1. The battle has recently reached such a fevered pitch that one writer described the March 2006 meeting of the American Association for the Advancement of Science as a "call to arms for American scientists, meant to recruit troops for the escalating war against creationism and its spinoff doctrine, intelligent design" (Richard Monastersky, "On the Front Lines in the War over Evolution," *Research and Books,* March 10, 2006).

2. Other court cases bearing on the issue include *Washington Ethical Society v. District of Columbia* (1957), *Smith v. Mississippi* (1970), *Wright v. Houston Independent School District* (1972), *Moore v. Gaston County Board of Education* (1973), *Steele v. Waters* (1975), and *Van Orden v. Perry* (2004).

has descended from a lower order of animals." The decision rendered by the Dayton, Tennessee court was that it was illegal to teach evolution, and John Scopes was found guilty of doing just that. The resulting fine of $100 was later overturned on a technicality: only a jury, not the judge, had the authority to assess the fine.

The *Epperson* Ruling (1968)

Tennessee was not the only state that had anti-evolution laws. Similar laws were passed in Oklahoma, Florida, and Texas. Between 1921 and 1929 such bills were introduced in some twenty states. Oklahoma repealed their law in 1926, but the Tennessee law stayed on the books until 1967. Arkansas too was a holdout, but their law was finally addressed by the U.S. Supreme Court in 1968. In this *Epperson v. Arkansas* decision the Court struck down the last state anti-evolutionary law. From the Court record we read:

> Appellant Epperson, an Arkansas public school teacher, brought this action for declaratory and injunctive relief challenging the constitutionality of Arkansas' "anti-evolution" statute. That statute makes it unlawful for a teacher in any state-supported school or university to teach or to use a textbook that teaches "that mankind ascended or descended from a lower order of animals".... The statute violates the Fourteenth Amendment, which embraces the First Amendment's prohibition of state laws respecting an establishment of religion.... The sole reason for the Arkansas law is that a particular religious group considers the evolution theory to conflict with the account of the origin of man set forth in the Book of Genesis.... The First Amendment mandates governmental neutrality between religion and religion, and between religion and non-religion. ... A State's right to prescribe the public school curriculum does not include the right to prohibit teaching a scientific theory or doctrine for reasons that run counter to the principles of the First Amendment.... The Arkansas law is not a manifestation of religious neutrality....[3]

3. *Epperson v. State of Arkansas,* 393 U.S. 97 (1968).

The Supreme Court ruled that it was a *violation of the First Amendment* to forbid the teaching of evolution in public schools.

The *Segraves* Ruling (1981)

In *Segraves v. State of California,* a California superior court ruled that the California State Board of Education's *Science Framework* provided adequate accommodation to Kelly Segraves's views, contrary to his argument that the discussion of evolution violated his children's freedom of religion. Further, the court demanded a policy that included all areas of science, not just origins. This ruling did not penetrate to the heart of the issue of whether teaching creation was a violation of the First Amendment. Determination of this issue would await the next two decisions.

The *McLean* Ruling (1982)

In *McLean v. Arkansas Board of Education,* the issue was whether it was legal for the state to mandate that, whenever evolution is taught, creation should be taught as well in a balanced treatment of both. The U.S. District Court ruled that this would constitute "... an establishment of religion prohibited by the First Amendment to the Constitution which is made applicable to the states by the Fourteenth Amendment." Why? In the judge's words, because, "In traditional Western religious thought, the conception of a creator of the world is a conception of God. Indeed, creation of the world 'out of nothing' is the ultimate religious statement because God is the only actor."[4] The case was never appealed, since Jon Buell of the Dallas-based Foundation for Thought and Ethics, which eventually produced a textbook (*Of Pandas and People*)[5] for teaching creation alongside evolution

4. *McLean v. Arkansas Board of Education,* 529 F. Supp. 1255 (E.D. Ark. 1982).
5. Percival Davis and Dean H. Kenyon, and Charles B. Thaxton, *Of Pandas and People: The Central Question of Biological Origins* (Dallas: Haughton, 1993).

in public schools, requested that the Arkansas attorney general not appeal the case. The Foundation believed that a similar law that had been enacted in Louisiana was better worded, had less baggage, could be better argued, and, therefore, had a better chance of success when appealed to the Supreme Court. I personally felt that the downside of this was that the *McLean* court decision, with all of its problems and weaknesses, would become a bad precedent for future decisions if left unappealed. This is precisely what happened when a case involving this issue went to the Supreme Court (*Edwards v. Aguillard,* 1987).

Mozert v. Hawkins County Board of Education (1987)

Students and parents had claimed that it was a violation of their First Amendment rights of free exercise of religion for the school board to be "forcing student-plaintiffs to read school books which teach or inculcate values in violation of their religious beliefs and convictions." Evolution was one such view to which they objected. This was upheld by the District Court but overruled by the Sixth Circuit Court. The latter court argued that even though students were offended, there was no evidence that anyone was "ever required to affirm his or her belief or disbelief in any idea or practice" taught in the text or class. The court insisted that there was a difference between "exposure" and being "coerced" to accept the ideas. They noted that the only way to avoid all offense was not to teach anything. They insisted that: "The lesson is clear: governmental actions that merely offend or cast doubt on religious beliefs do not on that account violate free exercise." They insisted that this exposure to offensive views was simply a matter of "civil tolerance" of other views and did not compel anyone to a "religious tolerance" whereby they were compelled to give equal status to other religious views. "It merely requires a recognition that in a pluralistic society we must 'live and let live.'"[6]

6. *Mozert v. Hawkins County Board of Education,* 827 F. 2d 1058 (1987).

The *Edwards* Ruling (1987)

The Louisiana law was shorter, but it too mandated that creation be taught in a balanced way whenever evolution is taught in public schools. When this law was tested in the highest court, the justices ruled (7 to 2)[7] in *Edwards v. Aguillard* (1987) that it was an unconstitutional violation of the First Amendment to mandate teaching creation in a balanced way whenever evolution is taught in public schools. In the Court's own words, "The Act impermissibly endorses religion by advancing the religious belief that a supernatural being created humankind."[8]

Since the time of *Edwards,* many creationists have clung to wording in the decision which allows for teaching "all scientific theories about the origins of humankind" or "any scientific theory that is based on established fact."[9] This they see as grounds for allowing creation (or intelligent design, as many now prefer to call it) along with evolution. However, focus shifted from state mandated laws to working with local school boards. Others have been satisfied with the *Edwards* court's statement that "We do not imply that a legislature could never require that scientific critiques of prevailing scientific theories be taught."[10] Thus, they have attempted a negative path of getting textbooks and schools to admit that evolution is only a theory, not a fact, and/or to allow critique of evolutionary views. Still other efforts have settled for simply getting creationist material into public school libraries and hopefully into the hands of biology teachers with the hope that they will voluntarily teach both evolution and creation.

More positive efforts to teach design alternatives to evolution have been organized under the name of the "intelligent design" ("ID") movement. Under the initiative of University of California at Berkeley law professor Phillip Johnson in his book *Darwin on Trial* (Regnery, 1991), the pace was set for attacking the naturalistic grounds for evolution with the hope that some form of intelligent design could be taught alongside evolution in public schools. Michael Behe's landmark volume, *Darwin's Black Box*

7. Rehnquist and Scalia dissented. See chapter 6.
8. *Edwards v. Aguillard,* 482 U.S. 578 (1987).
9. Ibid.
10. Ibid.

(Free Press, 1996), gave a scientific defense of intelligent design on the microbiological level. This, combined with a series of volumes by William Dembski (see his *Mere Creation: Science, Faith, and Intelligent Design* [InterVarsity, 1998]), forms the basis for this growing movement.

Differences between the ID movement and the earlier "scientific creationism" movement include several things.[11] First, ID as such is not committed to teaching a specific view of the age of the earth. The question is simply left open. Second, ID makes no affirmations about the nature or scope of Noah's flood. Third, ID advocates make no identification of the cause of intelligent design with God or any supernatural being. Fourth, they oppose laws mandating the teaching of creation or intelligent design. Rather, they concentrate only on showing that some intelligent cause (whether in or outside the universe) is a more likely cause for first life and new life forms. In this way they hope to escape the religious baggage of the "scientific creation" movement and avoid the wrath of the high court against mandating teaching about a creator or any supernatural cause. However, this hope was dashed in the first test of ID in the courts (*Dover,* 2005).

The *Webster* Ruling (1990)

In *Webster v. New Lenox School District* (see appendix 5) the tables were turned. Ray Webster, who taught social studies at the Oster-Oakview Junior High School in New Lenox, Illinois, sued the school for forbidding him to teach "creation science" in his social studies class. Webster claimed this was a violation of his First and Fourteenth Amendment rights.

The superintendent of the school claimed Webster was advocating a Christian viewpoint that was prohibited by the high court, and that he was instructed not to teach "creation science, because the teaching of this theory had been held by the federal courts to be religious advocacy.... In *Edwards v. Aguillard* ... (1987), the Supreme Court [had] determined

11. Also, because ID is less defined than most creationist efforts in the courts, it has a more diverse constituency, including proponents of Eastern Orthodoxy, Judaism, Roman Catholicism, and the Unification Church. Most creationists, however, would consider themselves Christian fundamentalists or evangelicals.

that creation science, as defined in the Louisiana act in question, was a nonevolutionary theory of origin that 'embodies the religious belief that a supernatural creator was responsible for the creation of humankind.'"[12]

The district court concluded that Webster did not have a First Amendment right to teach creation science in a public school and determined that the school board had the responsibility to ensure that the "Establishment Clause" of the First Amendment was not violated. "By relying on *Edwards v. Aguillard* (1987), the district court determined that teaching creation science would constitute religious advocacy in violation of the first amendment and that the school board correctly prohibited Mr. Webster from teaching such material." Strangely, the court added, "Webster has not been prohibited from teaching any nonevolutionary theories or from teaching anything regarding the historical relationship between church and state."[13] This failure on the part of the courts to see that the only "nonevolutionary" view is some form of creation (see appendix 6) continues to be a problem for the creationist cause, as is evident in the *Dover* decision (see chapter 7).

On the surface, it would appear that *Webster,* if left standing, would eliminate all possibility of teaching creation in public schools. However, there were mitigating circumstances in *Webster* (see appendix 6) that left a crack in the door for teaching ID in science classrooms. But that door was later slammed shut by the *Dover* decision (2005).

The *Peloza v. Capistrano* Ruling (1994)

In *Peloza v. Capistrano* the Ninth District Court of Appeals upheld the ruling that a teacher's freedom of religion was not violated by a school district's requirement that evolution be taught in biology classes. It ruled that the school district had the right to require a teacher to teach a scientific theory such as evolution in biology classes. Of course, this ruling did not state that creation could not be taught. For evolutionists, this had already been decided by the *Edwards* decision (1987). Most creationists disagreed,

12. *Webster v. New Lenox School District,* 917 F. 2d. 1004 (7th Cir. 1990).
13. Ibid.

claiming that creation could be taught as one of the alternate theories of origin allowed by *Edwards*. Other creationists, like myself, feared that the courts would see this as applying only to alternate naturalistic theories. The *Dover* decision (2005) confirmed this fear, at least on a local scale.

The *Freiler* Ruling (1997)

In *Freiler v. Tangipahoa Board of Education* the U.S. District Court of Louisiana rejected a policy that required that a disclaimer be read whenever evolution is taught, ostensibly to promote critical thinking. The court noted that this disclaimer applied only to evolution, not to creation, and therefore that, "in maintaining this disclaimer, the School Board is endorsing religion by disclaiming the teaching of evolution in such a manner as to convey the message that evolution is a religious viewpoint that runs counter to . . . other religious views."[14] Later, in 2000, the Fifth Circuit Court of Appeals affirmed the decision. The chilling effect of this ruling goes beyond this particular disclaimer and discourages other disclaimers as well, even though the actual decision does not rule out the possibility of other disclaimers regarding origins.

The *LeVake* Ruling (2000)

LeVake v. Independent School District came from the District Court for the Third Judicial District of the State of Minnesota. Rodney LeVake, a high school biology teacher, had argued for his right to teach "evidence both for and against the theory" of evolution. The school district contended that his proposal did not match the curriculum, which required teaching evolution. Given the precedent case law requiring a teacher to teach what he is hired to teach, the court ruled that LeVake's free speech rights did not override the required curriculum and the school district was not guilty of religious discrimination in denying his right to teach both for and against evolution. Interestingly, this is exactly the opposite of what evolutionists argued at the *Scopes* trial in 1925.

14. *Freiler v. Tangipahoa Board of Education*, No. 94-3577 (1997).

The *Dover* Ruling (2005)

The first test for teaching intelligent design (ID) hit the courts in the *Kitzmiller v. Dover Area School District* case. The Dover Area School District near Harrisburg, Pennsylvania, had adopted a policy requiring that students be read a statement that included the following:

> The Pennsylvania Academic Standards requires students to learn about Darwin's theory of evolution.... Because Darwin's theory is a theory.... the theory is not a fact.... Intelligent design is an explanation of the origin of life that differs from Darwin's view. The reference book, "Of Pandas and People," is available for students who might be interested in gaining an understanding of what intelligent design actually involves.[15]

This policy was not put forward by any group connected with the ID movement, such as the Seattle-based Discovery Institute, nor by the producers of the ID text for public schools, *Of Pandas and People*.[16] Indeed, the associate director of the Discovery Institute, John West, released a statement which read in part, "Discovery Institute strongly opposes the ACLU's effort to make discussions of intelligent design illegal. At the same time, we disagree with efforts to get the government to require the teaching of intelligent design."[17]

The Dover policy was opposed by the ACLU and Americans United for Separation of Church and State and defended by the Thomas More Law Center, a Christian law firm based in Ann Arbor, Michigan. The *Dover* case was heard by U.S. District Court Judge John Jones III between September 26 and November 4, 2005. The decision was rendered on December 20, 2005. It ruled that (1) the Dover School District policy is unconstitutional, (2) intelligent design and creation its progenitor are not science and should not be taught in Dover science classes, and (3) intelligent design and other forms of creation are essentially religious and are, therefore, a violation of the First Amendment establishment

15. *Kitzmiller v. Dover Area School District,* 400 F. Supp. 2d 707 (M.D. Pa. 2005).

16. See note 5, above.

17. See John G. West, "Discovery Institute's Position on Dover, PA 'Intelligent Design' Case," September 21, 2005, at http://www.discovery.org/scripts/viewDB/index.php?command=view&id=2847.

clause. In the words of the court, "For the reasons that follow, we hold that the ID [intelligent design] Policy is unconstitutional pursuant to the Establishment Clause of the First Amendment of the United States Constitution and Art. I, § 3 of the Pennsylvania Constitution."[18]

The *Dover* decision has not been appealed because the school board, which now has an anti-creation majority, does not want to appeal it. However, the issue inevitably will be raised again and eventually will be brought before the U.S. Supreme Court. How the Court will rule no one knows for sure. But if precedent is followed, it is unlikely that the high court will (1) allow any creation or design view to be mandated for schools, or (2) allow any view to be taught that implies a supernatural creator.

Meanwhile, the lessons of history may be gleaned to guide the future of this discussion. Having been an eyewitness of the famous "Scopes II" (*McLean,* 1982)[19] trial, I feel compelled to cast what light I can on this very important issue. Indeed, since the Arkansas courts refused to publish my testimony (given in 1981), which was crucial to the outcome of the trial, until after the Supreme Court ruled against teaching creation six years later (in 1987), there is a vital part of history that has been hitherto unknown that is now being revealed for the first time in this publication (see chapter 4). It is to these ends that I present this important but missing link in the history of the creation-evolution controversy, in the hope that it may cast some light on the issue as it is now again coming into the courts and—hopefully—have a positive influence on the outcome.

18. *Kitzmiller v. Dover Area School District,* 400 F. Supp. 2d 707 (M.D. Pa. 2005).
19. See our eyewitness account in Norman L. Geisler with A. F. Brooke II and Mark J. Keough, *The Creator in the Courtroom: "Scopes II"* (Milford, Mich.: Mott Media, 1982).

The *Scopes* Trial (1925)

Background of the Controversy

Charles Darwin started the evolution revolution. There were evolutionists before Darwin, even in ancient times, but Darwin was the first to propose a plausible scientific mechanism by which evolution could have occurred. Between the 1859 publication of his landmark volume *On the Origin of Species* and 1900, the naturalistic macroevolution theory literally conquered the intellectual scientific world of the West.

From the beginning, serious religious and moral implications were apparent in Darwin's theory. Darwin himself called it "my deity 'Natural Selection.'"[1] The very subtitle of his book, referring to the "preservation of favoured races in the struggle for life," has racial implications. Alfred Wallace, the "coinventor" of natural selection,

---

1. Darwin said, "I speak of natural selection as an active power or deity. . . . To believe in miraculous creations or in the 'continued intervention of creative power' is to make 'my deity "Natural Selection" superfluous' and to hold the Deity—if such there be—accountable for phenomena which are rightly attributed only to his magnificent laws" (Darwin, in a letter to Asa Gray, June 5, 1861 [in Francis Darwin, ed., *The Life and Letters of Charles Darwin,* 2 vols. (New York: Basic Books, 1959), 2:165]).

deified the very evolutionary process. "Wallace put more and more emphasis on the spiritual agency, so that in *The World of Life* it is described as 'a Mind not only adequate to direct and regulate all the forces at work in living organisms, but also the more fundamental forces of the whole material universe.' For many years Wallace was interested in spiritualism and psychical research."[2] Darwin's friend Karl Marx declared, "But nowadays, in our evolutionary conception of the universe, there is absolutely no room for either a creator or a ruler."[3] Henri Bergson deified the evolutionary process in his work *Creative Evolution* (1898), calling it a Life Force. Herbert Spencer, whom Darwin called "our great philosopher," made evolution into a cosmic process. In Germany, Ernst Haeckel, who developed social evolution from Darwin's theory, claimed that "the idea of 'design' has wholly disappeared from this vast province of science."[4] As Harvard paleontologist Stephen Jay Gould would later explain, "Evolution substituted a naturalistic explanation of cold comfort for our former conviction that a benevolent deity fashioned us directly in his own image. . . ."[5]

In America a few strong voices spoke against Darwin. In 1860 the famous Harvard zoologist Louis Agassiz wrote a critical review of *On the Origin of Species*.[6] At Princeton, Charles Hodge wrote a strong critique in 1878 titled *What Is Darwinism?* His answer was straight to the point: "What is Darwinism? It is Atheism. This does not mean that Mr. Darwin himself and all who adopt his views are atheists; but it means that his theory is atheistic, that the exclusion of design from nature is

2. "Wallace, Alfred," in Paul Edwards, ed., *The Encyclopedia of Philosophy,* 8 vols. (New York: Macmillan and The Free Press, 1967), 8:276.

3. Karl Marx and Friedrich Engels, *On Religion* (New York: Schocken, 1964), 295.

4. Ernst Haeckel, *The Riddle of the Universe at the Close of the Nineteenth Century* (New York: Harper & Brothers, 1900), 260.

5. Stephen Jay Gould, cited in Jonathan Wells, *The Politically Incorrect Guide to Darwinism and Intelligent Design* (Washington, D.C.: Regnery, 2006), 62.

6. Agassiz wrote in *American Journal of Science:* "[Darwin] has lost sight of the most striking of the features, and the one which pervades the whole, namely, that there runs throughout Nature unmistakable evidence of thought, corresponding to the mental operations of our own mind" ("Professor Agassiz on the Origin of Species," *American Journal of Science* 30 [June 1860]:143–147, 149–150).

... tantamount to atheism."[7] The logic is impeccable: no design, no designer; no creation, no creator. Evolution as a theory is atheistic, even though not all evolutionists are atheists.

Perhaps the most frightening consequences of Darwinism were the ethical ones. In 1924 a young Adolf Hitler wrote *Mein Kampf,* in which he proposed following the example of evolution and weeding out the weaker breeds of mankind. And he proceeded to put his proposal into action, exterminating those he considered less fit. Hitler justified his action by evolution, claiming, "If Nature does not wish that weaker individuals should mate with the stronger, she wishes even less that a superior race should intermingle with an inferior one; because in such a case all her efforts, throughout hundreds of thousands of years, to establish an evolutionary higher stage of being, may thus be rendered futile."[8]

The implications of Darwinism were not perceived quickly in America by the religious community in general.[9] In fact, it took some sixty years and a World War. But by the time of Hitler the implications were becoming clear. One year after Hitler's racist book, the people of Tennessee passed the Butler Act on March 13, 1925, forbidding the teaching of evolution in the public schools. Interestingly, the biology textbook that had been used in the schools before this taught a racism similar to Hitler's views. To quote from the book:

> At the present time there exist upon the earth five races.... These are the Ethiopian or negro type, originating in Africa; the Malay or brown race, from the islands of the Pacific; the American Indian; the Mongolian or yellow race, including the natives of China, Japan, and the Eskimos; and finally, *the highest type of all, the Caucasians,* represented by the civilized white inhabitants of Europe and America.[10]

7. Charles Hodge, "What Is Darwinism?" in *What Is Darwinism? And Other Writings on Science and Religion,* ed. Mark A. Noll and David N. Livingstone (Grand Rapids, Mich.: Baker, 1994), 177.

8. Hitler, *Mein Kampf* (New York: Reynal & Hitchcock, 1940), 161–162.

9. See David Livingstone, *Darwin's Forgotten Defenders* (Grand Rapids, Mich.: Eerdmans, 1987).

10. George William Hunter, *A Civic Biology* (New York: American Book Company, 1914), 196 (emphasis added).

Although such racist implications did not come out at the *Scopes* trial, it was clear from the speech prepared for the trial by William Jennings Bryan, leader of the anti-evolution movement, that both the theological and ethical implications of evolution were paramount in the minds of the anti-evolution forces. Two citations from the speech will make the point: "But it is not a laughing matter when one considers that evolution not only offers no suggestions as to a Creator but tends to put the creative act so far away as to cast doubt upon creation itself" (325).[11] Indeed, Bryan pointed to statistics showing that half of all scientists did not believe in God (329–330). He concluded: "If all the biologists of the world teach this doctrine—as Mr. Darrow says they do—then may heaven defend the youth of our land from their impious babblings" (333). Further, Bryan saw the serious ethical implications of evolution. He cited agnostic Clarence Darrow's defense of a young man who allegedly had committed murder. Darrow had argued that it was the influence of the atheist and evolutionist Friedrich Nietzsche on the young man that led him to do it (330–331). Bryan also cited Darwin himself (in *The Descent of Man*) approving of savage and barbarous acts in emulation of nature which weed out the weak and inferior breeds (335). Bryan summed up the issue this way: "Let us, then, hear the conclusion of the whole matter. Science is a magnificent material force, but it is not a teacher of morals. It can perfect machinery, but it adds no moral restraints to protect society from the misuse of the machine" (338).

Evolutionists, on the other hand, saw creationists' efforts as an attempt to squelch freedom and scientific progress. Darrow's concluding comments at the trial sum up their feelings: "I think this case will be remembered because it is the first case of this sort since we stopped trying people in America for witchcraft because here we have done our best to turn back the tide that has sought to force itself upon this—upon this modern world, of testing every fact in science by a religious dictum" (317).

11. All references to the trial transcript in this chapter are from William Hilleary and Oren W. Metzger, eds., *The World's Most Famous Court Trial: Tennessee Evolution Case* (Cincinnati, Ohio: National Book Company, 1925), which contains the trial transcript plus the "Text of Bryan's Proposed Address in Scopes Case" (321–339). The speech was prepared for delivery at the trial but not given because arguments to the jury by both sides were eliminated by mutual agreement.

Background of the *Scopes* Trial

It is in this context that what has been called "the world's most famous court trial"[12] occurred. The ACLU, eager for an opportunity to challenge the Tennessee law forbidding the teaching of evolution, advertised to get someone to break the law. John Scopes, a young teacher, volunteered to do so,[13] and the rest is history. Little Dayton, Tennessee, became a circus. The media of the world converged on the Rhea County Courthouse, where on a sultry July 10th the trial began. For the rest of the story, rather than referencing the popular movie *Inherit the Wind,* we can consult the actual stenographic record of the proceedings published in *The World's Most Famous Court Trial: Tennessee Evolution Case.*[14] Another excellent source is Edward J. Larson's Pulitzer Prize–winning book *Summer for the Gods,*[15] one of the best books ever written on the trial.

The Tennessee Law Forbidding the Teaching of Evolution

The focus of the *Scopes* trial was the Tennessee law forbidding the teaching of evolution which was enacted on March 21, 1925. It read in part:

> Section 1. Be it enacted by the General Assembly of the State of Tennessee, that it shall be unlawful for any teacher in any of the Universities, Normals and all other public schools of the State, which are supported in whole or in part by the public school funds of the state, to teach any theory that denies the story of the Divine Creation of man as taught in the Bible, and to teach instead that man has descended from a lower order of animals (5).

The case (No. 5232) was called *State of Tennessee v. John Thomas Scopes.* The trial lasted for eight days, from July 10 through July 21. Clarence

12. See note 11, above.
13. The indictment accused Scopes of teaching evolution on the specific day of April 24, 1925. Later, Scopes could not remember if he had actually taught evolution on that particular day. Nonetheless, the trial proceeded on the assumption that he had.
14. See note 11, above.
15. Edward J. Larson, *Summer for the Gods* (New York: Basic Books, 1997).

Darrow, famous agnostic ACLU lawyer, was lead attorney for the defense. William Jennings Bryan, one-time Democratic presidential candidate and defender of creation, was a visiting attorney for the state.

Highlights from the Trial

While the entire trial transcript is well worth reading, certain highlights are important for the ongoing saga of creation in the courts. The actual legal issue was: did or did not John Scopes "[teach] any theory that denies the story of the Divine creation of man as taught in the Bible, and . . . teach instead that man has descended from a lower order of animals" in violation of the law of the state of Tennessee?

First Day (Friday, July 10)

Opening Prayer[16]

The court was opened in prayer by Rev. Cartwright, who besought "God, our divine Father . . . the Supreme Ruler of the universe" for wisdom for the court and jury, justice for the defendant, reminding all in attendance that there is a day coming when "all of the nations of the earth shall stand before Thy judgment bar." The prayer was offered in "the cause of truth and righteousness." It concluded, "to Thy glory and grace for ever more. Amen" (3).

Introduction of Attorneys

Judge John T. Raulston asked Attorney General Tom Stewart to introduce the outside counsel for the state, William Jennings Bryan and his son (who was unnamed in the court transcript, since he "need[ed] no introduction"). For the defense Mr. (Judge) Neal, Clarence Darrow, Arthur Hays, Mr. Dudley Field Malone, and Mr. Thompson were introduced (4). Other attorneys for the state included Mr. McKenzie and Mr. Hicks.[17]

16. The crucial part of each prayer is included here since these prayers were disputed by the defense.

17. The court records included very few first names.

THE LAW THAT SCOPES IS ALLEGED TO
HAVE VIOLATED WAS READ

The law in question was Chapter 27 of the Acts of 1925 of the State of Tennessee, enacted on March 21, 1925. The act was read as follows:

> Section 1. Be it enacted by the General Assembly of the State of Tennessee, that it shall be unlawful for any teacher in any of the Universities, Normals and all other public schools of the State, which are supported in whole or in part by the public school funds of the state, to teach any theory that denies the story of the Divine Creation of man as taught in the Bible, and to teach instead that man has descended from a lower order of animals (5).

THE READING OF GENESIS CHAPTER ONE

Judge Neal then said, "Since the act involved in this investigation provides that it shall be unlawful to teach any theory that denies the divine creation of man as taught in the Bible, it is proper that I call your attention to the account of man's creation as taught in the Bible, it is proper that I call your attention to the first chapter of Genesis." The chapter was read in its entirety. The crucial parts are repeated here from the court record:

> In the beginning the Lord [*sic*] created the heaven and earth. . . . And God created great whales, and every living creature that moveth. . . . And God made the beasts of the earth after his kind, and cattle after their kind, and everything that creepeth upon the earth after his kind. . . . So God created man in His own image, in the image of God, created He him; male and female created He them (vv. 1, 21, 25, 27) (5–6).

THE CHARGE OF THE JUDGE TO THE GRAND JURY

Judge Neal charged: "You will bear in mind that in this investigation you are not interested to inquire into the policy or wisdom of this legislation. . . . Our constitution imposes upon the judicial branch the interpretation of statutes and upon the executive branch the enforcement of the law" (6). He told them the violation would only be a misdemeanor, but reminded them there are serious misdemeanors, such as those involving "the evil example of the teacher disregarding constituted authority in the very presence of the undeveloped mind whose thought and moral he directs and guides" (7).

A New Indictment Is Returned

Both sides agreed to quash the original indictment (No. 5231) and replace it with a new one (No. 5232). This was apparently to avoid its being overturned on a technicality. The judge named it *Case No. 5232 State of Tennessee v. John Thomas Scopes* (7).

The only other significant occurrence the first morning was concerning the competency of the witnesses. Darrow expressed his belief: "I think that scientists are competent evidence—or competent witnesses here, to explain what evolution is, and that they are competent on both sides" (8). Attorney General Stewart responded: "we think that it isn't competent as evidence; that is, it isn't competent to bring into this case scientists who testify as to what the theory of evolution is or interpret the Bible or anything of that sort" (8–9). He suggested, therefore, that they go immediately to qualify jury members so as not to pollute the jury pool by the discussion.

The rest of the day was spent interviewing potential jurors. When one prospective juror, Rev. Massingill, was asked by Darrow if he ever preached for or against evolution, he answered: "Well, I preached against it, of course! (Applause)." At this outburst the judge warned: "if you repeat that, ladies and gentlemen, you will be excluded" (14). There ensued a short disagreement over whether they should swear in the jurors immediately or wait until Monday morning.

Second Day (July 13)

Opening Prayer

The invocation on the second day of the trial was offered by Rev. Moffett to "God, our Father, Thou Who are the creator of the heaven and the earth. . . ." He prayed for "wise decisions" to be made and for "blessing" of the jury, the lawyers, the media, all involved in this case "in the name of our Lord and Saviour, Jesus Christ" (45).

Swearing In of Jury

Before the jury was sworn in, the judge had to call for order in the courtroom (45), saying, "we cannot proceed in the courtroom, as many people as there are without absolute order" (46). Before the jury could be sworn in the judge considered the motion to quash the indictment. The indictment was read first. In part it charged that: "John Thomas Scopes, heretofore on the 24th day of April, 1925, in the county aforesaid, then and there, unlawfully did wilfully teach in the public schools of Rhea county . . . a certain theory and theories that deny the story of the divine creation of man as taught in the Bible, and did teach instead thereof that man has descended from a lower order of animals . . ." (47).

The Defense Argument

The defense then made a motion to quash the indictment. They argued against both the indictment and the anti-evolution act on which it was based, citing a long list of reasons divided into three broad categories. First, they discussed constitutional issues:

a) The act is in violation of Section 17, Article II of the state constitution, which states that all bills must have only one subject and it be clearly stated in the title (47–48);

b) It violates Section 12, Article XI: "Education to be cherished," since it does not cherish a student's education in science.

c) It violates Section 18, Article II, which says, "No bill shall become a law until it shall have been read and passed, on three different days in each house, and shall have received, on its final passage, in each house, the assent of a majority. . . ." (48);

d) It violates Section 3, Article I, "That all men have a natural and indefeasible right to worship Almighty God according to the dictates of his own conscience" (48);

e) It violates Section 19, Article I, which states, "That the printing presses shall be free to every person. . . . The free communication of thoughts and opinions is one of the invaluable rights of man, and every citizen may freely speak, write and print on any subject . . ." (48–49).

Defense attorney Hays joined in the defense argument that the indictment was indefinite, insisting that Scopes was "charged in the caption of the act with one thing and in the body of the indictment it is put in another way" (55). It is also not clear, he said, what "teach" means. If it means simply exposing students to the theory, "I presume our teachers should be prepared to teach every theory on every subject. Not necessarily to teach a thing as a fact" (56). "It should not be wrong to teach evolution, or certain phases of evolution, but not as a fact" (56).

Attorney Hays suggested that the court consider a hypothetical law, parallel to the evolution law, this one forbidding the teaching of a heliocentric universe, which "denies the story that the earth is the center of the universe, as taught in the Bible, and [teaches] instead, that the earth and planets move around the sun" (56). He concluded: "My contention is that an act of that sort is clearly unconstitutional in that it is a restriction upon the liberties of the individual. . . . The only distinction you can draw between this statute and the one we are discussing is that evolution is as much a scientific fact as the Copernican theory, but the Copernican theory has been fully accepted, as this [theory of evolution] must be accepted" (56–57). Thus, "To my mind, the chief point against the constitutionality of this law is that it extends the police powers of the state unreasonably and is a restriction upon the liberty of the individual." It was unreasonable, he said, because "it would only be reasonable if it tended in some way to promote public morals" (57). And this is not possible unless we know what evolution is.

f) It violates Section 8, Article I, that, "No man can be disturbed but by law. That no man shall be taken . . . or deprived of his life, liberty or property but by the judgment of his peers or the law of the land" (49).

g) It also violates Section 9, Article I on "Rights of the accused in criminal prosecutions" (49).

h) It violates Section 14, Article I, which says "that no person shall be put to answer any criminal charge but by presentment, indictment or impeachment" (49).

i) It violates Section 8, Article II, which forbids passing laws "for the benefit of any particular individual, inconsistent with the general laws of the land" (49).

j) It violates Section 2, Article II, that "No person [is] to exercise powers of more than one department" (49).

Second, the defense charged that "the indictment is so vague as not to inform the defendant of the nature and cause of the accusation against him" (49).

Finally, they claimed that "the act and the indictment violate Section 1 of the Fourteenth amendment of the constitution of the United States," which says, "No state shall make or enforce any law which shall abridge the privileges or immunities of citizens of the United States" (49–50).

With the court's approval, the defense began to argue their points. The following highlights are instructive.

First, they argued that the law in question had two subjects: evolution and creation. The title of the act spoke of "evolution," but the body spoke of "any theory," not just the theory of evolution, which violated Section 17, Article II of the state constitution, that all Bills must have only one subject and that it be clearly stated in the title (47).

Second, they argued that the act violated Section 12, Article XI of the state constitution, which stated that education is to be cherished. The law clearly stated that this includes "literature and science" (51). But, "in no possible way can science be taught or science be studied without bringing in the doctrine of evolution, which this particular act attempts to make a crime." The defense went on to say, "Whether it is true or not true, all the important matters of science are expressed in the evolution nomenclature" (51).

Third, they promised to address later the charge of the alleged irregularity of the passage of the bill.

Fourth, the defense considered it "the most sacred provision of the constitution of Tennessee . . . that all men have a natural and indefeasible right to worship Almighty God according to the dictates of their own conscience; . . . that no human authority can, in any case whatever, control or interfere with the rights of conscience." This they called "the most important contention of the defence" (51–52). Hence, "Our contention, to be very brief, is that in this act there is made mandatory the teaching of a particular doctrine that comes from a particular religious book, and to that extent, . . . they contravene the provisions of our constitution" (52).

The jury retired in spite of the objection of the defense because the judge felt that "if you gentlemen are going to discuss matters that are vital to the issues in this case, before the court, it is in the discretion of the court to have the jury retire" (52–53).[18]

Fifth, the defense argued that the right to freedom of expression applies "whether the site of it is in a schoolhouse, or store, or street, or building, or any place . . . limited only by . . . responsibility under libel law" (53).

Sixth, in accord with Section 9, Article I of the state constitution, which demands a clear definition of the crime, the defense insisted that "the crime in this act—the definition is so indefinite that it is absolutely impossible for the defense to know exactly the nature of its charge—of the charge" (53). This is particularly true, they said, since it is speaking about "a doctrine in the Bible [which] is so indefinite that every man that reads the Bible will have a different interpretation as to exactly what that theory of creation is . . ." (54). Further, "we think that the indictment should set out just exactly what our defendant was supposed to have taught" (55).

Finally, they claimed "that *our main contention after all, may it please your honor, is that this is not a proper thing for any legislature . . . to make and assign a rule in regard to. In this law there is an attempt to pronounce a judgment and conclusion in the realm of science and in the realm of religion*" (55, emphasis added). In brief, they argued that it was not the province of the courts to make pronouncements in these areas.

STATE RESPONSE TO DEFENSE ARGUMENTS

The state offered two responses to the defense, the first by attorney McKenzie. He made two main points. First, he said, the Supreme Court of Tennessee had ruled too often on this issue. The language of the

18. Though the stenographer (or editor?) put a "?" mark at the end of the sentence, clearly the judge herein expressed his view and immediately ruled accordingly.

indictment was the language of the statute: "no particular religion can be taught in the schools. We cannot teach any religion in the schools, therefore, you cannot teach any evolution, or any doctrine that conflicts with the Bible. That sets them up exactly equal. No part of the constitution has been infringed by this act." Furthermore, he argued, the U.S. government recognizes the right of the state to regulate its own schools and sends it federal funds to do so.

As to the defense's hypothetical illustration involving the Copernican theory, this "was not at all a similar case to this act; it has no connection with it; no such act as that has ever passed through the fertile brain of a Tennessean" (57). In short, the state said, it was a false analogy.[19]

As for the clarity of the law, McKenzie argued in effect that titles do not have to be exact or complete descriptions of what is in the law, only accurate ones—good enough "to give notice to the legislature that they should prevent surprise and fraud in the enactment of laws" (58).

Again concerning the clarity of the law, McKenzie insisted that "you do not construe these statutes according to their technical sense, unless it is a technical statute; you construe them in common ordinary language, and give them an interpretation like the common people of this state can understand" (58). We do the same thing when we say that "Under the law you cannot teach in the common schools the Bible. Why should it be improper to provide that you cannot teach this other theory?" (58).

Further, as to their argument about the schools' right to cherish science, "the legislature under the constitutional provision may as well establish a uniform system of schools and a uniform administration of them . . ." (59). The state has the inherent right to control its schools. So, "if they think the teaching of evolution is harmful to the children of the state, . . . they may pass the act" (59). Further, even if they do not think it is harmful, as "the supreme head of the schools, . . . They can pass the law under the inherent powers vested in them" (60).

Finally, the state attorneys said, claiming an alleged right to teach anything under the right to worship law is "ridiculous." A teacher hired

19. This response is notably weak, since it does not give the strong dissimilarities to show that it is a false analogy. If evolution were an empirical science and creation were not, then it would have been a good analogy.

to teach mathematics cannot decide on his own to teach architecture. "The teaching in the schools has nothing whatever to do with religious worship, and as Mr. McKenzie brought out, he can preach as he wants to on the streets—his religious rights—but he cannot preach them in school" (60).

Attorney General Stewart Responds to the Motion to Quash

Stewart returned to the objection that the law and its caption did not coincide. He added that in Tennessee law the caption could be broader than the law but not the reverse. All that was necessary was that they be "germaine [sic] one to the other" (62). And both the caption and the law "deal with only one thing, and that is to prohibit the teaching in the public schools of Tennessee the evolutionary theory" (62). And as for the possibility that the law was broader than the caption in that it may be affirming that one cannot both teach evolution and also teach that the Bible is untrue, this would be eliminated by "the rule of construction in Tennessee which prohibits the court from placing an absurd construction on the act" (62).

He also added to the alleged "cherish . . . science" part of the constitution the argument of Justice White's dissenting opinion that this was merely a directive to the legislators that expressed a popular feeling of the people and was not a constitutional mandate to put science over everything else (62–63).

He then addressed the "free worship" argument, noting that "this [law] . . . does not even approach interference with religious worship" (65). It was addressed only to public school systems. "This does not prevent any man from worshiping God as his conscience directs and dictates" (65). It did not require anyone to join a particular denomination, contribute to a particular religion, or attend any given church.

At this point Clarence Darrow objected, claiming that the law stated that "no preference shall ever be given, by law, to any religious establishment." He insisted that the Tennessee anti-evolution law erred by "giving preference to the Bible." He asked, "Why not the Koran?" (65). Stewart's answer was: "The laws of the land recognize the Bible; the laws of the land recognize the law of God and Christianity as a part of the common law." In short, "We are not living in a heathen country." Stewart asked the ACLU attorney, Malone: "Do you say teaching the Bible in the public school is a religious matter?" Malone responded, "No." And he hastily added: however, "I would say to base a theory set forth in any version of the Bible to be taught in the public schools is an invasion of the rights of the citizen, whether exercised by police power or by the legislature" (66).

Stewart continued his argument by pointing out that "It is not an invasion of a man's religious rights. He can go to church on Sunday or any other day that there might be a meeting. . . ." Rather, "this is the authority, on the part of the legislature of the state of Tennessee, to direct the expenditure of the school funds of the state and through this act to require that the money shall not be spent in the teaching of the theories that conflict or contravene the Bible story of man's creation" (67).

Stewart then addressed the "freedom of speech" argument of the evolutionists, that John Scopes had a right to give his views on evolution anywhere he wanted, including in the public schools. Stewart responded, "Under that question, I say, Mr. Scopes might have taken his stand on the street corners and expounded until he became hoarse, as a result of his effort and we could not interfere with him." But "he cannot go into the public schools, or a school house, which is controlled by the legislature and supported by the public funds of the state and teach this theory" (67–68).

Darrow shifted the topic, inserting: "We claim the statute is void" because it was not specific as to what the crime was. Stewart responded, "The wording of the indictment complies with the wording of the statute. In such a case it is generally held to be good" (68). Further, in Tennessee law, "less strictness is required in indictments for misdeameanors [*sic*] than in felonies" (69). It was specific enough for the purpose. Everyone knew that Scopes wasn't indicted for "arson" or for "transporting liquor." Rather, "He is here for teaching a theory that denies the story of divine creation . . ." (69–70).

After looking over the original list of arguments the defense offered, Stewart narrowed the list to what he called "the principal one, I think on which this case rests. It is the Fourteenth Amendment to the United States Constitution" (70), which says, "Nor shall any state deprive any person of life, liberty or property without the due process of law, nor deny to any person within its jurisdiction the equal protection of the laws" (71). On this basis, Stewart said, evolutionists argue that the state (and its schools) has no right to abridge freedom of speech for the evolutionist view in schools. Stewart responded by citing a court precedent on the very issue in *Meyer v. State of Nebraska,* in which the court stated: "Nor has challenge been made to the state's power to prescribe a curriculum for institutions which it supports" (71). He added, "How much stronger could they make the language? How much more . . . would we have them say than to recognize the right of the state of Tennessee to direct and control the curriculum in the Rhea County High School?" (72).

CLARENCE DARROW'S SPEECH FOR THE DEFENSE

The next thirteen pages of the transcript record Clarence Darrow's famous anti-bigotry speech, in which he uses the terms "bigotry" and "bigoted" no less than eleven times. Along with this there is a liberal use of other pejorative terms, such as "fundamentalist" (79–80, 82, 86) and "fundamentalism" (87), "narrowness" (77), "not tolerant" (84), "hatred" (87), "venom" (80), "ignorance" (75, 79, 87) or "ignorant" (76). Searching for the thread of his argument is difficult, but a dominant theme is the need to preserve freedom of thought and speech. He makes the following points:

First, legislatures have the right to prescribe curriculum only within limits. "They could not prescribe it, . . . under your constitution, if it omitted arithmetic and geography and writing." Nor "could they prescribe it if the course of study was only to teach religion . . ." (75). Nor could they "establish a course in the public schools of teaching that the Christian religion as unfolded in the Bible, is true, and that every other religion, or mode or system of ethics is false . . ." (75).

Second, he argued: "And so it is, unless there is left enough of the spirit of freedom in the state of Tennessee, and in the United States, there is not a single line of any constitution that can withstand bigotry and ignorance when it seeks to destroy the rights of the individual; and bigotry and ignorance are ever active" (75).

Third, "I think the sooner we get rid of it in Tennessee the better for the peace of Tennessee, and the better for the pursuit of knowledge in the world . . ." (75).

Fourth, he insisted that "There is not a word said in the statute about evolution, there is not a word said in the statute about preventing the teaching of the theory of evolution—not a word," as there was in the caption. And, "Does the caption say anything about the Bible?" (76).

Fifth, the statute referred to the Bible as a "divine" book, "But the state of Tennessee under an honest and fair interpretation of the constitution has no more right to teach the Bible as a divine book than that the Koran is one, or the book of Mormons, or the book of Confucius, or the Buddha, or the Essays of Emerson, or any one of the other 10,000 books to which humans have gone for consolation and aid in their troubles" (77). "No legislature is strong enough in any state in the Union to characterize and pick any book as being divine" (77). Here Darrow attempted to show the Bible was a purely human book. "It is not a book of science. Never was and was never meant to be." In fact, "There are two conflicting accounts [of creation] in the first two chapters" (78). In addition, he said, there were some 500 sects or churches who did not agree among themselves as to how to interpret the Bible (79).

Sixth, Darrow argued, this law was inspired by "the fundamentalists [who] are after everybody that thinks. I know why he [John Scopes] is here. . . . because ignorance and bigotry are rampant, and it is a mighty strong combination, your Honor, it makes him fearful" (79).

Seventh, "Now as to the statute itself. It is full of weird, strange, impossible and imaginary provisions. Driven by bigotry and narrowness they come together and make this statute and bring this litigation. I cannot conceive anything greater" (77).

Eighth, Darrow argued that John Scopes should have taught evolution because "the doctrine of evolution . . . [is] . . . believed by every scientific man on earth" (80).

Ninth, "the indictment is void because it is uncertain, and gives no fact or information and it seems to me the main thing they did in bringing this case was to try to violate as many provisions of the constitution as they could, to say nothing about all the spirit of freedom and independence that has cost the best blood in the world for ages" (81).

Tenth, Darrow argued, the state by its constitution is committed to teaching science and "is committed to teaching the truth." And on no reading of "the spirit of the law"[20] concerning freedom of religion should the truth about evolution be kept out of our schools (82).

Eleventh, Darrow declared that the "fundamentalists" who inspired this law were enemies of "freedom" and that the law resulted in "tyranny"; and he added, "since man was created out of the dust of the earth [Gen. 2:7] . . . there is nothing else your Honor that has caused the difference of opinion, of bitterness, of hatred, of war, of cruelty, that religion has caused" (82).

Twelfth, he said again, there are over 500 sects or churches, all of them having their own interpretation of Scripture. Who is to say which one is right? Yet this law demands that one of these interpretations be correct in order for one to understand it. Yet it considers him a criminal if he breaks it (82–83).

Thirteenth, "Can a legislative body say 'You cannot read a book or take a lesson, or make a talk on science until you first find out whether you are saying [anything] against Genesis'?" (83).

Fourteenth, "It makes the Bible the yard stick to measure every man's intellect, to measure every man's intelligence and to measure every man's learning" (84). But this is to establish religion.

Fifteenth, "Yes, within limits they have [the right to establish curriculum]. We do not doubt it, but they probably cannot say writing and arithmetic could not be taught, and certainly they cannot say nothing can be taught unless it is first ascertained that it agrees with the Scriptures; certainly they cannot say that" (84–85).

20. Darrow is unwittingly quoting the Bible (2 Cor. 3:6) in support of his view, though he admitted he was unaware of his source.

Sixteenth, this law makes it a criminal act to teach evolution in a public school. If so, then it should be a criminal act to do it in a private school or to write it in a book or newspaper (86–87).

Finally, Darrow attributed the law in question to the "religious bigotry and hatred" of "fundamentalism." He insisted that "Ignorance and fanaticism is ever busy and needs feeding" (87) and pleaded that the law be overturned lest we go "marching backward to the glorious ages of the sixteenth century when bigots lighted fagots to burn the men who dared to bring any intelligence and enlightenment and culture to the human mind" (87).

Third Day (July 14)

The third day of the trial began with Darrow objecting to opening prayer on the grounds that it might bias the case. Stewart referred to him as "the agnostic counsel for the defense" (90) and said "this is a God fearing country." The judge affirmed he "has no purpose except to find the truth and do justice" (90) and overruled Darrow's objection on the grounds it had been his custom to open the court in prayer. Dr. Stribling then prayed to "Our Father," the source of all blessing, asking him to bless the proceedings of the court, and petitioning God that there may "be in every heart and in every mind a reverence to the Great Creator of the world" (91). Later a group of clergy from "other than fundamentalist churches" requested that they be allowed to pray too. The judge requested the local "pastor's association" to choose those who would lead in prayer (93).

Fourth Day (July 15)

OBJECTION ABOUT PRAYER

As the fourth day of the trial began, ACLU attorney Neal objected again about prayer on the grounds that it injected a religious atmosphere into the case. Mr. Hicks replied for the state: "They say, your honor, that evolution is not—does not contradict the Bible—does not contradict Christianity. Why are they objecting to prayers if it doesn't contradict the Bible—doesn't contradict Christianity," noting they had had a Unitarian, a Baptist, and a Methodist pray on different mornings. The judge replied, "The court believes that any religious society that is worthy of the name should believe in God and believe in divine guidance. . . . I don't think it hurts anybody and I think it may help somebody. So I overrule the objection" (96).

Stewart Apologizes About "Agnostic" Comment

Defense attorney Hays took exception to the previous day's comment about the "religious views of the counsel for the defense" (97). He had been referred to as "the agnostic counsel for the defense" (90). Stewart apologized, and Hays accepted his apology. The judge admonished the press about a news leak (97–98). Darrow said he considered it not an insult but a compliment to be called an agnostic (99).

Judge Overrules Motion to Quash

The judge rejected the ACLU motion to quash the indictment. He noted that "the caption covers all the legislation provided for in the body, and is germane thereto, and in no way obscures the legislation provided for" (100). He further noted that "The courts are not concerned in questions of public policy or the motive that prompts passage or enactment of any particular legislation." For "The policy, motive or wisdom of the statutes address themselves to the legislative department of the state, and not the judicial department" (101). Nor does it violate any freedom of thought or worship for the defendant since "there is no law in the state of Tennessee that undertakes to compel this defendant, or any other citizen, to accept employment in the public schools." Further, "The relations between the teacher and his employer are purely contractual and if his conscience constrains him to teach the evolution theory, he can find opportunities elsewhere . . ." (102). The other grounds of the motion to quash were rebutted as well, using precedent cases cited by the state and others such as *Pierce v. Society of Sisters*, *Leeper v. the State*, and *Meyer v. Nebraska*. The judge noted from the Meyer case the dictum: "Nor has challenge been made of the 'state's power to prescribe a curriculum for institutions which it supports'" (107). He concluded, "The court, having passed on each ground chronologically, and given the reasons therefor, is now pleased to overrule the whole motion, and require the defendant to plead further" (108).

THE PROSECUTION OF THE CASE BEGINS

Preliminaries being out of the way, the actual prosecution of the case began. The witnesses and jury were called (110–111). Mr. Neal pleaded "not guilty" on behalf of the defendant John Scopes (112).

MALONE OUTLINES DEFENSE CASE

Attorney Malone began the case for the defense with a quotation not identified but from John 4:24, declaring: "The defense believes that 'God is a spirit and they that worship Him must worship Him in spirit and in truth'" (112). He then gave the basic points of the defense as follows:

First, "The defense contends that to convict Scopes the prosecution must prove that Scopes not only taught the theory of evolution, but that he also, and at the same time, denied the theory of creation as set forth in the Bible" (113).

Second, he said, the defense also believed that "the prosecution must prove as part of its case what evolution is" (113).

Third, "the defense believes there is a direct conflict between the theory of evolution and the theories of creation set forth in the Book of Genesis" (113).

Fourth, "Neither do we believe that the stories of creation as set forth in the Bible are reconciliable or scientifically correct" (113).

Fifth, nonetheless, the defense would show that "there are millions of people who believe in evolution and in the stories of creation as set forth in the Bible and who find no conflict between the two" (113).

Sixth, "While the defense thinks there is a conflict between evolution and the Old Testament, we believe there is not conflict between evolution and Christianity" (113). "There may be a conflict between evolution and the peculiar ideas of Christianity, which are held by Mr.

Bryan as the evangelical leader of the prosecution, but we deny that the evangelical leader of the prosecution is an authorized spokesman for the Christians of the United States" (113).

Seventh, Malone cited Bryan as saying, "to compel people to accept a religious doctrine by act of law was to make not Christians but hypocrites" (114). For religion is a matter of love, not of force.

Eighth, he argued that "Christianity is bound up with no scientific theory, that it has survived 2,000 years in the face of all the discoveries of science and that Christianity will continue to grow in respect and influence if the people recognize that there is no conflict with science and Christianity" (115).

Ninth, he said the defense believed that "there is no branch of science which can be taught today without teaching the theory of evolution" (115).

Tenth, Malone also claimed that the defense would support evolution from science, offering embryological development as evidence. He cited "gill slits of an embryo baby" as one example, claiming "The embryo becomes a human being when it is born" (114–115).

Eleventh, he claimed the defense would show the practical benefits of evolution for mankind, in agriculture, in geology, and in "every branch of science" (116).

Twelfth, he said that "the book of Genesis is in part a hymn, in part an allegory and a work of religious interpretations written by men who believed that the earth was flat and whose authority cannot be accepted to control the teachings of science in our schools" (116).

Malone concluded his summary of what the defense intended to do by saying: "The narrow purpose of the defense is to establish the innocence of the defendant Scopes. The broad purpose of the defense will be to prove that the Bible is a work of religious aspiration and rules of conduct which must be kept in the field of theology" (116).

After an objection by the state to mentioning Bryan by name and Bryan saying he did not mind but would set the record straight about his views when he had an opportunity (117), the jury was sworn in by the court (119).

WITNESSES FOR THE STATE TAKE THE STAND

Mr. Walter White, superintendent of the Rhea County School District and the first witness called by the state, verified that Scopes was a science teacher, that he taught out of a textbook titled *A Civic Biology,* by George William Hunter,[21] that he had reviewed the whole book around April 21, and that he had remarked to White that "he couldn't teach biology without violating this law" (120) and that he [White] believed that Scopes did "teach" evolution from that text to the Rhea County students. ACLU attorney Hays objected to the King James Version of the Bible being offered as evidence for "the Bible" in the law, noting that there were numerous versions of the Bible, of different translations, and even the Catholic Bible with "80 books"[22] (123) in it as opposed to 66 in Protestant Bibles (123). A student in Scopes's class, Howard Morgan, answered the question about teaching evolution: "Did Prof. Scopes teach it to you?" by responding, "Yes, sir" (125). Another pupil, Harry Shelton, confirmed that Scopes had taught evolution to them (129). Mr. Robinson, member of the school board and owner of the store that sold the evolution biology books, also testified to a conversation with Scopes wherein he admitted that "any teacher in the state who was teaching Hunter's Biology was violating the law; that science teachers could not teach Hunter's Biology without violating the law" (129).

Under cross-examination, Darrow had Robinson read sections from Hunter's book about what evolution means, and that there are "over 500,000 species of animals" (131). State's attorney Stewart had Genesis 1 and 2 read in order to get it into the record, and the state rested its case.

The defense called Professor Maynard M. Metcalf, a zoologist from Oberlin College in Ohio, to the stand. He testified that, "I am absolutely convinced from personal knowledge that any one of these men [in my field] feel and believe, as a matter of course, that *evolution is a fact*" (137, emphasis added). He went on to say, "but I doubt very much if any two of

---

21. See note 10, above.

22. This is an error. Roman Catholics accept only 11 of the 14 Apocryphal books into their Bible, and only 7 of them are listed in the table of contents, with 4 additions being made to Daniel and Esther. This makes a total of 77 books in the Roman Catholic Bible but only 73 listed in the table of contents: 46 in the OT and 27 in the NT. See Norman Geisler and William Nix, *A General Introduction to the Bible* (Chicago: Moody, 1986), chapter 15.

them agree as to the exact method by which evolution has been brought about" (137). Later he described evolution as "a tremendous probability," which it "would be entirely impossible for any normal human being" to have "even for a moment the least doubt" about (143). The only evidence he alluded to, however, was similarities among animals and "varieties of human kind appearing earlier in the geological series" (143).

(The jury was retired while the attorneys argued about whether these scientific testimonies about evolution were relevant to the case.)

The witness continued: "The fact of evolution is a thing that is perfectly and absolutely clear . . . [but] the methods by which evolution has been brought about—that we are not yet in possession of scientific knowledge to answer" (139). When asked how old life is, his "guess" was "600,000,000 years" (141).

Fifth Day (July 16)

OPENING PRAYER

Dr. J. A. Allen, a Church of Christ pastor, opened in prayer to "Our Father who art in Heaven," that "Thy Word may be vindicated, and that Thy truth may be spread in the earth." This he prayed "in the name of Jesus. Amen" (145).

After more wrangling between the attorneys about the need for scientific testimony (145–147), the state moved to exclude the evidence on the grounds that "under the wording of the act and interpretation of the act, which we insist interprets itself, this evidence would be entirely incompetent" (147). To paraphrase, the law against teaching evolution is the law, regardless of the evidence for it or against it. So, "there is no issue left except the issue as to whether or not [what Scopes taught] conflicts with the Bible" (148).

BRYAN'S SON'S SPEECH ON THE DANGER OF EXPERT WITNESSES

The son of William Jennings Bryan then pleaded the case against expert testimony, arguing that it is "the weakest . . . and most dangerous" and there is no way to contradict it since it is only an opinion

(150). Another "danger involved in receiving the opinion of the witness is that the jury may substitute such opinion for their own" (151) even though it is "largely a field of speculation besought with pitfalls and uncertainties" (151). And "It is generally safer to take the judgment of unskilled jurors than the opinions of hired and generally biased experts" (150–151). Furthermore, "There is no issue of fact raised by evidence, the facts are agreed upon both sides" (152). So, "To permit an expert to testify upon this issue would be to substantiate [substitute?] trial by experts for trial by jury, and to announce to the world your honor's belief that this jury is too stupid to determine a simple question of fact" (153).

ACLU ATTORNEY HAYS RESPONDS

Defense attorney Hays responded that the defense agreed that Scopes taught evolution, "but as to whether that is contrary to . . . the Bible should be a matter of evidence" (154). Further, the jury needed to know the facts of science in order to know what evolution is. Further, evolution must be proven to be contrary to "the Bible." But which Bible? And whose interpretation of it? (156). Further, he said, the defense needed to be allowed to present the facts of evolution, which, he believed, were as firmly established as "the Copernican theory," which was "accepted by everyone today" (156). Further, for the court even to render an informed decision, "the court must take testimony and evidence on facts which are not matters of common knowledge" (157).

STATE'S ATTORNEY HICKS ARGUES FOR THE CLARITY OF THE LAW

Mr. Hicks, attorney for the state, argued that the words of the law itself "preclude the introduction of such testimony as they are trying to bring into the case" (161). The law says it is unlawful to teach "any theory that denies the story of divine creation . . . as taught in the Bible." That is clear. So, if the next phrase is not clear (that is, if "that man has descended from a lower order of animals" is not clear), then it must be understood in the light of the first phrase. For the courts have ruled that "if one clause of that statute, one part of it is vague, not definitely understood, . . . you must construe the whole statute together" (161). "They cannot take the first part of the statute and leave off the last, which Mr. Darrow endeavored to do here the other day in his great speech . . ." (162). Further, when "the language used is not entirely clear, the court may, to determine the meaning, and in aid of the interpretation, consider the spirit, intention and purpose of a law. . . ." And the purpose of the law "is to prevent the teaching in our schools that man descended from a lower order of animals, and when he [John Scopes] taught that, as has been proven by our proof in chief, he violated the law, and cannot get around it" (162).

State's Attorney McKenzie Argues "We Have Crossed the Rubicon"

State's attorney McKenzie observed that the court had already "crossed the Rubicon" when the judge ruled that the act was clear. "That never left anything on the face of the earth to determine, except as to the guilt or the innocence of the defendant at bar in violating that act" (166).

The judge then asked McKenzie if he believed the divine story of creation in the Bible was so clear that "no reasonable minds could differ as to the method of creation, that is, that man was created, complete by God." He answered "Yes" (166). The judge reinforced the question by saying, "And in one act, and not by a method of growth or development; is that your position?" McKenzie responded, "From lower animals—yes, that is exactly right" (166–167). Then the judge asked, "do you claim that if you meet the second clause, by implication of law you have met the requirement of the first?" McKenzie replied, "Yes, that is exactly it" (167).

The Speech of William Jennings Bryan

The afternoon of the fifth day began with a speech by William Jennings Bryan, who made the following main points.

First, "we believe the court should hold, that the [scientific] testimony that defense is now offering is not competent and not proper testimony . . ." (170).

Second, "our position is that the statute is sufficient. . . . The statute needs no interpretation" (171). The second part "was careful to define what it meant by the first part of the statute." It "removes all doubt" by pointing out "specifically what is meant" (171).

Third, "Mr Scopes knew what the law was and knew what evolution was, and knew that it violated the law, [and] he proceeded to violate the law. That is the evidence before this court, and we do not need any expert to tell us what that law means" (171).

Fourth, the opposition is saying in effect, "No, not the Bible, you see in this state they cannot teach the Bible. They can only teach things that declare it to be a lie, according to the learned counsel. These people in the state—Christian people—have tied their hands by their constitution" (172).

Fifth, "The question is can a minority in this state come in and compel a teacher to teach that the Bible is not true and make the parents of these children pay the expenses of the teacher to tell their children what these people believe is false and dangerous?" (172). "And the parents have a right to say that no teacher paid by their money shall rob their children of faith in God and send them back to their homes, skeptical, infidels, or agnostics, or atheists" (175).

Sixth, Bryan attacked evolution directly, asserting: "My contention is that the evolutionary hypothesis is not a theory, your honor" (176) because it has never been confirmed by fact that there is "a single species, the origin of which could be traced to another species" (177). He claimed, "the Christian believes man comes from above, but the evolutionist believes he must have come from below" (174). He showed the evolution tree in Hunter's *Civic Biology* book from which Scopes allegedly had taught (174). He cited Darwin's *Descent of Man* (1871), where Darwin said man came from the "new world . . . monkey" (176).

Seventh, Bryan affirmed his belief that [1] "the Bible is the Word of God . . . [2] the record of the Son of God, [3] the Saviour of the world, [4] born of the virgin Mary, [5] crucified and [6] risen again.[23] That Bible is not going to be driven out of this court by experts who come hundreds

23. Here Bryan states six of the fundamental doctrines that characterize a "fundamentalist."

of miles to testify that they can reconcile evolution with its ancestor in the jungle, with man made by God in His image . . ." (181–182).

CLARENCE DARROW'S RESPONSE

Darrow read a quote from Bryan, in which Bryan said, "It is the duty of the university . . . to be the great storehouse of the wisdom of the ages, and to let students go there, and learn, and choose." He continued the quote, "Every changed idea in the world has had its consequences. Every new religious doctrine has created its victims" (182). The implication seemed to have been that this was inconsistent with what Bryan was now arguing.

MALONE'S RESPONSE

ACLU attorney Malone made a variety of observations. His comments ranged from the trivial to the profound. The following is a summary of his main points.

First, he correctly noted that "it does seem to me that we have gone far afield in this discussion" (183).

Second, he then proceeded to criticize Bryan, whom he classed as "the leader of the prosecution," for being a "propagandist" and making a "speech against science" (183).

Third, he charged that creationists want everyone to believe the world is only "6,000 years old," "the world was flat," and the earth is "the center of the universe" (183).

Fourth, in response to the Darwin quote about man coming from monkeys, he noted the change in evolutionists' views, asking: "Haven't we learned anything in seventy-five years?" He also likened creationists to the Roman Catholic persecution of Galileo, who opposed the view that the sun moves around the earth (183).

Fifth, he perceived the conflict as one of ideas "by men of two frames of mind": theological and scientific. The theological mind he described as one that was closed, established by the revelation of God in the Bible, which it believed should be understood literally. The scientific mind, by contrast, was open, in progress, changing, and not based on any revelation from God. It believed that the Bible is only an inspiration and a guide, a set of ideas and sermons (184).

Sixth, "This theory of evolution, in one form or another, has been in Tennessee since 1832, and I think it is incumbent on the prosecution to introduce at least one person in the state of Tennessee whose morals have been affected by the teaching of this theory" (184).

Seventh, if the state was correct in its understanding of the anti-evolution law, then "or" and not "and" should have connected the two parts of it. But it does not, and so the state must prove two things, not just one.

Eighth, he asserted, the Bible is not a book of science. Hence, the state is wrong in claiming in effect that "only the Bible shall be taken as an authority on the subject of evolution in a course on biology" (185).

Ninth, in response to the judge's question he affirmed his belief that "the theory of evolution is reconcilable with the story of divine creation as taught in the Bible" (186). Hence, the defense does not believe that God created the first man "complete all at once" (186).

Tenth, Malone uttered one of the most profound lines in the trial: "For God's sake let the children have their minds kept open—close no doors to their knowledge; shut no door from them. Make the distinction between theology and science. Let them have both. Let them both be taught" (187).

Eleventh, Malone also made some profound statements about truth: "There is never a duel with the truth. The truth always wins and we are not afraid of it. The truth is no coward. The truth does not need the law. The truth does not need the forces of government. . . . The truth is imperishable, eternal and immortal and needs no human agency to support it" (187).

Twelfth, brimming with optimism, Malone proclaimed: "We are ready. We feel we stand with progress. We feel we stand with science. We feel we stand with intelligence. We feel we stand with fundamental freedom in America" (188).

Darrow Adds Some Comments

Clarence Darrow then added some thoughts of his own. First, "We say that God created man out of the dust of the earth is simply a figure of speech" (188).

Second, when asked: "[Do] you recognize God behind the first spark of life?" Darrow answered: "We expect most of our witnesses to take that view. As to me I don't pretend to have any opinion on it" (188).

Third, "there is no such thing as species—that is all nonsense. Science does not talk about species. . . . It is a process we are interested in and the Bible story is not inconsistent with that" (189).

Fourth, to the judge's question as to whether life has a "common source" of "one cell," Darrow answered, "Well, I am not quite so clear, but I think it did. It all came from protoplasm, which is a bearer of life and probably all came from one cell . . ." (189).

Fifth, Darrow admitted humans have reason "very much greater than any other animal," but never answered the judge's question as to where it came from (189).

Sixth, when asked about the evolutionists' view on immortality, he replied that "Evolution, as a theory, is concerned with the organism of man. Chemistry does not speak of immortality and hasn't anything to do with it" (189).

Stewart Refocuses the Issue

Attorney General Stewart tried to get the discussion back on track. He made several points.

First, he insisted that the purpose of the legislature in passing the law in question took precedence over any disputable construction in that law (190, 192, 193).

Second, he noted that there was nothing to which expert witnesses could testify, except to whether evolution was consistent with the Bible. But the people of Tennessee had already decided on that issue in the wording of the law (191–192).

Third, "it is the duty of the court to never place an absurd construction upon an act. And I submit that the construction, as I understand it, they insist upon would be absurd" (192).

Fourth, it is also a matter of precedent law that "In construing a statute the meaning is to be determined, not from special words in a single sentence or section but from the act taken as a whole . . . and viewing the legislation in the light of its general purpose" (193).

Fifth, "They say this is a battle between religion and science. If it is, I want to serve notice now, in the name of the great God, that I am on the side of religion" (197). "I say scientific investigation [about origins] is nothing but a theory and will never be anything but a theory" (198). "I say, bar the door, and not allow science to enter" (197).

Sixth, "There should not be any clash between science and religion. . . . How did it occur? It occurred from teaching that infidelity, that agnosticism, that which breeds in the soul of a child, infidelity, atheism, and drives him from the Bible that his father and mother raised him by, which . . . drives man's sole hope of happiness and of religion and of freedom of thought, and worship, and Almighty God, from him" (197).

Seventh, "Yes, discard that theory of the Bible [about creation]— throw it away, and let scientific development progress beyond man's origin. And the next thing you know, there will be a legal battle staged within the corners of this state, that challenges even permitting anyone to believe that Jesus Christ . . . was born of a virgin—challenge that, and the next step will be a battle staged denying the right to teach that there was a resurrection, until finally that precious book and its glorious teaching upon which this civilization has been built will be taken from us" (197–198).

Sixth Day (July 17)

OPENING PRAYER

On the sixth day of the *Scopes* trial, Dr. Eastwood opened with a prayer to "Our Father and our God," praying for "justice" in the courts and "blessings" on the court, jury, counsel, and the press "in the name of our Lord and Master Jesus Christ. Amen" (201).

The Ruling of the Judge About Expert Testimony

The conclusion of the judge's ruling on whether to allow expert testimony was as follows:

> In the final analysis this court, after a most earnest and careful consideration, has reached the conclusion that under the provisions of the act involved in this case, it is made unlawful thereby to teach in the public schools of the state of Tennessee the theory that man descended from a lower order of animals. If the court is correct in this, then the evidence of experts would shed no light on the issues. Therefore, the court is content to sustain the motion of the attorney general to exclude the expert testimony (203).

The Ensuing Discussion

After the defense insisted on getting the evolutionists' testimony into the record, Stewart charged that, "It is a known fact that the defense consider this a campaign of education to get before the people their ideas of evolution and scientific principles" (205). Defense attorney Malone denied this immediately.

Darrow's Angry Statement

After Bryan asked for and was given the right to cross-examine the expert witnesses, Darrow shot back: "We want to submit what we want to prove. That is all we want to do. If that will not enlighten the court cross-examination of Mr. Bryan would not enlighten the court" (206). He then added, "What we are interested in, counsel well knows what the judgment and verdict in this case will be. . . . I do not understand why . . . a bare suggestion of anything that is perfectly competent on our part should be immediately over-ruled." To this the judge retorted, "I hope you do not mean to reflect upon the court?" Darrow snapped: "Well, your honor has the right to hope" (206–207).

The court agreed, however, for the purposes of appeal, to allow the expert testimony to go on the record.[24] The question was left open as to whether the testimony would be written or oral, and court was dismissed early, at 10:30 a.m., until Monday morning.

Seventh Day (July 20)

OPENING PRAYER

A minister prayed to "Almighty God, our Father in Heaven," and gave thanks for "all the kindly influences" on our lives and acknowledged that "we have been stupid enough to match our human minds with revelations of the infinite and eternal." He prayed for God's "guidance and directing presence . . . in all things . . . we ask for Christ's sake. Amen" (211).

DARROW CITED FOR CONTEMPT OF COURT

The judge read a section from the previous day's record and concluded: "I feel that further forbearance would cease to be a virtue, and in an effort to protect the good name of my state, and to protect the dignity of the court over which I preside, I am constrained and impelled to call upon the said Darrow, to know what he has to say why he should not be dealt with for contempt" (212).

LETTER FROM GOVERNOR PEAY

The defense requested that they be allowed to read a letter from the governor in which he opined that, "It will be seen that this bill [the law that Scopes was accused of violating] does not require any particular theory or interpretation of the Bible regarding man's creation to be taught in the public schools." He further offered his view that "The widest latitude of interpretation will remain as to the time and manner of God's process in His creation of man" (213). He added, "After careful examination I can find nothing of consequence in the books now being

24. The *Scopes* verdict was appealed to the Tennessee Supreme Court, where it was upheld in 1927.

taught in our schools with which this bill will interfere in the slightest manner" (214).

The judge noted, "That is the governor's opinion about it," but added, "with all deference to Gov. Peay—[he] does not belong to the interpreting branch of the government. His opinion of what the law means . . . is of no consequence at all in the court, and could not have any bearing, and I exclude the statement" (214).

DEFENSE ATTEMPTS TO OFFER NEW TEXTBOOK AS EVIDENCE

ACLU attorney Hays offered as evidence a new science textbook that had been adopted for the schools since the *Scopes* trial had begun. Sections were read where Darwin is praised for having contributed to "a great part of [the world's] modern progress in biology" (215) and where it is explained how some primates "evolved (developed) along special lines of their own." But the book added, "none of them are to be thought of as the source or origin of the human species. It is futile, therefore, to look for the primitive stock of the human species in any existing animals" (215).[25]

FURTHER DISCUSSION OVER TESTIMONY

Continued wrangling over the law ensued, with defense attorney Hays charging that the law was "unreasonable" and, therefore, unconstitutional. He insisted that that was why they wanted to offer evidence (216). Attorney General Stewart continued to insist that the defense only wanted the evidence on the record for propaganda purposes: "I stated that the primary purpose of the defense is to go ahead with this lawsuit for the purpose of conducting an educational campaign and say to the publice [*sic*] through the press their idea of their theory" (218). The judge gave an hour for the defense to summarize for the court what their witnesses wanted to say before he made

25. It would appear that this statement was carefully crafted to support evolution while at the same time appearing to deny it. Three things are noteworthy in this regard: (1) The book speaks about the evolution of primates, (2) it does not deny the evolution of man but simply says man did not evolve from any "existing animals," and (3) it implies that scientists are still looking for "the source or origin of the human species."

his final decision on whether to allow their testimony in the record (though not for the jury, nor to decide the case, only for the record for appealing the case).

SUMMARY OF REV. WALTER C. WHITAKER'S TESTIMONY

Defense attorney Hays described Walter C. Whitaker, an Episcopal rector, as a "Christian and an evolutionist at the same time" (223). Hays said Whitaker's testimony would be as follows: "As one who for thirty years has preached Jesus Christ as the Son of God . . . I am unable to see any contradiction between evolution and Christianity." He also would say, "a man can be a Christian without taking every word of the Bible literally" (223).

SUMMARY OF SHAILER MATHEWS'S TESTIMONY

Shailer Mathews, Dean of the University of Chicago Divinity School, was quoted as saying, "a correct understanding of Genesis shows that its account of creation is no more denied by evolution than it is by the laws of light, electricity, and gravitation. The Bible deals with religion" (224). Further, "There are two accounts in Genesis of the creation of man. They are not identical and at points differ widely. It would be difficult to say which is the teaching of the Bible" (224). Further, "so far from opposing the Genesis account of the creation of man, the theory of evolution in some degree resembles it. But the book of Genesis is not intended to teach science, but to teach the activity of God in nature and the spiritual value of man" (224). Thus, "The theory of evolution is an attempt to explain the process in detail. . . . Genesis and evolution are complementary to each other, Genesis emphasizing the divine first cause and science the details of the process through which God works" (225). He noted that "This view that evolution is not contrary to Genesis is held by many conservative evangelical theologians, such as Strong, Hall, Micon, Harris and Johnson. Mullins also holds to theistic evolution" (225). Other statements were read into the record.

DARROW'S APOLOGY FOR CONTEMPT

After lunch, Clarence Darrow apologized to the judge, saying, "Of course, your honor will remember that whatever took place was hurried, one thing followed another and the truth is I did not know just how it looked until I read over the minutes as your honor did and when I read them over I was sorry that I had said it" (225). The judge replied in part, "My friends, and Col. Darrow, the Man that I believe came into the world to save man from sin, the Man that died on the cross that man might be redeemed, taught that it was godly to forgive. . . . The Savior died on the cross pleading with God for the men who crucified Him. I believe in that Christ. I believe in these principles. I accept Col. Darrow's apology" (226).

FURTHER TESTIMONY

A statement was taken from Rabbi Rosenwasser which included the notation that the King James translation was inaccurate, including "create" (from the Hebrew *bara*, which should be translated "set in motion") (228). He concluded: "If the Hebrew Bible were properly translated and understood, one would not find any conflict with the theory of evolution which would prevent him from accepting both" (229).

Dr. H. E. Murkett was also cited as saying: "We would also be able to prove that the Bible, properly interpreted, does not conflict with the theory of evolution . . ." (229). Other testimonies were taken on this same issue.

STATEMENT OF THE DEFENSE

The defense added their own statement: "Of course, the defense, as lawyers, take no position on the truth of the stories of the Bible, but we wish to state that we should be able to prove from learned Biblical scholars that the Bible is both a literal and figurative document, that God speaks by parables, allegories, sometimes literally and sometimes spiritually" (230). Citing Psalm 139:15–16 about God forming an embryo in the womb, they concluded: "Here there is a distinct statement that the human body was created by the process of evolution. Also Roman [*sic*] VIII 22 says: 'For we know that the whole creation groaneth and travaileth in pain together until now'" (230). "In other words, we should prove that the Bible is subject to various interpretations depending upon the learning and understanding of the individual, and that, if this is true, there is nothing necessarily inconsistent between one's understanding of the Bible and evolution." They added, "They may accept them as legends or parables, and thus not find them inconsistent with any scientific theory" (231). Strangely and ironically, the defense ended their statement with a quotation from 2 Timothy 4:3–4 (Goodspeed translation), which declares, "The time will come when they will not listen to wholesome instruction, but will overwhelm themselves with teachers to suit their whims and tickle their fancies, and they will turn from listening to the truth and wander off after fiction" (231)!

OTHER SCIENTISTS OFFER STATEMENTS

Anthropologist Fay-Cooper Cole argued that "evidence abundantly justifies" (235) evolution. He cited vestigial (useless) organs, similarities of animals, and human-like ancestors of man to support evolution. He referred to "Piltdown" man, subsequently exposed as a fraud (237), as well as "Neanderthal," "Java," and "Cromagnon." He concluded, "From the above it seems conclusive that it is impossible to teach anthropology or the prehistory of man without teaching evolution" (237–238).

Wilbur A. Nelson, Tennessee state geologist, reviewed the rock formations without mentioning a single "missing link," yet concluded that such information would not have been possible "unless the teaching of evolution had been permitted" (239). The only real evidence offered for evolution was that "the relative ages of the rocks correspond closely to the degrees of complexity of organization shown by the fossils in those rocks" (241).

One geologist, Kirtley F. Mather of Harvard, went so far as to say, "There are in truth no missing links in the record which connects man with other members of the order of primates" (247). He admitted that "it is possible to construct a mechanistic, evolutionary hypothesis which rules God out of the world," but it is not necessary because a theistic evolutionary model has both (248). He insisted that science and religion cannot conflict because the latter deals with the ultimate cause and the former with immediate causes. Hence, "Science has not even a guess as to the original source or sources of matter. . . . For science there is no beginning and no ending; all acceptable theories of earth origin are theories of rejuvenation rather than of creation—from nothing" (248). Yet he was convinced that "knowing the ages of the rocks has led to better knowledge of the Rock of Ages" (250).

Zoologist Maynard Metcalf contended that "intelligent teaching of biology or intelligent approach to any biological science is impossible if the established fact of evolution is omitted" (251). He added, "Not only has evolution occurred; it is occurring today and occurring even under man's control" (253). "Evolution is a present observable phenomenon as well as an established fact of past occurring" (253).

Zoologist Winterton C. Curtis of the University of Missouri admitted that creation of different types was not only a "possibility" but was actually held by some scientists: "One of the pre-Darwin ideas was that each animal, while created separately, was nevertheless formed in accordance with a certain type that the Creator had in mind, hence the resemblance" (257). Indeed, this view of a common Creator vs. a common ancestor continued after Darwin among some scientists (Louis Agassiz of Harvard being one) and is growing today. In spite of this, and in spite of the admission (by Curtis, quoting from a letter written to him) that "As to the nature of this process of evolution, we have many conjectures, but little positive knowledge," Curtis concluded, again quoting from the letter, "Let us then proclaim in precise and unmistakable language that our faith in evolution is unshaken" (259).

Horatio Hackett Newman, zoologist at the University of Chicago, argued from micro- to macroevolution while also acknowledging the difficulty of knowing the history of evolutionary development: "For the study of past evolutionary events we use the historical method so successfully employed in archaeology and ancient history; for the study of present evolution we make use of the methods of direct observation and experiment" (264). By contrast, "we admit that the evidences of past evolution are indirect and circumstantial . . ." (264). Strangely, he then proceeded to compare evolution to gravity, claiming that "The evidences upon which the law of gravity are [sic] based are no less indirect than those supporting the principle of evolution" (264).[26] He claimed there are 180 vestigial organs which are "evidence that man has descended from ancestors in which these organs were functional," including the "abbreviated tail" at the end of the backbone (268). He rejected the old creationists' view that "species" are a "fixed and definite assemblage such as one would expect it to be if specifically created as an immutable thing" (270). He called "special creation" a "rival explanation" to evolution (280).

Before the Jury Is Called Back into the Courtroom

Just before the jury was called back into the courtroom, Darrow protested the presence of a sign near the jury box which declared, "Read Your Bible" (280). State's attorney McKenzie asked, "Why should it be removed? It is their defense and stated before court, that they do not deny the Bible, that they expect to introduce proof to make it harmonize. Why should we remove the sign cautioning people to read the Word of God just to satisfy the others in the case?" (281). Darrow suggested balancing it with a sign on reading "Hunter's Biology" or "Read your evolution" (282). The court removed the sign, lest anyone be offended, and called for the jury.

The Defense Asks for Roman Catholic and Jewish Bibles as Evidence

The defense asked for Catholic and Jewish Bibles as evidence that there are differences in the Bible, not just in interpretations of it. The judge allowed for the Catholic Bible in English, but said "I don't believe it is worth fussing over. I don't think there is any conflict in it" (283). Stewart reminded the court that the "indictment was based on the

---

26. This is hardly the case, since gravity is a theory whose truth can be constantly and directly verified in the present by measuring the theory over against the observable and recurring laws of nature, whereas macroevolution cannot be so measured. It is a theory about past unobserved events of origin which are not recurring in the present and, hence, are no more observable than a historical event or archaeological event of which we have remains from the past.

King James Version of the Bible" (283), and that the Bible phrase in the indictment was not in question (284).

The Defense Calls Bryan as a Witness

In a surprise move, the defense called William Jennings Bryan as a witness, and he was willing to comply, though he was not actually sworn in as a witness. The next twenty pages containing Bryan's testimony were not an official part of the trial and were struck from the record the next day (304). Nonetheless, they contain fascinating exchanges that were highly sensationalized in the media. Bryan testified that he believed the Bible was the inspired Word of God and that "everything in the Bible should be accepted as it is given there; some of the Bible is given illustratively. For instance: 'Ye are the salt of the earth'" (285). He believed all the miracles in the Bible including that Jonah was literally swallowed by a great fish (285). He even went so far as to say he would believe the Bible, if it had said Jonah swallowed the whale, though he qualified it by saying, "the Bible doesn't make as extreme statements as evolutionists do" (285). Bryan confessed his belief that the sun stood still at Joshua's command, though he did not believe this was opposed to the scientific belief that the earth goes around the sun. It was a miracle that was written in "language that could be understood then" (286).

Although defense attorneys attempted to stop the irrelevant proceedings, since Bryan was willing the judge allowed his testimony to continue. Bryan charged that the ACLU attorneys "did not come here to try this case. They came to try revealed religion. I am here to defend it, and they can ask me any question they please" (288). Bryan accepted the historicity of Noah's flood (288–289), and the superiority of the Christian religion (291–292). He denied that the earth is only about 6,000 years old (298) and that the "days" of Genesis were only 24 hours long (299). As to whether the earth is young or old, Bryan said, "I do not think it important whether we believe one or the other" (302). When asked by Stewart what the purpose of the defense attorney's questions was, Bryan retorted: "The purpose is to cast ridicule on everybody who believes in the Bible, and I am perfectly willing that the world shall know that these gentlemen have no other purpose than ridiculing every Christian who believes in the Bible" (299). He added, "I am simply trying to protect the word of God against the greatest atheist or agnostic in the United States" (299). Bryan did not know where Cain got his wife but was content to believe it because the Bible said so (302). He believed in a literal Adam and Eve and a literal fall (303).

Bryan's last words were, "The only purpose Mr. Darrow has is to slur at the Bible. . . . I want the world to know that this man, who does not believe in a God, is trying to use a court in Tennessee . . . to slur at it, and while it will require time, I am willing to take it." Darrow's last words were: "I object to your statement. I am exempting you on your fool ideas that no intelligent Christian on earth believes" (304). With that the court adjourned for the day.

Eighth Day (July 21)

OPENING PRAYER

Dr. Camper prayed, "Oh God, our Heavenly Father. . . . We pray Thy blessing upon each one that has a part in this court here today. . . . We ask it in the name of Jesus Christ. Amen" (305).

BRYAN'S TESTIMONY STRUCK FROM THE RECORD

The judge expressed regret that he had allowed Bryan's testimony because of "an over-zeal to be absolutely fair to all parties" (305). He struck it from the record.

DARROW ENTERS PLEA OF GUILTY

Darrow claimed, "we have no witnesses to offer, no proof to offer on the issues that the court has laid down here. . . . I think to save time we will ask the court to bring in the jury and instruct the jury to find the defendant guilty" (306). Bryan pleaded with the press to be just in presenting his response to their report of his testimony the previous day, insisting that they should also print "the religious attitude of the people who come down here to deprive the people of Tennessee of the right to run their own schools" (308).

The Jury Is Brought in and Charged

The jury was then brought in and instructed as to the proper construction of the law: they were to understand the statute as only forbidding the teaching of evolution and making no assertion about what the Bible teaches about creation. The judge declared, "you are not concerned as to whether or not this is a theory denying the story of the divine creation of man as taught, for the issues as they have been finally made up in this case do not involve that question" (310). He pointed out that he had previously ruled that the second part of the statute merely explained the first; it did not make it necessary that the teacher also teach the biblical view on creation (whatever that may be).

The judge reminded the jury that the fine, if the defendant were found guilty, must be between $100 and $500. He defined the term "beyond reasonable doubt": not beyond all doubt, but beyond any doubt that "would prevent your mind resting easy as to the guilt of the defendant" (310).

Darrow told the jury that "there is no dispute about the facts. Scopes did not go on the stand, because he could not deny the statements made by [his students]" (311). Darrow added, "we cannot even explain to you that we think you should return a verdict of not guilty. We do not see how you could. We do not ask it. We think we will save our point and take it to the higher court . . ." (311).

Bryan's Last Speech

William Jennings Bryan's closing remarks are best summarized in the following two excerpts: "Here has been fought out a little case of little consequence as a case, but the world is interested because it raises an issue, and that issue will some day be settled right, whether it is settled on our side or the other side" (316). He added, "The people will determine this issue. They will take sides upon this issue. . . . no matter what our views may be, we ought not only desire, but pray, that that which is right will prevail, whether it be our way or somebody else's" (317).

DARROW'S LAST SPEECH

In his summary, Clarence Darrow said, "I think this case will be remembered because it is the first case of this sort since we stopped trying people in America for witchcraft because here we have done our best to turn back the tide that has sought to force itself upon this—upon this modern world, of testing every fact in science by a religious dictum" (317).

BENEDICTION

Dr. Jones closed in prayer, reciting 2 Corinthians 13:14: "May the grace of our Lord Jesus Christ, the love of God and the communion and fellowship of the Holy Ghost abide with you all. Amen" (319).

The Appeal of the Decision

Scopes was found guilty and ordered to pay a fine, but the fine was appealed and overturned on a technicality. The judge had issued the minimal fine of $100, but according to the law the jury should have set the amount, not the judge. Legally, the end of the case was like a tornado ending with a whimper. Of course, the issue lives on and perhaps will never die this side of eternity. The *Scopes* trial passed into history, but the legend survives, fueled by the fictional movie *Inherit the Wind,* from which the media show clips whenever the issue resurfaces.

Some Implications of the Trial

Important implications may be drawn from the *Scopes* trial for succeeding clashes in the courts. Several will be noted here, as they will bear on our further discussion.

1. The Framing of the Issue: Religion Against Science

By the very wording of the law at issue in the *Scopes* trial, the issue became framed from its inception as one of religion against science.

This unfortunate shadow has haunted every major creation/evolution trial since then, even though proponents of creation have strenuously attempted to make it a purely scientific issue by calling it "scientific creation" or "intelligent design" (see chapter 7). In the minds of the media and, through them, in the minds of the general public, the issue is still religion vs. science. Overcoming this mind-set has been one of the major challenges for the creationist movement. To date, the challenge has not been met. An important attempt to do this was squelched so as not to be available for the crucial Supreme Court decision in *Edwards* (1987). This will be discussed in detail in chapters 3, 4, and 7.

2. The Popularity of Science

Another important factor in this debate has been the popularity of science and the seizure of the "high ground" by the evolutionists. The successes of science are voluminous, and the practical effects of these successes are felt by everyone. Attacking science in the name of religion has not had great success in modern times. Since the vast majority of scientists embrace evolution, it is not popular in educated circles to attack evolution. Adding to the problem, most religious leaders, including early fundamentalists like A. A. Hodge, B. B. Warfield, James Orr, and even the Baptist theologian Augustus Strong have embraced theistic evolution as a viable solution to the problem. Having this option open makes it more difficult for those who claim that "evolution is against God." Meanwhile, naturalistic evolutionists have been successful in exploiting the courts to their advantage against the creation and intelligent design movements while at the same time convincing the courts that creation and intelligent design are no more than attempts by fundamentalists to get their religious views taught in public school. Again, this must be, but never has been, successfully overcome in a major court decision. A major hope to reverse this is found in my suppressed testimony (see chapter 4) and is spelled out in chapter 7.

3. The Ambiguity of the Term "Science"

Evolution is considered science and is even called a "fact" by evolution-ists. Creation, of course, is not thought of by the courts after *Scopes* as scientific but as a biblical and religious tenet. Given these premises implicit in the first major evolution/creation court case, the deck is loaded against creation, for its proponents acknowledge that it is something taught in a religious book—the Bible—while evolution is abstracted from any of its religious connotations and is portrayed as pure "science." However, there are two different kinds of science: origin science and operation science. Creation qualifies as a science under origin science (see chapter 8).

4. The Ambiguity of the Term "Evolution"

Another ambiguity in favor of macroevolution is the failure to clearly distinguish between microevolution, which is an empirical science, and macroevolution, which is being taught as if it too were an empirical science when it is not (see chapter 8). This equivocation has enabled evolution to survive the court tests of legitimacy while creation has not fared so well.

5. One-sided Use of Freedom of Speech

Another factor favoring evolution over creation in the public schools is the evolutionists' one-sided use of "freedom of speech" laws. Evolution-ists in *Scopes* and later have been able to convincingly apply this freedom to teaching their views while somehow forgetting that they should apply it equally to teaching creation. After all, the sword of free speech has two edges. It applies not only to the proponent (e.g., evolutionists) but also to his opponents (creationists).

Evolutionists have been successful in convincing the courts that it is not the province of the courts to make laws "in the realm of science and in the realm of religion" (55). Somehow, the higher courts since this time (that is, from 1968 to 2005) do not see that they have made pronouncements in these very areas, and in every case those pronouncements have favored one view over the other—just the opposite of the fairness for which they had pleaded in *Scopes!*

6. Emphasis on Minority Rights

Another issue creationists have not exploited is that of minority rights. Evolutionists were able to argue this convincingly in their favor at the *Scopes* trial. But creationists were not able to persuade the courts of this at the *McLean* case in Arkansas (1981–1982). Nor have subsequent cases utilized this argument effectively for teaching creation alongside evolution. For if evolution could gain its rights as a minority view in the schools while the creationist majority was passing laws against it, then why can't creationists do the same for their minority view now?

The Conclusion of the Trial

John Scopes was found guilty of violating the anti-evolution law of the state of Tennessee and was fined $100 by the judge. The trial adjourned, the world went home, but it has not been the same since. William Jennings Bryan died a short time later, but the controversy lives on.

In the *Scopes* trial of 1925, the legal victory was won by creationists, but the bigger and much more important public relations victory had been won by evolutionists—thanks in large part to a biased media. And even though it would be a whole generation before the Supreme Court in the 1968 *Epperson* case (see chapter 2) would strike down the last anti-evolution law, nonetheless, the theory of evolution, already accepted by the intellectual community, continued to gain ground in schools and, through them, in the wider public arena. And it was only a matter of time before this victory would work its way successfully through the courts (see chapters 3–7).

Additional Reading

Conkin, Paul M. *When All the Gods Trembled: Darwinism, Scopes, and American Intellectuals.* Rowman & Littlefield, 1998.

Geisler, Norman, with A. F. Brooke II and Mark J. Keough. *The Creator in the Courtroom: Scopes II*. Milford, Mich.: Mott Media, 1982.

Geisler, Norman, and Kerby Anderson. *Origin Science: A Proposal for the Creation-Evolution Controversy*. Grand Rapids, Mich.: Baker, 1987.

Hitchcock, James. *The Supreme Court and Religion in American Life*. Vol. 1. Princeton, N.J.: Princeton University Press, 2004.

Hodge, Charles. "What Is Darwinism?" In *What Is Darwinism? And Other Writings on Science and Religion*. Ed. Mark A. Noll and David N. Livingstone. Grand Rapids, Mich.: Baker, 1994.

Larson, Edward J. *Summer for the Gods*. New York: Basic Books, 1997.

———. *Trial and Error: The American Controversy over Creation and Evolution*. New York: Oxford University Press, 2003.

Moore, James R. *The Post-Darwinian Controversies*. New York: Cambridge University Press, 1979.

Roberts, Jon H. *Darwinism and the Divine in America: Protestant Intellectuals and Organic Evolution, 1859–1900*. Madison: University of Wisconsin Press, 1988; revised, Notre Dame, Ind.: University of Notre Dame Press, 2001.

The *Epperson* Supreme Court Ruling (1968)

Background

One of the most important Supreme Court cases about religious liberty is that of *Everson v. Board of Education* (1947).[1] The case involved a challenge to a New Jersey law allowing for parents who were sending their children to private schools to be reimbursed by local authorities for the cost of bus fare. Ironically, even though the law was upheld as constitutional, Justice Hugo Black, who wrote for the majority, set in motion a tide of thinking that would be felt down to the present day. James Hitchcock explains, "Black ended his opinion by pronouncing, 'The first amendment has erected a wall between church and state, that wall must be kept high and impregnable. We could not approve the slightest breach. New Jersey has not breached it here.' Thus Black revived [Thomas] Jefferson's metaphor after an oblivion of seventy years,

---

1. Not to be confused with the *Epperson* case of 1968, which is the subject of this chapter.

79

a revival that had crucial consequences for the modern understanding of the establishment clause."[2]

Hitchcock continues, "The *Everson* case was an instance where the specific issue—subsidized bus fares—was a rather minor one, but the case had implications far beyond the issue itself. In winning a small and temporary victory, proponents of religious schools lost the war because the case gave the court the opportunity to set forth, for the first time, an understanding of the first amendment based on the 'wall' metaphor, *an interpretation that virtually predetermined an increasingly stringent application of the Establishment Clause*"[3] (emphasis added). This helped set the stage for the first Supreme Court action on the creation/evolution controversy. For the first time this court decision took away the states' right to legislate their own religious matters and placed a wall of separation between the state and religion.

The Arkansas Supreme Court Upholds the Anti-evolution Law

The case known as *Epperson v. Arkansas* was heard by the U.S. Supreme Court on appeal from the Supreme Court of Arkansas. It was argued on October 16, 1968, and was decided a month later on November 12, 1968. Susan Epperson was an Arkansas public school teacher, hired in 1965, who challenged the constitutionality of Arkansas' so-called "anti-evolution" statute. That statute stated that it was unlawful for a teacher in any state-supported school to teach or to use a textbook that teaches "that mankind ascended or descended from a lower order of animals."[4]

The State Chancery Court held that the law was a violation of free speech and, thus, contrary to the First and Fourteenth Amendments of the U.S. Constitution. In a short two-sentence decision, the Arkansas Supreme Court upheld the anti-evolution law, saying: "Upon the

2. James Hitchcock, *The Supreme Court and Religion in American Life*, 2 vols. (Princeton, N.J.: Princeton University Press, 2004), 1:90.

3. Ibid., 91.

4. *Epperson v. State of Arkansas*, 393 U.S. 97 (1968).

principal issue, that of constitutionality, the court holds that Initiated Measure No. 1 of 1928 . . . is a valid exercise of the state's power to specify the curriculum in its public schools. The court expresses no opinion on the question whether the Act prohibits any explanation of the theory of evolution or merely prohibits teaching that the theory is true; the answer not being necessary to a decision in the case, and the issue not having been raised."[5]

The U.S. Supreme Court Decision in *Epperson* (1968)

The U.S. Supreme Court overturned the Arkansas Supreme Court and ruled that the statute "violates the Fourteenth Amendment, which embraces the First Amendment's prohibition of state laws respecting an establishment of religion." In the Court's words:

(a) The Court does not decide whether the statute is unconstitutionally vague, since, whether it is construed to prohibit explaining the Darwinian theory or teaching that it is true, the law conflicts with the Establishment Clause. . . .

(b) The sole reason for the Arkansas law is that a particular religious group considers the evolution theory to conflict with the account of the origin of man set forth in the Book of Genesis. . . .

(c) The First Amendment mandates governmental neutrality between religion and religion, and between religion and nonreligion. . . .

(d) A State's right to prescribe the public school curriculum does not include the right to prohibit teaching a scientific theory or doctrine for reasons that run counter to the principles of the First Amendment. . . .

(e) The Arkansas law is not a manifestation of religious neutrality.

The Court went on to say, "This appeal challenges the constitutionality of the 'anti-evolution' statute which the State of Arkansas adopted

5. Ibid.

in 1928 to prohibit the teaching in its public schools and universities
of the theory that man evolved from other species of life. The statute
was a product of the upsurge of 'fundamentalist' religious fervor of the
twenties." They believed that, "The Arkansas statute was an adaptation
of the famous Tennessee 'monkey law' which that State adopted in 1925.
The constitutionality of the Tennessee law was upheld by the Tennessee
Supreme Court in the celebrated Scopes case in 1927." This law made
"it unlawful for a teacher in any state-supported school or university
'to teach the theory or doctrine that mankind ascended or descended
from a lower order of animals,' or 'to adopt or use in any such institu-
tion a textbook that teaches' this theory. Violation is a misdemeanor
and subjects the violator to dismissal from his position."[6]

The Supreme Court Ruling

Following is the text of the *Epperson* decision, omitting the footnotes.
After giving background information in Part I, the Court stated:

II. At the outset, it is urged upon us that the challenged statute is vague
and uncertain and therefore within the condemnation of the Due Process
Clause of the Fourteenth Amendment. The contention that the Act is
vague and uncertain is supported by language in the brief opinion of
Arkansas' Supreme Court. That court, perhaps reflecting the discomfort
which the statute's quixotic prohibition necessarily engenders in the
modern mind, stated that it "expresses no opinion" as to whether the
Act prohibits "explanation" of the theory of evolution or merely forbids
"teaching that the theory is true." Regardless of this uncertainty, the
court held that the statute is constitutional.

On the other hand, counsel for the State, in oral argument in this
Court, candidly stated that, despite the State Supreme Court's equivocation, Arkansas would interpret the statute "to mean that to make a
student aware of the theory . . . just to teach that there was such a theory"
would be grounds for dismissal and for prosecution under the statute;
and he said "that the Supreme Court of Arkansas' opinion should be

6. *Epperson v. State of Arkansas,* 393 U.S. 97 (1968).

interpreted in that manner." He said: "If Mrs. Epperson would tell her students that 'Here is Darwin's theory, that man ascended or descended from a lower form of being,' then I think she would be under this statute liable for prosecution." In any event, we do not rest our decision upon the asserted vagueness of the statute. On either interpretation of its language, Arkansas' statute cannot stand. It is of no moment whether the law is deemed to prohibit mention of Darwin's theory, or to forbid any or all of the infinite varieties of communication embraced within the term "teaching." Under either interpretation, the law must be stricken because of its conflict with the constitutional prohibition of state laws respecting an establishment of religion or prohibiting the free exercise thereof. The overriding fact is that Arkansas' law selects from the body of knowledge a particular segment which it proscribes for the sole reason that it is deemed to conflict with a particular religious doctrine; that is, with a particular interpretation of the Book of Genesis by a particular religious group.

III. The antecedents of today's decision are many and unmistakable. They are rooted in the foundation soil of our Nation. They are fundamental to freedom.

Government in our democracy, state and national, must be neutral in matters of religious theory, doctrine, and practice. It may not be hostile to any religion or to the advocacy of no-religion; and it may not aid, foster, or promote one religion or religious theory against another or even against the militant opposite. The First Amendment mandates governmental neutrality between religion and religion, and between religion and nonreligion.

As early as 1872, this Court said: "The law knows no heresy, and is committed to the support of no dogma, the establishment of no sect." *Watson v. Jones.* . . . This has been the interpretation of the great First Amendment which this Court has applied in the many and subtle problems which the ferment of our national life has presented for decision within the Amendment's broad command.

Judicial interposition in the operation of the public school system of the Nation raises problems requiring care and restraint. Our courts, however, have not failed to apply the First Amendment's mandate in our educational system where essential to safeguard the fundamental values of freedom of speech and inquiry and of belief. By and large, public education in our Nation is committed to the control of state and local authorities. Courts do not and cannot intervene in the resolution of conflicts which arise in the daily operation of school systems and which do not directly and sharply implicate basic constitutional values. On the other hand, "the vigilant protection of constitutional freedoms is nowhere more vital than in the community of American schools" *Shelton v. Tucker*... (1960). As this Court said in *Keyishian v. Board of Regents*, the First Amendment "does not tolerate laws that cast a pall of orthodoxy over the classroom"... (1967).

The earliest cases in this Court on the subject of the impact of constitutional guarantees upon the classroom were decided before the Court expressly applied the specific prohibitions of the First Amendment to the States. But as early as 1923, the Court did not hesitate to condemn under the Due Process Clause "arbitrary" restrictions upon the freedom of teachers to teach and of students to learn. In that year, the Court, in an opinion by Justice McReynolds, held unconstitutional an Act of the State of Nebraska making it a crime to teach any subject in any language other than English to pupils who had not passed the eighth grade. The State's purpose in enacting the law was to promote civic cohesiveness by encouraging the learning of English and to combat the "baneful effect" of permitting foreigners to rear and educate their children in the language of the parents' native land. The Court recognized these purposes, and it acknowledged the State's power to prescribe the school curriculum, but it held that these were not adequate to support the restriction upon the liberty of teacher and pupil. The challenged statute, it held, unconstitutionally interfered with the right of the individual, guaranteed by the Due Process Clause, to engage in any of the common occupations of life and to acquire useful knowledge. *Meyer v. Nebraska*... (1923). See also *Bartels v. Iowa*... (1923)....

There is and can be no doubt that the First Amendment does not permit the State to require that teaching and learning must be tailored to the principles or prohibitions of any religious sect or dogma. In *Everson v. Board of Education*, this Court, in upholding a state law to provide free bus service to school children, including those attending parochial schools, said: "Neither [a state nor the federal government] can pass laws which aid one religion, aid all religions, or prefer one religion over another"... (1947).

At the following Term of Court, in *McCollum v. Board of Education* ... (1948), the Court held that Illinois could not release pupils from class to attend classes of instruction in the school buildings in the religion of their choice. This, it said, would involve the State in using tax-supported property for religious purposes, thereby breaching the "wall of separation" which, according to Jefferson, the First Amendment was intended to erect between church and state.... See also *Engel v. Vitale*... (1962); *Abington School District v. Schempp*... (1963). While study of religions and of the Bible from a literary and historic viewpoint, presented objectively as part of a secular program of education, need not collide with the First Amendment's prohibition, the State may not adopt programs or practices in its public schools or colleges which "aid or oppose" any religion.... This prohibition is absolute. It forbids alike the preference of a religious doctrine or the prohibition of theory which is deemed antagonistic to a particular dogma. As Mr. Justice Clark stated in *Joseph Burstyn, Inc. v. Wilson*, "the state has no legitimate interest in protecting any or all religions from views distasteful to them ..." (1952). The test was stated as follows in *Abington School District v. Schempp* ... "What are the purpose and the primary effect of the enactment? If either is the advancement or inhibition of religion then the enactment exceeds the scope of legislative power as circumscribed by the Constitution."

These precedents inevitably determine the result in the present case. The State's undoubted right to prescribe the curriculum for its public schools does not carry with it the right to prohibit, on pain of criminal penalty, the teaching of a scientific theory or doctrine where that prohibition is based upon reasons that violate the First Amendment. It is much too late to argue that the State may impose upon the teachers in its schools any conditions that it chooses, however restrictive they may be of constitutional guarantees. *Keyishian v. Board of Regents* ... (1967).

In the present case, there can be no doubt that Arkansas has sought to prevent its teachers from discussing the theory of evolution because it is contrary to the belief of some that the Book of Genesis must be the exclusive source of doctrine as to the origin of man. No suggestion has been made that Arkansas' law may be justified by considerations of state policy other than the religious views of some of its citizens. It is clear that fundamentalist sectarian conviction was and is the law's reason for existence. Its antecedent, Tennessee's "monkey law," candidly stated its purpose: to make it unlawful "to teach any theory that denies the story of the Divine Creation of man as taught in the Bible, and to teach instead that man has descended from a lower order of animals." Perhaps the sensational publicity attendant upon the Scopes trial induced Arkansas to adopt less explicit language. It eliminated Tennessee's reference to "the story of the Divine Creation of man" as taught in the Bible, but there is no doubt that the motivation for the law was the same: to suppress the teaching of a theory which, it was thought, "denied" the divine creation of man.

Arkansas' law cannot be defended as an act of religious neutrality. Arkansas did not seek to excise from the curricula of its schools and universities all discussion of the origin of man. The law's effort was confined to an attempt to blot out a particular theory because of its supposed conflict with the Biblical account, literally read. Plainly, the law is contrary to the mandate of the First, and in violation of the Fourteenth, Amendment to the Constitution.

The judgment of the Supreme Court of Arkansas is Reversed.[7]

An Evaluation of the *Epperson* Decision

Several observations are in order regarding the *Epperson* Decision. They will be helpful in moving toward our final conclusions (in chapters 8 and 9).

First, before the famous *Everson* case (1947) the states still had the right to legislate their own religious matters. For the First Amendment of the Constitution mandated only that "Congress" (i.e., the federal government) could not "establish religion." Indeed, five of the thirteen colonies that ratified the First Amendment had their own state religions. None of them were required to disestablish their religions. However, with *Everson* (1947) the high court reversed this. Then, using *Everson* as a precedent, *Epperson* (1968) declared that "the [Arkansas] statute violates the Fourteenth Amendment, which embraces the First Amendment's prohibition of state laws respecting an establishment of religion." This gave new powers to the federal government to interfere in a state's affairs as it applies to religious liberties. Thus, a state can use its

7. Ibid.

constitutional religious freedoms to overturn state laws that they deem have interfered with these rights. This power was used in *Epperson* and in the creation decisions after *Epperson*. It is obvious in these decisions that this power is both misdirected and overextended. Strangely, the Court made no attempt to define religion, yet it pronounced that the law forbidding evolution was motivated by religion.

Second, the *Epperson* court misused the religious neutrality test. The way it applied this test, almost anything even indirectly connected with a religion can be ruled unconstitutional. By logical extension this would include most moral principles and all good laws which by their very nature religious people are motivated to pass. For what good person would not be moved by his religious beliefs to protect the innocent against theft, abuse, or murder? So, by the same kind of argument used in *Epperson* virtually all good laws providing protection against crime could be ruled unconstitutional.

Third, to claim that "the sole reason for the Arkansas law is that a particular religious group considers the evolution theory to conflict with the account of the origin of man set forth in the Book of Genesis" is flatly contrary to what the law states and would demand that the Supreme Court divine the intention of the lawmakers, rather than examine the law they made. Similar arguments could be made against other laws, if the legislators, whether Buddhist, Muslim, or Hindu, voted for laws that happened to be in accord with their holy books.

Fourth, one of the reasons for this misdirected decision is the venerable and misused principle of precedent (*stare decisis,* "to stand by the decisions"). The influence of the *Scopes* trial (1925) in *Epperson* is both evident and admitted. Even though the Arkansas anti-evolution law is shorter and less objectionable than the Tennessee *Scopes* law was, having no mention of any religious book or beliefs, nonetheless it is summarily dismissed by *Epperson* on the same grounds. Clearly, the Court is not looking at the face of the Act, or at its social and educational benefits. Rather, it is attempting to divine evil intent on the part of those who wrote the law.

Fifth, as we see in this case and will see in ensuing cases, the alleged "fundamentalist" religious motivation is read into this Arkansas legislation as well. The Court fails to distinguish between religious motives, which are not in themselves bad and are behind most good laws, and religious intent in the law itself (see chapter 6). There is certainly nothing wrong with tax-paying citizens not wanting public schools supported by them to teach theories of origins to their students contrary to their beliefs. And for a court to rule contrary to the beliefs of citizens and the laws they enact is a classic case of "taxation without representation."

Sixth, if one makes it a matter of religious freedom not to oppose evolution, then why is it not also a matter of *establishing* religion to favor a view (e.g., evolution) that is in accord with most nontheistic religions? Does not the high court in effect establish one set of religions (nontheistic ones) in its attempt to avoid favoring another, namely, theistic religions? This certainly is not a neutral stance on religion on the part of the Court.

Seventh, one can sense a disdain for fundamentalist religions in the thrust and tenor of the decision. The very term "fundamentalism" that the Court used has bad connotations. And, is not "fundamentalism" a religion protected by the Constitution? Why should the courts be hostile to fundamentalism?[8] Indeed, in their zealous opposition to fundamentalism the courts have helped establish an opposing religion of secularism, which *Abington* (1963) forbids.

Eighth, the use of the *Watson v. Jones* (1872) decree by the Court, that: "The law knows no heresy, and is committed to the support of no dogma, the establishment of no sect" is totally misplaced. How can forbidding what the opposition calls a purely scientific theory (namely, evolution) be a religious heresy? If anything, the reverse can be argued: by insisting that evolution, which is contrary to the religious beliefs of many, cannot be forbidden, has not the Court established a religion? If it is religious to oppose evolution, why is it not religious to affirm it? Can the Court really be neutral in ruling to favor beliefs that favor one religion but not another?

Ninth, one has to be judicially and historically blind to mandate that evolution—a theory that clearly opposes creation—can be taught and

8. David Limbaugh documents the bias of the courts against conservative Christians in his book *Persecution* (New York: Perennial, 2004).

yet claim that this has no implications for our life as a nation, when our founding document itself affirmed that "all men are created" by a "Creator." In effect, the high court has ruled that *The Declaration of Independence* is unconstitutional, and that opposing views, such as evolution, are constitutional. They have stood the Constitution on its head. No wonder they cannot read it right side up! Were the founding fathers to know about such constitutional twisting, they would be shocked beyond belief.

Summary

Much of the faulty reasoning in *Epperson* will reappear in succeeding court decisions (see chapters 3, 4, 7). Thus, by the misapplications of legal precedent (*stare decisis*) the courts continue to compound their errors, exclude First Amendment rights for tax-paying creationists, and help establish opposing religious beliefs. Just how to rectify these bad court decisions is the subject of the final chapters (8 and 9).

3

The *McLean* Trial (1982)

The *Scopes* trial had turned the tide of public opinion in favor of teaching evolution in public schools, and the *Epperson* case, citing the separation of church and state, prohibited states from mandating that evolution could *not* be taught in public schools. As a result, Arkansas passed a law (Act 590) stating that if either evolution or creation were taught, then a balanced presentation should be given of the opposing view. The ensuing trial, *McLean v. Arkansas Board of Education,* became known as "Scopes II."

Introduction: History of Act 590

The history of the Arkansas creation-evolution Act 590 is as follows: (1) In 1977 Paul Ellwanger, a Roman Catholic layman from South Carolina, formed "Citizens for Fairness in Education," a group that introduced bills relating to the creation-evolution controversy in numerous state legislatures. (2) Using a model bill prepared by Wendell Bird, staff attorney for the Institute for Creation Research, Ellwanger drafted Act 590. (3) On February 24, 1981, Senator James L. Holsted introduced it as Bill 482 in the Arkansas State Senate, where it was read for the first and second time. (4) On March 3, 1981, the Senate Judiciary Committee recommended that Bill 482 receive a "do pass." (5) On March 12, 1981, the bill was read for the third and final time and passed by a vote of 22 to 2. (6) On March 12 the bill was read for the first time in the Arkansas State House. (7) On March 13 the bill was read for the second time. (8) On March 13 the House Education Committee held a brief hearing on the bill. (9) On March 17 the bill was read for a third and final time in the House of Representatives. It passed by a vote of 69 to 18. (10) On March 19, 1981, Governor Frank White signed the bill into law. (11) On May 27, 1981, the American Civil Liberties Union filed suit challenging the constitutionality of Act 590. (12) On December 7–17, 1981, the trial was held in Federal Judge William Overton's court, Little Rock, Arkansas. (13) On January 5, 1982, Judge Overton ruled the bill was an unconstitutional violation of the First Amendment. (14) On February 4, 1982, one day before the deadline for appeal to the 8th Circuit Court of Appeals (St. Louis), the attorney general, Steve Clark, announced that the state would not appeal the ruling.

The Contents of Act 590 (1981)

The Arkansas law at issue in "Scopes II" reads as follows:

An act to require balanced treatment of creation-science and evolution-science in public schools; to protect academic freedom by providing student choice; to ensure freedom of religious exercise; to guarantee freedom of belief and speech; to prevent establishment of religion; to prohibit religious instruction concerning origins; to bar discrimination on the basis of creationist or evolutionist belief; to provide definitions and clarifications; to declare the legislative purpose and legislative findings of fact; to provide for severability of provisions; to provide for repeal of contrary laws; and to set forth an effective date.

Be it enacted by the General Assembly of the State of Arkansas:

SECTION 1. Requirement for Balanced Treatment. Public schools within this State shall give balanced treatment to creation-science and to evolution-science. Balanced treatment to these two models shall be given in classroom lectures taken as a whole for each course, in textbook materials taken as a whole for each course, in library materials taken as a whole for the sciences and taken as a whole for the humanities, and in other educational programs in public schools, to the extent that such lectures, textbooks, library materials, or educational programs deal in any way with the subject of the origin of man, life, the earth, or the universe.

SECTION 2. Prohibition against Religious Instruction. Treatment of either evolution-science or creation-science shall be limited to scientific evidences for each model and inferences from those scientific evidences, and must not include any religious instruction or references to religious writings.

SECTION 3. Requirement for Nondiscrimination. Public schools within this State, or their personnel, shall not discriminate, by reducing a grade of a student or by singling out and making public criticism, against any student who demonstrates a satisfactory understanding of both evolution-science and creation-science and who accepts or rejects either model in whole or part.

SECTION 4. Definitions. As used in this Act:

(a) "Creation-science" means the scientific evidences for creation and inferences from those scientific evidences. Creation-science includes the scientific evidences and related inferences that indicate: (1) Sudden creation of the universe, energy, and life from nothing; (2) The insufficiency of mutation and natural selection in bringing about development of all living kinds from a single organism; (3) Changes only within fixed limits of originally created kinds of plants and animals; (4) Separate ancestry for man and apes; (5) Explanation of the earth's geology by catastrophism, including the occurrence of a worldwide flood; and (6) A relatively recent inception of the earth and living kinds.

(b) "Evolution-science" means the scientific evidences for evolution and inferences from those scientific evidences. Evolution-science includes the scientific evidences and related inferences that indicate: (1) Emergence by naturalistic processes of the universe from disordered matter and emergence of life from nonlife; (2) The sufficiency of mutation and natural selection in bringing about the development of present living kinds from simple earlier kinds; (3) Emergence by mutation and natural selection of present living kinds from simple earlier kinds; (4) Emergence of man from a common ancestor with apes; (5) Explanation of the earth's geology and the evolutionary sequence by uniformitarianism; and (6) An inception several billion years ago of the earth and somewhat later of life.

(c) "Public schools" means public secondary and elementary schools.

SECTION 5. Clarifications. This Act does not require or permit instruction in any religious doctrine or materials. This Act does not require any instruction in the subject of origins, but simply requires instruction in both scientific models (of evolution-science and creation-science) if public schools choose to teach either. This Act does not require each individual textbook or library book to give balanced treatment to the models of evolution-science and creation-science; it does not require any school books to be discarded. This Act does not require each individual classroom lecture in a course to give such balanced treatment, but simply requires the lectures as a whole to give balanced treatment; it permits some lectures to present evolution-science and other lectures to present creation-science.

SECTION 6. Legislative Declaration of Purpose. This Legislature enacts this Act for public schools with the purpose of protecting academic freedom for students' differing values and beliefs; ensuring neutrality toward students' diverse religious convictions; ensuring freedom of religious exercise for students and their parents; guaranteeing freedom of belief and speech for students; preventing establishment of Theologically Liberal, Humanist, Nontheist, or Atheist religions; preventing discrimination against students on the basis of their personal beliefs concerning creation and evolution; and assisting students in their search for truth. This Legislature does not have the purpose of causing instruction in religious concepts or making an establishment of religion.

SECTION 7. Legislative Findings of Fact. This Legislature finds that:

(a) The subject of the origin of the universe, earth, life, and man is treated within many public school courses, such as biology, life science, anthropology, sociology, and often also in physics, chemistry, world history, philosophy, and social studies.

(b) Only evolution-science is presented to students in virtually all of those courses that discuss the subject of origins. Public schools generally censor creation-science and evidence contrary to evolution.

(c) Evolution-science is not an unquestionable fact of science, because evolution cannot be experimentally observed, fully verified, or logically falsified, and because evolution-science is not accepted by some scientists.

(d) Evolution-science is contrary to the religious convictions or moral values or philosophical beliefs of many students and parents, including individuals of many different religious faiths and with diverse moral values and philosophical beliefs.

(e) Public school presentation of only evolution-science without any alternative model of origins abridges the United States Constitution's protections of freedom of religious exercise and of freedom of belief and speech for students and parents, because it undermines their religious convictions and moral or philosophical values, compels their unconscionable professions of belief, and hinders religious training and moral training by parents.

(f) Public school presentation of only evolution-science furthermore abridges the Constitution's prohibition against establishment of religion, because it produces hostility toward many Theistic religions and brings preference to Theological Liberalism, Humanism, Nontheistic religions, and Atheism, in that these religious faiths generally include a religious belief in evolution.

(g) Public school instruction in only evolution-science also violates the principle of academic freedom, because it denies students a choice between scientific models and instead indoctrinates them in evolution-science alone.

(h) Presentation of only one model rather than alternative scientific models of origins is not required by any compelling interest of the State, and exemption of such students from a course or class presenting only evolution-science does not provide an adequate remedy because of teacher influence and student pressure to remain in that course or class.

(i) Attendance of those students who are at public schools is compelled by law, and school taxes from their parents and other citizens are mandated by law.

(j) Creation-science is an alternative scientific model of origins and can be presented from a strictly scientific standpoint without any religious doctrine just as evolution-science can, because there are scientists who conclude that scientific data best support creation-science and because scientific evidences and inferences have been presented for creation-science.

(k) Public school presentation of both evolution-science and creation-science would not violate the Constitution's prohibition against establishment of religion, because it would involve presentation of the scientific evidences and related inferences for each model rather than any religious instruction.

(l) Most citizens, whatever their religious beliefs about origins, favor balanced treatment in public schools of alternative scientific models of origins for better guiding students in their search for knowledge, and they favor a neutral approach toward subjects affecting the religious and moral and philosophical convictions of students.

SECTION 8. Short Title. This Act shall be known as the "Balanced Treatment for Creation-Science and Evolution-Science Act."

SECTION 9. Severability of Provisions. If any provision of this Act is held invalid, that invalidity shall not affect other provisions that can be applied in the absence of the invalidated provisions, and the provisions of this Act are declared to be severable.

SECTION 10. Repeal of Contrary Laws. All State laws or parts of State laws in conflict with this Act are hereby repealed.

SECTION 11. Effective Date. The requirements of the Act shall be met by and may be met before the beginning of the next school year if that is more than six months from the date of enactment, or otherwise one year after the beginning of the next school year, and in all subsequent school years.

Approved,
Frank White (Governor) 3-19-81[1]

The Judge's Decision Against the Creation-Evolution Act

Even though it appeared to be an eminently fair law with clear social and educational benefits and aversion to teaching religion, the Arkansas law was ruled unconstitutional. Because of its historic importance, the complete contents of the judge's decision follows:

1. Act 590 of 1981, General Acts, 73rd General Assembly, State of Arkansas.

MEMORANDUM OPINION
Introduction

On March 19, 1981, the Governor of Arkansas signed into law Act 590 of 1981, entitled the "Balanced Treatment for Creation-Science and Evolution-Science Act." The Act is codified as Ark. Stat. Ann. §80-1663, et seq., (1981 Supp). Its essential mandate is stated in its first sentence: "Public schools within this state shall give balanced treatment to creation-science and to evolution-science." On May 27, 1981, this suit was filed challenging the constitutional validity of Act 590 on three distinct grounds.

First, it is contended that Act 590 constitutes an establishment of religion prohibited by the First Amendment to the Constitution, which is made applicable to the states by the Fourteenth Amendment. Second, the plaintiffs argue the Act violates a right to academic freedom which they say is guaranteed to students and teachers by the Free Speech Clause of the First Amendment. Third, plaintiffs allege the Act is impermissibly vague and thereby violates the Due Process Clause of the Fourteenth Amendment.

The individual plaintiffs include the resident Arkansas Bishops of the United Methodist, Episcopal, Roman Catholic, and African Methodist Episcopal Churches, the principal official of the Presbyterian Churches in Arkansas, other United Methodist, Southern Baptist, and Presbyterian clergy, as well as several persons who sue as parents and next friends of minor children attending Arkansas public schools. One plaintiff is a high school biology teacher. All are also Arkansas taxpayers. Among the organizational plaintiffs are the American Jewish Congress, the Union of American Hebrew Congregations, the American Jewish Committee, the Arkansas Education Association, the National Association of Biology Teachers and the National Coalition for Public Education and Religious Liberty, all of which sue on behalf of members living in Arkansas.

The defendants include the Arkansas Board of Education and its members, the Director of the Department of Education, and the State Textbooks and Instructional Materials Selecting Committee. The Pulaski County Special School District and its Directors and Superintendent were voluntarily dismissed by the plaintiffs at the pretrial conference held October 1, 1981.

The trial commenced December 7, 1981, and continued through December 17, 1981. This Memorandum Opinion constitutes the Court's findings of fact and conclusions of law. Further orders and judgments will be in conformity with this opinion.

I.

There is no controversy over the legal standards under which the Establishment Clause portion of this case must be judged. The Supreme Court has on a number of occasions expounded on the meaning of the clause, and the pronouncements are clear. Often the issue has arisen in the context of public education, as it has here. In *Everson v. Board of Education* . . . (1947), Justice Black stated:

> The "establishment of religion" clause of the First Amendment means at least this: Neither a state nor the Federal Government can set up a church. Neither can pass laws which aid one religion, aid all religions, or prefer one religion over another. Neither can force nor influence a person to go to or to remain away from church against his will or force him to profess a belief or disbelief in any religion. No person can be punished for entertaining or professing religious beliefs or disbeliefs, for church attendance or non-attendance. No tax, large or small, can be levied to support any religious activities or institutions, whatever they may be called, or whatever form they may adopt to teach or practice religion. Neither a state nor the Federal Government can, openly or secretly, participate in the affairs of any religious organizations or groups and vice versa. In the words of Jefferson, the clause . . . was intended to erect "a wall of separation between church and State."

The Establishment Clause thus enshrines two central values: voluntarism and pluralism. And it is in the area of the public schools that these values must be guarded most vigilantly.

> Designed to serve as perhaps the most powerful agency for promoting cohesion among a heterogeneous democratic people, the public school must keep scrupulously free from entanglement in the strife of sects. The preservation of the community from divisive conflicts, of Government from irreconcilable pressures by religious

groups, of religion from censorship and coercion however subtly exercised, requires strict confinement of the State to instruction other than religious, leaving to the individual's church and home, indoctrination in the faith of his choice. (*McCollum v. Board of Education* . . . [1948], [Opinion of Frankfurter, J., joined by Jackson, Burton and Rutledge, J.J.]).

The specific formulation of the establishment prohibition has been refined over the years, but its meaning has not varied from the principles articulated by Justice Black in *Everson*. In *Abington School District v. Schempp* . . . (1963), Justice Clark stated that "to withstand the strictures of the Establishment Clause there must be a secular legislative purpose and a primary effect that neither advances nor inhibits religion." The Court found it quite clear that the First Amendment does not permit a state to require the daily reading of the Bible in public schools, for "surely the place of the Bible as an instrument of religion cannot be gainsaid." . . . Similarly, in *Engel v. Vitale* . . . (1962), the Court held that the First Amendment prohibited the New York Board of Regents from requiring the daily recitation of a certain prayer in the schools. With characteristic succinctness, Justice Black wrote, "Under [the First] Amendment's prohibition against governmental establishment of religion, as reinforced by the provisions of the Fourteenth Amendment, government in this country, be it state or federal, is without power to prescribe by law any particular form of prayer which is to be used as an official prayer in carrying on any program of governmentally sponsored religious activity." Black also identified the objective at which the Establishment Clause was aimed: "Its first and most immediate purpose rested on the belief that a union of government and religion tends to destroy government and to degrade religion."

Most recently, the Supreme Court has held that the clause prohibits a state from requiring the posting of the Ten Commandments in public school classrooms for the same reasons that officially imposed daily Bible reading is prohibited. *Stone v. Graham* . . . (1980). The opinion in Stone relies on the most recent formulation of the Establishment Clause test, that of *Lemon v. Kurtzman* . . . (1971):

First, the statute must have a secular legislative purpose; second, its principal or primary effect must be one that neither advances nor inhibits religion . . . finally, the statute must not foster "an excessive government entanglement with religion." *Stone v. Graham.* . . .

It is under this three-part test that the evidence in this case must be judged. Failure on any of these grounds is fatal to the enactment.

II.

The religious movement known as Fundamentalism began in nineteenth century America as part of evangelical Protestantism's response to social changes, new religious thought and Darwinism. Fundamentalists viewed these developments as attacks on the Bible and as responsible for a decline in traditional values.

The various manifestations of Fundamentalism have had a number of common characteristics, but a central premise was always a literal interpretation of the Bible and a belief in the inerrancy of the Scriptures. Following World War I, there was again a perceived decline in traditional morality, and Fundamentalism focused on evolution as responsible for the decline. One aspect of their efforts, particularly in the South, was the promotion of statutes prohibiting the teaching of evolution in public schools. In Arkansas, this resulted in the adoption of Initiated Act 1 of 1929.

Between the 1920s and early 1960s, anti-evolutionary sentiment had a subtle but pervasive influence on the teaching of biology in public schools. Generally, textbooks avoided the topic of evolution and did not mention the name of Darwin. Following the launch of the Sputnik satellite by the Soviet Union in 1957, the National Science Foundation funded several programs designed to modernize the teaching of science in the nation's schools. The Biological Sciences Curriculum Study (BSCS), a nonprofit organization, was among those receiving grants for curriculum study and revision. Working with scientists and teachers, BSCS developed a series of biology texts which, although emphasizing different aspects of biology, incorporated the theory of evolution as a major theme. The success of the BSCS effort is shown by the fact that fifty percent of American school children currently use BSCS books directly and the curriculum is incorporated indirectly in virtually all biology texts. (Testimony of Mayer; Nelkin, Pg 1)

In the early 1960s, there was again a resurgence of concern among Fundamentalists about the loss of traditional values and a fear of growing secularism in society. The Fundamentalist movement became more active and has steadily grown in numbers and political influence. There is an emphasis among current Fundamentalists on the literal interpretation of the Bible and the Book of Genesis as the sole source of knowledge about origins.

The term "scientific creationism" first gained currency around 1965 following publication of *The Genesis Flood* in 1961 by Whitcomb and Morris. There is undoubtedly some connection between the appearance of the BSCS texts emphasizing evolutionary thought and efforts by Fundamentalists to attack the theory. (Mayer)

In the 1960s and early 1970s, several Fundamentalist organizations were formed to promote the idea that the Book of Genesis was supported by scientific data. The terms "creation science" and "scientific creationism" have been adopted by these Fundamentalists as descriptive of their study of creation and the origins of man. Perhaps the leading creationist organization is the Institute for Creation Research (ICR), which is affiliated with the Christian Heritage College and supported by the Scott Memorial Baptist Church in San Diego, California. The ICR, through the Creation-Life Publishing Company, is the leading publisher of creation science material. Other creation science organizations include the Creation Science Research Center (CSRC) of San Diego and the Bible Science Association of Minneapolis, Minnesota. In 1963, the Creation Research Society (CRS) was formed from a schism in the American Scientific Affiliation (ASA). It is an organization of literal Fundamentalists who have the equivalent of a master's degree in some recognized area of science. A purpose of the organization is "to reach all people with the vital message of the scientific and historic truth about creation." Nelkin, The Science Textbook Controversies and the Politics of Equal Time, 66. Similarly, the CSRC was formed in 1970 from a split in the CRS. Its aim has been "to reach the 63 million children of the United States with the scientific teaching of Biblical creationism."[2]

It is true, as defendants argue, that courts should look to legislative statements of a statute's purpose in Establishment Clause cases and accord such pronouncements great deference. See, e.g., *Committee for Public Education & Religious Liberty v. Nyquist* ... (1973) and *McGowan v.*

---

2. A section elaborating the judge's views of the religious motivation of those in favor of creation science follows here. It and the footnotes of the ruling have been omitted for lack of space.

Maryland ... (1961). Defendants also correctly state the principle that remarks by the sponsor or author of a bill are not considered controlling in analyzing legislative intent. See, e.g., *United States* v. *Emmons* ... (1973) and *Chrysler Corp.* v. *Brown* ... (1979).

Courts are not bound, however, by legislative statements of purpose or legislative disclaimers. *Stone v. Graham* ... (1980), *Abington School Dist.* v. *Schempp* ... (1963). In determining the legislative purpose of a statute, courts may consider evidence of the historical context of the Act, *Epperson v. Arkansas* ... (1968); the specific sequence of events leading up to passage of the Act; departures from normal procedural sequences; substantive departures from the normal, *Village of Arlington Heights v. Metropolitan Housing Corp.* ... (1977); and contemporaneous statements of the legislative sponsor, *Fed. Energy Admin. v. Algonquin SNG, Inc.* ... (1976).

The unusual circumstances surrounding the passage of Act 590, as well as the substantive law of the First Amendment, warrant an inquiry into the stated legislative purposes. The author of the Act had publicly proclaimed the sectarian purpose of the proposal. The Arkansas residents who sought legislative sponsorship of the bill did so for a purely sectarian purpose. These circumstances alone may not be particularly persuasive, but when considered with the publicly announced motives of the legislative sponsor made contemporaneously with the legislative process; the lack of any legislative investigation, debate, or consultation with any educators or scientists; the unprecedented intrusion in school curriculum; and official history of the State of Arkansas on the subject, it is obvious that the statement of purposes has little, if any, support in fact. The State failed to produce any evidence which would warrant an inference or conclusion that at any point in the process anyone considered the legitimate educational value of the Act. It was simply and purely an effort to introduce the biblical version of creation into the public school curricula. The only inference which can be drawn from these circumstances is that the Act was passed with the specific purpose by the General Assembly of advancing religion. The Act therefore fails the first prong of the three-pronged test, that of secular legislative purpose, as articulated in *Lemon v. Kurtzman, supra,* and *Stone v. Graham, supra.*

III.

If the defendants are correct and the Court is limited to an examination of the language of the Act, the evidence is overwhelming that both the purpose and effect of Act 590 is the advancement of religion in the public schools.

Section 4 of the Act provides:

Definitions, as used in this Act:

(a) "Creation-science" means the scientific evidences for creation and inferences from those scientific evidences. Creation-science includes the scientific evidences and related inferences that indicate: (1) Sudden creation of the universe, energy, and life from nothing; (2) The insufficiency of mutation and natural selection in bringing about development of all living kinds from a single organism; (3) Changes only within fixed limits of originally created kinds of plants and animals; (4) Separate ancestry for man and apes; (5) Explanation of the earth's geology by catastrophism, including the occurrence of a worldwide flood; and (6) A relatively recent inception of the earth and living kinds.

(b) "Evolution-science" means the scientific evidences for evolution and inferences from those scientific evidences. Evolution-science includes the scientific evidences and related inferences that indicate: (1) Emergence by naturalistic processes of the universe from disordered matter and emergence of life from nonlife; (2) The sufficiency of mutation and natural selection in bringing about development of present living kinds from simple earlier kinds; (3) Emergence by mutation and natural selection of present living kinds from simple earlier kinds; (4) Emergence of man from a common ancestor with apes; (5) Explanation of the earth's geology and the evolutionary sequence by uniformitarianism; and (6) An inception several billion years ago of the earth and somewhat later of life.

(c) "Public schools" means public secondary and elementary schools.

The evidence establishes that the definition of "creation science" contained in 4(a) has as its unmentioned reference the first 11 chapters of the Book of Genesis. Among the many creation epics in human history, the account of sudden creation from nothing, or *creatio ex nihilo,* and subsequent destruction of the world by flood is unique to Genesis. The concepts of 4(a) are the literal Fundamentalists' view of Genesis. Section 4(a) is unquestionably a statement of religion, with the exception of 4(a)(2) which is a negative thrust aimed at what the creationists understand to be the theory of evolution.

Both the concepts and wording of Section 4(a) convey an inescapable religiosity. Section 4(a)(l) describes "sudden creation of the universe, energy and life from nothing." Every theologian who testified, including defense witnesses, expressed the opinion that the statement referred to a supernatural creation which was performed by God.

Defendants argue that: (1) the fact that 4(a) conveys ideas similar to the literal interpretation of Genesis does not make it conclusively a statement of religion; (2) that reference to a creation from nothing is not necessarily a religious concept since the Act only suggests a creator who has power, intelligence, and a sense of design and not necessarily the attributes of love, compassion, and justice; and (3) that simply teaching about the concept of a creator is not a religious exercise unless the student is required to make a commitment to the concept of a creator.

The evidence fully answers these arguments. The ideas of 4(a)(l) are not merely similar to the literal interpretation of Genesis; they are identical and parallel to no other story of creation.

The argument that creation from nothing in 4(a)(l) does not involve a supernatural deity has no evidentiary or rational support. To the contrary, "creation out of nothing" is a concept unique to Western religions. In traditional Western religious thought, the conception of a creator of the world is a conception of God. Indeed, creation of the world "out of nothing" is the ultimate religious statement because God is the only actor. As Dr. Langdon Gilkey noted, the Act refers to one who has the power to bring all of the universe into existence from nothing. The only "one" who has this power is God.

The leading creationist writers, Morris and Gish, acknowledge that the idea of creation described in 4(a)(1) is the concept of creation by God and make no pretense to the contrary. The idea of sudden creation from nothing, or *creatio ex nihilo*, is an inherently religious concept. (Vawter, Gilkey, Geisler, Ayala, Blount, Hicks.)

The argument advanced by defendants' witness, Dr. Norman Geisler, that teaching the existence of God is not religious unless the teaching seeks a commitment, is contrary to common understanding and contradicts settled case law. *Stone* v. *Graham* ... (1980); *Abington School District* v. *Schempp* ... (1963).

The facts that creation science is inspired by the book of Genesis and that Section 4(a) is consistent with a literal interpretation of Genesis leave no doubt that a major effect of the Act is the advancement of particular religious beliefs. The legal impact of this conclusion will be discussed further at the conclusion of the Court's evaluation of the scientific merit of creation science.

IV.(A)

The approach to teaching "creation science" and "evolution science" found in Act 590 is identical to the two-model approach espoused by the Institute for Creation Research and is taken almost verbatim from ICR writings. It is an extension of Fundamentalists' view that one must either accept the literal interpretation of Genesis or else believe in the godless system of evolution.

The two model approach of the creationists is simply a contrived dualism which has no scientific factual basis or legitimate educational purpose. It assumes only two explanations for the origins of life and existence of man, plants, and animals: it was either the work of a creator or it was not. Application of these two models, according to creationists, and the defendants, dictates that all scientific evidence which fails to support the theory of evolution is necessarily scientific evidence in support of creationism and is, therefore, creation science "evidence" in support of Section 4(a).

IV.(B)

The emphasis on origins as an aspect of the theory of evolution is peculiar to creationist literature. Although the subject of origins of life is within the province of biology, the scientific community does not consider origins of life a part of evolutionary theory. The theory of evolution assumes the existence of life and is directed to an explanation of how life evolved. Evolution does not presuppose the absence of a creator or God and the plain inference conveyed by Section 4 is erroneous.

As a statement of the theory of evolution, Section 4(b) is simply a hodgepodge of limited assertions, many of which are factually inaccurate.

For example, although 4(b)(2) asserts, as a tenet of evolutionary theory, "sufficiency of mutation and natural selection in bringing about the development of present living kinds from simple earlier kinds," Drs. Ayala and Gould both stated that biologists know that these two processes do not account for all significant evolutionary change. They testified to such phenomena as recombination, the founder effect, genetic drift and the theory of punctuated equilibrium, which are believed to play important evolutionary roles. Section 4(b) omits any reference to these. Moreover, 4(b) utilizes the term "kinds" which all scientists said is not a word of science and has no fixed meaning. Additionally, the Act presents both evolution and creation science as "package deals." Thus, evidence critical to some aspect of what the creationists define as evolution is taken as support for a theory which includes a worldwide flood and a relatively young earth.

IV.(C)

In addition to the fallacious pedagogy of the two-model approach, Section 4(a) lacks legitimate educational value because "creation-science" as defined in that section is simply not science. Several witnesses suggested definitions of science. A descriptive definition was said to be that science is what is "accepted by the scientific community" and is "what scientists do." The obvious implication of this description is that, in a free society, knowledge does not require the imprimatur of legislation in order to become science.

More precisely, the essential characteristics of science are:

(1) It is guided by natural law;
(2) It has to be explanatory by reference to natural law;
(3) It is testable against the empirical world;
(4) Its conclusions are tentative, i.e., are not necessarily the final word; and
(5) It is falsifiable. (Ruse and other science witnesses.)

Creation science as described in Section 4(a) fails to meet these essential characteristics. First, the section revolves around 4(a)(1) which asserts a sudden creation "from nothing." Such a concept is not science because it depends upon a supernatural intervention which is not guided by natural law. It is not explanatory by reference to natural law, is not testable and is not falsifiable.

If the unifying idea of supernatural creation by God is removed from Section 4, the remaining parts of the section explain nothing and are meaningless assertions.

Section 4(a)(2), relating to the "insufficiency of mutation and natural selection in bringing about development of all living kinds from a single organism," is an incomplete negative generalization directed at the theory of evolution.

Section 4(a)(3) which describes "changes only within fixed limits of originally created kinds of plants and animals" fails to conform to the essential characteristics of science for several reasons. First, there is no scientific definition of "kinds" and none of the witnesses was able to point to any scientific authority which recognized the term or knew how many "kinds" existed. One defense witness suggested there may be 100 to 10,000 different "kinds." Another believes there were "about 10,000, give or take a few thousand." Second, the assertion appears to be an effort to establish outer limits of changes within species. There is no scientific explanation for these limits which is guided by natural law and the limitations, whatever they are, cannot be explained by natural law.

The statement in 4(a)(4) of "separate ancestry of man and apes" is a bald assertion. It explains nothing and refers to no scientific fact or theory.

Section 4(a)(5) refers to "explanation of the earth's geology by catastrophism, including the occurrence of a worldwide flood." This assertion completely fails as science. The Act is referring to the Noachian flood described in the Book of Genesis. The creationist writers concede that *any* kind of Genesis Flood depends upon supernatural intervention. A worldwide flood as an explanation of the world's geology is not the product of natural law, nor can its occurrence be explained by natural law.

Section 4(a)(6) equally fails to meet the standards of science. "Relatively recent inception" has no scientific meaning. It can only be given meaning in reference to creationist writings which place the age at between 6,000 and 20,000 years because of the genealogy of the Old Testament. . . . Such a reasoning process is not the product of natural law; not explainable by natural law; nor is it tentative.

Creation science, as defined in Section 4(a), not only fails to follow the canons of dealing with scientific theory, it also fails to fit the more general descriptions of "what scientists think" and "what scientists do." The scientific community consists of individuals and groups, nationally and internationally, who work independently in such varied fields as biology, paleontology, geology and astronomy. Their work is published and subject to review and testing by their peers. The journals for publication are both numerous and varied. There is, however, not one recognized scientific journal which has published an article espousing the creation science theory described in Section 4(a). Some of the State's witnesses suggested that the scientific community was "closed-minded" on the subject of creationism and that explained the lack of acceptance of the creation science arguments. Yet no witness produced a scientific article for which publication had been refused. Perhaps some members of the scientific community are resistant to new ideas. It is, however, inconceivable that such a loose knit group of independent thinkers in all the varied fields of science could, or would, so effectively censor new scientific thought.

The creationists have difficulty maintaining among their ranks consistency in the claim that creationism is science. The author of Act 590, Ellwanger, said that neither evolution nor creationism was science. He thinks both are religious. Duane Gish recently responded to an article in *Discover* critical of creationism by stating: "Stephen Jay Gould states that creationists claim creation is a scientific theory. This is a false accusation. Creationists have repeatedly stated that neither creation nor evolution is a scientific theory (and each is equally religious)": Gish letter to editor of *Discover*, July, 1981, App. 30 to Plaintiffs' Pretrial Brief.

The methodology employed by creationists is another factor which is indicative that their work is not science. A scientific theory must be tentative and always subject to revision or abandonment in light of facts that are inconsistent with, or falsify, the theory. A theory that is by its own terms dogmatic, absolutist and never subject to revision is not a scientific theory.

The creationists' methods do not take data, weigh it against the opposing scientific data, and thereafter reach the conclusions stated in Section 4(a). Instead, they take the literal wording of the Book of Genesis and attempt to find scientific support for it. The method is best explained in the language of Morris in his book (Px 31) *Studies in the Bible and Science* at page 114:

> ... it is ... quite impossible to determine anything about Creation through a study of present processes, because present processes are not creative in character. If man wished to know anything about Creation (the time of Creation, the duration of Creation, the order of Creation, the methods of Creation, or anything else) his sole source of true information is that of divine revelation. God was there when it happened. We were not there. . . . Therefore, we are completely limited to what God has seen fit to tell us, and this information is in His written Word. This is our textbook on the science of Creation!

The Creation Research Society employs the same unscientific approach to the issue of creationism. Its applicants for membership must subscribe to the belief that the Book of Genesis is "historically and scientifically true in all of the original autographs." The Court would never criticize or discredit any person's testimony based on his or her religious beliefs. While anybody is free to approach a scientific inquiry in any fashion they choose, they cannot properly describe the methodology used as scientific, if they start with a conclusion and refuse to change it regardless of the evidence developed during the course of the investigation.

IV.(D)

In efforts to establish "evidence" in support of creation science, the defendants relied upon the same false premise as the two-model approach contained in Section 4, i.e., all evidence which criticized evolutionary theory was proof in support of creation science. For example, the defendants established that the mathematical probability of a chance chemical combination resulting in life from non-life is so remote that such an occurrence is almost beyond imagination. Those mathematical facts, the defendants argue, are scientific evidences that life was the product of a creator. While the statistical figures may be impressive evidence against the theory of chance chemical combinations as an explanation of origins, it requires a leap of faith to interpret those figures so as to support a complex doctrine which includes a sudden creation from nothing, a worldwide flood, separate ancestry of man and apes, and a young earth.

The defendants' argument would be more persuasive, if, in fact, there were only two theories or ideas about the origins of life and the world. That there are a number of theories was acknowledged by the State's witnesses, Dr. Wickramasinghe and Dr. Geisler. Dr. Wickramasinghe testified at length in support of a theory that life on earth was "seeded" by comets which delivered genetic material and perhaps organisms to the earth's surface from interstellar dust far outside the solar system. The "seeding" theory further hypothesizes that the earth remains under the continuing influence of genetic material from space which continues to affect life. While Wickramasinghe's theory about the origins of life on earth has not received general acceptance within the scientific community, he has, at least, used scientific methodology to produce a theory of origins which meets the essential characteristics of science.

. . . Perhaps [Dr. Wickramasinghe was called as a witness] because he was generally critical of the theory of evolution and the scientific community, a tactic consistent with the strategy of the defense. Unfortunately for the defense, he demonstrated that the simplistic approach of the two model analysis of the origins of life is false. Furthermore, he corroborated the plaintiffs' witnesses by concluding that "no rational scientist" would believe the earth's geology could be explained by reference to a worldwide flood or that the earth was less than one million years old.

The proof in support of creation science consisted almost entirely of efforts to discredit the theory of evolution through a rehash of data and theories which have been before the scientific community for decades. The arguments asserted by creationists are not based upon new scientific evidence or laboratory data which has been ignored by the scientific community.

Robert Gentry's discovery of radioactive polonium halos in granite and coalified woods is, perhaps, the most recent scientific work which the creationists use as argument for a "relatively recent inception" of the earth and a "worldwide flood." The existence of polonium halos in granite and coalified wood is thought to be inconsistent with radiometric dating methods based upon constant radioactive decay rates. Mr. Gentry's findings were published almost ten years ago and have been the subject of some discussion in the scientific community. The discoveries have not, however, led to the formulation of any scientific hypothesis or theory which would explain a relatively recent inception of the earth or a worldwide flood. Gentry's discovery has been treated as a minor mystery which will eventually be explained. It may deserve further investigation, but the National Science Foundation has not deemed it to be of sufficient import to support further funding.

The testimony of Marianne Wilson was persuasive evidence that creation science is not science. Ms. Wilson is in charge of the science curriculum for Pulaski County Special School District, the largest school district in the State of Arkansas. Prior to the passage of Act 590, Larry Fisher, a science teacher in the District, using materials from the ICR, convinced the School Board that it should voluntarily adopt creation science as part of its science curriculum. The District Superintendent assigned Ms. Wilson the job of producing a creation science curriculum guide. Ms. Wilson's testimony about the project was particularly convincing because she obviously approached the assignment with an open mind and no preconceived notions about the subject. She had not heard of creation science until about a year ago and did not know its meaning before she began research.

Ms. Wilson worked with a committee of science teachers appointed from the District. They reviewed practically all of the creationist literature. Ms. Wilson and the committee members reached the unanimous conclusion that creationism is not science; it is religion. They so reported to the Board. The Board ignored the recommendation and insisted that a curriculum guide be prepared.

In researching the subject, Ms. Wilson sought the assistance of Mr. Fisher who initiated the Board action and asked professors in the science departments of the University of Arkansas at Little Rock and the University of Central Arkansas for reference material and assistance, and attended a workshop conducted at Central Baptist College by Dr. Richard Bliss of the ICR staff. Act 590 became law during the course of her work so she used Section 4(a) as a format for her curriculum guide.

Ms. Wilson found all available creationists' materials unacceptable because they were permeated with religious references and reliance upon religious beliefs.

It is easy to understand why Ms. Wilson and other educators find the creationists' textbook material and teaching guides unacceptable. The materials misstate the theory of evolution in the same fashion as Section

4(b) of the Act, with emphasis on the alternative mutually exclusive nature of creationism and evolution. Students are constantly encouraged to compare and make a choice between the two models, and the material is not presented in an accurate manner.

A typical example is Origins (Px 76) by Richard B. Bliss, Director of Curriculum Development of the ICR. The presentation begins with a chart describing "preconceived ideas about origins" which suggests that some people believe that evolution is atheistic. Concepts of evolution, such as "adaptive radiation," are erroneously presented. At page 11, figure 1.6, of the text, a chart purports to illustrate this "very important" part of the evolution model. The chart conveys the idea that such diverse mammals as a whale, bear, bat, and monkey all evolved from a shrew through the process of adaptive radiation. Such a suggestion is, of course, a totally erroneous and misleading application of the theory. Even more objectionable, especially when viewed in light of the emphasis on asking the student to elect one of the models, is the chart presentation at page 17, figure 1.6. That chart purports to illustrate the evolutionists' belief that man evolved from bacteria to fish to reptile to mammals and, thereafter, into man. The illustration indicates, however, that the mammal from which man evolved was *a rat*.

Biology, A Search for Order in Complexity is a high school biology text typical of creationists' materials. The following quotations are illustrative:

> Flowers and roots do not have a mind to have purpose of their own; therefore, this planning must have been done for them by the Creator. (at page 12)

> The exquisite beauty of color and shape in flowers exceeds the skill of poet, artist, and king. Jesus said (from Matthew's gospel), 'Consider the lilies in [*sic*] the field, how they grow; they toil not, neither do they spin. . . .' (Px 129 at page 363)

The "public school edition" texts written by creationists simply omit Biblical references but the content and message remain the same. For example: *Evolution—The Fossils Say No!* contains the following:

Creation. By creation we mean the bringing into being by a supernatural Creator of the basic kinds of plants and animals by the process of sudden, or fiat, creation.

We do not know how the Creator created, what processes He used, *for He used processes which are not now operating anywhere in the natural universe.* This is why we refer to creation as Special Creation. We cannot discover by scientific investigation anything about the creative processes used by the Creator. (page 40)

Gish's book also portrays the large majority of evolutionists as "materialistic atheists or agnostics."

Scientific Creationism (Public School Edition) by Morris, is another text reviewed by Ms. Wilson's committee and rejected as unacceptable. The following quotes illustrate the purpose and theme of the text:

Foreword

Parents and youth leaders today, and even many scientists and educators, have become concerned about the prevalence and influence of evolutionary philosophy in modern curriculum. Not only is this system inimical to orthodox Christianity and Judaism, but also, as many are convinced, to a healthy society and true science as well. (at page iii)

The rationalist of course finds the concept of special creation insufferably naive, even 'incredible.' Such a judgment, however, is warranted only if one categorically dismisses the existence of an omnipotent God. (at page 17)

Without using creationist literature, Ms. Wilson was unable to locate one genuinely scientific article or work which supported Section 4(a). In order to comply with the mandate of the Board she used such materials as an article from Readers Digest about "atomic clocks" which inferentially suggested that the earth was less than 4 ½ billion years old. She was unable to locate any substantive teaching material for some parts of Section 4 such as the worldwide flood. The curriculum guide which she prepared cannot be taught and has no educational value as science. The defendants did not produce any text or writing in response to this evidence which they claimed was usable in the public school classroom.

The conclusion that creation science has no scientific merit or educational value as science has legal significance in light of the Court's previous conclusion that creation science has, as one major effect, the advancement of religion. The second part of the three-pronged test for establishment reaches only those statutes having as their *primary* effect the advancement of religion. Secondary effects which advance religion are not constitutionally fatal. Since creation science is not science, the conclusion is inescapable that the *only* real effect of Act 590 is the advancement of religion. The Act therefore fails both the first and second portions of the test in *Lemon v. Kurtzman* (1971).

IV.(E)

Act 590 mandates "balanced treatment" for creation science and evolution science. The Act prohibits instruction in any religious doctrine or references to religious writings. The Act is self-contradictory and compliance is impossible unless the public schools elect to forego significant portions of subjects such as biology, world history, geology, zoology, botany, psychology, anthropology, sociology, philosophy, physics, and chemistry. Presently, the concepts of evolutionary theory as described in 4(b) permeate the public [school] textbooks. There is no way teachers can teach the Genesis account of creation in a secular manner.

The State Department of Education, through its textbook selection committee, school boards and school administrators will be required to constantly monitor materials to avoid using religious references. The school boards, administrators and teachers face an impossible task. How is the teacher to respond to questions about a creation suddenly and out of nothing? How will a teacher explain the occurrence of a worldwide flood? How will a teacher explain the concept of a relatively recent age of the earth? The answer is obvious because the only source of this information is ultimately contained in the Book of Genesis.

References to the pervasive nature of religious concepts in creation science texts amply demonstrate why State entanglement with religion is inevitable under Act 590. Involvement of the State in screening texts for impermissible religious references will require State officials to make delicate religious judgments. The need to monitor classroom discussion in order to uphold the Act's prohibition against religious instruction will necessarily involve administrators in questions concerning religion. These continuing involvements of State officials in questions and issues of religion create an excessive and prohibited entanglement with religion. *Brandon v. Board of Education* . . . (2nd Cir. 1980).

V.

These conclusions are dispositive of the case and there is no need to reach legal conclusions with respect to the remaining issues. The plaintiffs raise two other issues questioning the constitutionality of the Act and, insofar as the factual findings relevant to these issues are not covered in the preceding discussion, the Court will address these issues. Additionally, the defendants raised two other issues which warrant discussion.

V.(A)

First, plaintiff teachers argue the Act is unconstitutionally vague to the extent that they cannot comply with its mandate of "balanced" treatment without jeopardizing their employment. The argument centers around the lack of a precise definition in the Act for the word "balanced." Several witnesses expressed opinions that the word has such meanings as equal time, equal weight, or equal legitimacy. Although the Act could have been more explicit, "balanced" is a word subject to ordinary understanding. The proof is not convincing that a teacher using a reasonably acceptable understanding of the word and making a good faith effort to comply with the Act will be in jeopardy of termination. Other portions of the Act are arguably vague; such as the "relatively recent" inception of the earth and life. The evidence establishes, however, that relatively recent means from 6,000 to 20,000 years, as commonly understood in creation science literature. The meaning of this phrase, like Section 4(a) generally, is, for purposes of the Establishment Clause, all too clear.

V.(B)

The plaintiffs' other argument revolves around the alleged infringement by the defendants upon the academic freedom of teachers and students. It is contended this unprecedented intrusion in the curriculum by the State prohibits teachers from teaching what they believe should be taught or requires them to teach that which they do not believe is proper. The evidence reflects that traditionally the State Department of

Education, local school boards and administration officials exercise little, if any, influence upon the subject matter taught by classroom teachers. Teachers have been given freedom to teach and emphasize those portions of subjects the individual teacher considered important. The limits to this discretion have generally been derived from the approval of textbooks by the State Department and preparation of curriculum guides by the school districts.

Several witnesses testified that academic freedom for the teacher means, in substance, that the individual teacher should be permitted unlimited discretion subject only to the bounds of professional ethics. The Court is not prepare[d] to adopt such a broad view of academic freedom in the public schools.

In any event, if Act 590 is implemented, many teachers will be required to teach material in support of creation science which they do not consider academically sound. Many teachers will simply forego teaching subjects which might trigger the "balanced treatment" aspects of Act 590 even though they think the subjects are important to a proper presentation of a course.

Implementation of Act 590 will have serious and untoward consequences for students, particularly those planning to attend college. Evolution is the cornerstone of modern biology, and many courses in public schools contain subject matter relating to such varied topics as the age of the earth, geology, and relationships among living things. Any student who is deprived of instruction as to the prevailing scientific thought on these topics will be denied a significant part of science education. Such a deprivation through the high school level would undoubtedly have an impact upon the quality of education in the State's colleges and universities, especially including the pre-professional and professional programs in the health sciences.

V.(C)

The defendants argue in their brief that evolution is, in effect, a religion, and that by teaching a religion which is contrary to some students' religious views, the State is infringing upon the student's free exercise rights under the First Amendment. Mr. Ellwanger's legislative findings, which were adopted as a finding of fact by the Arkansas Legislature in Act 590, provides:

> Evolution-science is contrary to the religious convictions or moral values or philosophical beliefs of many students and parents, including individuals of many different religious faiths and with diverse moral and philosophical beliefs. Act 590, §7(d).

The defendants argue that the teaching of evolution alone presents both a free exercise problem and an establishment problem which can only be redressed by giving balanced treatment to creation science, which is admittedly consistent with some religious beliefs. This argument appears to have its genesis in a student note written by Mr. Wendell Bird, "Freedom of Religion and Science Instruction in Public Schools" (1978). The argument has no legal merit.

If creation science is, in fact, science and not religion, as the defendants claim, it is difficult to see how the teaching of such a science could "neutralize" the religious nature of evolution.

Assuming for the purposes of argument, however, that evolution is a religion or religious tenet, the remedy is to stop the teaching of evolution; not establish another religion in opposition to it. Yet it is clearly established in the case law, and perhaps also in common sense, that evolution is not a religion and that teaching evolution does not violate the Establishment Clause, *Epperson v. Arkansas*, supra, *Willoughby v. Stever* . . . (May 18, 1973); . . . cert. denied . . . (1975); *Wright v. Houston Indep. School Dist.* . . . (1978); . . . cert. denied . . . (1974).

V.(D)

The defendants presented Dr. Larry Parker, a specialist in devising curricula for public schools. He testified that the public school's curriculum should reflect the subjects the public wants taught in schools. The witness said that polls indicated a significant majority of the American public thought creation science should be taught if evolution was taught. The point of this testimony was never placed in a legal context. No doubt a sizeable majority of Americans believe in the concept of a Creator or, at least, are not opposed to the concept and see nothing wrong with teaching school children about the idea.

The application and content of First Amendment principles are not determined by public opinion polls or by a majority vote. Whether the proponents of Act 590 constitute the majority or the minority is quite irrelevant under a constitutional system of government. No group, no matter how large or small, may use the organs of government, of which the public schools are the most conspicuous and influential, to foist its religious beliefs on others.

The Court closes this opinion with a thought expressed eloquently by the great Justice Frankfurter:

> We renew our conviction that "we have stake[d] the very existence of our country on the faith that complete separation between the state and religion is best for the state and best for religion." *Everson v. Board of Education*, 330 U.S. at 59. If nowhere else, in the relation between Church and State, "good fences make good neighbors" . . . *McCollum v. Board of Education* . . . (1948).

An injunction will be entered permanently prohibiting enforcement of Act 590.

It is so ordered this January 5, 1982.

(signed) William Overton
UNITED STATES DISTRICT JUDGE[3]

Implications of the Arkansas Case

Several aspects of the trial and the judge's decision require comment. I shall limit my observations to only those aspects which in view of potential historic significance and public reaction seem most worthy of inclusion. These will include the media, the bill, the trial attorneys, the judge, and the ruling.

Comments on the Media Coverage[4]

Reporters swarmed into the Little Rock courtroom from all over the world. Excitement was high, especially for the first few days. This enthusiasm often faded as the long, highly technical testimony contin-

---

3. *McLean v. Arkansas Board of Education*, 529 F. Supp. 1255 (E.D. Ark. 1982).
4. See appendices 1 and 2 for more on the media coverage of this trial.

ued. By the last few days of the trial there were plenty of empty seats in the courtroom.

Since I have no access to records of television and radio coverage, and since these did not vary significantly from the printed media, I will base my comments largely on the printed record. In a single word, the media reporting was largely slanted. It was pitched to the "religion vs. science" theme even before the trial began.

No sooner had the bill been signed into law (March 19, 1981) than the *Arkansas Gazette* headlined a story (March 22, 1981) "'Creation-science' *Bill Prompted by Religious Beliefs,*[5] Sponsor Says." The sponsor, Senator Holsted, is quoted in bold print under his picture as saying, "I can't separate the bill from that belief in a Creator." He is further cited as saying, "The bill probably does favor *the viewpoint of religious fundamentalists.*" The article then narrates Holsted's "born again" conversion and his agreement with the Moral Majority, even though he was not a member of that organization.

Even when the article later grudgingly admitted that Holsted affirmed that the bill was against establishing religion, the *Arkansas Gazette* quickly added: "But he could not explain why the bill does not state that *the intent also is to prevent the establishment of conservative or fundamentalist religions.*"

Similar slanted reporting persisted during and after the trial, despite the Associated Press's reporting an NBC poll (November 18, 1981) a month before the trial showing that "three of four Americans say they believe that both the scientific theory of evolution and the *Biblical theory of creation* should be taught in public schools. . . ."[6]

As the trial began, the same "religion vs. science" motif continued. Scientific evidence for creation was usually referred to in quotation marks. For example, the *Dallas Times Herald* (December 9, 1981) headline read "Scientists Ridicule 'Evidence' of Creationists." The *Arkansas Gazette* (December 11, 1981) headed its articles *"Creation-*

5. All emphasis in these quotes is added.
6. Even this poll used the slanted words "biblical" versus "scientific" to describe the views, rather than acknowledging that many Americans believe that creationism has a legitimate scientific basis.

ism Is Bound to Religion, Educators Say in 4th Day of Trial," and "Creationism Can't Be Divorced from Religion, Educators Say in Act 590 Trial."

When the defense witnesses took the stand the press invariably sensationalized the irrelevant. The judge correctly noted in his ruling that "the court would never criticize or discredit any person's testimony based on his or her religious beliefs." Unfortunately, however, the mostly undiscerning public does not always grant this same courtesy, and the press knows it. In effect, they count on it.

Typical of the reporting was *The Milwaukee Journal* (December 12, 1981) headline: "Trial zeros in on *fundamentalist Christian beliefs.*" *The Arkansas Democrat* gave this front-page headline to the first creation scientists called to testify: "Clark to Call *7 Avowed Bible Believers.*" This despite the fact that no witness so described himself. The witnesses were asked irrelevant questions (over the objections of defense attorneys) about their religious beliefs. The papers almost unanimously described these witnesses by pejorative terms such as "biblical literalist." The following is a summary of what happened in this regard.

The defense attorneys protested on several occasions the ACLU references to the religious beliefs of creationists and defense witnesses.

First, it was done during the pretrial depositions (preliminary statement of testimony). For example, here is an excerpt from the deposition of one witness:

> Mr. Campbell: For the record, I object to these questions on the occult, as to their relevance.
> Mr. Siano [ACLU attorney]: Your objection is noted.

Second, the defense attorneys made this same objection to the judge during a pretrial discovery conference on November 16, 1981, but the judge overruled it.

Third, at least twice during the trial defense attorney David Williams objected to using the personal religious beliefs of creationists in testimony. He cited federal rule of evidence 610.[7] The judge overruled his objection.

Fourth, Williams asked for a *continued objection* to be recorded for the rest of the trial instead of bringing it up each time, and this objection was noted in the official court record. In view of these factors, the defense attorneys did not bring it up again later when ACLU lawyers raised the issues of the occult, demons, and UFOs, which I had mentioned briefly in my pretrial deposition.

Despite days of scientific testimony by creation scientists, the *Arkansas Democrat* (December 15, 1981) described that testimony in headlines as "Salvationist View of Human Origins." *Time* magazine headed their article "Darwin vs. the Bible" and put creation science in quotation marks, suggesting that it is merely an alleged science. When zoologist Harold Coffin gave abundant scientific evidence for the creationists' view, the *Dallas Times Herald* (December 16, 1981) reported: "Zoologist Bases Belief of Origins on Bible." The *Arkansas Gazette* (December 16, 1981) headed their article on the scientific testimony: *"Religious Dimensions of 'Creation Science'. . . ."*

Other bias was evident. *The Wall Street Journal* article (December 28, 1981) claimed creation science was not really a science. When we responded in a letter to the editor (January 14, 1982) with evidence to the contrary (see chapter 8), they headed the section containing the letter with an indirect retort: "World's Beginning Stirs No End of Creative Theorizing." This again alerts the reader to beware of the opinions expressed.

One of the most scientific and factual testimonies for creationism was that of Donald Chittick. Despite his unwillingness to assent to the contents of a *Bible Science Association* newsletter written by someone else, the *Arkansas Democrat* (December 16, 1981), in the lead paragraph about him, stated: "But one witness confirmed he was a member of the Bible Science Association, which was *putting 'Christ and the Bible and the power of the Holy Spirit back into science* as one of the most powerful methods of witnessing in the church today.'" This was a flagrant case of

---

7. This rule states that evidence of the beliefs or opinions of a witness on matters of religion is not admissible for the purpose of showing that by reason of their nature the witness's credibility is impaired or enhanced.

guilt by association. Numerous more examples of such bias are given below (in appendices 1 and 2).

In several other ways the media generally and effectively distorted the issue of the Arkansas trial:[8] (1) They failed to stress the solid credentials of the scientists who were witnesses for the defense, even though both the court and the ACLU recognized them all as "experts." (2) They neglected to report the anti-creation bias of the ACLU witnesses, though many of these were active in organizations with an anti-creationist agenda. (3) The media usually failed to report that many pro-evolution witnesses agreed that scientific evidence for creationism should be taught in the schools. (4) The media omitted mention of the religious or philosophical beliefs of the evolutionists; most were either liberal, agnostic, atheistic, or Marxist.

The reason for the media bias was stated well by Robert Lichter, Stanley Rothman, and Linda Lichter in their 1986 book *The Media Elite*. Their surveys revealed:

> A distinctive characteristic of the media elite is its secular outlook. Exactly half eschew any religious affiliation. Another 14 percent are Jewish, and almost one in four (23 percent) was raised in a Jewish household. Only one in five identify as Protestant, and one in eight as Catholic. Very few are regular churchgoers. Only 8 percent go to church or synagogue weekly, and 86 percent seldom or never attend religious services. . . . A majority see themselves as liberals. Fifty-four percent place themselves to the left of center, compared to only 17 percent who choose the right side of the spectrum.[9]

8. This exaggeration and literary embellishment led someone halfway around the world to write the *Washington Post* saying: "Dear Sir: The main daily newspaper in this part of the world, 'The West Australian,' based at the city of Perth, included a report on December 15 by your reporter Mr. Philip J. Hilts on the court case in Arkansas concerning the teaching of creation science in public schools. A copy of the report, which is enclosed, attributes to the opening creationist witness 'a spectacular courtroom fireworks display. . . .' Most of the report reads fairly objectively, but one looks in vain for the alleged 'spectacular' courtroom fireworks display. Was it perhaps the fancy of Mr. Hilts? It seems so. Evidently, he is personally opposed to creation-science. While he is quite free to hold that view, why does he use his supposedly factual report to discredit the opening witness?"

9. S. Robert Lichter, Stanley Rothman, and Linda S. Lichter, *The Media Elite* (Bethesda, Md.: Adler & Adler, 1986), 22, 28.

A blatant example of this bias is found in the *Chemistry and Engineering News* (January 18, 1982), which so distorted the testimony of an agnostic evolutionist who testified for the Arkansas creation-evolution act that he wrote this in a letter to the editor:

> Sir:
>
> Rudy M. Baum in his article on "Science confronts creationist assault" (*C&EN*, Jan. 18, page 12) characterizes my testimony in the Arkansas trial as consisting "of self serving diatribes." He needs to consult his dictionary. What I spoke in defense of was "openness of inquiry" and "fair-play for minority opinion in regard to controversial issues." Considering that I am agnostic and an evolutionist—both included in my testimony but neglected by the media generally—the "self-serving" factor is obscure at best.
>
> Apparently any spoken response in open court above that of a Caspar Milquetoast qualifies as a diatribe, unless, of course, one represents the camp of entrenched opinion. As a "news analyst" Baum qualifies for the "Paul Goebbels" award, which is granted only to those showing expertise in (1) belittlement, (2) innuendo, (3) prejudice, and (4) reporting out of context. . . .
>
> W. Scot Morrow
> Associate Professor of Chemistry
> Wofford College, Spartanburg, S.C.[10]

There is little doubt that the unquestionably slanted, biased, and even incorrect media coverage before, during, and after the trial has given the American public a distorted picture of what actually occurred at this historic event. I hope this book will help correct this situation.

An Evaluation of the Arkansas Law

My positive comments on Act 590 were summed up in an article for *Christianity Today* (see appendix 3), which I will summarize here. First,

10. W. Scot Morrow, letter to the editor, *Chemistry and Engineering News,* March 29, 1982.

I commented on some misconceptions about the Act and then I gave a rationale for why I supported it.

MISCONCEPTIONS ABOUT ACT 590

There were many misconceptions about Act 590, most of which were due to media distortion of the issue and ignorance of the facts. It was generally misconceived that:

1) The Act mandates teaching the biblical account of creation. (It actually forbids that.)

2) It is opposed to teaching evolution. (It actually mandates teaching evolution alongside creation.)

3) It refers to God or religious concepts. (There is no reference to God and it forbids teaching religion.)

4) It forces teachers who are opposed to creation to teach it anyway. (Actually, the teacher doesn't have to teach anything about origins and/or they can have someone else teach the lectures they do not want to teach.)

5) It is a "fundamentalist" Act. (Actually, the "fundamentalists" of the 1920s were categorically opposed to teaching evolution and in favor of teaching only the Genesis account of creation [see chapter 1 above]. This Act is contrary to both of these stands of the 1920s "fundamentalists.") Further, the promoter of the Act was a Roman Catholic layman, Paul Ellwanger, not a Protestant "fundamentalist."

RATIONALE FOR SUPPORTING THE ACT

First, I argued, as did the ACLU at the 1925 *Scopes* trial, that it is "bigotry" for public schools to teach only one theory of origins. In their own words, "For God's sake let the children have their minds kept open—close no doors to their knowledge; shut no door from them. . . . Let them have both. Let them both be taught."[11] And if it was bigotry to teach only one view when only creation was being taught, then why is it not still bigotry when only evolution is being taught?

11. Dudley Field Malone, quoted in William Hilleary and Oren W. Metzger, eds., *The World's Most Famous Court Trial: Tennessee Evolution Case* (Cincinnati: National Book Company, 1925), 187.

Second, I insisted that in the interest of openness to the scientific endeavor the "loyal opposition" should be permitted their "day in court." In fact, many court decisions would have been premature (and even wrong) had they not waited to hear both sides of the issue. The value of the adversarial system should be obvious to anyone in the legal profession.

Third, teaching scientific creationism is no more nor no less teaching religion than is teaching evolution from a scientific perspective. Both are consistent with certain religious worldviews, but neither is the essence of their respective religion. Either could be used to imply certain religious conclusions, but neither should be excluded simply because it has been so used (or misused).

Fourth, scientific progress depends on allowing the presentation of alternative theories. Copernicus's view that the earth revolves around the sun was once a minority view. So was Einstein's theory of relativity; yet without this theory much of modern physics would not have been possible.

In short, the Act was clear (even the judge agreed), fair (in that it permitted both sides of the controversy to be taught), and not unconstitutional on its face.

SOME DIFFICULTIES WITH THE WORDING OF THE ACT

Even though creationism is science and not religion, it would seem that Act 590 could have avoided any appearance of being religious if it had done the following: First, instead of speaking of "creation out of nothing" it could have used the words "the sudden appearance of the universe" or of life.

Second, it could have avoided similarity with Genesis 1 by substituting for the word "kinds" of life a less objectionable and more scientific term such as "forms" or "types." ("Species" could not be used, since creationists do not believe in the fixity of the taxonomical category called "species.")

Third, the inclusion of points 5 and 6 (catastrophism and young earth) was an unnecessary red flag for those opposed to the Act. As many creation scientists have observed, a "long time" is not really help-ful to the evolutionist view, but it does not hurt the creationist's view. Dropping colored paper from an airplane at 10,000 feet is less likely to spell your name on your roof than dropping it from 5,000 (where it has less time to fall). Regardless of how much time is allowed, how-ever, intelligent intervention into these randomly moving elements is needed in order to direct them and "inform" them exactly what they are to spell out.

In view of the actual irrelevance of long time periods to the basic arguments for creation, it is ill-advised to wave unnecessary red flags in front of evolutionists. Why provide them with one more excuse to proclaim the creationists' view religious (since many believe only the Bible teaches a young earth)? After all, if creationism is taught, then there will be ample opportunity to present the scientific evidence for a young earth even if it is not spelled out in detail.

Fourth, the Arkansas Act unnecessarily gives the impression that one must choose between one of two complete "packaged" positions, each containing six points. Technically, the Act does not say this. It simply contrasts six major areas of disagreement to which either an "evolution" or a "creation" interpretive model may be applied. It thus leaves the door open for one to choose some explanations from one side and some from the other. However, the way the two views are separated does make it possible that some may read the Act as detail-ing two mutually exclusive packages where one must choose all of one or all of the other.

Fifth, the Act could have been improved by mentioning theistic re-ligions among those it opposes being established. By failing to make such allowance, the Act leaves itself open to the charge that it may favor theistic religions despite the fact that it explicitly states its opposition to establishing any religion.

In brief, Act 590 could have been improved. Indeed, subsequent acts (such as *Edwards,* 1982) have been better. Nonetheless, Act 590 was fair and, in my opinion, it was not unconstitutional.

Comments on the Trial Attorneys

Attorneys for the Defense

The press gave much attention to the charges by certain groups that the attorney general, Steve Clark, and his staff (attorneys David Williams, Rick Campbell, and Callis Childs; and Assistants Tim Humphries, Cindy English, and W. W. "Dub" Elrod) did not do a good job of defending the law. This conclusion is based on several allegations made by attorney Wendell R. Bird.[12] The allegations of poor defense centered mainly around the following situations reported by the media (see appendix 6). It was alleged: (1) that Clark had refused expert legal help from the attorneys Wendell Bird and John Whitehead; (2) that Clark's defense was not adequately prepared; (3) that Clark was not dedicated to defending the law, having (allegedly) sold out to the ACLU as evidenced by a gift of $25 to the ACLU a few weeks before the trial.

As far as we can tell, all of these allegations are false. Before we can draw implications, let us discern the facts of the matter. (1) First, Clark did not turn down all legal help from the ICR. What he turned down was their attorney's request to be the "counsels of record," which means official trial attorneys. (2) Second, Steve Clark did not give the ACLU a gift of $25 as alleged. What he did do was give two free lunches for the purpose of a raffle. (3) The main attorneys for the defense (and the ones who signed the defense brief) were Dave Williams and Rick Campbell, both of whom are evangelical Christians.

It is my impression, based on firsthand observations of the entire trial and direct communication with the attorneys before, during, and after the trial that: (1) They executed their duties well. This was the unanimously expressed opinion of all the defense witnesses at the trial, and of Duane Gish, who was there as an observer. (2) The attorney general was penetrating in his cross-examining of those ACLU witnesses he handled.

12. See appendix 7 of Norman L. Geisler with A. F. Brooke II and Mark J. Keough, *The Creator in the Courtroom: "Scopes II"* (Milford, Mich.: Mott Media, 1982) for a statement of the Creation Science Legal Defense Fund (Wendell Bird, Legal Counsel) on the alleged mishandling of the case by the state's attorney.

(3) There was no question in our minds about the dedication of the defense attorneys, though they were far outnumbered by the ACLU.

THE ACLU ATTORNEYS

The lead attorney for the ACLU was Robert M. Cearley, Jr. (of Cearley, Gitchel, Mitchell, and Bryant, P.A., Little Rock, Arkansas). Immediately following the trial, twelve ACLU attorneys posed for the *Arkansas Democrat* (December 18, 1981). The plaintiffs' brief lists the following (nine) names: Robert Cearley, Philip Kaplan (of Kaplan, Brewer, and Bilheimer, P.A., Little Rock), Bruce Ennis, Jr. and Jack Novick (of ACLU Foundation, N.Y.), and Peggy L. Kerr, Gary E. Crawford, and Mark E. Herlichy (listed as "of counsel"). In addition, acknowledgment is given to two legal students (of Fordham University School of Law), Kathryn Keneally and Kathryn S. Reimann. The media reported that there were a total of seventeen, and one source reported as many as twenty-two ACLU lawyers and assistants who worked on the case. Compared with four defense attorneys and their three legal assistants, the ACLU outnumbered the state by about three to one.

Furthermore, it appears obvious that with this larger staff (twenty in all) than the defense (about six), the attorneys of the ACLU had a definite legal advantage. And judging from the volumes of books and exhibits presented at the trial, it was clear that the ACLU legal staff had done their homework.

Another interesting feature of the ACLU attorneys was their obvious theatrical ability. They understood playing to the press (by bringing up irrelevant but sensational matters, like UFOs), and appealing to the court (by frequently mentioning the religious background and associations of those in favor of the creation-evolution Act). Probably most observers (whatever side they were on) would agree that the ACLU simply presented a more persuasive case than the attorney general. In order to do this, however, the ACLU attorneys had to twist, distort, and even misrepresent the facts. For example, they carefully concealed the unfalsifiable nature of the general theory of evolution; they hid the scientific support for the creationist viewpoint. They also successfully painted supporters of creationism as Protestant "fundamentalists," though many were agnostics, Buddhists, Roman Catholics, evangelical Protestants, and other beliefs.

In some cases, the ACLU flatly misrepresented the facts. For example, they represented one witness as teaching a "science" class at Dallas Seminary, despite his clear disavowal of this in his deposition, where he said, "This is a theology course." And by presenting the class in *religious* anthropology as though it were *scientific* anthropology, the ACLU could make his five religious views about origins look as if it contradicted the position of Act 590, which lists two scientific *positions* on each point of origins (see plaintiffs' brief). The full text reads like this:

Q. "And all of the references there in this anthropology course are to the Bible in that section?"

A. "That's correct."

Q. "And there are no—in that section there are no scientific statements whatsoever?"

A. "That's correct. This is a theology course."

There is no question that the ACLU lawyers were well trained at twisting and distorting the facts, a talent the defense did not exercise. In short, the ACLU lawyers continued the "religion vs. science" scenario the media had already presented, and the judge bought it.

Comments on the Judge

Some have implied that Judge Overton accepted the ACLU "story" because he was part of their plot. I don't think that was the case. He did, however, give clear evidence of being biased against creationism. Consider the following:

1) The judge was a theologically liberal Methodist who did not believe in creationism as defined by Act 590.

2) He was the son of an evolutionary biology teacher, who attended every session of the trial, who sat behind me at the trial, and whom I

saw express her disdain at the creationist cause from time to time at the trial.

3) His theologically liberal Methodist bishop was the first witness against teaching creationism. Some felt that this fact alone should have disqualified the judge. One person wrote a letter to the editor of the *Arkansas Democrat* (December 15, 1981) saying:

> In the creation science trial, there is a question of neutrality on the part of Judge Overton. When the Methodist bishop of Arkansas testified for the ACLU, how could the judge not be influenced. After all, he is a Methodist and surely must respect the head Methodist of the state. You can be well assured that if the Judge were a "fundamentalist Christian" the ACLU would cry and scream "partiality."

4) The judge manifested bias against creationism by several outbursts of personal opinion during the trial. Once, he chided a high school science teacher. The court record reads as follows:

> Witness [Townley]: "why narrow your possibilities to only one when—"
> The court [the judge, interrupting]: "Well, because it's not Sunday school. You're trying to teach about science."[13]

5) He denied a motion by the defense which would have eliminated irrelevant religious opinions being included in the record (and thus being reported by the press).[14]

6) Before the trial the judge said he would rule from the bench (as though his mind were made up), but he later reversed course when he was criticized by witnesses and citizens as being biased.

7) Despite nearly a week of testimony from numerous Ph.D.'s in science (some of whom were evolutionists) insisting that creationism is as scientific as evolution and is not based on the Bible, the judge still referred to *scientific* creationism as "the *biblical* view of creation." His

13. *McLean v. Arkansas Board of Education,* 529 F. Supp. 1255 (E.D. Ark. 1982). See chapter 4 for another example of such an obvious public display of bias.

14. See appendix 1.

basic mind-set had never been changed: evolution is to be learned in the public school, and creation is what you learned in Sunday school.

8) The judge's decision reveals an absolutistic naturalistic bias, as will be clearly seen in the following discussion on the ruling.

9) Scot Morrow, an evolutionist who was a witness for teaching creation along with evolution, was interrupted and verbally chastised by the judge. He later said he thought the judge was closed-minded.[15]

Comments on the Judge's Ruling

It was the almost unanimous opinion of those present on both sides after the trial that the judge would rule for the plaintiffs. No one was greatly surprised, then, on January 5, 1982, when Judge Overton struck down Act 590 and ruled it an unconstitutional violation of the First Amendment. We will divide our comments on this ruling into several sections: factual, logical, legal, and religious.

THE FACTUAL ERRORS

There are a number of factual errors worthy of note in the ruling. First, the judge is clearly wrong in saying the term "scientific creationism" did not gain currency until around 1965, after the publication of *The Genesis Flood* in 1961. In fact, the term did not come into common use till around 1974, following the publication of Henry Morris's book *Scientific Creationism.*

Second, the judge is wrong in asserting that Paul Ellwanger was "motivated by . . . [the] desire to see the Biblical version of creation taught in the public schools." Ellwanger desired that a *scientific* version of creation be taught in the schools.

Third, the judge is mistaken in believing that creation and flood stories are unique to Genesis. They are found in many ancient cultures, including Babylonian and Sumerian.

Fourth, the creationists' concept of a "recent earth" is not based on the genealogy of the Old Testament but on their scientific arguments for a young earth.

15. Cited in Geisler, *Creator in the Courtroom*, 133.

Fifth, it is not true that no witness gave evidence of refusal to publish creationists' articles. Robert Gentry gave ample evidence of this in his testimony.

Sixth, the judge wrongly affirms that Mr. Ellwanger believes "both evolution and creation are religion." Ellwanger believes both are scientific views.

Seventh, the ruling incorrectly affirms that the improbability argument is used by creationists to support "a worldwide flood . . . and a young earth." It was used only to show the need for positing a designer of life.

Eighth, the judge misrepresents my testimony about fundamentalists' beliefs in "Five Fundamentals." In fact, I testified that there were two overlapping sets of five, which made six "Fundamentals."[16]

Ninth, he incorrectly asserts that the scientific community does not consider the origin of life as part of the overall theory of evolution. Spontaneous generation of life is often discussed by evolutionists as an explanation of how life began in the primeval "soup."

Tenth, the judge falsely asserts that a defense witness testified that there were more than two basic scientific positions on origins. The witness affirmed that there were only two scientific views on the various points of origin (either life and life forms began by chance or they began by a creator), but that there are many religious ways to conceive of this "creator."

These are only some of the more obvious mistakes. The ruling as a whole badly distorts many statements crucial to the case. Close examina-

16. The judge wrongly asserted (in footnote 4 of his ruling) that: "Dr. Geisler testified to the widely held view that there are five beliefs characteristic of all Fundamentalist movements, in addition, of course, to the inerrancy of Scripture: (1) belief in the virgin birth of Christ, (2) belief in the deity of Christ, (3) belief in the substitutional atonement of Christ, (4) belief in the second coming of Christ, and (5) belief in the physical resurrection of all departed souls."

What I actually had said in the deposition testimony was: "And those essential doctrines were: (1) the virgin birth of Christ, that Jesus was virgin born; (2) the deity of Christ, that Jesus was God; (3) the atonement of Christ, that Christ died on the cross for the sins of the world; (4) the bodily resurrection, that Jesus bodily rose from the grave; (5) and the inspiration of the Bible, that the Bible is the word of God. (6) Now, some added a 6th one, but these were the five fundamentals. The 6th one that they added is that Jesus is going to return to this earth someday, the Second Coming of Christ."

The judge made two mistakes. He confused the bodily resurrection of Christ with the bodily resurrection of all believers. And he didn't add correctly, since the "five" he noted plus the inspiration of Scripture equals six fundamentals, as I had said.

tion would indicate that the ruling is based on the pretrial mind-set of the judge, since he sometimes cites the witnesses' ideas from their pretrial depositions rather than from the more clearly thought out statements they later gave in court testimony. In fact the judge's opinion seems to be based largely on the ACLU brief.

THE LOGICAL FALLACIES

The ruling is a field day for fallacy hunters. First of all, the heart of the legal opinion is the genetic fallacy. This fallacy argues that since the source of creationism is a religious book (Genesis) then creationism must be religious. But as had been pointed out in testimony from both sides (Ruse for evolution and others for creation), the source of a scientific theory has nothing to do with its status as science. No one ever rejected the Kekule model of the benzene molecule or Tesla's alternating current motor because they came from visions, or Socrates' views simply because he credits the oracle of Delphi as his inspiration for those views.

The source of a scientific idea is quite irrelevant; it is justifiability that counts. If one is to throw away a scientific viewpoint because its inspiration comes from the Judeo-Christian Bible, then much of early modern science should be discarded since Bacon, Kelvin, Newton, and others admitted their source was the biblical view of creation. This is a widely held understanding even by non-creationists, from Alfred N. Whitehead to Ian Barbour. Furthermore, if a scientific view is ruled illegal because its source is the Bible, then much of Near Eastern archaeology should be likewise prohibited because the source and inspiration for much of it came from the Bible. But despite the fact that this was all carefully pointed out to the judge in precise testimony, he still ruled that the bill was religious because its source was Genesis.

Second, the fallacy of *misimplication* is evident. The judge stated and implied that many would draw religious implications from teachings about creation. But the same also applies to evolution. For if creationism should be rejected because it is consistent with the beliefs of "fundamentalists" (though it was never one of the stated "fundamentals"), then evolution should also be rejected because it is one of the stated beliefs of religious humanists (indeed, it is one of their fundamental beliefs). Furthermore, many scientists have elevated evolution itself into a "god" or the equivalent. Later in life, for example, Darwin referred to "my deity 'Natural Selection'" as replacing the function of the Deity in creating the species.[17] Ernst Haeckel deified the process of evolution, as did Alfred Wallace.[18] Julian Huxley refers to his religion as the "religion of evolutionary humanism."[19] Now, so far as we know, there are no informed creationists who have ever made creationism into a god or religion (though it is a part of the religious beliefs of many). In view of this, one could argue that there is a greater danger of the theory of evolution becoming a religion than of creationism becoming a religion.

Third, one notices the fallacy of *emphasizing the accidental*. The classic example of this logic is the man who became intoxicated whether he drank wine and water, whiskey and water, or gin and water. He reasoned that the water was the cause of his intoxication, since it was the common element in the three scenarios. Judge Overton has said in essence that since all fundamentalists have creationism as part of their religious belief then it must be the essence of their religious belief. This does not logically follow. For what is only accidental to a system (even if it is always present) is not necessarily the essence of that system. And creationism has never been declared the essence of any fundamentalist religion. In fact, not all fundamentalists believe in creationism as defined in Act 590. Most historians acknowledge that one of the characteristics of much of modern fundamentalism is the belief in dispensationalism. The most widespread version of this was largely influenced by the Scofield Bible. Yet this reference Bible accepts the Gap Theory, that there may be long geological ages in the alleged "gap" between the first two verses of Genesis, which is in conflict with points 5 and 6 in Act 590's definition of creationism. Furthermore, some of the earliest fundamentalists who

17. Charles Darwin, in a letter to Asa Gray, June 5, 1861 (in Francis Darwin, ed., *The Life and Letters of Charles Darwin*, 2 vols. [New York: Basic Books, 1959], 2:165).

18. Wallace said, "natural selection is supreme" and operates like a "mind" that can "regulate all the forces at work in living organisms" (see "Wallace, Alfred," in Paul Edwards, ed., *The Encyclopedia of Philosophy*, 8 vols. [New York: Macmillan and The Free Press, 1967], 8:276).

19. Julian Huxley, *Religion Without Revelation* (New York: Harper, 1957), 203ff.

wrote in the famous book called *The Fundamentals*[20] (such as James Orr, B. B. Warfield, and G. F. Wright) were willing to accept modified evolutionary positions. So if creationism (as defined in Act 590) is not even universally held among fundamentalists—to say nothing of essential to fundamentalism—then the judge erred in rejecting creationism on the grounds it was essentially religious.

Fourth, the judge's ruling commits the fallacy of *overlooking the essential*. The essence of religion is worship or *commitment* to an ultimate (whether God, a person, or an idea). Religion is not simply acknowledging that there is a first cause to the universe. This is no more a religious act than recognizing that some person would make a good spouse makes one married. It takes *commitment* to make religion (or marriage). If approaching an object in a purely scientific way represents religion, then the study of Christ from the evidence of history is automatically teaching "religion." The judge has failed to account for one of the most fundamental distinctions of the courts in this matter: the teaching *of* religion is wrong in public school, but not the teaching *about* religion. In like manner, the teaching about an *object* of a religion (e.g., the Creator) is not the essence of that religion. Rather, it is presenting some alleged teachings of the Creator. In short, belief that God exists does not automatically constitute a religious belief. (Aristotle believed that God existed but did not worship him.) It is belief *in* God (trust, commitment) that is religious.

Fifth, since the judge failed to make the above essential distinction, a *reductio ad absurdum* follows. The absurd consequence of the judge's position that a creator cannot be implied as an explanation of the origin of life is that even Darwin's *Origin of Species* cannot be taught in public schools, since the last lines of that book refer to the creator of the first form (or forms) of life.[21]

---

20. R. A. Torrey, ed. *The Fundamentals* (Los Angeles: Bible Institute of Los Angeles, 1917).

21. Darwin's actual closing words were as follows: "There is grandeur in this view of life, with its several powers, having been originally breathed by the Creator into a few forms or into one; and that, whilst this planet has gone cycling on according to the fixed law of gravity, from so simple a beginning endless forms most beautiful and most wonderful have been, and

Sixth, the fallacy of *equivocation* is committed concerning the word "science." Strictly defined, science has to do with things that are observable, repeatable, and falsifiable. On this view neither the general theory of macroevolution nor creation is science, since origin events were not observed and have not been repeated. In the broad sense of origin science that reconstructs past unobserved events the way a forensic scientist would, both macroevolution and creation are scientific. The judge failed to recognize this point.

Seventh, the judge's ruling also contains cases of special pleading. Suppose we accept the widely held belief reflected by the judge that creation *ex nihilo* (out of nothing) is unique to certain Judeo-Christian views. Even so, it is special pleading to make this "an inherently religious concept" any more than making creation *ex deo* (out of God), as in pantheistic systems, or creation *ex materia* (out of preexisting stuff), as in dualistic systems, inherently religious concepts. Why single out only one of the three basic views of origins—the one represented by "creation-science" in the Act—and make it alone "inherently religious"? Is this not a clear bias against one view of origins?

Eighth, Judge Overton violates the *law of the excluded middle,* which demands that there can be only two views when one is the logical opposite of the other. Both witnesses and defense attorneys insisted that on any given point of origin the beginning was either (a) caused by natural forces or (b) caused by some supernatural force. Despite this logically obvious distinction, Overton insisted that there could be more than two theories about origins. He ignored the obvious fact that things either began by chance or else by design—a fact that even evolutionists acknowledge (see appendix 6).

Ninth, there are *non sequiturs* (things that do not follow logically) in the ruling. For example, the judge insists that Section 4 of Act 590 is wrong because "evolution does not presuppose the absence of a creator or God...." By this Judge Overton apparently means that Act 590 wrongly assumes that evolution implies atheism. This of course is not true, since theistic evolution is a logical possibility. What Section 4 implies is that,

---

are being evolved" (*The Origin of Species,* introduction by W. R. Thompson [reprint, London: Dent, 1967], 463).

according to evolution, there is no direct involvement of any supreme being in the origin of the various forms of life. It does not imply that all evolutionists believe there is no God at all or that one could not be indirectly involved in the evolutionary process.

Tenth, there is *petitio principii* (begging the question). The judge defines any discussion of a Creator as an "inescapably religious discussion." He then easily concludes that such a discussion is unconstitutional. He says the same of "creation out of nothing." But when these concepts are prejudged to be religious and this conclusion is then used as the basis for determining whether they are a religious violation of the First Amendment, the judge has used his conclusion as his premise. This is the logical fallacy of begging the question.

THE LEGAL IMPLICATIONS

Judge Overton's ruling also raises some serious legal questions. The debate turns on two different interpretations of what the First Amendment means. One view is that it entails a wall of separation between church and state. This view is clearly reflected in the judge's ruling, as is evidenced by his closing quotation about "good fences make good neighbors," his ruling out any supernaturalistic interpretation of scientific data, and his conclusion that any reference to or implication of a "creation" is automatically religious.

The other interpretation is that the First Amendment intended no "wall of separation" between church and state but was designed to guarantee "religious neutrality" on the part of the state toward religion by opposing the "establishment" of any one religion over others. This view is reflected in articles by Wendell Bird and John Whitehead, who together defended the Louisiana creation/evolution case that we will look at in chapter 5.[22] The essence of their argument is that the First Amendment is not for completely *separating* church and state but is against *establishing* or favoring any one religion above others by the aid of the state.

22. See Wendell R. Bird, "Freedom of Religion and Science Instruction in Public Schools," *Yale Law Journal* 87/3 (January 1978): 515–570; idem, "Freedom from Establishment and Unneutrality in Public School Instruction and Religion School Regulation," *Harvard Journal of Law and Public Policy* (June 1979): 143-154; John W. Whitehead, *The Separation Illusion* (Milford, Mich.: Mott Media, 1982).

The First Amendment reads: *"Congress shall make no law respecting an establishment of religion, or prohibiting the free exercise thereof."* And in the famous *Everson* case (1947), Supreme Court Justice Black stated that this means "neither a state nor the Federal Government can set up a church." And neither can it "pass laws which aid one religion . . . or prefer one religion over another."

Now if the First Amendment is really an anti-establishment clause, as it says, and not a complete separation clause, as it does not say, then the basis for the judge's ruling is wrong. One thing seems certain: if the Constitution meant to separate God and government, then *The Declaration of Independence* is unconstitutional, for it speaks of the "unalienable rights" granted to all humans by the "Creator." And since pronouncing *The Declaration of Independence* unconstitutional is absurd on its face, we are left with the only reasonable conclusion: that the Constitution does not separate God from government or from government-sponsored public schools.

But let us suppose for the sake of argument that the First Amendment could be understood as a separation clause (and not an anti-establishment clause). Even on this interpretation Judge Overton's decision is contrary to the First Amendment, since it allows only a naturalistic evolutionary view to be taught, which view favors the beliefs of religious humanists. In fact the judge's decision not only favors the religion of humanism but favors it exclusively. For the ruling allows only nontheistic evolutionistic and naturalistic views, which accord precisely with the views of religious humanists, to be taught.

In brief, if one takes an "anti-establishment" interpretation of the First Amendment, then the Arkansas creation-evolution act is constitutional, since it does not establish any one view or religion over another but mandates teaching both views. And if one takes a "wall of separation" view (as Overton apparently does), then his ruling is a violation of the First Amendment, since it not only allows but favors nontheistic religions over theistic ones. In either case, the ruling seems to violate the Constitution, not uphold it.

Judge Overton rejected this anti-establishment interpretation, saying that "the argument has no legal merit." He dismissively referred to

Bird's scholarly article in the *Yale Law Review*[23] as "a student note." It is difficult for non-lawyers to enter this battle on the meaning of the Constitution. It seems that much of the current legal "reading" of the Constitution is contrary to a commonsense interpretation. Certainly experience shows that the vast majority of people expect readers to understand by their words what they meant by them, not what the reader would like them to mean. Now, from what we can discern from the statements of the framers of the Constitution, and its understood meaning by contemporaries and immediate successors, the anti-establishment interpretation of the First Amendment seems to be the correct one. If this is so, Judge Overton's decision is based on a misinterpretation of the Constitution.

For those who defend the interpretation of the First Amendment more in terms of what it means to us today rather than what the framers meant by it, I ask the following question: Do these interpreters want their words to be interpreted by succeeding generations according to what they meant by them or according to what the future readers will decide they mean to *them*? If these interpreters expect us to accept their meaning (and not read ours into it), then should they not give the original framers of the First Amendment the same courtesy?

The Religious Implications

Judge Overton ruled that Act 590 would establish the religion of "fundamentalism" in public schools and was thereby unconstitutional. But in ruling the way he did the judge has in effect established the religion of "secular humanism" in the public schools. Judge Overton accomplished the opposite of what he thought he was doing. For in trying to avoid giving what he called "fundamentalist" beliefs one voice (among two voices), he gave "humanists" the only voice.

Two Overlooked Factors

There are two significant factors to keep in mind which Judge Overton apparently overlooked. First, in a balanced-treatment, two-model

23. See note 22, above.

approach (such as Act 590 provided for), there is no way one can reasonably argue that only one view is being favored. The Act mandates teaching both views (if either is taught). So if Overton's reasoning is right, then the Act is also unconstitutional because it mandates teaching evolution (which is consistent with a humanistic religious system). But the judge clearly acknowledged (via his citing of the *Epperson* case, 1968) that teaching evolution is not teaching religion. If the Act equally mandates teaching both (if either), then it is unreasonable to reject the Act because it allegedly favors one of two equally mandated views.

Second, there is no way Act 590 could establish one view over another, since it doesn't mandate teaching either. It is only an "if, then" law. It says that if one view is taught—and it need not be—then the opposing view must also be taught. How can a law mandating the teaching of *nothing* be establishing *anything*?

Of course, it is argued that with such an Act many teachers would opt not to teach either view and would thereby rob the student of a valid educational experience. But the possibility of missing "a valid educational experience" is neither unconstitutional nor uncommon (there is simply far too much knowledge to teach everything).

THE ESTABLISHMENT OF A HUMANISTIC RELIGION

Granting as I do the good intentions of Judge Overton, his decision has in effect done exactly the opposite of what he desired. The judge wished to uphold the First Amendment by avoiding the "establishment" of religion in Arkansas public schools. This is a noble task for which he was trained and took the oath of office. Unfortunately, the judge has accomplished the reverse of his stated desires. For by trying to avoid favoring the religion of "fundamentalism" he has in effect "established" the religion of "humanism."

Let us outline the reasoning for this conclusion:

1. Humanism has been defined as a religion by the U.S. Supreme Court.
2. Nontheism, evolution, naturalism, and relativism are the central beliefs of religious humanists.

3. Overton's decision in effect exclusively favors the teaching of the above beliefs.
4. But whatever in effect favors the central beliefs of one religion over another is a violation of the First Amendment.
5. Therefore, Overton's decision in effect is a violation of the First Amendment.

Now let us examine each of these premises:

Humanism is a religion. Humanism is a "religion" by its own acclaim and by legal recognition. This is evidenced by the following facts: (1) The *Humanist Manifesto I* (1933) declares: "to establish such a religion [of humanism] is a major necessity of the present." The words "religion" or "religious" occur some twenty-nine times in the six-page Manifesto. (2) The *Humanist Manifesto II* (1973) continues to expound the belief that humanism is a religion, using the words "religion" or "religious" some nineteen times. It proclaims that "Faith, commensurate with advancing knowledge, is also necessary."[24] (3) An influential journal is dedicated to these beliefs; it is called the *Religious Humanist.* (4) Many proponents of humanism have written books and articles describing their humanistic beliefs as a religion. Julian Huxley called his beliefs "the religion of evolutionary humanism."[25] Konstantin Kolenda's book on humanistic religion is entitled *Religion Without God* (Prometheus, 1976).

Not only do humanists recognize humanism as a religion (or as religious), but the Supreme Court has also recognized the term "secular humanism" as describing a religion. The process of this recognition came about gradually when many agnostics and atheists claimed First Amendment protection for their beliefs against discrimination in jobs or in the military. The Supreme Court ruled (in the *Everson* case, 1947) that "neither a State nor the Federal Government can constitutionally force a person to profess a belief or disbelief in any religion. Neither can [it] constitutionally pass laws or impose requirements which aid

24. Paul Kurtz, ed., *Humanist Manifestos I and II* (Buffalo, N.Y.: Prometheus, 1973), 13. "Humanist Manifesto I" first appeared in *The New Humanist* 6/3 (May/June 1933). "Humanist Manifesto II" first appeared in *The Humanist* 33/5 (September/October 1973).
25. See Huxley, *Religion Without Revelation,* 203ff.

all religions as against non-believers."[26] Also, the Court ruled (*Torcaso,* 1961) that those who do not believe in God can still have a conscientious objector status on religious grounds (i.e., on the grounds of the First Amendment). The record of the *Torcaso* case specifies some nontheistic religions, saying, "Among religions in this country which do not teach what would generally be considered a belief in the existence of God are Buddhism, Taoism, Ethical Culture, Secular Humanism, and others."[27]

So not only do humanists claim there is such a religion as secular humanism, but the Supreme Court has officially noted this religion by name.

Nontheism, evolutionism, and naturalism are the central beliefs of humanism. There are four central beliefs of religious humanism: (1) nontheism, (2) evolution, (3) naturalism, and (4) relativism (of human values). These beliefs are confessed in *Manifestos I* and *II* and throughout the writings of most humanists.

Manifesto I begins,

> We therefore affirm the following:
> First: Religious humanists regard the universe as self-existing and not created [non-theism].
> Second: Humanism believes that man is a part of nature [naturalism] and that he has emerged as the result of a continuous process [evolution].[28]

Thirdly, the *Humanist Manifesto* denies any supernatural explanations (see points 3, 4, 5, 6, and 11).[29] The *Humanist Manifesto II* (1973) reaffirms these same three beliefs (see "Preface" and "Religion," sections 1 and 2).[30]

The *Secular Humanist Declaration* (1980) again reaffirms these exact beliefs in points 4, 6, 8, and 9. Under the last point they say, "There

26. *Everson v. Board of Education of Ewing,* 330 U.S. 1 (1947).
27. *Torcaso v. Watkins,* 367 U.S. 488 (1961).
28. Kurtz, ed., *Humanist Manifestos I and II,* 8.
29. Ibid., 8–9.
30. Ibid., 13–17.

may be some significant differences among scientists concerning the mechanics of evolution; yet the evolution of the species is supported so strongly by the weight of evidence that it is difficult to reject it." It concludes, "Secular humanism places trust in human intelligence rather than in divine guidance."[31] Again, secular humanism acknowledges no need for God, a naturalistic explanation for everything, and a belief in evolution. So far as we can determine, all secular humanists hold these three essential beliefs which form the core of the religion of humanism. Indeed, if one appealed to God, the supernatural, and/or creation, he would by definition be excluded as a secular humanist; he would in fact be some kind of theist.

In addition to these three beliefs—nontheism, evolution, and naturalism—secular humanism believes in the relativity of human values. *Manifesto I* (point 5) reads: "Humanism asserts that the nature of the universe depicted by modern science makes unacceptable any supernatural or cosmic guarantee of human values."[32] If this is so, then *Manifesto II* correctly notes, "Ethics is autonomous and situational, needing no theological or ideological sanction" (point 3).[33] In short, if God is not needed for the origin of life, then godliness is likewise not needed as the basis for living life. Each person must decide his or her own values. Thus, the first three central beliefs of secular humanism imply the fourth. And these four are core beliefs of the religion of secular humanism.

Overton's ruling favors religious humanists' beliefs. Of the four central premises of secular humanism, Judge Overton directly ruled that three of them (and, by implication, the fourth as well) are the only religious beliefs that can be taught in Arkansas science classes. For he ruled that teaching any non-naturalistic or non-evolutionary theory would be unconstitutional. He ruled that even the implication of a "creator" or supernatural cause is a violation of the First Amendment. In the judge's own words, scientific creationism "is not science because it depends upon supernatural intervention which is not guided by natural law." It

---

31. *The Secular Humanist Declaration* (Buffalo, N.Y.: Prometheus, 1980), 21, 24. The book's cover describes it as having been "drafted by Paul Kurtz and endorsed by 58 prominent scholars and writers."

32. Ibid., 8.

33. Ibid., 17.

cannot be science, the judge added, because "it is not explanatory by reference to natural law. . . ." In fact, the judge pontificated, "there is *no* scientific explanation for these limits [of created kinds of animals] which is guided by natural law and the limitations, whatever they are, *cannot* be explained by natural law" (emphasis added). And as for the creationist contention for separate origins for ape and human, the judge ruled that this "explains *nothing* and refers to *no* scientific fact or theory" (emphasis added). In addition, the judge said, "the concepts and wording convey an *inescapable* religiosity" (emphasis added). Indeed, he called the scientific claim for "creation of the world" the ultimate religious statement because "God is the only actor." And "concepts concerning . . . a supreme being of some sort are manifestly religious" (see chapter 8, passim).

Favoring one religion violates the First Amendment. The First Amendment of the United States Constitution says nothing about the separation of church and state. It does, however, forbid the "establishment" of a religion by the federal government. It reads: "Congress shall make no law respecting an establishment of religion, or prohibiting the free exercise thereof. . . ." Later, in the *Everson* case (1947), Supreme Court Justice Black stated that this means "neither a state nor the Federal Government can set up a church." And neither can it "pass laws which aid one religion . . . or prefer one religion over another." Thus any judicial decision which so aids one religion over another is a clear violation of the First Amendment.

Some may not consider humanism a religion. But even here the Supreme Court has ruled (*Abington,* 1963) that "the State may not establish a 'religion of Secularism' in the sense of affirmatively opposing or showing hostility to religion" and thereby "preferring those who believe in no religion over those who do believe."[34] Further, in the *Reed* case (1965), a district court similarly ruled that for government "to espouse a particular philosophy of secularism, or secularism in general"[35] may be a violation of the First Amendment.

34. *Abington School District v. Schempp,* 374 U.S. 203 (1963).
35. *Reed v. Van Hoven,* 237 F. Supp. 48 (W. D. MI 1965).

A Misunderstanding of Religion

That Judge Overton misunderstood the nature of religion is clear from his statement that, "The argument advanced by defendants' witness, Dr. Norman Geisler, that teaching the existence of God is not religious unless the teaching seeks a commitment, is contrary to common understanding and contradicts settled case law. *Stone* v. *Graham* . . . (1980); *Abington School District* v. *Schempp* . . . (1963)."

First of all, Overton does not state precisely what it is in these laws that demands that one cannot refer to a rational inference from scientific evidence, without any call to or implication of devotion to or worship of this first cause, without making that first cause an object of religious worship. A careful examination of these cases reveals that no such implication is there.

Second, he overlooks the fact that in my testimony (see chapter 4) I cite an expert witness on the side of teaching only evolution (Langdon Gilkey) who supports the very point I made.

Third, likewise, the judge ignores the fact that in the *Torcaso* case (1961), Paul Tillich, whom I cite in support of this same point, was used as an authority by the Court in helping to define religion. And Tillich testified that religion involves a commitment to what is "ultimate," even if one does not believe in God.

Finally, if the mere reference to a creator is *ipso facto* religious and unconstitutional, then so are *The Declaration of Independence,* "under God" in our Pledge of Allegiance, presidential oaths, and numerous other parts of our heritage that have never been ruled unconstitutional (see chapter 6).

Missing the Point

The judge missed the main point of my testimony (see chapter 4) and ignored the rest. He dismissed my point (that science is an objective approach to a first cause, while religion calls for devotion or commitment to such a cause) in a single sentence: "It is contrary to common understanding and contradicts settled case law." He does not explain *how* it is contrary, and the cases he cites (*Stone* [1980] and *Abington* [1963]) do not address this issue. The majority of my testimony is not even addressed, yet according to expert eyewitnesses (see the foreword and preface to this book) it destroyed the ACLU case.

The Inescapable Conclusion

On January 5, 1982, federal court judge William Overton in effect established secular humanism as a religion in the Arkansas public schools. For he ruled that only humanist beliefs, including nontheism, evolution, and naturalism, can be taught in public school science classes. These beliefs not only favor humanism but are central beliefs of the religion of secular humanism. Perhaps the judge did not intend to do this, but this is nonetheless the effect of his decision. History will record that in Judge Overton's federal court (December 7–17, 1981) the Creator "lost"! The irony of history was that this very court which dishonorably dismissed God began each day by the U.S. marshal praying, "God save the United States and this honorable court." To this we can only add, Amen![36]

Further Reading

Geisler, Norman L., with A. F. Brooke II and Mark J. Keough. *The Creator in the Courtroom: "Scopes II"*. Milford, Mich.: Mott Media, 1982.

Gentry, Robert. *Creation's Tiny Mystery*. Knoxville: Earth Science Association, 1988.

Gilkey, Langdon. *Creationism on Trial: Evolution and God at Little Rock*. Minneapolis: Winston, 1998.

Hilleary, William, and Oren W. Metzger, eds. *The World's Most Famous Court Trial: Tennessee Evolution Case*. Cincinnati: National Book Company, 1925.

Scalia, Antonin. *Dissenting Opinion in Edwards* (1987) (excerpted in chapter 6 of this book).

36. For further evaluation of the case see chapters 8 and 9.

The Testimony They Refused to Transcribe

The circumstances surrounding my own testimony in the Arkansas *McLean* trial are strange and suspicious. The testimony went to the heart of the issue of whether creation science is religion or science, and yet it was almost completely ignored by ACLU cross-examination (see appendix 4). Further, the court refused to transcribe the testimony until after the Supreme Court ruled on the issue of whether creation science is religion or science, which was five whole years later.

Another eyewitness at the trial (Wayne Frair) has spoken to the strange circumstances in which testimonies in favor of teaching creation were not transcribed and made available to higher courts or the general public until after it was too late to influence their decision. He failed to ever get his testimony transcribed, despite repeated and frustrating attempts (see the preface to this book).

My testimony was eventually transcribed and sent to me by the Arkansas attorney general's office. The testimony was given on December

11, 1981, but it was not until after the Supreme Court ruled on the issue, on June 19, 1987, that I received the transcript. This strange situation has challenged my normally anti-conspiratorial beliefs!

According to other eyewitnesses at the trial, my testimony was crucial to the case and harmful to the ACLU's cause against teaching creation alongside evolution in public schools. Duane Gish, an eyewitness of the event, wrote: "Geisler was not only present during the trial; he was the lead witness for the creationist side. . . . His testimony, in my view (I was present during the entire trial), effectively demolished the most important thrust of the case by the ACLU" (see the foreword to this book).

Another witness at the trial (Wayne Frair) confirmed Gish's comments, saying, "Geisler's presentation was superb, . . . and at its end Gish was absolutely exuberant. . . . In no uncertain words he declared to me that Geisler successfully had demolished every one of the arguments presented by ACLU witnesses during their preceding five days of testimony" (see the preface to this book).

In spite of the crucial nature of it in the creationists' cause, my testimony was not available for any higher court to see until too late. And, sadly, the Supreme Court (in *Edwards,* 1987) and later courts like *Webster* (1990) and *Dover* (2005) cite *McLean* as a precedent opposed to allowing creation into public schools. What follows is the complete unedited transcript of my testimony in *McLean v. Arkansas Board of Education* (1982), now being made available for the very first time:[1]

IN THE UNITED STATES DISTRICT COURT
EASTERN DISTRICT OF ARKANSAS
WESTERN DIVISION

McLean, Plaintiff, vs.
Board of Education, Defendant.
Docket No. LR-C-81-322

---

1. All corrections of errors are in brackets. All comments on the text are in footnotes. The complete "Cross-Examination" is found in appendix 4.

Friday, December 11, 1981
Little Rock, Arkansas, 9:00 a.m.

PARTIAL TRANSCRIPT OF PROCEEDINGS
BEFORE THE HON. WILLIAM R. OVERTON

TRANSCRIPT OF TESTIMONY OF DR. GEISLER

REPORTED BY: JAMES TAYLOR
TRANSCRIBED BY: PEGGE MERKEL

NORMAN GEISLER, DEFENDANTS' WITNESS SWORN
DIRECT EXAMINATION

BY MR. CAMPBELL:

Q Would you please state your name and address?

A My name is Norman Leo Geisler, 9551 Mill Trail Drive, Dallas, Texas.

Q And what is your occupation, Dr. Geisler?

A I'm a professor at Dallas Theological Seminary.

Q I'd like to show you what's been marked as defendants' exhibit no. 9 [8] for identification and ask you if this is a copy of your curriculum vitae?

A Yes, it is.

MR. CAMPBELL: Your Honor, at this time the State would move the introduction into evidence of defendants' exhibit 9 [8].

MR. SIANO: No objection.

MR. CAMPBELL: Your Honor, that's defendants' exhibit no. 8.

(Defendants' exhibit 8 received into evidence.)

BY MR. CAMPBELL:

Q Dr. Geisler, are there any additions to your curriculum vitae that you'd like to make?

A Yes, there are a couple. First of all, I belong to the American Scientific Affiliation. Also, I noted that the list of some of the articles that I've written is not complete.

   There are a couple articles from "Scholarly Journals" that aren't included. I can mention them now if you want, or I can—

Q Mention those for the record if you know right offhand.

A Okay. One is "The Missing Premise in the Ontological Argument" which was published in "Religious Studies"; the other is "The Missing Premise in the Cosmological Argument," which was published in the "New Scholastism" [Scholasticism].

Q Dr. Geisler, where did you receive your Ph.D.?

A I received my Ph.D. in philosophy from Loyolla [Loyola] University in Chicago.

Q And what was the subject of your dissertation?

A My dissertation dealt with the—What is Religion? What is the nature of religion and religious experience as it bears on the borderline areas of science and philosophy and the interrelationships between them.

Q And how long have you been employed by the Dallas Theological Seminary?

A This is my third year.

Q Where were you previously employed?

A Previously I was a chairman of the Philosophy of Religion Department at Trinity Evangelical Divinity School in Deerfield, Illinois and then just previous to that chairman of the Philosophy Department at Trinity College in Deerfield, Illinois.

Q What classes do you teach at the Dallas Theological Seminary?

A I teach classes in philosophy, philosophy of religion, methodology, philosophical methodology and theology.

Q And what are your areas of expertise?

A My areas of expertise are the very areas that I mentioned in those classes and describing my dissertation areas of religion, philosophy and the relationship between them and science and the border lying [borderline] areas.

Q How many books have you written?

A I'm not sure but I think about 14 or 15 are published.

MR. CAMPBELL: Your Honor, the State would tender Dr. Geisler as an expert in the areas of philosophy, religion and theology and how the two interrelate with science.

MR. SIANO: No objection, Your Honor.

BY MR. CAMPBELL:

Q Dr. Geisler, how would you define religion?

A Religion is a very difficult term to define, and it's really part of our problem. First of all, what I did was an examination of the nature of religious experience, and I discovered that probably the one common denominator in all religious experience is some kind of a commitment to something that goes beyond the immediate emperical [empirical] experience of an individual. This is what we call transcendence, more than the immediate emperical [empirical] experience, and I discovered in doing that, that the reason that one religion thought other religions weren't religion is they were transcending in different directions. So, the tendency was that if someone transcended, let's say upward and thought that God was up there, and then someone else denied that God was up there and thought that God was a ground being [ground of being], that one had a tendency to think the other one was not religious, but he was transcending in another direction.

So, what I did was work out an examination of what I called the typology or classifications of different ways you could transcend or go beyond your immediate experience. I studied Eliadi [Eliade] and the "Myths of Origin," and their [there] religion is thought to be a transcendence backwards, that you move beyond your immediate experience by going back to origins.

I also studied people like Plotinus who said you transcend upward, you move from the emperical [empirical] experience to higher spiritual experience until you get to the top.

In the modern world there was a movement against the God out there or up there by Bishop Robinson and others in the Death of God movement, and they denied that God is up there, and they transcended downward to a ground of being. Someone satirized it by saving [saying] we should probably take the steeples off of the churches and make cisterns now because they were transcending in depth.

Then I discovered that there were people who transcended forward, that is, they thought of God or the equivalent of God as moving in a forward direction. Hagle [Hegel], for example, and the process theologians, along with Herbert Spencer and the evolutionary philosophies that think of the ultimate or the transcended as moving forward.

Then I also discovered that some people attempt to transcend inward to a center. Chardin, Tellarde Chardin [Teilhard de Chardin], the famous Roman Catholic theologian who said we transcend, in his book "The Divine Millieu" [Milieu] inward.

Then there were those who transcended just kind of outward to the periphery of the universe. Then I found those who transcended in kind of a circle like Netue (phonetic) [Nietzsche] who was thought to be an atheist said that he willed the eternal recurrence of the same state of affairs.

So my conclusion was that religion doesn't necessarily involve God. Religion doesn't necessarily involve someone up there or someone at the beginning. It could be a depth, it could be a commitment to a center, could be a commitment to an outer or it could be a commitment to something moving forward, a progressive evolutionary thing, in which case there are really evolutionary religions.

Q You talked about this transcending. What does—what does transcendence or transcendent value, what does that mean?

A Well, transcendence means more than. Let me try and give some illustrations from Ian Ramsey in his book "Religious Language." He says that transcendence is you could take the same object, say, the same emperical [empirical] object and when suddenly it has disclosure power, when it suddenly tells you more than emperical [empirical]. One of the illustrations he gives is of a judge passing out sentences and then finally he recognizes in one of the people that he's passing out a sentence to, a former lover of his. And he says that has disclosure power, because the normal emperical [empirical] understanding of that takes on a new dimension, it takes on a transcendent dimension.

Other illustrations he gives is the experience that many scientists have had when they make a discovery. The insight, the flash of creative insight that they get or the discovery that people have when they look at lines on a page and they realize that suddenly that's not just 16 lines, that's a cube and it takes on depth. So, transcendence means that ability to see more than or to go beyond the immediate emperical [empirical] data and get something that is a comprehensive model by which someone can order their life.

Q For the court reporter, Dr. Geisler, you may want to slow down just a little bit. Does a religion demand a belief in a deity?

A No, it doesn't. There are many religions that have no belief in God at all. Certain forms of Buddhism do not have a belief in God but they do have a transcendent. Nervannah [Nirvana] becomes their transcendent. There are religions of atheism. Altheiser [Altizer] in the Death of God movement said that God is dead. He transcended forward, moving forward. There are humanistic religions that have no God whatsoever. In fact, they deny the existence of God or at least a need for an existence of God, but they nevertheless have a commitment to something that they consider to be of transcendent value and ultimate importance to them.

I think the best way to define religion is the way that Dr. Paul Tillick [Tillich] of Harvard defined it, one of the foremost American theologians. He said, really religion is an ultimate commitment, and you don't need to have a God or a deity to make an ultimate commitment. You could make an ultimate commitment to a country. He calls this patriology [Patriolatry]. My country, right or wrong, is an ultimate commitment to a country, and he says that would be a religious commitment. Or you could have an ultimate commitment to an ideal. John Dewey, the father of American education so called, is someone who had a had a [sic] definition of religion in his book, "[A] Common Faith" in which he said religion or the religious is the way he described it, is a commitment to an ideal, an enduring ideal, that's worth pursuing even over obstacles. So, it's not necessary to have God at all in a religion.

Q What is a humanistic religion?

A Well, a humanistic religion is a religion that centers its commitment in man. That is, it's committed to something it thinks is of transcendent value, more than an individual man, it's a commitment to man and man's progress.

For example, in evolutionary humanist religions such as Huxley, the commitment is to the process of evolution which produced man and man's future. So that it's a commitment to something that centers in human values rather than something that centers in traditional divine or theistic values.

Q I'd like to show you what's been marked for identification purposes as defendants' exhibit no. 9 for identification and ask if you can identify that?

A Yes. This is the Humanist Manifesto I and II that I provided.

Q Where did you get that?

A I bought that in a book store in Dallas.

Q Would it assit [assist] you in your testimony today to use this?

A Yes. May I use my copy here? I think I have some notes on it that will be—I mean, some marks that will be easier to find passages.

Q Looking at the exhibit, Dr. Geisler, are there any references which you relied upon in concluding that humanism is religion?

A Yes. First of all, this is the Humanist Manifestos I and II, which were published in 1933 and 1973 respectively, and this particular edition comes from Crometheist [Prometheus] Books, which publishes a lot of humanistic material.

In the preface it says in the very first line on page 3, "Humanism is a philosophical religious and moral point of view as old as human civilization itself."

Then without reading more of this part I counted some 28 times in the first manifesto the use of the word religion, most of which was a positive use describing a humanist point of view.

Then if you note on page 4 in the last paragraph there about four lines down, it says, "They are intended not as new dogmas," referring to this manifesto, "for an age of confusion, but as the expression of a quest for values and goals that we can work for and that can help us to take new direction. Humanists are committed to building a world that is significant, not only for the individual's quest for meaning but for the whole of human kind." I think that's a good description of what I discovered a religion to be. They describe it as a religion. It is a commitment to something that is of transcendent value for them.

Then I noted on the first page, page 7 really, Humanist Manifesto I on the bottom, it speaks several times on that page, line 2, religion, line 5 religion, down through the page about six times, and the last line refers to abiding values. So they are committed to these abiding values.

Then on the next page, page 8, the first full paragraph, at the end of that paragraph the third line up from the end of that paragraph reads, "To establish such a religion is a major necessity of the present. It is a responsibility which rests upon this generation. We, therefore, affirm the following." And then they give their humanistic beliefs.

So, the Humanist Manifesto claims to be an expression of a religion called Humanism that has certain component parts that they describe.

MR. CAMPBELL: Your Honor, then I would move the introduction into evidence of defendants' exhibit no. 9.

THE COURT: Let it be received.

(Defendants' exhibit 9 received into evidence.)

BY MR. CAMPBELL:

Q Dr. Geisler, I'd like to show you what's been marked as defendants' exhibit no. 10 for indentification [identification] and ask if you can identify this.

A Yes. This is an article in "The Humanist," which is a humanist journal that I took from the journal in the library at Southern Methodist University in Dallas.

Q Would it assist you in your testimony today to refer to this?

A Yes, it would.

Q Looking at defendants' exhibit no. 10 for identification, are there any references which you have relied upon in concluding that humanism is religion?

A Yes. I might note first that this is January and February 1962 and on the front page the first article is entitled "The New Religion of Humanism," and that is by Julian Huxley. The J. is cut off by memeograph [mimeograph] machine, something overlapped it there. And then inside, the page 3, the title of the article is "The Coming New Religion of Humanism," by Sir Julian Huxley.

Then on the bottom of page 4, the last paragraph, the beginning of the last paragraph, it says, "The new framework of ideas on which any new dominant religion will be based is at once evolutionary and humanistic. For evolutionary humanism Gods are creations of man, not vice versa." So, I've done a study—

MR. SIANO: Your Honor, if I might, I would like an offer of proof at this time based upon the memorandum the plaintiffs have submitted earlier in this case. We think the line of inquiry at this point is inappropriate and we would object.

THE COURT: That will be overruled.

THE WITNESS: Then on page 5, on the bottom right hand column, a paragraph entitled "Evolution Humanism.["] ["]The beliefs of this religion of evolutionary humanism are not based on revelation in the supernatural sense but on the revelations that science and learning have given us about man and the universe. A humanist believes with full assurance that man is not alien to nature but a part of nature albeit a unique one. He is made of the same matter and works by the same energy as the rest of the universe."

That's one of the central tenants [tenets] of the humanistic belief is that either there is no God or God is not involved in any direct way in the world and that the world is to be understood in a total naturalistic way without any reference to any supernatural intervention. Humanists are naturalists as opposed to supernaturalists.

MR. CAMPBELL: Your Honor, I move the introduction of defendants' exhibit no. 10 for identification into evidence.

THE COURT: It will be received.

(Defendants' exhibit 10 received into evidence.)

BY MR. CAMPBELL:

Q Dr. Geisler, what are evolutionary religions?

A In 1859 when Darwin published the "Origin of the Species," there were immediately a number of people who took the biological ideal or model or theory of evolution and made it into a religion in the sense in which I have just defined it. For example, Herbert Spencer took Darwin's concept, and he developed it into a complete cosmic philosophy which was the equivalent of the ultimate and to which of course he and those who followed him made an ultimate commitment. So, it became a religion. The evolutionary process itself became a religion. That was the transcendent.

At the same time many philosophers of religion and scientists, Heckle [Haeckel] in Germany, took the evolutionary hypothesis and used it to attack God, to say it was anti-theistic to attack miracles and to attack the supernatural or any belief therein. Even Darwin himself who started out as a believer in God as he referred to in the last line of the "Origin of the Species," but he was a believer I might add in a deistic God, a God who created the world and from there on the world ran by natural processes, God didn't intervene again after he had created the first simple form or few forms of life. But Darwin became increasingly sceptical [skeptical] over his life; that is, after he started to apply his theory of evolution consistently, he came to the conclusion that you couldn't even have grounds for believing in God, and in his letters, which incidentally, are published, and also there's an excellent book by James Moore I think referred to by George Marsdin [Marsden] in his witness as well. This book by James Moore documents that—it's called the "Post Darwinian Controversy," by the way, and it's published by Cambridge. It's probably the most definitive and scholarly work on this topic in print today published just a few years ago. In this book he narrates the fact that Darwin became increasingly sceptical [skeptical] and in his later years said, and this is paraphrasing Darwin, "Natural selection is my deity."

So even Darwin himself thought of the process of natural selection as a deity and he was not at all sure that there could be another one.

So, Spencer, Heckel [Haeckel], Wallace, who was a colleague and actually co-inventor, co-formulator of the theory of natural selection with Darwin, Wallace himself made the process of evolution into a God. So, simultaneously with the origin [Origin] of the species [Species] in 1859 and following, there developed a whole religion which made the evolutionary process of development of life into higher forms into a God to which people made their ultimate commitment.

Q Is belief in a supreme being or a Creator or that a supreme being or Creator exists necessarily religious?

A No. As a matter of fact, you can believe in God without any religious, or at least you can believe that there is a God. I would distinguish between belief in and belief that. You can believe that there is a God and have no religious significance whatsoever. Let me give a few historic examples and then a few contemporary ones. Aristotle, the famous Greek philosopher, argued that if there are things that are moving in the world, there must be a cause of that Motion and ultimately, since you can't have an infinite regress of causes, there must be a first unmoved mover. Now, the first unmoved mover for Aristotle had no religious significance whatsoever. This was just a cosmic explanation. It was the result of starting with what he could observe scientifically and carrying through a scientific principle, the principle of causality, that every event must have a cause. And if you take this principle that every event has a cause and start carrying it through, you end up as the logical conclusion Aristotle said, of this process that begins with science of positing an unmoved mover, an uncaused cause.

But Aristotle didn't worship this cause, it wasn't his religious object, it was just a scientific or metaphysical explanation.

Same thing was true of Plato, the ancient Greek philosopher. He posited a demiergoss [*Demiurgos*], a Creator who looked at the ultimate. The ultimate in Plato's philosophy was called the Good, not God, and this demiergoss [*Demiurgos*] looked at the good and used that as a pattern to form the world. So that you have a former looking at the ultimate form and forming the unformed world.

Now, the demiergoss [*Demiurgos*] has no necessary religious connotations at all in Plato. It serves a cosmic function to explain the origin of the universe. And I might add that in Christian belief, which includes the belief in the historic sense, historic Christians, who—take, for example, Roman Catholic, Protestants in the historic sense until the turn of the century in America or just before that, traditionally believed that there was a God and that he had created angels and that some of these angels rebeled [rebelled] and became demons. The leader of this rebellion was called Satan, and they believed that he was a real person who has great powers who can deceive people in the world. The occult is usually connected, as it is in the Scriptures, to this belief that occult practices like moving physical objects through the air such as maybe you might see in "The Empire Strikes Back" Luke Skywalker learning to do this. This would be an occult power, and the belief in Satan in this Christian context in no way automatically means that the God that that [*sic*] Satan recognizes is an object of his worship.

For example, there's a verse in the Bible that says Satan believes in God, believes that there is a God but he trembles. In other words, God is not the ultimate object of his worship. So, though he knows there is a God in this Christian tradition and though he believes that God exists, he doesn't believe in God, he's not making God an object of his commitment.

So, it's entirely possible to have a belief that there is a God, that there is a Creator, with no religious significance whatsoever. In fact, Paul Tillick [Tillich] I think put it very well when he said unless you make a commitment to it, unless you make it the ultimate commitment, make it the object of your devotion or your ultimate pursuit or your overall explanation of everything, it has no religious significance whatsoever. And he gives this kind of description. He said philosophy and religion are two different ways of approaching the same object. If you approach the object from the standpoint of reason, that's philosophical. If you approach it from the standpoint of faith, that's religious. If you approach it just to explain it, that's philosophy. If you approach it to believe in it, that's religion.

And Dr. Gilkey, who testified here earlier, who was a student of Paul Tillick [Tillich], gave an excellent illustration of this in his book, "Maker of Heaven and Earth." He said on page 35, I believe it was, in "Maker of Heaven and Earth," that it's like mountain climbers going up two sides of the same mountain. They are headed for the same peak but they are approaching it differently. One is approaching it philosophically, just from the standpoint of reason and what can be tested and proven. The other is approaching it religiously, but it's one and the same peak. We don't have two peaks. There's only one peak because you can only have one highest. And I think this is an excellent illustration of what Paul Tillick [Tillich] meant and what I've discovered in my writings to be the distinction between belief that and belief in.

Now, let me elaborate that distinction, because it brings out this point. Belief that there is a Creator has no religious significance whatsoever anymore [any more] than the devil's belief that there is a God makes God the object of his worship.

Belief that there is a Creator has no religious significance at all anymore [any more] than Aristotle's belief that there was a Creator was the object of his religion.

THE COURT: Are you saying that if I believe in a Creator that has no religious significance at all?

THE WITNESS: No, I didn't, your Honor. I said if you believe that there is a Creator has no religious significance.

THE COURT: Oh, excuse me. I misunderstood.

THE WITNESS: Yes. And that's the distinction I want to now make. The belief that there is a Creator has no religious significance at all. It's only if you commit yourself to it. The devil believes that there is a Creator. In fact, he knows because he was created by him in the Christian tradition. But God has no religious significance to the devil because he's totally opposed to God. And Aristotle and Plato were the other illustrations. They believed that there was a God but they didn't believe in this God as the object of their religion.

Now, let me distinguish this, if I may, in terms of a commitment today. Suppose I believe that there is a lovely young lady who would make a nice wife for me. I know that she is available; I know that she can cook. I know that she would make a nice companion. That will not automatically make me married to her.

I must make a commitment to her; I must believe in and make a commitment. So that one and the same object can be approached in two different ways.

I might approach it this way. Let's suppose I am a studier of statistical tables of death and I'm doing actuary work for a life insurance company and I'm looking at these tables of death. And one of the—they are all numbers and I'm adding them up and seeing how many people die on this occasion and what the patterns are. Then suddenly across my desk comes a new number which happens to be the number of my mother's death. That takes on new significance. It's not just a number. It's—I had a personal relationship there. I had—I was involved. Paul Tillick [Tillich] says this, the difference between a religious attitude toward the same object and a non-religious attitude is are you involved, are you committed to it, are you worshiping it, is it the object of your devotion? If not, it's just like another statistic.

Now, let's suppose that same person whose mother's name came across the desk, two days later, it's just one of the numbers in the pile and it's part of the statistics. Now his mother is approached in a detached way, just a number not committed to it. So one and the same mother can be approached in two different ways, one from a statistical objective analysis, another from an involved committed analysis, and what they are saying is that just the belief that there is a God is not in and of itself religious unless you say I'm going to worship that or I want to commit myself to it as the ultimate.

Just as the belief in biological evolution is not in and of itself a God, but if one makes biological evolution the explanatory model of all and commits himself to it, then it has become a God to him.

So what I would say is something like this. If the belief that there is an ultimate is automatically in and of itself a religious commitment, then the belief that there is evolution would automatically in and of itself be a religious commitment. Of course, that would be unfair to say that somebody who believes in evolution has automatically made evolution his God. Huxley did; Spencer did; Wallace did. But all evolutionists do not and it can be taught strictly in a scientific way.

I want to make this point one other way because it's an important point. Suppose in a history class in school we study Jesus of Nazareth. Now, as a Christian sitting in that class who believes that Jesus is God, that is, he believes that Jesus is God in carnate [incarnate], in human form, which is the traditional Christian belief, Roman Catholic and Protestant until modern times. Now, when they look at one and the same object, Jesus, could it possibly become a religious object to them?

Well, it's conceivable that it might trigger in their thought something they learned in church and that's my God, and any historical evidence that would be presented for the existence of Jesus might possibly lead them to be further confirmed in their faith, but still the study of Jesus as a historical person has merit in an [and] of itself provided that the teacher doesn't say Jesus should be worshipped commit yourself to Jesus. Provided it's studied in an objective detached way rather than calling for commitment. Jesus is a religious object to a Christian. Stones are religious objects to some people. They are worshipped. But we wouldn't rule out a stone from a geology class just because some people have worshipped stones. And we don't rule out God from a science class just because some people have worshipped God.

Q What do you mean by worship?

A Make the object of your ultimate commitment.

THE COURT: Mr. Campbell, why don't we take a recess until one o'clock.

MR. CAMPBELL: All right, sir.

(Recess.)

BY MR. CAMPBELL:

Q Dr. Geisler, before the break we had been discussing or you had been distinguishing for the Court between a belief in a Creator and a belief that a Creator exists. Do you have an opinion as to whether one can refer to a Creator without teaching religion?

A   Yes, I do. And may I apologize for speaking so rapidly. I'll try and slow down a little bit. The belief that there is a Creator is not essentially religious. If someone turns that object into an object of their devotion or worship, then it becomes religious, the way someone turns a rock or country or an ideal into the object of their ultimate commitment, it, too, becomes a religion when they make that kind of commitment to it. I might also say that surely incidental references to a Creator are not essentially religious, or if they are, then surely the pledge under God, the pledge [of] allegiance under God or in God we trust on coins or the Declaration of Independence, which refers to the inalienable rights of the Creator, those references to the Creator would automatically thereby be religious if simply referring to a God.

But if someone says this God is someone that you should believe in and this God is someone worthy to be worshipped, then that becomes essentially religious.

Q   You studied the history of philosophy and religion.

A   That's correct.

Q   And I believe you also said you studied the history of science and the religion debate.

A   As it relates to the tension between them, yes.

Q   Based on your studies what gave rise to modern science as we know it today?

A   Well, many contemporary students of this issue who are not Christian in the traditional sense at all, they are just studying it historically, have acknowledged that the Christian view of a Creator and a Creation was the motivating force for much of the rise of modern science.

For example, many of the earliest scientists were themselves believers in a Creator, and they looked at the Creation and they said if He created it and it operates regularly according to known patterns, then it's subject to scientific scrutiny. So, it's really this that led people like Sir Isaac Newton and Calvin [Kelvin] and many of the—Francis Bacon, for instance, in "Novum Organum," his classic work that gave rise to much of the modern inductive experimental method explicitly states that it was the mandate in Genesis 1, and he was referring to the mandate to subdue the world, that gave rise to the scientific or at least gave some sort of inspiration for the scientific method.

Alfred North Whitehead, who wrote a book with Bertran[d] Russell "Principia Mathematica," which was a massive work, also wrote another book entitled "Science in the Modern World," and Alfred North Whitehead said that Christianity is the mother of science; that is, it was only within this Christian world view that it was possible for science to arise. So, I think it's widely acknowledged that it was Christianity or the Christian view of a Creator [and] Creation that was the impotus [impetus] for the rise of much modern science.

There are other factors as well, but that was one of the dominant factors.

Q Are there other early Christians who were in science?

A Yes. Many of the early scientists were themselves committed Christians; that is, they believed in God in terms of their personal religious convictions. But they studied the world objectively in a detached way. They were coming, as it were, up the other side of that mountain when they were working as scientists and they felt no contradiction at all between their personal religious beliefs in God and approaching Creation objectively and scientifically to see what in it was capable of scientific scrutiny.

Q Do you know whether the scientific views of these men were rejected by the scientific community of their day because the source of some of their views was religious?

A I think it's safe to say that scarcely any reputable scientist ever
rejected a scientific view simply because of the religious source of
those beliefs. In other words, simply because Newton believed in
God, I don't recall reading about anybody who ever rejected the
theory of gravitation because Newton believed in God. Or Pascal
or Pasteur or Calvin [Kelvin] or any of the other men.

You see, in science, as one of the earlier witnesses testified to,
I think it was Prof. Ruse, you distinguish between the source of
your model and the justification of that model, and the source,
that is, where you got the model, has nothing whatsoever to do
with the scientific justifiability of the model.

There are a number of interesting illustrations in the history of
philosophy that I might bring to your attention that have very
weird sources. They were philosophical or scientific people who
were not composing religious models, but their models came from
very odd sources.

For instance, it's well known that Socrates, in his philosophy,
that the impetus for his philosophy came from the oracle of Delphi. In other words, a prophet has told him that he was the wisest
of men. But now I don't really recall ever reading a historian of
philosophy who rejected Socrates' philosophy simply because a
prophet has told him.

The same thing is true, they scrutinized it on philosophical grounds,
they reasoned about it. The same thing is true of many of the people.
For example, I mentioned Francis Bacon. He admits in the "New
Organ" that this inspiration came from Genesis, the mandate that
God had given. But nobody rejected Bacon, they hailed him as the
father of modern science in many respects because of it.

DeCart [Descartes], a famous rationalist philosopher who said
that you have to prove everything by reason, either axioms or what
is reducable [reducible] to axioms, received the impetus for his
philosophy in three dreams. He had three successive dreams in
which there was lightening [lightning] and a watermelon and
somebody giving a little voice to him.

Now, I've never ever heard of a philosopher rejecting DeCart's [Descartes'] philosophy simply because he had three dreams to get him going.

There's a man named Kecule (phonetic) [Kekule] who is the inventor of the benzyne [benzene] molecule, and this is one of the most fascinating stories in the history of science. Kecule [Kekule] got his idea for the benzyne [benzene] molecule in a dream or a vision in which he saw a snake biting its own tail, and that model of the snake biting its own tail suggested to him the model of the benzyne [benzene] molecule which was accepted by the scientific community, and to my knowledge no one has ever rejected his model of the benzyne [benzene] molecule simply because he got it in a dream or a vision seeing a snake.

There's another man named Tessla (phonetic) [Tesla] who invented the internal motor, the alternating current motor, and he received his inspiration or his model when he was reading the German poet Gerta [Goethe] on Sunday morning, I believe it was, and suddenly the inspiration came to him, and he saw a vision in which he saw the internal workings of this motor and he built it and it worked. And no one, so far as I know, has ever rejected his motor simply because he got it in a vision while he was reading Gerta [Goethe]. Spencer, the famous philosopher—

THE COURT: You don't need to site [cite] anymore [any more] examples. I got the picture.[2]

BY MR. CAMPBELL:

Q Dr. Geisler, how would you define science?

A Well, there's a narrow definition of science and a broad definition, and a lot of the ambiguity that occurs on the topic is because we fail to distinguish those two types.

The narrow definition of science, science has observability or to observe some phenomena in the world. It has repeatability.

2. Apparently the judge did not want any more of these illustrations in the record. He said, "I got the picture," but his ruling shows that he didn't get it, since he ruled that creation is religious because it came from a religious source (the Bible).

It's something that you have to be able to repeat somehow. It has testability, something that has to be tested, a model or theory that is falsifiable, and these are characteristics of something that is the narrow definition of science; that is, something that we can do now. It deals with the present. You can observe it, you make theories about it, you can test it, you can extrapolate on the basis of it.

In the broad definition of science, if you're dealing with things in the past, then obviously repeatability is not one of the essential characteristics, because we can't repeat origins. We can't say to the fossils, for example, would you repeat that death, run that through again for me. We can't say to the origin of the universe, could I see this explosion again, for example, the big bang theory. We can't repeat.

So, in a sense, when you're dealing with origins repeatability and natural law, that is, a natural process that is often used in the scientific process in the present, doesn't apply. Because in dealing with origins, you have to make inferences built on analogy. Some of the earlier witnesses I think said the same thing. That you observe things in the present, you make a model that is testable, make some predictions that are testable, falsifiable, but you have to make an inference of what is likely to have been the case at the beginning where you couldn't observe. See, observability and repeatability aren't possible for origins.

I think it's something like this. Origins, scientific study of origins is something like forensic medicine. You look at certain scientific data and you try and reconstruct the original situation. But, of course, you can't do it with absolute definitiveness, because you can only make probable models that can be tested. And I think when we're talking about origins, we can't talk about the fact of evolution or the fact of creation, because it's really only an extrapolation or an inference built on observation to try and reconstruct that [what] we can't repeat and observe.

Q What is a scientific model?

A Well, scientific model is a structure or framework by which we understand the scientific data. It's something like looking at the stars at night and you've seen these astrological charts that have all the interesting lines between them and you see the big bear and all of these lines. Well, actually the lines aren't there. All that we have is stars. Now, stars are like facts in this illustration. Science draws the lines between those stars. The lines don't exist, and in fact, not only can I not see the big bear, I have a hard time seeing the big dipper sometimes when I look at the sky, because those are constructions of the mind put on reality.

Now, a scientific model is a construction. We've all seen these charts in books, either Creation books or evolution and there will be lines drawn between the various species on the chart. Now, the lines don't exist that way in nature. There aren't any lines there. Those lines exist only in theories or constructs or models that scientists put on them, because that's how they suppose they are related.

Q In what way can science deal with ultimate origins?

A Well, one of the ways that science can deal with ultimate origins is by analogy. It has to take things that we know to be true in the present and suppose that they were also true in the past or argue from analogy.

For example, if you know something to be true in the present that this kind of product is produced by intelligent activity. Say, for example, a dictionary is normally produced by intelligent activity, not [an] explosion in a printing shop.

Now, you take that kind of analogy and you apply it toward the beginning. But you can't be absolutely sure. It may or may not apply. Analogy, inference built on present observation and experience.

Q How many views are there on the ultimate origins of the universe?

A Well, it all depends on whether you're talking about religious views or philosophical views. Religiously there are many views. No God created it, that a finite God created it, that an infinite

God created it. This infinite God was a pantheistic God identical to the universe, that he wasn't identical to the universe, that many Gods—see, there are many religious views, but philosophically there are only two. Either the origin of the universe, the origin of life and the origin of new kinds of life, new forms of life.

These three things either happened by intelligent intervention or not by intelligent intervention. There are only two chances.

And it's not only philosophers who think two alternatives. It's not only philosophers who think that way, but if you read the scientific literature, many scientists say the same thing. For example, Robert Gestro [Jastrow] says the same thing in his book about either life started by Creation or spontaneous generation. Either the universe was eternal or it came to be.

So, philosophically there are only two, but if you want to ask about the nature, the religious nature of the cause or no cause, then you get into all kinds of religious differences.

Q How do philosophers apart from religion talk about ultimate origins?

A Well, philosophers apart from religion talk about ultimate origins in terms of the term God. As one philosopher put it, western philosophy has borne the burden of this term God. It's with us, we can't avoid it. So, they talk about proofs for the existence of God or disproofs for the existence of God as no religious connotation to them at all. The journals, both pro and con on this topic of ultimate origin from a philosophical point of view, you'll find a reference to God all the time.

Q What is your own view as to the ultimate origin of the universe?

A Well, my own view from a philosophical standpoint is very similar to that of Thomas Aquinas, the famous 13th century Christian philosopher who said that if every event has a cause, then there must be an ultimate first cause of the universe, because you can't have an infinite regress of causes; therefore, it's necessary to postulate an ultimate first cause.

Q As a theologian what would the model of Creation or the scient[ific]—model of Creation imply to you?

A I'm not sure I understand the question. Could you rephrase that?

Q Well, how does the science model of Creation imply the existence of God to you?

A Well, the science model of Creation implies the existence of God to me the way that a moral law implies the existence of a moral law given [giver]. If you tell me you ought to do this, that's a prescriptive statement, not a descriptive statement. A descriptive statement is this is the way it is being done. But a prescriptive statement is this is the way it ought to be done.

When you make a prescriptive command to me, you ought to do this, that implies a prescriber. See, that's a logical inference I make that all prescriptions come from prescribers.

Now, in the same way, if you say to me this is Creation, that logically implies to me a Creator. I might add not everybody comes to the same conclusion. There are people who believe that there are moral laws with no moral law givers, and there's a Creation with no Creator. But that's a logical inference that I make philosophically from the Creation to the Creator.

Q Why would you necessarily believe that the Creator was or was not God?

A Well, the term God can be taken in two senses. As I said, it's a common term. Philosophers use it even when they are talking from a philosophical perspective, but theologians use it when they're talking from a theological perspective. It's convenient that they do, because as Dr. Gilkey put it, there's only one peak on this mountain and you can come at it from two different directions. But the term used of the peak is often used interchangeably. So I would say in the sense that scientific creation implies a Creator and the term God is commonly used of the Creator, then scientific creationism would imply a God in that sense but only belief that there is a God, not belief in God. Unless, of course, somebody teaches you should believe in Him as well as believing that he is there.

Q I'd like to show you a copy of Act 590. I believe it's plaintiff's exhibit no. 29.

A Could I use my copy of this?

Q Yes. What does Act 590 say about references to religion and the use of religious materials?

A It explicitly prohibits the use of religious materials or references to religion.

Q Under the provisions of the Act, in what way could a Creator be referred to?

A Well, I think a Creator could be referred to as a logical inference of Creation or a Creator could be referred to as an end of a process of reasoning that posits something that is necessary to account for it. For example, if the only way you could account for a certain scientific data is to postulate an intelligent intervention, then I think it would certainly permit that.

Q How long have you taught theological and Biblical subjects?
A Twenty-two years.

Q During that time have you had an opportunity to study the original languages of the Bible?
A Yes, I have.

Q Have you studied the various interpretations of Genesis?
A Yes, I have.

Q Can you describe some of those interpretations?
A Well, I'm glad you said some. There really is a spectrum of interpretations from very literal to very allegorical, and there are all kinds of shades in between, but generally speaking there are those who take Genesis at face value. They take it as a historical literal account, and then there are those who take it as a myth or

an allegory spiritual meaning to it, reference not to any literal historical based on facts, and then there are some who kind of combine those in between.

Q How is Biblical literalism distinguished from inerrancy?

A Well, the belief in inerrancy, inerrancy means without terror [error], and those who accept the inerrancy of the Bible say that nothing that the Bible teaches is mistaken, that whenever the Bible teaches something it teaches it truly. Whatever the Bible affirms, God affirms. So that's the nature of the Bible. Whatever the Bible teaches is true. That would be inerrancy.

The other question, literalism, is how do you interpret that truth? You see, it's one thing to say the Bible is completely true and another thing to say how you should interpret that truth. So often these two questions are confused, and I think they should be clearly distinguished because many people believe in inerrancy who do not take Genesis literally. And there are people who take Genesis literally who don't necessarily believe in inerrancy.

Q How does a literalist's interpretation of Genesis relate to the origins issue?

A Well, if you were interpreting, now as a theologian with a literal method[,] the book of Genesis[,] it would come out I think something like the fundamentalists have traditionally interpreted it from around 1920 to 1930 and following. Number one, that there was a God who created the universe in the beginning, that this God created the universe out of nothing and that he directly created every new species or kind of thing that came into existence and that he took a handful of dust and he breathed in it and made Adam and then he took a rib out of Adam and he made Eve out of this rib, that he brought the animals before Adam and he gave names to all of these animals. All of this is taken literally, and that he did this whole thing in 144 hours, six 24 hour days.

Q What do other interpretations of Genesis say about origins?

A Well, there are those who say that this is basically a religious story that is intended to evoke our response to a Creator but not describe Creation, that the language there is basically evocatove [evocative] and not descriptive, that it's a kind of a religious story, a model, a myth by which we can become related to a who God, but not a scientific description of a how process.

Q You mentioned fundamentalist a moment ago. What is fundamentalist?

A That's a difficult term. I feel a little bit like a previous witness who said I don't prefer labels but unfortunately they're there, and let me try and describe fundamentalism.

Fundamentalism is a movement that began around the turn of the century, and it began because, as the result of the new religions that were arising in the world, atheism and skepticism, the religion of humanism and evolutionism, that had attacked their beliefs, the beliefs I just described a moment ago. The fundamentalist[s] stated their basic beliefs in terms of five or six fundamentals. They said these things are fundamental and essential to Christianity and these we'll defend. The Virgin birth of Christ; the deity of Christ, that he is God; the substitutionary atonement, that he died for the sins of mankind; the bodily resurrection of Christ from the grave; the second coming of Christ and the inspiration of the Bible.

Now, the reason I mention six and normally they are thought of as five is because there were two sets of five. One was by the Presbyterian church and the other by a Baptist church and they overlap on one. So it turns out to be six really rather than five.

So, these people believed in the fundamentals. That's what I would call early fundamentalists from let's say beginning anywhere around 1858 and '59 with the revivalism movement, moving right on up to 1900. Charles Hodge, A. A. Hodge, B. B. Warfield are people who would represent this view.

What happened, and the reason they were called fundamentalists is there came to be people in the church that had traditionally believed those, that due to the influence of some of these modern philosophies, denied one or more of those fundamentals, and they didn't want these people to be part of their church. So they said if you won't believe these fundamentals, then you can't be part of the church.

And a man by the name of Briggs was defrocked of his position, and the fundamentalist movement began about that time.

However, that's early fundamentalism. Later fundamentalism is a little different than this, and I'd like to characterize the difference. It's not often clarified. Later fundamentalism really began around 1920 as George Marzdan [Marsden] puts in his book. About 1920—what happened between the 1890's and 1920 was very significant. The growth of evolutionary philosophy was very strong.

Spencer's philosophy of evolutionism was very strong in the United States, it was being taught in the schools, and these people perceived it as a threat to their faith, because indeed it was. Their faith said all these things are literally true and this philosophy said they aren't true.

As a result of that after the Second [First] World War, 1918, when people saw the barbarism that had occurred as a result of this war and when Hitler in 1924 wrote Mein Kampf and declared that evolution was to be used as a mean [means] to prove that the Arian [Aryan] race was superior and that natural selection was used by him to justify annihilation of Jews, then people began to react against this and say this whole thing is bad.

That started a swing toward 1918 when Reilly [Riley[3]] gave a famous sermon on this having come back from abroad saying we've got to fight this thing. That started a swing toward what I call more radical fundamentalism or later fundamentalism as described in Marzdan's [Marsden's] book. And this took on a new characteristic. It became militant where the early fundamentalism was not militant. It became separatistic where the early fundamentalism

3. William Bell Riley (1861–1947), pastor of First Baptist Church of Minneapolis.

was not separatistic, it was the liberals who were separating from the orthodox, not the reverse.

Q Let me ask you. Have you prepared an outline of the history of Darwinism and fundamentalism for me?

A Yes, I have. I don't have a copy of that.

Q I show you what has been marked as defendants' exhibit no. 11 for identification and ask if you can identify that.

A Yes, this is the one I prepared.

Q Would this assist you in your testimony today?

A Yes. Yes, it will.

Q Can you tell me what caused the split between these—between the early and late fundamentalists that you just discussed?

A It was not really a split, it was an evolution. What happened to the later fundamentalists is as a result of what they perceived to be the philosophy of evolution, not the biology or science of evolution, they perceived it as a religious threat, and indeed, it was a religion, because as we testified earlier, Spencer and Wallace and these men had made it into one. So what happened is the earlier fundamentalists were not anti-Darwin categorically. Many of these early fundamentalists wrote books saying biological evolution is okay.

In fact, one of the interesting things is that the book, "The Fundamentals," which was put out if you will note here on the chart, "The Fundamentals" was published 1910 to 1915, that book had three authors in it who were part of this early fundamentalist group who said that evolution in the biological sense is fine. We can accommodate that into our Christian beliefs. So they were not militantly anti-evolutionists and some of them weren't in fact anti-biological evolution.

But then after 1918 when it was perceived in a social philosophical and religious sense, then this group became very militant and it started to—well, look on the chart in 1921 William J. Bryant [Bryan] adopts anti-evolution campaign; 1921 fundamental fellowship adopts five fundamentals; 1924 Hitler wrote Mein Kampf which had a strong Darwinian antisemetic [anti-Semitic] flavor. Then 1925 the fundamentalists anti-evolution lobbies began. They decided to fight against all kinds of evolution, social, religious, scientific, and I think what happened is that they threw the baby out with the bath water, meaning by that that they threw scientific evolution out with their overreaction against religious evolution, and then of course, following that there were several states, 1926 and following, that adopted anti-evolution laws, one of which wasn't revoked until sometime in the 1960's.

Then immediately following that the "Humanist Manifesto" 1933 in which evolution was adopted as one of the tenants [tenets] of humanistic religion. There are about four basic tenants [tenets]: no God, evolution, naturalistic process and everything is relative in terms of ethics. That was adopted in humanism.

Julian Huxley in 1962 pronounced evolutionary humanism a religion and then 1973 the "Humanist Manifesto II" followed it up saying it's still a religion.

In 1981, interestingly enough, the secular humanist declaration omits all references to religion entirely. And I think what happened there in that period is that they decided that because humanism was a religion, evolution was part of it, and it's wrong to teach religion in the schools, that they would back off calling it a religion.

Q As I understand your testimony, then, early fundamentalists would have had no disagreement with the teaching of evolution, is that correct?

A Biological evolution as a science, the early fundamentalists were willing to accommodate themselves to it. Because Warfield, Wright[4] and James Orr, who were three men who wrote that book, "The Fundamentals," all believed in some form of theistic evolution. But the later fundamentalists adopted anti-evolution of all kinds

4. B. B. Warfield (1851–1921) and George Frederick Wright (1838–1921).

as part of their militant campaign against—and evolution became a large [bad] word.

And I might add that the thing that characterized these later fundamentalists from the early fundamentalists not only were they militant and anti every kind of evolution, but they were narrow and often bigoted and were people who I think really brought disrepute on the full cause of the earlier fundamentalists who were educated. There [They] were also anti-intellectual where the early fundamentalists were the teachers at Princeton and the major schools in the east. So, they were militant, narrow, often bigoted anti-intellectual and threw all kinds of evolution out. That's quite different from the early fundamentalists.

Q Do you have an opinion as to whether Act 590 reflects late fundamentalist attitudes?

A Yes, I do have an opinion on that.

Q What is your opinion?

A It seems to me that Act 590 reflects far more of the earlier fundamentalists than the later fundamentalist, because Act 590 says to me teach both sides. Well, you would never get a fundamentalist of the 1920, 1930 variety saying let's teach evolution. Where Act 590 says let's teach evolution as a scientific theory right alongside creation. So, I don't see this [meaning] we're totally against all kinds of evolution. This is an Act to me that says both should be taught.

Another thing. I don't see the anti-intellectual attitude you had from these fundamentalists, because this is saying let's teach it as a scientific theory, which would imply we're going to have to have scientists who have degrees that aren't just attacking everybody who went away and got a Ph.D. and saying well, he's just phenomenally dumb or the kind of satires that the fundamentalists would take on. The later fundamentalists would take on people who got education. So I see this—let me put it this way. If this reflects later fundamentalists they repent [repented of] it.

Q What relationship is there between the definition of creation science in section 4(a) of Act 590 and the book of Genesis?

A Well, I think in all honesty that the people who devised this probably got their model from the book of Genesis. I think that the inspiration and the model for this came from the book of Genesis, just as the inspiration and model I described of many of the other people came from oracles or snakes or what have you.

Q What significance is it that the book of Genesis may have been a source of the scientific model of creation science?

A I don't think it's any significance at all, because the source does not matter. It's the justification. Can you provide a scientific theory and model that can be justified? That's all science should be concerned about.

Q Can you think of examples where the Bible may have been the source of some scientific discovery in the past?

A Yes, I can think of a number of these. For example, the Bible talks about many historical events that happened. Now, those are subject to historical verification because when you say, for example, Hesekiah [Hezekiah] built a tunnel, people can go digging around Jerusalem to see if they can find Hesekiah's [Hezekiah's] tunnel, and as a matter of fact, that's exactly what has happened. They have unearthed, by the science of archeology, many of the very things mentioned in the Bible. So the Bible has actually been a source for finding these things mentioned in the Bible.

The simple fact that the Hittites are mentioned in the Bible. Now, a generation or so ago scholars used to laugh and say Hittites, they are not mentioned anywhere in the world outside the Bible. The only book in the world Hittites are mentioned is the Bible. They didn't exist, the Bible created them.

Now, every scholar knows that the whole Hittite library has been found and the Hittites were a people from ancient time, they accept it as part of history. So they got their clue from the Bible and then they tested it scientifically.

As far as I know no one has thrown out the principles of archeology because the inspiration for much of it came from the Bible.

MR. CAMPBELL: Your Honor, I'd like to move the admission of defendants' exhibit no. 12 for identification into evidence.

THE COURT: It will be received.

(Defendants' exhibit 12 received into evidence.)

BY MR. CAMPBELL:

Q Dr. Geisler, do you have an opinion as to whether it is legitimate to derive a scientific model from a religious source?

A Yes, I do.

Q And what is your opinion?

A My opinion is that it's perfectly legitimate, it's done many times.

MR. CAMPBELL: Thank you. I have no further questions.

Brief Comments on My Testimony

As will be shown in chapter 8, much of my testimony was to the heart of the issue, namely, what is religion? And is creation science religious? The answers to these questions determine whether or not it is an unconstitutional violation of the First Amendment to teach creation science in a public school. Since the Arkansas judge largely ignored the force of the arguments and they were not available for Supreme Court review (since the Arkansas authorities refused to transcribe them), I will briefly comment on the issue here. A fuller treatment is found in chapter 8.

First, the judge didn't get (or got and didn't like) my point that the mere fact that an idea came from a religious source does not make it religious, since many scientific ideas, including evolution, came from religious sources. This destroyed one of the ACLU's main arguments—that creation is religious because it comes from a religious source, the Bible.

Second, the judged failed to take seriously my argument that a Creator can be referred to objectively in a scientific or philosophical way without establishing religion, as did Aristotle, Plato, and others. I even referred to one of the evolutionist expert witnesses, Langdon Gilkey, in support of the point. I also referred to Paul Tillich, whom the Supreme Court used to help define religion (in *Torcaso,* 1961), and who made the same point in his writings. But the judge entirely ignored this.

Third, the judge totally ignored my distinction between empirical science (which neither macroevolution nor creation is) that deals with regular observable events and science in a forensic sense (which both macroevolution and creation are) which deals with past, unobserved events relating to the origin of the universe, life, and new life forms. If he had pondered this point, he would not have ruled that evolution is science in an empirical, observable sense and creation is not.

On these three points the whole case hinged. And the Supreme Court never had my testimony with these arguments before them, for the Arkansas authorities refused to transcribe them for five years, until after the Supreme Court made its ruling against teaching creation in schools based in part on the Arkansas case. This is a very strange and suspicious fact. In any event, the Arkansas judge either missed or ignored my arguments and ruled against creation being taught alongside evolution in public schools (see chapter 3). All of these issues will be addressed in more detail later (in chapter 8). First, in chapters 5 through 7, we will examine the disastrous consequences of Judge Overton's decision in subsequent court cases.

5

The *Edwards* Supreme Court Ruling (1987)

The 1987 case of *Edwards v. Aguillard* is the only creation/evolution case to reach the Supreme Court to date since *Epperson* (1968). As such, it is very important and precedent-setting. We will look first at the background of the ruling and then at the decision itself. Finally, we will evaluate its conclusions. The insightful and strong dissenting opinion to this ruling by Supreme Court Justice Antonin Scalia is discussed in the next chapter.

Background of the Ruling

After the Arkansas decision (1982), Jon Buell and Charles Thaxton of the Foundation for Thought and Ethics in the Dallas area pleaded with the attorney general of Arkansas not to appeal the *McLean* decision against creation on the grounds that Act 590 was not the best-constructed law. Louisiana had a better law, and it seemed better to appeal that one. I was of the opinion that it would be harmful to let this bad decision stand as precedent in the record, knowing how the courts use precedents. Further, the Arkansas law, while it could have been constructed better, was not unconstitutional. As we will see, the better-constructed Louisiana law fared no better and was rejected for many of the same basic reasons, citing the Arkansas *McLean* decision as a precedent, just as I had feared.

Louisiana's "Creationism Act," like the Arkansas law, was a "balanced" approach. It allowed that schools could opt not to teach on origins at all. However, it demanded that if they chose to teach one view of origins, then the other view should be presented in a balanced way as well. It defined the theories as "the scientific evidences for [creation or evolution] and inferences from those scientific evidences."[1]

The challenge to the Louisiana law came from Louisiana parents, teachers, and religious leaders in a federal district court, which granted summary judgment, holding that the Act violated the Establishment Clause of the First Amendment. The case then went to the court of appeals, and from there to the Supreme Court.

The *Edwards* Supreme Court Ruling (1987)

The U.S. Supreme Court held that:

1. The Act is facially invalid as violative of the Establishment Clause of the First Amendment, because it lacks a clear secular purpose. Pp. 585-594.

(a) The Act does not further its stated secular purpose of "protecting academic freedom." It does not enhance the freedom of teachers to teach what they choose and fails to further the goal of "teaching all of the evidence." Forbidding the teaching of evolution when creation science is not also taught undermines the provision of a comprehensive scientific education. Moreover, requiring the teaching of creation science with evolution does not give schoolteachers a flexibility that they did not already possess to supplant the present science curriculum with the presentation of theories, besides evolution, about the origin of life.

1. *Edwards v. Aguillard*, 482 U.S. 578 (1987).

Furthermore, the contention that the Act furthers a "basic concept of fairness" by requiring the teaching of all of the evidence on the subject is without merit. Indeed, the Act evinces a discriminatory preference for the teaching of creation science and against the teaching of evolution by requiring that curriculum guides be developed and resource services supplied for teaching creationism but not for teaching evolution, by limiting membership on the resource services panel to "creation scientists," and by forbidding school boards to discriminate against anyone who "chooses to be a creation-scientist" or to teach creation science, while failing to protect those who choose to teach other theories or who refuse to teach creation science. A law intended to maximize the comprehensiveness and effectiveness of science instruction would encourage the teaching of all scientific theories about human origins. Instead, this Act has the distinctly different purpose of discrediting evolution by counterbalancing its teaching at every turn with the teaching of creationism.

(b) The Act impermissibly endorses religion by advancing the religious belief that a supernatural being created humankind. The legislative history demonstrates that the term "creation science," as contemplated by the state legislature, embraces this religious teaching. The Act's primary purpose was to change the public school science curriculum to provide persuasive advantage to a particular religious doctrine that rejects the factual basis of evolution in its entirety. Thus, the Act is designed either to promote the theory of creation science that embodies a particular religious tenet or to prohibit the teaching of a scientific theory disfavored by certain religious sects. In either case, the Act violates the First Amendment. Pp. 589-594.

2. The District Court did not err in granting summary judgment upon a finding that appellants had failed to raise a genuine issue of material fact. Appellants relied on the "uncontroverted" affidavits of scientists, theologians, and an education administrator defining creation science as "origin through abrupt appearance in complex form" and alleging that such a viewpoint constitutes a true scientific theory. The District Court, in its discretion, properly concluded that the postenactment testimony of these experts concerning the possible technical meanings of the Act's terms would not illuminate the contemporaneous purpose of the state legislature when it passed the Act. None of the persons making

the affidavits produced by appellants participated in or contributed to
the enactment of the law.[2]

Wendell R. Bird, Special Assistant Attorney General of Georgia, argued the case for the appellants. With him on the briefs were A. Morgan
Brian, Jr., and Thomas T. Anderson, Special Assistant Attorney General, Kendall L. Vick, and Patricia Nalley Bowers, Assistant Attorney
General of Louisiana.

Jay Topkis argued the case for appellees. With him on the brief was
John DiGiulio, Samuel I. Rosenberg, Allen Blumstein, Gerard E. Harper,
Jack D. Novik, Burt Neuborne, Norman Dorsen, John Sexton, and
Ron Wilson.

The Court voted 7-2 against teaching creation along with evolution—only Scalia and Rehnquist dissented. Brennan wrote the opinion
of the Court, in which Marshall, Blackmun, Powell, and Stevens joined,
and in all but Part II of which O'Connor joined. Powell filed a concurring opinion, in which O'Connor joined. White, filed an opinion
concurring in the judgment.

Justice Brennan delivered the opinion of the Court:[3] (1)

I

The question for decision is whether Louisiana's "Balanced Treatment
for Creation-Science and Evolution-Science in Public School Instruction" Act (Creationism Act) . . . (1982), is facially invalid as violative of
the Establishment Clause of the First Amendment.

The Creationism Act forbids the teaching of the theory of evolution
in public schools unless accompanied by instruction in "creation science."
No school is required to teach evolution or creation science. If either
is taught, however, the other must also be taught. Ibid. The theories of
evolution and creation science are statutorily defined as "the scientific
evidences for [creation or evolution] and inferences from those scientific
evidences."

Appellees, who include parents of children attending Louisiana
public schools, Louisiana teachers, and religious leaders, challenged

2. Ibid.
3. Technical references have been largely eliminated.

the constitutionality of the Act in District Court, seeking an injunction and declaratory relief (2). Appellants, Louisiana officials charged with implementing the Act, defended on the ground that the purpose of the Act is to protect a legitimate secular interest, namely, academic freedom (3). Appellees attacked the Act as facially invalid because it violated the Establishment Clause and made a motion for summary judgment. The District Court granted the motion. *Aguillard* v. *Treen* ... (1983). The court held that there can be no valid secular reason for prohibiting the teaching of evolution, a theory historically opposed by some religious denominations. The court further concluded that "the teaching of 'creation-science' and 'creationism,' as contemplated by the statute, involves teaching 'tailored to the principles' of a particular religious sect or group of sects" ... (citing *Epperson* v. *Arkansas* ... (1968). The District Court therefore held that the Creationism Act violated the Establishment Clause either because it prohibited the teaching of evolution or because it required the teaching of creation science with the purpose of advancing a particular religious doctrine.

The court of Appeals affirmed. The court observed that the statute's avowed purpose of protecting academic freedom was inconsistent with requiring, upon risk of sanction, the teaching of creation science whenever evolution is taught. ... The court found that the Louisiana Legislature's actual intent was "to discredit evolution by counterbalancing its teaching at every turn with the teaching of creationism, a religious belief." ... Because the Creationism Act was thus a law furthering a particular religious belief, the Court of Appeals held that the Act violated the Establishment Clause. A suggestion for rehearing en banc[4] was denied over a dissent. We noted probable jurisdiction ... (1986), and now affirm.

II

The Establishment Clause forbids the enactment of any law "respecting an establishment of religion" (4). The Court has applied a three-pronged test to determine whether legislation comports with the Establishment Clause. First, the legislature must have adopted the law with a secular purpose. Second, the statute's principal or primary effect must be one

4. With a full court; with full judiciary authority.

that neither advances nor inhibits religion. Third, the statute must not result in an excessive entanglement of government with religion. *Lemon* v. *Kurtzman* . . . (1971) (5). State action violates the Establishment Clause if it fails to satisfy any of these prongs.

In this case, the Court must determine whether the Establishment Clause was violated in the special context of the public elementary and secondary school system. States and local school boards are generally afforded considerable discretion in operating public schools. See *Bethel School Dist. No. 403* v. *Fraser* . . . (1986) . . . (BRENNAN, J., concurring in judgment); *Tinker* v. *Des Moines Independent Community School Dist* . . . (1969). "At the same time . . . we have necessarily recognized that the discretion of the States and local school boards in matters of education must be exercised in a manner that comports with the transcendent imperatives of the First Amendment." Board of Education, Island Trees Union Free School Dist . . . (1982).

The Court has been particularly vigilant in monitoring compliance with the Establishment Clause in elementary and secondary schools. Families entrust public schools with the education of their children, but condition their trust on the understanding that the classroom will not purposely be used to advance religious views that may conflict with the private beliefs of the student and his or her family. Students in such institutions are impressionable and their attendance is involuntary. See, e. g., *Grand Rapids School Dist.* v. *Ball* . . . (1985); *Wallace* v. *Jaffree* . . . (1985); *Meek* v. *Pittenger* . . . (1975); *Abington School Dist.* v. *Schempp* . . . (1963) (BRENNAN, J., concurring). The State exerts great authority and coercive power through mandatory attendance requirements, and because of the students' emulation of teachers as role models and the children's susceptibility to peer pressure (6). . . . Furthermore, "the public school is at once the symbol of our democracy and the most pervasive means for promoting our common destiny. In no activity of the State is it more vital to keep out divisive forces than in its schools . . ." *Illinois ex rel. McCollum* v. *Board of Education* . . . (1948) (opinion of Frankfurter, J.).

Consequently, the Court has been required often to invalidate statutes which advance religion in public elementary and secondary schools. See, e. g., *Grand Rapids School Dist.* v. *Ball*, supra (school district's use of religious school teachers in public schools); *Wallace* v. *Jaffree*, supra (Alabama statute authorizing moment of silence for school prayer); *Stone*

v. *Graham* . . . (1980) (posting copy of Ten Commandments on public classroom wall); *Epperson* v. *Arkansas* . . . (1968) (statute forbidding teaching of evolution); *Abington School Dist.* v. *Schempp*, supra (daily reading of Bible); *Engel* v. *Vitale* . . . (1962) (recitation of "denominationally neutral" prayer).

Therefore, in employing the three-pronged *Lemon* test, we must do so mindful of the particular concerns that arise in the context of public elementary and secondary schools. We now turn to the evaluation of the Act under the *Lemon* test.

III

Lemon's first prong focuses on the purpose that animated adoption of the Act. "The purpose prong of the *Lemon* test asks whether government's actual purpose is to endorse or disapprove of religion." *Lynch* v. *Donnelly* . . . (1984) (O'CONNOR, J., concurring). A governmental intention to promote religion is clear when the State enacts a law to serve a religious purpose. This intention may be evidenced by promotion of religion in general, see *Wallace* v. *Jaffree* . . . (Establishment Clause protects individual freedom of conscience "to select any religious faith or none at all"), or by advancement of a particular religious belief, e. g., *Stone* v. *Graham* . . . (invalidating requirement to post Ten Commandments, which are "undeniably a sacred text in the Jewish and Christian faiths") [footnote omitted]; *Epperson* v. *Arkansas* (holding that banning the teaching of evolution in public schools violates the First Amendment since "teaching and learning" must not "be tailored to the principles or prohibitions of any religious sect or dogma"). If the law was enacted for the purpose of endorsing religion, "no consideration of the second or third criteria [of *Lemon*] is necessary." *Wallace* v. *Jaffree.* . . . In this case, appellants have identified no clear secular purpose for the Louisiana Act.

True, the Act's stated purpose is to protect academic freedom. . . . This phrase might, in common parlance, be understood as referring to enhancing the freedom of teachers to teach what they will. The Court of Appeals, however, correctly concluded that the Act was not designed to further that goal (7). We find no merit in the State's argument that the "legislature may not [have] used the terms 'academic freedom' in the correct legal sense. They might have [had] in mind, instead, a basic concept of fairness; teaching all of the evidence." . . . Even if "academic freedom" is read to mean "teaching all of the evidence" with respect to the origin of human beings, the Act does not further this purpose. The goal of providing a more comprehensive science curriculum is not furthered either by outlawing the teaching of evolution or by requiring the teaching of creation science.

III A

While the Court is normally deferential to a State's articulation of a secular purpose, it is required that the statement of such purpose be sincere and not a sham. See *Wallace* v. *Jaffree* . . . (POWELL, J., concurring); . . . (O'CONNOR, J., concurring in judgment); *Stone* v. *Graham* . . . ; *Abington School Dist.* v. *Schempp.* . . . As JUSTICE O'CONNOR stated in *Wallace*: "It is not a trivial matter, however, to require that the legislature manifest a secular purpose and omit all sectarian endorsements from its laws. That requirement is precisely tailored to the Establishment Clause's purpose of assuring that Government not intentionally endorse religion or a religious practice."

It is clear from the legislative history that the purpose of the legislative sponsor, Senator Bill Keith, was to narrow the science curriculum. During the legislative hearings, Senator Keith stated: "My preference would be that neither [creationism nor evolution] be taught." Such a ban on teaching does not promote—indeed, it undermines—the provision of a comprehensive scientific education.

It is equally clear that requiring schools to teach creation science with evolution does not advance academic freedom. The Act does not grant teachers a flexibility that they did not already possess to supplant the present science curriculum with the presentation of theories, besides evolution, about the origin of life. Indeed, the Court of Appeals found that no law prohibited Louisiana public school teachers from teaching any scientific theory. As the president of the Louisiana Science Teachers Association testified, "any scientific concept that's based on established fact can be included in our curriculum already, and no legislation allowing this is necessary." The Act provides Louisiana schoolteachers with no new authority. Thus the stated purpose is not furthered by it.

The Alabama statute held unconstitutional in *Wallace* v. *Jaffree*, supra, is analogous. In *Wallace*, the State characterized its new law as one designed to provide a 1-minute period for meditation. We rejected that stated purpose as insufficient, because a previously adopted Alabama law already provided for such a 1-minute period. Thus, in this case, as in *Wallace*, "appellants have not identified any secular purpose that was not fully served by [existing state law] before the enactment of [the statute in question]."

Furthermore, the goal of basic "fairness" is hardly furthered by the Act's discriminatory preference for the teaching of creation science and against the teaching of evolution (8). While requiring that curriculum guides be developed for creation science, the Act says nothing of comparable guides for evolution.... Similarly, resource services are supplied for creation science but not for evolution. Only "creation scientists" can serve on the panel that supplies the resource services. Ibid. The Act forbids school boards to discriminate against anyone who "chooses to be a creation-scientist" or to teach "creationism," but fails to protect those who choose to teach evolution or any other non-creation science theory, or who refuse to teach creation science.

If the Louisiana Legislature's purpose was solely to maximize the comprehensiveness and effectiveness of science instruction, it would have encouraged the teaching of all scientific theories about the origins of humankind (9). But under the Act's requirements, teachers who were once free to teach any and all facets of this subject are now unable to do so. Moreover, the Act fails even to ensure that creation science will be taught, but instead requires the teaching of this theory only when the theory of evolution is taught. Thus we agree with the Court of Appeals' conclusion that the Act does not serve to protect academic freedom, but has the distinctly different purpose of discrediting "evolution by counterbalancing its teaching at every turn with the teaching of creationism...."

III B

Stone v. *Graham* invalidated the State's requirement that the Ten Commandments be posted in public classrooms. "The Ten Commandments are undeniably a sacred text in the Jewish and Christian faiths, and no legislative recitation of a supposed secular purpose can blind us to that fact."... As a result, the contention that the law was designed to provide instruction on a "fundamental legal code" was "not sufficient to avoid conflict with the First Amendment." Ibid. Similarly *Abington School Dist.* v. *Schempp* held unconstitutional a statute "requiring the selection and reading at the opening of the school day of verses from the Holy Bible and the recitation of the Lord's Prayer by the students in unison," despite the proffer of such secular purposes as the "promotion of moral values, the contradiction to the materialistic trends of our times, the perpetuation of our institutions and the teaching of literature." . . .

As in *Stone* and *Abington*, we need not be blind in this case to the legislature's preeminent religious purpose in enacting this statute. There is a historic and contemporaneous link between the teachings of certain religious denominations and the teaching of evolution (10). It was this link that concerned the Court in *Epperson* v. *Arkansas* . . . (1968), which also involved a facial challenge to a statute regulating the teaching of evolution. In that case, the Court reviewed an Arkansas statute that made it unlawful for an instructor to teach evolution or to use a textbook that referred to this scientific theory. Although the Arkansas antievolution law did not explicitly state its predominate religious purpose, the Court could not ignore that "the statute was a product of the upsurge of 'fundamentalist' religious fervor" that has long viewed this particular scientific theory as contradicting the literal interpretation of the Bible. . . . (11). After reviewing the history of antievolution statutes, the Court determined that "there can be no doubt that the motivation for the [Arkansas] law was the same [as other antievolution statutes]: to suppress the teaching of a theory which, it was thought, 'denied' the divine creation of man." . . . The Court found that there can be no legitimate state interest in protecting particular religions from scientific views "distasteful to them," . . . (citation omitted), and concluded "that the First Amendment does not permit the State to require that teaching and learning must be tailored to the principles or prohibitions of any religious sect or dogma," . . .

These same historic and contemporaneous antagonisms between the teachings of certain religious denominations and the teaching of evolution are present in this case. The preeminent purpose of the Louisiana Legislature was clearly to advance the religious viewpoint that a supernatural being created humankind (12). The term "creation science" was defined as embracing this particular religious doctrine by those responsible for the passage of the Creationism Act. Senator Keith's leading expert on creation science, Edward Boudreaux, testified at the legislative hearings that the theory of creation science included belief in the existence of a supernatural creator (noting that "creation scientists" point to high probability that life was "created by an intelligent mind") (13).

Senator Keith also cited testimony from other experts to support the creation-science view that "a creator [was] responsible for the universe and everything in it." ... (14). The legislative history therefore reveals that the term "creation science," as contemplated by the legislature that adopted this Act, embodies the religious belief that a supernatural creator was responsible for the creation of humankind.

Furthermore, it is not happenstance that the legislature required the teaching of a theory that coincided with this religious view. The legislative history documents that the Act's primary purpose was to change the science curriculum of public schools in order to provide persuasive advantage to a particular religious doctrine that rejects the factual basis of evolution in its entirety. The sponsor of the Creationism Act, Senator Keith, explained during the legislative hearings that his disdain for the theory of evolution resulted from the support that evolution supplied to views contrary to his own religious beliefs. According to Senator Keith, the theory of evolution was consonant with the "cardinal principle[s] of religious humanism, secular humanism, theological liberalism, aetheistism [*sic*]." ... The state senator repeatedly stated that scientific evidence supporting his religious views should be included in the public school curriculum to redress the fact that the theory of evolution incidentally coincided with what he characterized as religious beliefs antithetical to his own (15). The legislation therefore sought to alter the science curriculum to reflect endorsement of a religious view that is antagonistic to the theory of evolution.

In this case, the purpose of the Creationism Act was to restructure the science curriculum to conform with a particular religious viewpoint. Out of many possible science subjects taught in the public schools, the legislature chose to affect the teaching of the one scientific theory that historically has been opposed by certain religious sects. As in *Epperson*, the legislature passed the Act to give preference to those religious groups which have as one of their tenets the creation of humankind by a divine creator. The "overriding fact" that confronted the Court in *Epperson* was "that Arkansas' law selects from the body of knowledge a particular segment which it proscribes for the sole reason that it is deemed to conflict with ... a particular interpretation of the Book of Genesis by a particular religious group." ... Similarly, the Creationism Act is designed either to promote the theory of creation science which embodies a particular religious tenet by requiring that creation science be taught whenever evolution is taught or to prohibit the teaching of a scientific theory disfavored by certain religious sects by forbidding the teaching of evolution when creation science is not also taught. The Establishment Clause, however, "forbids *alike* the preference of a religious doctrine or the prohibition of theory which is deemed antagonistic to a particular dogma." . . . (emphasis added). Because the primary purpose of the Creationism Act is to advance a particular religious belief, the Act endorses religion in violation of the First Amendment.

We do not imply that a legislature could never require that scientific critiques of prevailing scientific theories be taught. Indeed, the Court acknowledged in Stone that its decision forbidding the posting of the Ten Commandments did not mean that no use could ever be made of the Ten Commandments, or that the Ten Commandments played an exclusively religious role in the history of Western Civilization. . . . In a similar way, teaching a variety of scientific theories about the origins of humankind to schoolchildren might be validly done with the clear secular intent of enhancing the effectiveness of science instruction. But because the primary purpose of the Creationism Act is to endorse a particular religious doctrine, the Act furthers religion in violation of the Establishment Clause (16).

IV

Appellants contend that genuine issues of material fact remain in dispute, and therefore the District Court erred in granting summary judgment. Federal Rule of Civil Procedure 56(c) provides that summary judgment "shall be rendered forthwith if the pleadings, depositions, answers to interrogatories, and admissions on file, together with the affidavits, if any, show that there is no genuine issue as to any material fact and that the moving party is entitled to a judgment as a matter of law." A court's finding of improper purpose behind a statute is appropriately determined by the statute on its face, its legislative history, or its interpretation by a responsible administrative agency. See, e. g., *Wallace v. Jaffree* . . . ; *Stone* v. *Graham* . . . ; *Epperson* v. *Arkansas*. . . . The plain meaning of the statute's words, enlightened by their context and the contemporaneous legislative history, can control the determination of legislative purpose. See *Wallace* v. *Jaffree* . . . (O'CONNOR, J., concurring in judgment); *Richards* v. *United States* . . . (1962); *Jay* v. *Boyd* . . . (1956). Moreover, in determining the legislative purpose of a statute, the Court has also considered the historical context of the statute, e. g., *Epperson* v. *Arkansas*, supra, and the specific sequence of events leading to passage of the statute, e. g., *Arlington Heights* v. *Metropolitan Housing Dev. Corp.* . . . (1977).

In this case, appellees' motion for summary judgment rested on the plain language of the Creationism Act, the legislative history and historical context of the Act, the specific sequence of events leading to the passage of the Act, the State Board's report on a survey of school superintendents, and the correspondence between the Act's legislative sponsor and its key witnesses. Appellants contend that affidavits made by two scientists, two theologians, and an education administrator raise a genuine issue of material fact and that summary judgment was therefore barred. The affidavits define creation science as "origin through abrupt appearance in complex form" and allege that such a viewpoint constitutes a true scientific theory. See App. to Brief for Appellants A-7 to A-40.

We agree with the lower courts that these affidavits do not raise a genuine issue of material fact. The existence of "uncontroverted affidavits" does not bar summary judgment (17). Moreover, the postenactment testimony of outside experts is of little use in determining the Louisiana Legislature's purpose in enacting this statute. The Louisiana Legislature did hear and rely on scientific experts in passing the bill (18), but none of the persons making the affidavits produced by the appellants participated in or contributed to the enactment of the law or its implementation (19). The District Court, in its discretion, properly concluded that a Monday-morning "battle of the experts" over possible technical meanings of terms in the statute would not illuminate the contemporaneous purpose of the Louisiana Legislature when it made the law (20). We therefore conclude that the District Court did not err in finding that appellants failed to raise a genuine issue of material fact, and in granting summary judgment (21).

V

The Louisiana Creationism Act advances a religious doctrine by requiring either the banishment of the theory of evolution from public school classrooms or the presentation of a religious viewpoint that rejects evolution in its entirety. The Act violates the Establishment Clause of the First Amendment because it seeks to employ the symbolic and financial support of government to achieve a religious purpose. The judgment of the Court of Appeals therefore is Affirmed.

Notes:

1 JUSTICE O'CONNOR joins all but Part II of this opinion.

2 Appellants, the Louisiana Governor, the Attorney General, the State Superintendent, the State Department of Education and the St. Tammany Parish School Board, agreed not to implement the Creationism Act pending the final outcome of this litigation. The Louisiana Board of Elementary and Secondary Education, and the Orleans Parish School Board were among the original defendants in the suit but both later realigned as plaintiffs.

3 The District Court initially stayed the action pending the resolution of a separate lawsuit brought by the Act's legislative sponsor and others for declaratory and injunctive relief. After the separate suit was dismissed on jurisdictional grounds, *Keith* v. *Louisiana Department of Education* . . . (1982), the District Court lifted its stay in this case and held that the Creationism Act violated the Louisiana Constitution. The court ruled that the State Constitution grants authority over the public school system to the Board of Elementary and Secondary Education rather than the state legislature. On appeal, the Court of Appeals certified the question to the Louisiana Supreme Court, which found the Creationism Act did not violate the State Constitution, *Aguillard* v. *Treen* . . . (1983). The Court of Appeals then remanded the case to the District Court to determine whether the Creationism Act violates the Federal Constitution. *Aguillard* v. *Treen* . . . (1983).

4 The First Amendment states: "Congress shall make no law respecting an establishment of religion. . . ." Under the Fourteenth Amendment, this "fundamental concept of liberty" applies to the States. *Cantwell* v. *Connecticut* . . . (1940).

5 The *Lemon* test has been applied in all cases since its adoption in 1971, except in *Marsh* v. *Chambers* . . . (1983), where the Court held that the Nebraska Legislature's practice of opening a session with a prayer by a chaplain paid by the State did not violate the Establishment Clause. The Court based its conclusion in that case on the historical acceptance of the practice. Such a historical approach is not useful in determining the proper roles of church and state in public schools, since free public education was virtually nonexistent at the time the Constitution was

adopted. See *Wallace* v. *Jaffree* . . . (1985) (O'CONNOR, J., concurring in judgment) (citing *Abington School Dist.* v. *Schempp* . . . (1963)
(BRENNAN, J., concurring)).

6 The potential for undue influence is far less significant with regard
to college students who voluntarily enroll in courses. "This distinction
warrants a difference in constitutional results." *Abington School Dist.* v.
Schempp . . . (BRENNAN, J., concurring). Thus, for instance, the Court
has not questioned the authority of state colleges and universities to
offer courses on religion or theology. See *Widmar* v. *Vincent* . . . (1981)
(POWELL, J.); . . . (STEVENS, J., concurring in judgment).

7 The Court of Appeals stated that "academic freedom embodies the
principle that individual instructors are at liberty to teach that which
they deem to be appropriate in the exercise of their professional judgment." . . . But, in the State of Louisiana, courses in public schools are
prescribed by the State Board of Education and teachers are not free,
absent permission, to teach courses different from what is required.
. . . "Academic freedom," at least as it is commonly understood, is not
a relevant concept in this context. Moreover, as the Court of Appeals
explained, the Act "requires, presumably upon risk of sanction or dismissal for failure to comply, the teaching of creation-science whenever
evolution is taught. Although states may prescribe public school curriculum concerning science instruction under ordinary circumstances,
the compulsion inherent in the Balanced Treatment Act is, on its face,
inconsistent with the idea of academic freedom as it is universally understood." . . . The Act actually serves to diminish academic freedom by
removing the flexibility to teach evolution without also teaching creation
science, even if teachers determine that such curriculum results in less
effective and comprehensive science instruction.

8 Creationism Act's provisions appear among other provisions prescribing
the courses of study in Louisiana's public schools. These other provisions,
similar to those in other States, prescribe courses of study in such topics
as driver training, civics, the Constitution, and free enterprise. None of
these other provisions, apart from those associated with the Creationism
Act, nominally mandates "equal time" for opposing opinions within a
specific area of learning. See, e. g., La. Rev. Stat. Ann. . . . (1987).

9 The dissent [of Scalia] concludes that the Act's purpose was to protect
the academic freedom of students, and not that of teachers. Post, at 628.
Such a view is not at odds with our conclusion that if the Act's purpose

was to provide comprehensive scientific education (a concern shared by students and teachers, as well as parents), that purpose was not advanced by the statute's provisions. . . .

Moreover, it is astonishing that the dissent, to prove its assertion, relies on a section of the legislation that was eventually deleted by the legislature. . . . The dissent contends that this deleted section—which was explicitly rejected by the Louisiana Legislature—reveals the legislature's "obviously intended meaning of the statutory terms 'academic freedom.'" Post, at 628.

Quite to the contrary, Boudreaux, the main expert relied on by the sponsor of the Act, cautioned the legislature that the words "academic freedom" meant "freedom to teach science." . . . His testimony was given at the time the legislature was deciding whether to delete this section of the Act.

10 See *McLean* v. *Arkansas Bd. of Ed.* . . . (1982) (reviewing historical and contemporary antagonisms between the theory of evolution and religious movements).

11 The Court evaluated the statute in light of a series of antievolution statutes adopted by state legislatures dating back to the Tennessee statute that was the focus of the celebrated Scopes trial in 1925. *Epperson* v. *Arkansas.* . . . The Court found the Arkansas statute comparable to this Tennessee "monkey law," since both gave preference to "'religious establishments which have as one of their tenets or dogmas the instantaneous creation of man.'" . . . (quoting *Scopes* v. *State* . . . (1927) (Chambliss, J., concurring)).

12 While the belief in the instantaneous creation of humankind by a supernatural creator may require the rejection of every aspect of the theory of evolution, an individual instead may choose to accept some or all of this scientific theory as compatible with his or her spiritual outlook. . . .

13 Boudreaux repeatedly defined creation science in terms of a theory that supports the existence of a supernatural creator. . . . (equating creation science with a theory pointing "to conditions of a creator"); . . . ("Creation . . . requires the direct involvement of a supernatural intelligence"). The lead witness at the hearings introducing the original bill, Luther Sunderland, described creation science as postulating "that everything was created by some intelligence or power external to the universe."

14 Senator Keith believed that creation science embodied this view: "One concept is that a creator however you define a creator was responsible for everything that is in this world. The other concept is that it just evolved." . . . Besides Senator Keith, several of the most vocal legislators also revealed their religious motives for supporting the bill in the official legislative history. . . . (Sen. Saunders noting that bill was amended so that teachers could refer to the Bible and other religious texts to support the creation-science theory); . . . (Rep. Jenkins contending that the existence of God was a scientific fact).

15 See, e. g., . . . (noting that evolution is contrary to his family's religious beliefs); . . . (contending that evolution advances religions contrary to his own); . . . (stating that evolution is "almost a religion" to science teachers); . . . (arguing that evolution is cornerstone of some religions contrary to his own); . . . (author of model bill, from which Act is derived, sent copy of the model bill to Senator Keith and advised that "I view this whole battle as one between God and anti-God forces. . . . If evolution is permitted to continue . . . it will continue to be made to appear that a Supreme Being is unnecessary . . .").

16 Neither the District Court nor the Court of Appeals found a clear secular purpose, while both agreed that the Creationism Act's primary purpose was to advance religion. "When both courts below are unable to discern an arguably valid secular purpose, this Court normally should hesitate to find one." *Wallace* v. *Jaffree* . . . (POWELL, J., concurring).

17 There is "no express or implied requirement in Rule 56 that the moving party support its motion with affidavits or other similar materials negating the opponent's claim." *Celotex Corp.* v. *Catrett* . . . (1986).

18 The experts, who were relied upon by the sponsor of the bill and the legislation's other supporters, testified that creation science embodies the religious view that there is a supernatural creator of the universe. . . .

19 Appellants contend that the affidavits are relevant because the term "creation science" is a technical term similar to that found in statutes that regulate certain scientific or technological developments. Even assuming, arguendo, that "creation science" is a term of art as represented by appellants, the definition provided by the relevant agency provides a better insight than the affidavits submitted by appellants in this case. In a 1981 survey conducted by the Louisiana Department of Education, the school superintendents in charge of implementing the provisions of the Creationism Act were asked to interpret the meaning of "creation

science" as used in the statute. About 75 percent of Louisiana's superintendents stated that they understood "creation science" to be a religious doctrine. . . . Of this group, the largest proportion of superintendents interpreted creation science, as defined by the Act, to mean the literal interpretation of the Book of Genesis. The remaining superintendents believed that the Act required teaching the view that "the universe was made by a creator. . . ."

20 The Court has previously found the postenactment elucidation of the meaning of a statute to be of little relevance in determining the intent of the legislature contemporaneous to the passage of the statute. See *Wallace v. Jaffree* . . . (O'CONNOR, J., concurring in judgment).

21 Numerous other Establishment Clause cases that found state statutes to be unconstitutional have been disposed of without trial. E. g., *Larkin* v. *Grendel's Den, Inc.* . . . (1982); *Lemon* v. *Kurtzman* . . . (1971); *Engel* v. *Vitale*, . . . (1962).[5]

Comments on the *Edwards* Court Decision

A careful reading of the high court's decision reveals some important things about the creation/evolution issue in the courts. The following is a summary. It sets the stage for the *Dover* court decision (2005) and for future battles in the courts.

First of all, precedent plays an important role in the Court's decision. Appeal was made, as feared, to the *Epperson* case (1968) as well as the *McLean* decision (1982). But both of these decisions were seriously flawed (see chapters 2 and 3).

Second, as in *McLean,* the teaching of creation is considered inherently religious. Any references to a "creator," even as a first cause or explanation of scientific evidence, seem to be taboo for the Court. To quote, "(b) The Act impermissibly endorses religion by advancing the religious belief that a supernatural being created humankind."[6]

Third, the reference to the legitimacy of teaching other views of origins seems to mean in context only other naturalistic views, since reference

5. *Edwards v. Aguillard,* 482 U.S. 578 (1987).
6. Ibid.

to a "creator" is considered inherently religious. Hence, it is a sham to claim, as the Court does, that "we do not imply that a legislature could never require that scientific critiques of prevailing scientific theories be taught." There is no other view than evolution except creation, and that is the one the Court is not allowing. Further, if the legislature has the right to "require" some "scientific critiques" of "prevailing scientific theories,"[7] then why are they forbidding creation, which does precisely this by way of contrast?

Fourth, it is ludicrous to claim that "the teaching of 'creation-science' and 'creationism,' as contemplated by the statute, involves teaching 'tailored to the principles' of a particular religious sect or group of sects."[8] How can a law that forbids teaching both views (if either one is denied a hearing) be considered favorable to only one set of religious beliefs? Just the opposite is the case. In fact, teaching only evolution is favorable to nontheistic religions.

Fifth, the religious history and motivation behind the law are, for the Court, telling arguments against its constitutionality. Here again, the Court overlooks the nature and legislative purpose of the law and divines religious motives it deems sufficient to discard it on First Amendment grounds.

Sixth, the ruling states a very positive thing in a very negative way: It says, "The Creationism Act forbids the teaching of the theory of evolution in public schools unless accompanied by instruction in 'creation science.'"[9] First of all, it is not a "Creationism Act." It is an act to teach both creation and evolution, if either are taught. Second, it is misleading to say it "forbids teaching the theory of evolution." It does not; it encourages teaching it along with creation in a balanced way. To put it positively, it is an Act that encourages teaching evolution, along with creation, in a way that enhances student understanding and choices.

Seventh, it is also absurd to claim that "the Louisiana Legislature's actual intent was 'to discredit evolution by counterbalancing its teach-

7. Ibid.
8. Ibid.
9. Ibid.

ing at every turn with the teaching of creationism, a religious belief.'"[10] For one thing, creationism is not a "religious belief." It is just as much a scientific theory about origins as is evolution. Further, it is no more a "discredit" to evolution than is teaching evolution a discredit to teaching creation. It is, however, a discredit to academic freedom, educational excellence, and constitutional rights not to allow creation a place in the curriculum.

Eighth, it is also wrongheaded to argue that "the Court has been particularly vigilant in monitoring compliance with the Establishment Clause in elementary and secondary schools" because "students in such institutions are impressionable and their attendance is involuntary."[11] If this is so, then it is even worse to expose these impressionable minds to only one theory of origins, one which conflicts at some points with most parents' beliefs! For surveys show that the vast majority of parents believe there is a creator of the universe and of life.[12]

Ninth, it misappropriates and misapplies the *Lemon* test for constitutionality. The test is not really an appropriate test, and the way it is applied to this (and many other) cases is illegitimate, as even some Supreme Court justices have observed (see chapters 6 and 9).

Tenth, it is either contradictory or a sham for the Court to speak of "a teacher's flexibility"[13] that the teachers allegedly had without this law. In fact, there was no real "flexibility" to teach creation, as is evident from the fact that creation was ruled inherently religious by virtue of its implication that there was a creator.

Finally, it is incredible that the Court could claim that this balanced treatment act, which would have allowed both creation and evolution to be taught, "advances a religious doctrine by requiring either the banishment of the theory of evolution from public school classrooms or the presentation of a religious viewpoint that rejects evolution in its entirety."[14] Perhaps the best way to untwist this distorted logic is to change only one word, which I have highlighted in what follows, and insist that the

10. Ibid.
11. Ibid.
12. Some 95 percent of Americans say that they believe in God (see chapter 9, note 17).
13. *Edwards v. Aguillard,* 482 U.S. 578 (1987).
14. Ibid.

present law (via *Epperson*) that protects only the teaching of evolution "advances a religious doctrine by requiring either the banishment of the theory of *creation* from public school classrooms or the presentation of a religious viewpoint that rejects *creation* in its entirety."

6

Scalia's Dissenting Opinion in the *Edwards* Case (1987)

Excerpts from Scalia's Dissent[1]

Justice Antonin Scalia issued a penetrating dissent in the *Edwards* case. One can only regret that it was not the majority ruling. Following are some excerpts along with comments.

First, Scalia notes correctly that it is a "questionable premise that legislation can be invalidated under the Establishment Clause on the basis of its motivation alone." And this is precisely what the Court did here and has done elsewhere in the creation/evolution issue.

Second, Scalia is also right in saying it is insufficient for the Court to invalidate laws on the basis of "its visceral knowledge regarding what must have motivated the legislators." It is dangerous to discard a law simply on the basis of what one imagines the motives for the law to have been.

1. All excerpts are quoted from *Edwards v. Aguillard,* 482 U.S. 578 (1987).

Third, he points out that, since the expert creationist witnesses claimed that "creation science is a strictly scientific concept that can be presented without religious reference. . . . then, we must assume that the Balanced Treatment Act does not require the presentation of religious doctrine."

Fourth, Scalia insightfully notes that "we surely would not strike down a law providing money to feed the hungry or shelter the homeless if it could be demonstrated that, but for the religious beliefs of the legislators, the funds would not have been approved. Also, political activism by the religiously motivated is part of our heritage." He adds, "Today's religious activism may give us the Balanced Treatment Act, but yesterday's resulted in the abolition of slavery, and tomorrow's may bring relief for famine victims."

Fifth, "similarly, we will not presume that a law's purpose is to advance religion merely because it 'happens to coincide or harmonize with the tenets of some or all religions.'" After all, teaching evolution harmonizes with the religious beliefs of all nontheistic religions that believe in evolution.

Sixth, he adds, "The witnesses repeatedly assured committee members that 'hundreds and hundreds' of highly respected, internationally renowned scientists believed in creation science and would support their testimony." This should be sufficient to show that creation science is a scientific teaching.

Seventh, "there are two and only two scientific explanations for the beginning of life—evolution and creation science. . . . Both are bona fide 'sciences.'" Forbidding one and allowing only the other is favoring those religions with which evolution is compatible.

Eighth, "since there are only two possible explanations of the origin of life, any evidence that tends to disprove the theory of evolution necessarily tends to prove the theory of creation science, and vice versa. For example, the abrupt appearance in the fossil record of complex life, and the extreme rarity of transitional life forms in that record, are evidence for creation science." So, disallowing creation science is in effect disallowing the primary objections to evolution and establishing it and its religious implications.

Ninth, "creation science is educationally valuable. Students exposed to it better understand the current state of scientific evidence about the origin of life. . . . Those students even have a better understanding of evolution. . . . Creation science can and should be presented to children without any religious content."

Tenth, testimony shows that "teachers have been brainwashed by an entrenched scientific establishment composed almost exclusively of scientists to whom evolution is like a 'religion.' These scientists discriminate against creation scientists so as to prevent evolution's weaknesses from being exposed."

Eleventh, "even with nothing more than this legislative history to go on, I think it would be extraordinary to invalidate the Balanced Treatment Act for lack of a valid secular purpose. Striking down a law approved by the democratically elected representatives of the people is no minor matter."

Twelfth, "the Louisiana Legislature explicitly set forth its secular purpose ("protecting academic freedom") in the very text of the Act. . . . We have in the past repeatedly relied upon or deferred to such expressions. . . ." But, "The Court seeks to evade the force of this expression of purpose by stubbornly misinterpreting it, and then finding that the provisions of the Act do not advance that misinterpreted purpose, thereby showing it to be a sham."

Thirteenth, "the Act's reference to 'creation' is not convincing evidence of religious purpose. The Act defines creation science as 'scientific evidenc[e],' . . . and Senator Keith and his witnesses repeatedly stressed that the subject can and should be presented without religious content. . . . We have no basis on the record to conclude that creation science need be anything other than a collection of scientific data supporting the theory that life abruptly appeared on earth. . . . Creation science, its proponents insist, no more must explain whence life came than evolution must explain whence came the inanimate materials from which it says life evolved."

Fourteenth, "to posit a past creator is not to posit the eternal and personal God who is the object of religious veneration. Indeed, it is not even to posit the 'unmoved mover' hypothesized by Aristotle and other notably nonfundamentalist philosophers." This is the same point I made in my suppressed testimony in the Arkansas case (see chapter 4).

Fifteenth, "the legislative history gives ample evidence of the sincerity of the Balanced Treatment Act's articulated purpose. Witness after witness urged the legislators to support the Act so that students would not be 'indoctrinated' but would instead be free to decide for themselves, based upon a fair presentation of the scientific evidence, about the origin of life."

Sixteenth, Scalia noted that "even appellees concede that a valid secular purpose is not rendered impermissible simply because its pursuit is prompted by concern for religious sensitivities.... If a history teacher falsely told her students that the bones of Jesus Christ had been discovered, or a physics teacher that the Shroud of Turin had been conclusively established to be inexplicable on the basis of natural causes, I cannot believe (despite the majority's implication to the contrary...) that legislators or school board members would be constitutionally prohibited from taking corrective action, simply because that action was prompted by concern for the religious beliefs of the misinstructed students."

Seventeenth, "In sum, even if one concedes, for the sake of argument, that a majority of the Louisiana Legislature voted for the Balanced Treatment Act partly in order to foster (rather than merely eliminate discrimination against) Christian fundamentalist beliefs, our cases establish that that alone would not suffice to invalidate the Act, so long as there was a genuine secular purpose as well."

Eighteenth, "I have to this point assumed the validity of the *Lemon* 'purpose' test. In fact, however, I think the pessimistic evaluation that THE CHIEF JUSTICE made of the totality of *Lemon* is particularly applicable to the 'purpose' prong: it is 'a constitutional theory [that] has no basis in the history of the amendment it seeks to interpret, is difficult to apply and yields unprincipled results...' *Wallace* v. *Jaffree* ... (REHNQUIST, J., dissenting). Our cases interpreting and applying the purpose test have made such a maze of the Establishment Clause that even the most conscientious governmental officials can only guess what motives will be held unconstitutional."

Concluding Comments

Scalia's dissent needs no elaboration. He hits on most of the key points in the controversy and backs it up with case references and sound judicial reasoning. Since only one other justice joined with him (Rehnquist) and since, while they are conservative, we do not know how the two recently appointed Supreme Court justices (Roberts and Alito) would vote on such issues, it is reasonable to assume that the high court is not yet prepared to overturn this decision. Thus, it is very important to get the information contained in this book out to the general public, scholars, lawyers, and courts.

Notes [for Scalia's Dissent]:[2]

1. Article VI, cl. 3, of the Constitution provides that "the Members of the several State Legislatures . . . shall be bound by Oath or Affirmation, to support this Constitution."

2. Thus the popular dictionary definitions cited by JUSTICE POW-ELL, ante, at 598-599 (concurring opinion), and appellees, see Brief for Appellees 25, 26; . . . are utterly irrelevant, as are the views of the school superintendents cited by the majority. . . . Three-quarters of those surveyed had "no" or "limited" knowledge of "creation-science theory," and not a single superintendent claimed "extensive" knowledge of the subject. . . .

3. Although creation scientists and evolutionists also disagree about the origin of the physical universe, both proponents and opponents of Senator Keith's bill focused on the question of the beginning of life.

4. Although appellees and amici dismiss the testimony of Senator Keith and his witnesses as pure fantasy, they did not bother to submit evidence of that to the District Court, making it difficult for us to agree with them. The State, by contrast, submitted the affidavits of two scientists, a philosopher, a theologian, and an educator, whose academic credentials are rather impressive. . . . Like Senator Keith and his witnesses, the affiants swear that evolution and creation science are the only two scientific explanations for the origin of life. . . . that creation science is strictly

---

2. Most of the specific text of Scalia's dissent to which these notes refer is not included in the foregoing. I have included the notes, however, because they are interesting in their own right. They also are quoted from *Edwards v. Aguillard,* 482 U.S. 578 (1987).

scientific . . . ; that creation science is simply a collection of scientific data that supports the hypothesis that life appeared on earth suddenly and has changed little . . . ; that hundreds of respected scientists believe in creation science . . . ; that evidence for creation science is as strong as evidence for evolution . . . ; that creation science is educationally valuable . . . ; that creation science can be presented without religious content . . . ; and that creation science is now censored from classrooms while evolution is misrepresented as proven fact. . . . It is difficult to conclude on the basis of these affidavits—the only substantive evidence in the record—that the laymen serving in the Louisiana Legislature must have disbelieved Senator Keith or his witnesses.

5. The majority finds it "astonishing" that I would cite a portion of Senator Keith's original bill that was later deleted as evidence of the legislature's understanding of the phrase "academic freedom." . . . What is astonishing is the majority's implication that the deletion of that section deprives it of value as a clear indication of what the phrase meant—there and in the other, retained, sections of the bill. The Senate Committee on Education deleted most of the lengthy "purpose" section of the bill (with Senator Keith's consent) because it resembled legislative "findings of fact," which, committee members felt, should generally not be incorporated in legislation. The deletion had absolutely nothing to do with the manner in which the section described "academic freedom." . . .

6. As the majority recognizes . . . Senator Keith sincerely believed that "secular humanism is a bona fide religion" . . . and that "evolution is the cornerstone of that religion," . . . . The Senator even told his colleagues that this Court had "held" that secular humanism was a religion. . . . (In *Torcaso v. Watkins* . . . (1961), we did indeed refer to "Secular Humanism" as a "religio[n].") Senator Keith and his supporters raised the "religion" of secular humanism not, as the majority suggests, to explain the source of their "disdain for the theory of evolution," . . . but to convince the legislature that the State of Louisiana was violating the Establishment Clause because its teachers were misrepresenting evolution as fact and depriving students of the information necessary to question that theory. . . . The Senator repeatedly urged his colleagues to pass his bill to remedy this Establishment Clause violation by ensuring state neutrality in religious matters . . . , surely a permissible purpose under *Lemon*. Senator Keith's argument may be questionable, but nothing in the statute

or its legislative history gives us reason to doubt his sincerity or that of his supporters.

7. Professor Choper summarized our school aid cases thusly:

"[A] provision for therapeutic and diagnostic health services to parochial school pupils by public employees is invalid if provided in the parochial school, but not if offered at a neutral site, even if in a mobile unit adjacent to the parochial school. Reimbursement to parochial schools for the expense of administering teacher-prepared tests required by state law is invalid, but the state may reimburse parochial schools for the expense of administering state-prepared tests. The state may lend school textbooks to parochial school pupils because, the Court has explained, the books can be checked in advance for religious content and are 'self-policing'; but the state may not lend other seemingly self-policing instructional items such as tape recorders and maps. The state may pay the cost of bus transportation to parochial schools, which the Court has ruled are 'permeated' with religion; but the state is forbidden to pay for field trip transportation visits 'to governmental, industrial, cultural, and scientific centers designed to enrich the secular studies of students.'" Choper, The Religion Clauses of the First Amendment: Reconciling the Conflict . . . (1980).

Since that was written, more decisions on the subject have been rendered, but they leave the theme of chaos securely unimpaired. See, e. g., *Aguilar* v. *Felton* . . . (1985); *Grand Rapids School District* v. *Ball* . . . (1985).

7

The *Dover* Case (2005)

Introduction

The plaintiff in the 2005 *Dover* case was Tammy Kitzmiller and the defendant was the Dover Area School District, in Dover, Pennsylvania. On October 18, 2004, the defendant Dover Area School Board of Directors passed by a 6-3 vote the following resolution:

> Students will be made aware of gaps/problems in Darwin's theory and of other theories of evolution including, but not limited to, intelligent design. Note: Origins of Life will not be taught.[1]

On November 19, 2004, the defendant Dover Area School District announced by press release that, beginning in January 2005, teachers

1. *Kitzmiller v. Dover Area School District,* 400 F. Supp. 2d 707 (M.D. Pa. 2005).

would be required to read the following statement to students in the ninth-grade biology class at Dover High School:

> The Pennsylvania Academic Standards require students to learn about Darwin's Theory of Evolution and eventually to take a standardized test of which evolution is a part. Because Darwin's Theory is a theory, it continues to be tested as new evidence is discovered. The Theory is not a fact. Gaps in the Theory exist for which there is no evidence. A theory is defined as a well-tested explanation that unifies a broad range of observations. Intelligent Design is an explanation of the origin of life that differs from Darwin's view. The reference book, *Of Pandas and People*, is available for students who might be interested in gaining an understanding of what Intelligent Design actually involves. With respect to any theory, students are encouraged to keep an open mind. The school leaves the discussion of the Origins of Life to individual students and their families. As a Standards-driven district, class instruction focuses upon preparing students to achieve proficiency on Standards-based assessments.[2]

The Court Ruling

Summary of the Ruling

On December 20, 2005, the United States District Court for the Middle District of Pennsylvania ruled that: (1) The Dover School District policy was unconstitutional; (2) intelligent design and creation its progenitor were not science and should not be taught in Dover science classes; and (3) intelligent design and other forms of creation are essentially religious and are, therefore, a violation of the First Amendment establishment clause.

In the words of the court, "For the reasons that follow, we hold that the ID [intelligent design] Policy is unconstitutional pursuant to the Establishment Clause of the First Amendment of the United States Constitution and Art. I, § 3 of the Pennsylvania Constitution."[3]

2. Ibid.
3. Ibid.

History of the Ruling

The *Dover* trial began September 26, 2005, and continued through November 4. The ruling was not expected until early 2006, but a surprisingly long (139-page) ruling came very quickly on December 20, 2005, in little over a month. Coming as it did on that date, the announcement, which could have been expected to cause widespread reaction, was overshadowed by the holiday season.

Evidential Basis of the Ruling

According to the court, "This Memorandum Opinion constitutes the Court's findings of fact and conclusions of law which are based upon the Court's review of the evidence presented at trial, the testimony of the witnesses at trial, the parties' proposed findings of fact and conclusions of law with supporting briefs, other documents and evidence in the record, and applicable law. Further orders and judgments will be in conformity with this opinion."[4]

The Tests Used for the Ruling

The *Dover* court acknowledged that the "Constitution provides that 'Congress shall make no law respecting an establishment of religion, or prohibiting the free exercise thereof.'" They go on to note that "the prohibition against the establishment of religion applies to the states through the Fourteenth Amendment" as is evident in *Modrovich v. Allegheny County* (2004) and *Wallace v. Jaffree* (1985). The court concluded: "After a searching review of Supreme Court and Third Circuit Court of Appeals precedent, it is apparent to this Court that both the endorsement test and the *Lemon* test should be employed in this case to analyze the constitutionality of the ID Policy under the Establishment Clause. . . . We will therefore initially analyze the constitutionality of the ID Policy under the endorsement test and will then proceed to the *Lemon* test as it applies to this case."[5]

4. Ibid.
5. Ibid.

Applying the Endorsement Test
to the Dover ID Policy

First, the court applied the endorsement test to the Dover school policy. We will examine the nature of the endorsement test and its application to teaching ID in public school science classes.

The nature of the endorsement test itself. According to the *Dover* court, "The endorsement test recognizes that when government transgresses the limits of neutrality and acts in ways that show religious favoritism or sponsorship, it violates the Establishment Clause." . . . "The central issue in this case is whether [the government] has endorsed [religion] by its [actions]. To answer that question, we must examine both what [the government] intended to communicate . . . and what message [its conduct] actually conveyed. The purpose and effect prongs of the *Lemon* test represent these two aspects of the meaning of the [government's] action. . . . The test consists of the reviewing court determining what message a challenged governmental policy or enactment conveys to a reasonable, objective observer who knows the policy's language, origins, and legislative history, as well as the history of the community and the broader social and historical context in which the policy arose." To make this determination, a hypothetical "objective observer" who is "familiar with the origins and context of the government-sponsored message at issue and the history of the community where the message is displayed" is posited. This "reasonable observer is [assumed to be] an informed citizen who is more knowledgeable than the average passerby." So, "the observer looks to that evidence to ascertain whether the policy 'in fact conveys a message of endorsement or disapproval' of religion, irrespective of what the government might have intended by it."[6]

The application of the endorsement policy. The court ruling listed several reasons why the Dover school board policy violated this test. It concluded that, "An Objective Observer Would Know that ID and Teaching About 'Gaps' and 'Problems' in Evolutionary Theory are Creationist, Religious Strategies that Evolved from Earlier Forms of Creationism."[7]

6. Ibid.
7. Ibid.

This conclusion was supported by appealing both to legislative history showing religious motivation behind the Dover law and to precedent cases like *Epperson* (1968), *McLean* (1982), and *Edwards* (1987). From these earlier cases the court noted that, "The Supreme Court further held that the belief that a supernatural creator was responsible for the creation of human kind is a religious viewpoint and that the Act at issue 'advances a religious doctrine by requiring either the banishment of the theory of evolution from public school classrooms or the presentation of a religious viewpoint that rejects evolution in its entirety.' Id. At 591, 596. Therefore, as noted, the import of *Edwards* (1987) is that the Supreme Court made national the prohibition against teaching creation science in the public school system."[8]

The court then noted, "The concept of intelligent design (hereinafter 'ID'), in its current form, came into existence after the *Edwards* case was decided in 1987. For the reasons that follow, we conclude that the religious nature of ID would be readily apparent to an objective observer, adult or child."[9]

The court cited John Haught, a theologian who testified that the ID argument "traced this argument back to at least Thomas Aquinas in the 13th century, who framed the argument as a syllogism: Wherever complex design exists, there must have been a designer; nature is complex; therefore nature must have had an intelligent designer," noting that Aquinas added, "Everyone understands [this] to be God." The court observed through testimony that this is the same argument that William Paley advanced early in the nineteenth century and that ID proponents admit that Paley's argument is basically the same as their argument, namely, that "purposeful arrangement of parts" is evidence of a designer.[10]

The only apparent difference between the argument made by Paley and the argument for ID, as expressed by defense expert witnesses Michael Behe and Minnich, is that ID's "official position" does not acknowledge that the designer is God. "However, as Dr. Haught testified, anyone familiar with

8. Ibid.
9. Ibid.
10. Ibid.

Western religious thought would immediately make the association that the tactically unnamed designer is God." Further, the court argued that even the proposed ID text, *Of Pandas and People,*[11] described the designer as "'master intellect,' strongly suggesting a supernatural deity as opposed to any intelligent actor known to exist in the natural world."[12]

Furthermore, the court noted that "it is notable that both Professors Behe and Minnich admitted their personal view is that the designer is God and Professor Minnich testified that he understands many leading advocates of ID to believe the designer to be God." And "although proponents of the IDM [Intelligent Design Movement] occasionally suggest that the designer could be a space alien or a time-traveling cell biologist, no serious alternative to God as the designer has been proposed by members of the IDM, including Defendants' expert witnesses.... In fact, an explicit concession that the intelligent designer works outside the laws of nature and science and a direct reference to religion is *Pandas'* rhetorical statement, 'what kind of intelligent agent was it [the designer]' and answer: 'On its own science cannot answer this question. It must leave it to religion and philosophy.'"[13] For further support the court cited ID leaders Phillip Johnson and William Dembski's religious beliefs that the intelligent designer is a "theistic" type of "God." Then they went back to the *McLean* case and pointed out that Duane Gish and Henry Morris, earlier creationists, also identify God with a theistic God.

The court also concluded that "dramatic evidence of ID's religious nature and aspirations is found in what is referred to as the 'Wedge Document'"[14] when the authors of this document state their "Governing Goals" are to "defeat scientific materialism and its destructive moral, cultural, and political legacies" and "to replace materialistic explanations with the theistic understanding that nature and human beings are created by God." In addition, "ID's religious nature is evident because it involves a supernatural designer. The courts in *Edwards* and *McLean* expressly

11. Percival Davis and Dean H. Kenyon, and Charles B. Thaxton, *Of Pandas and People: The Central Question of Biological Origins* (Dallas: Haughton, 1993).
12. *Kitzmiller v. Dover Area School District,* 400 F. Supp. 2d 707 (M.D. Pa. 2005).
13. Ibid.
14. See Phillip E. Johnson, *The Wedge of Truth: Splitting the Foundations of Naturalism* (Downers Grove, Ill.: InterVarsity Press, 2002) for elaboration.

found that this characteristic removed creationism from the realm of science and made it a religious proposition.... Prominent ID proponents have made abundantly clear that the designer is supernatural.

Defendants' expert witness ID proponents confirmed that the existence of a supernatural designer is a hallmark of ID. First, Professor Behe has written that by ID he means 'not designed by the laws of nature,' and that it is 'implausible that the designer is a natural entity.'" The court noted that "Professor Minnich testified that for ID to be considered science, the ground rules of science have to be broadened so that supernatural forces can be considered.... Professor Steven William Fuller testified that it is ID's project to change the ground rules of science to include the supernatural...." Indeed, one of the "leading ID proponents, Johnson, has concluded that science must be redefined to include the supernatural if religious challenges to evolution are to get a hearing.... Additionally, Dembski agrees that science is ruled by methodological naturalism and argues that this rule must be overturned if ID is to prosper."[15]

Further, the court stated that "support for the proposition that ID requires supernatural creation is found in the book *Pandas,* to which students in Dover's ninth grade biology class are directed. *Pandas* indicates that there are two kinds of causes, natural and intelligent, which demonstrate that intelligent causes are beyond nature.... Professor Haught, who as noted was the only theologian to testify in this case, explained that in Western intellectual tradition, non-natural causes occupy a space reserved for ultimate religious explanations.... Robert Pennock, Plaintiffs' expert in the philosophy of science, concurred with Professor Haught and concluded that because its basic proposition is that the features of the natural world are produced by a transcendent, immaterial, non-natural being, ID is a religious proposition regardless of whether that religious proposition is given a recognized religious label.... It is notable that not one defense expert was able to explain how the supernatural action suggested by ID could be anything other than an inherently religious proposition. Accordingly, we find that ID's

15. *Kitzmiller v. Dover Area School District,* 400 F. Supp. 2d 707 (M.D. Pa. 2005).

religious nature would be further evident to our objective observer because it directly involves a supernatural designer."[16]

Finally, "by comparing the pre and post *Edwards* drafts of *Pandas,* three astonishing points emerge: (1) the definition for creation science in early drafts is identical to the definition of ID; (2) cognates of the word creation (creationism and creationist), which appeared approximately 150 times were deliberately and systematically replaced with the phrase ID." And "(3) the changes occurred shortly after the Supreme Court held that creation science is religious and cannot be taught in public school science classes in *Edwards.*" Thus, "this word substitution is telling, significant, and reveals that a purposeful change of *words* was effected without any corresponding change in *content.* . . ." This "directly refutes FTE's [Foundation for Thought and Ethics] argument that by merely disregarding the words 'creation' and 'creationism,' FTE expressly rejected creationism in *Pandas.*"[17] For "in early pre-*Edwards* drafts of *Pandas,* the term 'creation' was defined as 'various forms of life that began abruptly through an intelligent agency with their distinctive features intact—fish with fins and scales, birds with feathers, beaks, and wings, etc.,' the very same way in which ID is defined in the subsequent published versions."[18]

The court also noted that "the sole argument Defendants made to distinguish creationism from ID was their assertion that the term 'creationism' applies only to arguments based on the Book of Genesis, a young earth, and a catastrophic Noaich flood; however, substantial evidence established that this is only one form of creationism, including the chart that was distributed to the Board Curriculum Committee, as will be described below."[19]

Responding to the Dover school board's disclaimer of the religious nature of their resolution, the *Dover* court noted that the Supreme Court (in *Edwards*) stated that: "Families entrust public schools with the education of their children, but condition their trust on the understanding that

16. Ibid.
17. Davis and Kenyon, *Of Pandas and People* (see note 9, above).
18. *Kitzmiller v. Dover Area School District,* 400 F. Supp. 2d 707 (M.D. Pa. 2005).
19. Ibid.

the classroom will not purposely be used to advance religious views that may conflict with the private beliefs of the student and his or her family," and added, "Students in such institutions are impressionable and their attendance is involuntary." Further, the court noted, "the overwhelming evidence at trial established that ID is a religious view, a mere re-labeling of creationism, and not a scientific theory. As the Fifth Circuit Court of Appeals held in *Freiler,* an educator's 'reading of a disclaimer that not only disavows endorsement of educational materials but also juxtaposes that disavowal with an urging to contemplate alternative religious concepts implies School Board approval of religious principles.'" Further, "encouraging students to keep an open mind and explore alternatives to evolution, it offers no scientific alternative; instead, the only alternative offered is an inherently religious one, namely, ID." So, "a thorough review of the disclaimer's plain language therefore conveys a strong message of religious endorsement to an objective Dover ninth grade student." In summary, the court claimed that "the disclaimer singles out the theory of evolution for special treatment, misrepresents its status in the scientific community, causes students to doubt its validity without scientific justification, presents students with a religious alternative masquerading as a scientific theory, directs them to consult a creationist text as though it were a science resource, and instructs students to forego scientific inquiry in the public school classroom and instead to seek out religious instruction elsewhere." Furthermore, "as Drs. Alters and Miller testified, introducing ID necessarily invites religion into the science classroom as it sets up what will be perceived by students as a 'God-friendly' science, the one that explicitly mentions an intelligent designer, and that the 'other science,' evolution, takes no position on religion."[20] The same logic was applied to what an objective Dover parent or citizen might believe, and the conclusion was the same—ID is religion.

"Intelligent Design Theory Is Not Science"

Not only did the *Dover* court conclude that ID was religion, they also insisted that it was not science. They wrote, "After a searching review of

20. Ibid.

the record and applicable case law, we find that while ID arguments may be true, a proposition on which the Court takes no position, ID is not science." Why? "We find that ID fails on three different levels, any one of which is sufficient to preclude a determination that ID is science." First, "ID violates the centuries-old ground rules of science by invoking and permitting supernatural causation." Second, "the argument of irreducible complexity, central to ID, employs the same flawed and illogical contrived dualism that doomed creation science in the 1980's." Third, "ID's negative attacks on evolution have been refuted by the scientific community. As we will discuss in more detail below, it is additionally important to note that ID has failed to gain acceptance in the scientific community, it has not generated peer-reviewed publications, nor has it been the subject of testing and research."[21]

"Science Is Limited to Natural Causes"

In support of their first conclusion, the court depended on naturalistic evolutionist testimony that claimed "that since the scientific revolution of the 16th and 17th centuries, science has been limited to the search for natural causes to explain natural phenomena.... This revolution entailed the rejection of the appeal to authority, and by extension, revelation, in favor of empirical evidence.... Since that time period, science has been a discipline in which testability, rather than any ecclesiastical authority or philosophical coherence, has been the measure of a scientific idea's worth." They added, "In deliberately omitting theological or 'ultimate' explanations for the existence or characteristics of the natural world, science does not consider issues of 'meaning' and 'purpose' in the world. ..." And "while supernatural explanations may be important and have merit, they are not part of science."[22]

"Science Is Empirical and Testable"

The court admitted that "this self-imposed convention of science, which limits inquiry to testable, natural explanations about the natural world, is referred to by philosophers as 'methodological naturalism'

21. Ibid.
22. Ibid.

and is sometimes known as the scientific method. . . . Methodological naturalism is a 'ground rule' of science today which requires scientists to seek explanations in the world around us based upon what we can observe, test, replicate, and verify."[23]

They cited the National Academy of Sciences (NAS) as "in agreement that science is limited to empirical, observable and ultimately testable data." It is restricted to what "can be inferred from the confirmable data—the results obtained through observations and experiments that can be substantiated by other scientists. Anything that can be observed or measured is amenable to scientific investigation. Explanations that cannot be based upon empirical evidence are not part of science."[24]

"INTELLIGENT DESIGN IS A 'SCIENCE STOPPER'"

The court concluded: "This rigorous attachment to 'natural' explanations is an essential attribute to science by definition and by convention. . . . We are in agreement with Plaintiffs' lead expert Dr. Miller, that from a practical perspective, attributing unsolved problems about nature to causes and forces that lie outside the natural world is a 'science stopper.'" For "once you attribute a cause to an untestable supernatural force, a proposition that cannot be disproven, there is no reason to continue seeking natural explanations as we have our answer. . . .

"ID is predicated on supernatural causation, as we previously explained and as various expert testimony revealed. . . . ID takes a natural phenomenon and, instead of accepting or seeking a natural explanation, argues that the explanation is supernatural. Further support for the conclusion that ID is predicated on supernatural causation is found in [the ID reference book *Of Pandas and People,* which states]: 'Darwinists object to the view of intelligent design *because it does not give a natural cause explanation* of how the various forms of life started in the first place. Intelligent design means that various forms of life began abruptly, through an intelligent agency.' . . . Stated another way, ID posits that

23. Ibid.
24. Ibid.

animals did not evolve naturally through evolutionary means but were created abruptly by a non-natural, or supernatural, designer."[25]

"ID ATTEMPTS TO CHANGE THE GROUND RULES OF SCIENCE"

The court stated: "It is notable that [the] defense experts' own mission, which mirrors that of the IDM itself, is to change the ground rules of science to allow supernatural causation of the natural world, which the Supreme Court in *Edwards* and the court in *McLean* correctly recognized as an inherently religious concept." And "Professor Behe admitted that his broadened definition of science, which encompasses ID, would also embrace astrology. . . ." Also ID Professor Minnich acknowledged, "that for ID to be considered science, the ground rules of science have to be broadened to allow consideration of supernatural forces." William Dembski, an ID leader, "proclaims that science is ruled by methodological naturalism and argues that this rule must be overturned if ID is to prosper." Indeed, the ID *"Wedge Document* acknowledges as 'Governing Goals' to 'defeat scientific materialism and its destructive moral, cultural and political legacies' and to 'replace materialistic explanations with the theistic understanding that nature and human beings are created by God.'"[26]

"ALL MAJOR SCIENTIFIC ORGANIZATIONS DENY THAT ID IS SCIENCE"

"Notably, every major scientific association that has taken a position on the issue of whether ID is science has concluded that ID is not, and cannot be considered as such." The most prestigious one (NAS) views ID as follows: "Creationism, intelligent design, and other claims of supernatural intervention in the origin of life or of species are not science because they are not testable by the methods of science. These claims subordinate observed data to statements based on authority, revelation, or religious belief." NAS goes on to claim that "documentation offered in support of these claims is typically limited to the special publications

25. Ibid.
26. Ibid.

of their advocates. These publications do not offer hypotheses subject to change in light of new data, new interpretations, or demonstration of error. This contrasts with science, where any hypothesis or theory always remains subject to the possibility of rejection or modification in the light of new knowledge."[27]

"ID Is Based on a False Dichotomy"

The court contended that "ID is at bottom premised upon a false dichotomy, namely, that to the extent evolutionary theory is discredited, ID is confirmed. (5:41 (Pennock)). This argument is not brought to this Court anew, and in fact, the same argument, termed 'contrived dualism' in *McLean*, was employed by creationists in the 1980's to support 'creation science.' The court in McLean noted the 'fallacious pedagogy of the two model approach' and that 'in efforts to establish "evidence" in support of creation science, the defendants relied upon the same false premise as the two model approach . . . all evidence which criticized evolutionary theory was proof in support of creation science.'" . . . "However, we believe that arguments against evolution are not arguments for design. Expert testimony revealed that just because scientists cannot explain today how biological systems evolved does not mean that they cannot, and will not, be able to explain them tomorrow. (2:36-37 (Miller)). As Dr. Padian aptly noted, 'Absence of evidence is not evidence of absence.'" The court added, "Just because scientists cannot explain every evolutionary detail does not undermine its validity as a scientific theory as no theory in science is fully understood."[28]

"Irreducible Complexity Does Not Prove ID"

The court then attacked the very heart of the ID movement—the argument from irreducible complexity. It claimed that Behe admits making a mistake in reasoning that he has not yet corrected. And Drs. Miller and Padian testified, "Professor Behe's concept of irreducible complexity depends on ignoring ways in which evolution is known to occur." Just because an organism does not function in the same way

27. Ibid.
28. Ibid.

without all the parts does not mean it cannot operate in another way. "For example, in the case of the bacterial flagellum, removal of a part may prevent it from acting as a rotary motor. However, Professor Behe excludes, by definition, the possibility that a precursor to the bacterial flagellum functioned not as a rotary motor, but in some other way, for example as a secretory system." So, "the qualification on what is meant by 'irreducible complexity' renders it meaningless as a criticism of evolution. . . . In fact, the theory of evolution proffers exaptation as a well-recognized, well-documented explanation for how systems with multiple parts could have evolved through natural means. Exaptation means that some precursor of the subject system had a different, select-able function before experiencing the change or addition that resulted in the subject system with its present function. . . . The NAS has rejected Professor Behe's claim for irreducible complexity by using the following cogent reasoning:

> "'Structures and processes that are claimed to be "irreducibly" complex typically are not on closer inspection. . . . The evolution of complex molecular systems can occur in several ways. Natural selection can bring together parts of a system for one function at one time and then, at a later time, recombine those parts with other systems of components to produce a system that has a different function. Genes can be duplicated, altered, and then amplified through natural selection. The complex biochemical cascade resulting in blood clotting has been explained in this fashion.'"[29]

"THE ALLEGED POSITIVE ARGUMENT FOR DESIGN FAILS"

As for the alleged "positive argument" for design in which the "pur-poseful arrangement of parts" is alleged to prove an intelligent designer, the court retorted: "Expert testimony revealed that this inductive ar-gument is not scientific and as admitted by Professor Behe, [a natural cause] can never be ruled out." Indeed, the argument is based upon an analogy to human design.

29. Ibid.

But "Professor Behe testified that the strength of the analogy depends upon the degree of similarity entailed in the two propositions; however, if this is the test, ID completely fails." For, "Unlike biological systems, human artifacts do not live and reproduce over time. They are non-replicable, they do not undergo genetic recombination, and they are not driven by natural selection." Further, in "human artifacts, we know the designer's identity, human, and the mechanism of design, as we have experience based upon empirical evidence that humans can make such things, as well as many other attributes including the designer's abilities, needs, and desires." The court concluded "that the only attribute of design that biological systems appear to share with human artifacts is their complex appearance, i.e. if it looks complex or designed, it must have been designed. . . .This inference to design based upon the appearance of a 'purposeful arrangement of parts' is a completely subjective proposition, determined in the eye of each beholder and his/her viewpoint concerning the complexity of a system." Accordingly, "the purported positive argument for ID does not satisfy the ground rules of science which require testable hypotheses based upon natural explanations. . . . ID is reliant upon forces acting outside of the natural world, forces that we cannot see, replicate, control or test, which have produced changes in this world. While we take no position on whether such forces exist, they are simply not testable by scientific means and therefore cannot qualify as part of the scientific process or as a scientific theory."[30]

"GAPS IN EVOLUTIONARY THEORY DON'T HELP ID"

The court concluded that proponents supported their assertion that evolutionary theory cannot account for "real gaps in scientific knowledge, which indisputably exist in all scientific theories," but also that they "[misrepresented] well-established scientific propositions." Beside this, "an overwhelming number of scientists, as reflected by every scientific association that has spoken on the matter, have rejected the ID proponents' challenge to evolution. Moreover, . . . Dr. Miller . . .

30. Ibid.

provided unrebutted testimony that evolution, including common descent and natural selection, is 'overwhelmingly accepted' by the scientific community and that every major scientific association agrees. (1:94–100 (Miller))." What is more, the court claimed that the ID text *Of Pandas and People* contained several distortions of evolution. "First, [it] misrepresents the 'dominant form of understanding relationships' between organisms, namely, the tree of life, represented by classification determined via the method of cladistics. . . ." Second, [it] "misrepresents 'homology,' the 'central concept of comparative biology,' that allowed scientists to evaluate comparable parts among organisms for classification purposes for hundreds of years. Third, *Pandas* fails to address the well-established biological concept of exaptation, which involves a structure changing function, such as fish fins evolving fingers and bones to become legs for weight-bearing land animals. . . . Finally, Dr. Padian's unrebutted testimony demonstrates that *Pandas* distorts and misrepresents evidence in the fossil record about pre-Cambrian-era fossils, the evolution of fish to amphibians, the evolution of small carnivorous dinosaurs into birds, the evolution of the mammalian middle ear, and the evolution of whales from land animals.

"In addition to Dr. Padian, Dr. Miller also testified that [ID's] treatment of biochemical similarities between organisms is 'inaccurate and downright false' and explained how *Pandas* misrepresents basic molecular biology concepts to advance design theory. . . . In addition, Dr. Miller refuted *Pandas'* claim that evolution cannot account for new genetic information and pointed to more than three dozen peer-reviewed scientific publications showing the origin of new genetic information by evolutionary processes.

"A final indicator of how ID has failed to demonstrate scientific warrant is the complete absence of peer-reviewed publications supporting the theory. Expert testimony revealed that the peer review process is 'exquisitely important' in the scientific process. It is a way for scientists to write up their empirical research and to share the work with fellow experts in the field, opening up the hypotheses to study, testing, and criticism."[31]

31. Ibid.

The Court's Conclusion

Finally, the *Dover* court concluded: "After this searching and careful review of ID as espoused by its proponents, as elaborated upon in submissions to the Court, and as scrutinized over a six week trial, we find that ID is not science and cannot be adjudged a valid, accepted scientific theory as it has failed to publish in peer-reviewed journals, engage in research and testing, and gain acceptance in the scientific community. ID, as noted, is grounded in theology, not science. Accepting for the sake of argument its proponents', as well as Defendants' argument that to introduce ID to students will encourage critical thinking, it still has utterly no place in a science curriculum."[32]

Application of the Lemon Test to the ID Policy

The court continued, "Although we have found that Defendants' conduct conveys a strong message of endorsement of the Board members' particular religious view, pursuant to the endorsement test, the better practice in this Circuit is for this Court to also evaluate the challenged conduct separately under the *Lemon* test."[33]

THE THREE PRONGS OF THE *LEMON* TEST

As articulated by the Supreme Court, the *Lemon* test determines that something "violates the Establishment Clause of the First Amendment if: (1) it does not have a secular purpose; (2) its principal or primary effect advances or inhibits religion; or (3) it creates an excessive entanglement of the government with religion. . . . As the *Lemon* test is disjunctive, either an improper purpose or an improper effect renders the ID Policy invalid under the Establishment Clause."[34]

After going over much of the same material and argumentation, the court concluded that "Defendants Presented No Convincing Evidence that They were Motived [*sic*] by Any Valid Secular Purpose." Indeed,

32. Ibid.
33. Ibid.
34. Ibid.

"their asserted purposes are a sham, and they are accordingly unavailing, for the reasons that follow.

"We initially note that the Supreme Court has instructed that while courts are 'normally deferential to a State's articulation of a secular purpose, it is required that the statement of such purpose be sincere and not a sham.' (*Edwards*).... "Moreover, Defendants' asserted secular purpose of improving science education is belied by the fact that most if not all of the Board members who voted in favor of the biology curriculum change conceded that they still do not know, nor have they ever known, precisely what ID is. To assert a secular purpose against this backdrop is ludicrous.

"Finally, although Defendants have unceasingly attempted in vain to distance themselves from their own actions and statements, which culminated in repetitious, untruthful testimony, such a strategy constitutes additional strong evidence of improper purpose under the first prong of the *Lemon* test."

Thus, "any asserted secular purposes by the Board are a sham and are merely secondary to a religious objective."

Accordingly, "we find that the secular purposes claimed by the Board amount to a pretext for the Board's real purpose, which was to promote religion in the public school classroom, in violation of the Establishment Clause."[35]

THE COURT'S CONCLUSION

The court concluded: "Although Defendants' actions have failed to pass constitutional muster under the endorsement test and pursuant to the purpose prong of *Lemon,* thus making further inquiry unnecessary, we will briefly address the final *Lemon* prong relevant to our inquiry, which is effect, in the interest of completeness.... Moreover, because the *Lemon* effect test largely covers the same ground as the endorsement test, we will incorporate our extensive factual findings and legal conclusions made under the endorsement analysis by reference here, in accordance with Third Circuit practice." ...

35. Ibid.

"Since ID is not science, the conclusion is inescapable that the only real effect of the ID Policy is the advancement of religion. . . . Second, the disclaimer read to students 'has the effect of implicitly bolstering alternative religious theories of origin by suggesting that evolution is a problematic theory even in the field of science.'" So, "the effect of Defendants' actions in adopting the curriculum change was to impose a religious view of biological origins into the biology course, in violation of the Establishment Clause."[36]

In an aggressive, wide-reaching, and final conclusion the court declared that, "The proper application of both the endorsement and *Lemon* tests to the facts of this case makes it abundantly clear that the Board's ID Policy violates the Establishment Clause. In making this determination, we have addressed the seminal question of whether ID is science. We have concluded that it is not, and moreover that ID cannot uncouple itself from its creationist, and thus religious, antecedents.

"Both Defendants and many of the leading proponents of ID make a bedrock assumption which is utterly false. Their presupposition is that evolutionary theory is antithetical to a belief in the existence of a supreme being and to religion in general. Repeatedly in this trial, Plaintiffs' scientific experts testified that the theory of evolution represents good science, is overwhelmingly accepted by the scientific community, and that it in no way conflicts with, nor does it deny, the existence of a divine creator.

"To be sure, Darwin's theory of evolution is imperfect. However, the fact that a scientific theory cannot yet render an explanation on every point should not be used as a pretext to thrust an untestable alternative hypothesis grounded in religion into the science classroom or to misrepresent well-established scientific propositions.

"The citizens of the Dover area were poorly served by the members of the Board who voted for the ID Policy. It is ironic that several of these individuals, who so staunchly and proudly touted their religious convictions in public, would time and again lie to cover their tracks and disguise the real purpose behind the ID Policy."[37]

36. Ibid.
37. Ibid.

The court added, "With that said, we do not question that many of the leading advocates of ID have bona fide and deeply held beliefs which drive their scholarly endeavors. Nor do we controvert that ID should continue to be studied, debated, and discussed. As stated, our conclusion today is that it is unconstitutional to teach ID as an alternative to evolution in a public school science classroom."

They added, "Those who disagree with our holding will likely mark it as the product of an activist judge. If so, they will have erred as this is manifestly not an activist Court. Rather, this case came to us as the result of the activism of an ill-informed faction on a school board, aided by a national public interest law firm eager to find a constitutional test case on ID, who in combination drove the Board to adopt an imprudent and ultimately unconstitutional policy. The breathtaking inanity of the Board's decision is evident when considered against the factual backdrop which has now been fully revealed through this trial. The students, parents, and teachers of the Dover Area School District deserved better than to be dragged into this legal maelstrom, with its resulting utter waste of monetary and personal resources."

And "to preserve the separation of church and state mandated by the Establishment Clause of the First Amendment to the United States Constitution, and Art. I, § 3 of the Pennsylvania Constitution, we will enter an order permanently enjoining Defendants from maintaining the ID Policy in any school within the Dover Area School District, from requiring teachers to denigrate or disparage the scientific theory of evolution, and from requiring teachers to refer to a religious, alternative theory known as ID. We will also issue a declaratory judgment that Plaintiffs' rights under the Constitutions of the United States and the Commonwealth of Pennsylvania have been violated by Defendants' actions. Defendants' actions in violation of Plaintiffs' civil rights as guaranteed to them by the Constitution of the United States and 42 U.S.C. § 1983 subject Defendants to liability with respect to injunctive and declaratory relief, but also for nominal damages and the reasonable value of Plaintiffs' attorneys' services and costs incurred in vindicating Plaintiffs' constitutional rights."[38]

38. Ibid.

A Response to the *Dover* Court's Ruling

Refutation of the ruling is left for the next chapter. Here it will suffice to summarize the major points of the ruling and to challenge some major premises. First, some general comments.

General Comments

(1) This 139-page ruling (book?) is a tour de force for evolution.[39] (2) It is wide-ranging, going well beyond what was necessary for the court to do in this particular case. (3) It ruled not only that the Dover school board policy as mandated was unconstitutional, but that teaching ID in any form is a violation of the First Amendment. (4) It also ruled, unlike the Supreme Court *Edwards* case, that ID and so-called "scientific creation" is inherently religious and, thereby, forbidden to be taught by any science teacher in a public school science class. It is in fact an ID creationist's worst nightmare. If left standing, the *Dover* ruling will forever squelch the teaching of creation in any form in public school science classes.[40]

Specific Comments

Some specific points also need to be briefly stated. Again, no attempt will be made here to refute any of these claims. For this, see chapter 8.

---

39. According to a report in *World* magazine, the wording of the *Dover* ruling relied heavily on a document submitted to the court by the ACLU (see Mark Bergin, "Aped Decision," *World,* December 23, 2006).

40. "Meanwhile, back in Ohio, the Darwinists had not given up in their relentless efforts to eliminate the critical analysis of evolution from that state's science curriculum. In February 2006, the Ohio State Board of Education finally caved in to the Darwinists and deleted it. The move was spearheaded by board member Martha Wise, who reportedly once claimed that God told her that critical analysis of evolution was wrong. On February 22, 2006, she wrote: 'I believe in God the creator. I believe in freedom, I believe in America, and the state of Ohio, and the Republican Party, fiscal conservatism, fairness, and honesty. These values guided me last week to lead the Ohio Board of Education to remove creationism from our state's Science Standards'" (Jonathan Wells, *The Politically Incorrect Guide to Darwinism and Intelligent Design* [Washington, D.C.: Regnery, 2006], 153–154).

First, the *Dover* court defined science in strictly naturalistic terms. Any reference to or implication of a supernatural cause is strictly unscientific as defined by the court. The only way intelligent design could possibly be justified is to change the very ground rules of science, which demand that only natural causes be considered. Another point, to be explained in chapter 8, is that one and the same object—the first cause—can be the object of both religious devotion and scientific exploration. If it is presented exclusively as the latter, it is not a violation of the First Amendment. By not recognizing this distinction, the *Dover* court has in effect established naturalistic religions.

Second, the *Dover* court considered the ID proponents' use of more neutral sounding terms like "cause," "first cause," "intelligent cause," and "designer" to be merely a guise for the more obviously religious term "God." Given this, and the historic use of "Creator," there is no reason we should forsake this venerable term, which has been part of our national legal heritage from the beginning.

Third, the *Dover* decision forces the supernatural/natural debate into the open. Supernaturalism is considered the enemy of science. It is in their words a "science-stopper." Thus, for the *Dover* court, any attempt to promote ID is an attack on science. This, of course, is not true, but is a confusion of the two kinds of science, empirical and forensic (see chapter 8).

Fourth, the court claims that ID cannot be separated from its mother "scientific creationism," which repeatedly has been found unconstitutional in the courts (*Epperson* [1968], *McLean* [1982], and *Edwards* [1987]). Both have been pronounced "inherent[ly] religious" because of their inference of a supernatural creator into the natural domain of science. As we shall see (chapter 8), even if true, this does not mean that either one or both of these approaches to origins should not be taught. However, scientific creationism and ID are *not* identical, as was shown earlier (introduction) and will be demonstrated in the section immediately following (in the FTE response).

Fifth, the concept of irreducible complexity, which is at the very heart of the ID proposal, was challenged by the court, which agreed with the evolutionists' arguments that apparent complex design can be explained on purely naturalistic grounds.

Sixth, the widely used ID book *Of Pandas and People* was singled out for condemnation on the grounds that it was not only bad science but also inherently religious. This would seem to mean its use would be forbidden under any conditions in a public school science class. Thankfully, this was only a local decision and has not been ratified by the Supreme Court.

Seventh, there is nothing contrived about positing only two basic views of origins. There are only two views on each point of origin (see appendix 6), and what argues for one, argues against the other. Besides this, there is positive evidence for creation (see chapter 8).

In short, it is hard to conceive of how things could have gone worse for the creationist cause in public school science classes than it did in the *Dover* case.

Response of the Foundation for Thought and Ethics (FTE)

The publishers of the book *Of Pandas and People* attempted unsuccessfully by way of an amicus (friend of the court) brief to salvage their text from the wrath of the *Dover* court. Here is their own summary of their brief:

> Plaintiffs attack the theory of intelligent design as a form of creationism, and urge this Court to proscribe even its mention in public school science classes. They do so based in part on a false characterization of the early intelligent design textbook *Of Pandas and People* ("*Pandas*"), which has been designated as a resource for students in the Dover Area School District. Plaintiffs' claims against *Pandas* rest on (1) a false equivalence of intelligent design and "creationism"; (2) a reliance on the *post hoc, ergo propter hoc* fallacy, assuming that because *Pandas* followed *Edwards* it was a result of it; and (3) an abandonment of ordinary textual interpretation in favor of language that was abandoned in the final draft of the book. Moreover, the fixation on *Pandas* ignores the rapid progress in the scholarship of intelligent design theorists since its publication.
>
> First, intelligent design, as presented in *Pandas,* differs from "creationism" in methodology and propositional content. With regard to methodology, courts have recognized that creationism bases its claims

upon faith, doctrine, or religious scripture. Yet *Pandas* offers a scientific theory of intelligent design which makes its claims based on empirical evidence and scientific methods. With regard to propositional content, the Supreme Court has recognized that creationism entails religious beliefs in a "supernatural creator." Yet *Pandas* advocates a theory of intelligent design which is conceptually distinct from creationism in that it does not address religious questions such as the identity of the designer, nor does it speculate about the existence of a supernatural creator. *Pandas'* claims are empirically based and do not go beyond what can be inferred through scientific investigation.

Second, plaintiffs present a misleading portrait of the historical record by suggesting that the scientific debate over design in nature originated with Biblical "creationism" or as an effort to circumvent the ruling in *Edwards v. Aguillard*. The debate over whether design is empirically detectable began with ancient Greek and Roman philosophers. Moreover, scientists and natural philosophers contemporary with Darwin debated whether nature displays evidence of design. Instead of being considered the descendant of twentieth-century Biblical "creationism," the current theory of "intelligent design" is most accurately understood as the revival and extension of a longstanding intellectual tradition within Western science and natural philosophy.

Third, plaintiffs place inappropriate reliance on what they claim is creationist language in early drafts of *Pandas* to establish the "true meaning" of the book. With regard to this case, only actions of the school board or perceptions of the students are relevant to the constitutionality of the school board's policy, and pre-publication drafts of *Pandas* are irrelevant to either question. Additionally, early drafts of *Pandas* which used the term "creation" made clear that "there is no basis in uniform experience for going from nature to the supernatural." *Pandas* authors eventually concluded that the term "creation" did not accurately convey their meaning, and therefore utilized the term, "intelligent design," that did.

Finally, Amicus observes that the modern theory of intelligent design does not rely upon *Pandas* as authoritative. Written on a high school level and published in its first edition more than 15 years ago, *Pandas* has been superseded by a host of significant academic monographs and science journal articles explicating the contemporary theory of intelligent design. Accordingly, the substantive content of intelligent design today should be ascertained primarily through the scholarship produced by scientists and other scholars supportive of intelligent design, not the content of an early textbook, or its unpublished drafts.[41]

Clearly, the noble attempt of FTE to put distance between themselves and their forerunner, "creation science," did not work. There are several reasons for this: historical, legal, and logical. *Historically,* the ID movement is seen in continuity with the creation movement. *Legally,* the courts have depended heavily on precedent cases (*stare decisis*). *Logically,* creation implies a creator and design implies a designer. So, it is difficult to totally disassociate the two. There is also a problem *tactically.* By making ID more general and devoid of any implication of a supernatural creator, ID proponents risk a hollow victory, if any, and fall prey to the long-standing evolutionists' claim that only natural causes (i.e., those inside the universe) count as scientific. But this kind of metaphysical and/or methodological naturalism is the very thing the ID movement was designed to avoid from the beginning.[42] As we testified in *McLean* (see chapter 3) and show below (see chapter 8), there is no justifiable reason to avoid use of terms like "creator" or admission of the implications of a "supernatural" creator, if the evidence calls for it. These are not inherently religious concepts, as expert testimony, legal history, and constitutional analysis reveal (see chapter 6).

Is There Any Light at the End of the Tunnel?

In the light of *Dover,* is there any hope for getting court approval for teaching creation science or ID in public schools? Yes, there is hope, but it is dim in view of the long series of court cases against creation and ID. There are significant obstacles to overcome in order to pave the way for future victories for creation in the courts. Just how to do this is the subject of our next two chapters.

41. See http://www.discovery.org/scripts/viewDB/filesDB-download.php?command=download&id=648.
42. See Phillip Johnson, *Darwin on Trial* (Washington, D.C.: Regnery, 1991).

8

Should Creation Be Taught as Science in Public Schools?

Introduction

Two main reasons have been given by the courts for not allowing the teaching of creation alongside evolution in public school science classes: (1) Creation is not science and, therefore, has no more place in a science class than does astrology, the flat earth view,[1] or the demon theory of sickness. (2) Creation and intelligent design (hereafter ID)[2] are essentially religious and, therefore, violate the First Amendment prohibition against establishing religion. Before these objections can be addressed, we must define some crucial terms of the debate.

1. For a corrective to the myth that most medieval people believed in a "flat earth," see Jeffrey Burton Russell, *Inventing the Flat Earth: Columbus and Modern Historians* (Westport, Conn.: Praeger, 1997).

2. ID proponents add the word "intelligent" to "design" to indicate they are not referring to apparent design caused by natural processes (like waves make in the sand) but to real design that can be made only by an intelligent cause.

Definitions

Creation: For the purposes of this discussion "creation" or "ID,"[3] as many now call it, will be defined as it was in the *McLean* (1982) case: "'Creation science' means the scientific evidences for creation and inferences from these scientific evidences" *(McLean*, Section 4).

More specifically, ID has been described as follows:

1. The information needed for life is contained in a molecule known as DNA. This information can be analyzed with a field of science called information theory.
2. The complexity of life is a measure of the information in its DNA. Information and complexity are synonyms.
3. Natural selection does not create information. It only modifies existing information. Thus, new information must be created by genetic drift—random changes to DNA.
4. The odds associated with [the occurrence of] events in the past (like the origin and evolution of life) can be accurately determined using information and probability theory.
5. If the odds associated with [the occurrence of] the origin and evolution of life are too small, then design is implicated, and it may be inferred.[4]

In this chapter we will discuss whether the reasons given for rejecting the teaching of the scientific evidence for creation in public schools in *McLean* (1982), *Edwards* (1987), and *Dover* (2005) are insufficient and whether, therefore, creation or ID should be permitted in public schools.

3. Of course, intelligent design advocates have defined ID more broadly than creation advocates have typically defined creation, avoiding references to a Creator, creation, the age of the earth, and a flood. They prefer terms like design, Designer, and Intelligent Cause. The courts, nonetheless, see this as a thinly disguised form of creationism (see chapter 7). Also, some creationists distinguish their views from ID. See Stephen C. Meyer, "Intelligent Design Is Not Creationism," *Daily Telegraph,* January 28, 2006; and Henry Morris, "Intelligent Design and/or Scientific Creationism," at http://www.icr.org/article/2708/.

4. Stuart Pullen, *The Tenets of Intelligent Design* (Jan. 1, 2001), at http://www.theory-of-evolution.org/Introduction/design.htm.

It should be noted here that the term "creation" is used as a shorthand for presenting the scientific evidences for and reasonable inferences from creation, and the term "school" refers to its being presented in public school science classes. Further, "creation" does not imply that any religious implications should be drawn from this in these classes nor that anything but scientific evidence and reasonable inferences should be discussed. Likewise, private schools are not in view here, nor any other classes than science classes in public schools. Whether and how creation may be discussed in other classes and in other than public schools is not the topic under discussion here.[5] It is assumed also that terms like cause, first cause, primary cause, intelligent cause, designer, and creator are appropriate to use in connection with this discussion,[6] however references to religion, religious sources, prayer, devotion, commitment, and worship are not allowed since the latter have clear and direct religious connotations.

Further, "creation" is used with reference to intelligent intervention at any one or more of three points: (1) the origin of the universe, (2) the origin of first life, (3) the origin of new life forms. Those who hold an intelligent cause for only the first of these may be called "mere creationists," and those who hold all three may be called "full creationists," but all are creationists. And all should be able to provide scientific and rational arguments for their views.

Evolution: By "evolution" is meant the view of common ancestry whereby all higher forms of life evolved by purely natural processes, without intelligent intervention, from lower forms which came ultimately from one simple form of life. Naturalistic evolutionists also believe that this first life came into existence by spontaneous generation

5. It is wisely agreed by both sides that religious views of origins, properly balanced and objectively discussed, may be presented in non-science classes such as history, philosophy, or sociology.

6. As I pointed out in my testimony (see chapter 4), even the use of terms like "God" and "Supreme Being" need not violate the First Amendment unless one is called on to give religious devotion or worship to him. However, admittedly, these terms carry more religious baggage. Hence, tactically, it may be advisable to avoid them in the context of referring to an intelligent cause of the universe and first life in a science class.

from nonliving material. As Richard Dawkins put it, natural selection is a "Blind Watchmaker."[7]

"Evolution" is understood here as macro or large-scale evolution between different basic types or forms of life. In contrast to creation, which affirms a common *creator* of all basic forms of life, macroevolutionists believe in a common *ancestor* of all forms of life. Darwin's five tenets of evolution are accepted by most evolutionists: (1) Variation exists within members of the same species, which is a group of interbreeding animals or plants. (2) Variation can be inherited by parents passing on their traits to their offspring. (3) Animals and plants compete for limited resources like food, water, and shelter. (4) Natural selection is a direct result of the first three tenets. Since natural resources are limited, individuals with favorable traits are more likely to survive and reproduce. Because these individual(s) pass on favorable traits to their descendants, nature selects those with favorable characteristics and preserves them. This process is called natural selection or survival of the fittest. (5) Under the guidance of natural selection, simple life evolved into complex life. Darwin extrapolated that if small changes could occur by natural selection over short time, then large changes could occur over long time. Creationists object to the fifth tenet, noting that it is based on speculation and not observation.

Opposition by creationists to evolution in this general sense does not eliminate microevolution, which both views affirm. Microevolution refers to changes within basic forms of life on a small scale, such as the existence of a couple hundred different kinds of dogs, from the little Chihuahua to the Great Dane, which are all part of the canine family of animals. This kind of small-scale "evolution" is observable and repeatable and, hence, comes within the domain of empirical science in the present and, thus, is not part of the dispute; it is acceptable to both creationists and macroevolutionists. Creationism, therefore, as a theory is opposed only to macroevolution, or large-scale evolution

7. See Richard Dawkins, *The Blind Watchmaker: Why the Evidence of Evolution Reveals a Universe Without Design* (New York: Norton, 1996). Some theistic evolutionists are willing to posit God as the creator of first life but agree that naturalistic macroevolution took place from that point on.

from microbe to man. Hence, the term "evolution" in the following discussion is to be understood as macroevolution.

The term "evolution" covers more than just biological evolution. A naturalistic view of the origin of the universe is called "cosmic evolution." A naturalistic view of the origin of first life is called "chemical evolution." And the naturalistic view of the origin of new life forms is called "biological evolution." Again, scientific and rational arguments for all three of these kinds of evolution should be permitted in public schools, provided the evidence for the opposing view is also allowed.

A Response to Reasons Given for Not Teaching Creation

As we have seen in earlier chapters, the two basic reasons given by the courts for not allowing the teaching of creation are that it is not science and that it is religious. Both of these reasons have been used to exclude creation from the science curriculum in public schools. *McLean* (1982) used both, *Edwards* (1987) used only the latter, and *Dover* (2005) used both, though it defined science differently.

A Response to the Scientific Arguments Against Teaching Creation

The *McLean* (1982) court argued that creation is not science,[8] as did *Dover* (2005), though they defined "science" differently. This sentiment that creation is not science is commonly echoed in the scientific community.

"CREATION DOES NOT MEET THE CRITERIA OF SCIENCE"

The difficulty with this objection is in gaining a universally agreeable definition of science. Even *Dover* (2005) and *McLean* (1982) do not agree on the definition, and *Edwards* (1987) declined defining science in ruling on this point. *Dover* and *McLean* agree that science is observable and repeatable, and involves only natural causes. *McLean* added that it must also be tentative and falsifiable, but these latter two tests

8. See chapter 3 above for the details.

are clearly problematic since many evolutionists claim that evolution is a fact, and facts are not falsifiable. Yet evolutionists at *McLean* argued that all scientific views must be falsifiable (see chapter 3). Furthermore, both *Dover* and *McLean* are wrong in assuming that science about origin events must be observable and repeatable. Origin events are by nature unobserved and unrepeated past events. They can be approached only by way of forensic science, which uses the principles of causality and uniformity to reconstruct events we cannot observe. Likewise, this definition wrongly assumes, as some courts have, that only natural causes count as scientific explanations of events. However, many sciences use intelligent causes, for example cryptology, archaeology, and the SETI ("Search for Extra-terrestrial Intelligence") program. Why then should an intelligent cause be ruled out in origin science? Only an incurable commitment to naturalism (anti-supernaturalism) can account for this arbitrary misdefinition of a scientific approach to origins.

Even if some broad criterion like "testability" or confirmability is used, this objection fares no better since the sword cuts both ways. In the broad sense of an origin (forensic) science both creation and evolution are testable by whether they meet the principles of causality and uniformity. In a narrow sense of current empirical testability (that is, observable and repeatable), neither evolution nor creation is testable. Also, in this connection, there is a logical irony in the evolutionist's argument. Many contend that the creation or ID view is not testable, but they also claim to have tested it and found it false![9]

"NOTHING MAKES SENSE IN SCIENCE APART FROM EVOLUTION"

A common refrain in the courts is the claim by evolutionists that nothing makes sense in science apart from the theory of macroevolution. But if this were true then how did it happen that most major biological disciplines were begun either before Darwin or by scientists who rejected his theory? As Jonathan Wells aptly put it, "Why do Darwinists claim

9. Evolutionists Jerry Coyne, Russell Doolittle, and Kenneth Miller make this kind of claim about the ID argument from irreducible complexity. See Jonathan Wells, *The Politically Incorrect Guide to Darwinism and Intelligent Design* (Washington, D.C.: Regnery, 2006), 139.

that their hypothesis is indispensable to agriculture, when it was Darwin who needed farmers—not farmers who needed Darwin? . . . In what way is Darwinism indispensable to medicine, when the modern decline in infectious diseases resulted from public health measures and scientific disciplines that owe nothing to Darwin's theory?"[10]

In fact, a highly under-advertised fact is that Darwin opposed giving vaccinations, saying: "With savages, the weak in body or mind are soon eliminated; and those that survive commonly exhibit a vigorous state of health. We civilized men, on the other hand, do our utmost to check the process of elimination [by natural selection]; we build asylums for the imbecile, the maimed, and the sick; we institute poor laws; and our medical men exert their utmost skill to save the life of everyone to the last moment. There is reason to believe that vaccination has preserved thousands, who from a weak constitution would formerly have succumbed to small-pox. Thus the weak members of civilized societies propagate their kind."[11] Hence, Darwin himself admitted that his theory was opposed to public health.

The truth is that biology as an empirical science with all of its laws from which predictions can be made is completely understandable as such without any direct reference to speculations about how life may or may not have originated. Like the laws of physics and chemistry, things operate uniformly in biology and life goes on regardless of whether one is a theist, atheist, or pantheist. Speculations about worldview or origin do not change the law of gravity nor the laws of how life operates. And biological speculations that deal with origins (like evolution or creation) are not an empirical science. They work more like a forensic science and speak only to *how life got here*, not *how it operates* in the present. The present operation of life is the object of observation and repetition in the biological world. The study of this realm is the same no matter what theory of origins one has.

If anything, one can argue the reverse, namely, that assuming life was designed makes more sense in biology than assuming it is an accidental result of a "blind watchmaker." For as microbiology has shown, intelli-

10. Wells, *Politically Incorrect Guide,* 82.
11. Charles Darwin, *The Descent of Man,* in *On the Origin of Species and the Descent of Man,* vol. 49 of Great Books of the Western World (Chicago: University of Chicago Press, 1952), 323.

gent design is reflected in the irreducible and specified complexity in the natural world. This kind of order in the biological world is best explained by there being a mind behind it all. It can be argued that with this kind of assumption one can make more sense out of the biological world than without it. One example of this is the so-called vestigial organs, of which nearly two hundred were posited in Darwin's day. Assuming there was design for them, even when it was not known, had a greater heuristic value than assuming they were merely the products of chance. It prompted scientific investigations that have led to the discovery of a purpose for virtually all of these once-thought-useless organs supposedly left over from our evolutionary past.[12]

"CREATION IS REJECTED BY THE SCIENTIFIC COMMUNITY"

Another reason sometimes given for not teaching creation in schools is that it is rejected by the majority in the scientific community. But it is also true that evolution was once rejected by the majority in the scientific community. If minority views were not allowed a hearing, then students would never have heard about evolution in their schools. In fact, this is precisely what was argued at the 1925 *Scopes* trial (see chapter 1), when evolutionists' views were being excluded. Further, using current majority opinion to define science is tantamount to saying "science is what current scientists say it is." But this is simply to determine what is right by majority vote, and it will only add to an already painful history of unacceptable consequences. Science, of all disciplines, should have learned by now to tolerate minority views. In fact, virtually all scientific views now accepted by the majority of scientists were once minority views.[13] To do otherwise is to resort to some form of the fallacy of "cre-

12. See Jerry Bergman and George Howe, *"Vestigial Organs" Are Fully Functional: A History and Evaluation of the Vestigial Organ Origins Concept* (Kansas City: Creation Research Society Books, 1993).

13. The absence of peer review for creationists' literature is sometimes given as evidence that creationists' views are not credible science, but this is groundless for many reasons. First, virtually all the major science journals are biased against creationists' views. Second, creationists have published in "peer" journals that are open to creationists' views. Third, some ID literature (like that of Behe and Dembski) is found in peer journals.

dentialism" or "expertism." But real science does not have to do this; it can always provide evidence.

What is more, virtually all the founders of modern science were creationists. This includes Kepler, Pascal, Boyle, Newton, Faraday, Agassiz, Maxwell, Pasteur, and Kelvin. If creation is disallowed in our schools, then we have disregarded a large part of our intellectual heritage. Surely there is something incongruous about claiming that Kepler, Newton, and Pasteur were not scientific in their views about origins. It is a twisted logic for the children of modern science to disclaim the legitimacy of their own parentage. And it leads to the patent absurdity that, when it comes to scientific views about origins, the great founders of modern science would be barred from speaking in American public school science classes!

In addition, the kindred argument that most experts in the field reject creation and ID only reflects the weakness of the evolutionists' position. This resort to "credentialism" or "expertism" is not science; it is sociology. Real science never had to resort to this; it provides good evidence and good reasons for its views. As Orson Scott Card said, "expertism is 'the "trust us, you poor fools" defense.'"[14] Besides this, there are an increasing number of scientific scholars who reject Darwinian evolution. What is more, given the opposition to and suppression of creation by the evolution dominated scientific establishment, it is no surprise that creation is only a minority view. Wells lists numerous examples of suppression of creationists:

> The Darwinists who harassed Richard Sternberg at the Smithsonian; president Timothy White of the University of Idaho; Hector Avalos at Iowa State University; the school administrators who drove out Roger DeHart; Brian Leiter at the University of Texas; Paul Z. Myers at the University of Minnesota; Brian McEnnis, Steve Rissing, and Jeffrey McKee at Ohio State University; and the Mississippi University for Women Darwinists who dismissed Nancy Bryson—all public employees.[15]

14. Orson Scott Card, cited in Wells, *Politically Incorrect Guide,* 200.
15. Ibid., 190–191.

The truth is that articles attacking evolution are regularly rejected by the science journals, and articles defending evolution are regularly accepted. Until this bias changes we cannot expect creation to become more widely accepted in the scientific community.

Finally, allowing minority views is the very key to scientific progress. For science progresses by new ideas. Thus, to disbar minority scientific creationists from having a voice in school science classrooms is antithetical to the best procedure for scientific progress. If positing an intelligent cause was fruitful in the origin of science, why should it be barred in the development of science?

"Creation Is Not Observable or Repeatable"

Evolutionists often insist that creation is not science because it is not observable or repeatable. They believe that allowing creation to be taught in schools is like permitting the flat earth view to be taught. But this argument is based on a misunderstanding of two different kinds of science: empirical science and origin science. Admittedly, creation or ID is not an empirical science, which is based on the two basic principles of observation and repetition; but neither is macroevolution empirical science. The criterion of empirical science is that one's theories can be measured over against some observable and recurring pattern of events in the empirical world. But since both creation and macroevolution are unobserved events that would have occurred in the past and are not being repeated in the present, it follows that neither of them is an empirical science. So, if evolutionists insist on narrowly defining all science as empirical science, then they have eliminated macroevolution from the realm of science as well.

However, there is a widely used and broader sense of the word "science" which includes forensic science and other sciences dealing with the past. In origin science, as opposed to empirical science, we are dealing with past unobserved and unrepeated events for which we have evidence remaining in the present by which we can build a plausible scenario of what probably happened. Indeed, sometimes the forensic evidence (like fingerprints and DNA) is strong enough to convict a person of murder. And it is in this sense of the term "science" that both macroevolution and creation qualify as explanations of past events relating to origins. Dealing with past events has long been given the name "science" by scientists, as is evident from the sciences of paleontology, archaeology, and astrophysics. What is more, some of these sciences deal with intelligent causes—for example archaeology, cryptology, computer science, information theory, and SETI. If naturalistic evolutionists wish to eliminate all intelligent causes from science, then they must disavow these sciences as well.

The principles of origin science (like forensic science) cannot be based on direct observation and repetition of past events. Rather, they operate on two reasonable scientific premises: (1) *the principle of causality,* that every event must have an adequate cause; and (2) *the principle of uniformity,* which, applied to causes, affirms that causes of particular events in the past are like causes of like events in the present. For example, repeated observation informs us that it takes an intelligent being to produce an arrowhead from a piece of flint in the present. Hence, archaeologists do not hesitate to postulate an intelligent cause of similar arrowheads from the past. Likewise, when scientists look at the evidence that a single-cell organism has enough specified complexity in the genetic code to fill a thousand complete sets of encyclopedias,[16] they can reasonably postulate (by way of the principle of uniformity)[17] that an intelligent cause produced the first living cell. The insistence that one can allow an inference only to natural (non-intelligent) causes is like claiming that all those encyclopedia volumes must have happened by something like an explosion in a print shop! To insist on a natural cause in the face of evident marks of intelligence, is as absurd as a geology teacher insisting that her class must explain the presidential faces on Mt. Rushmore by some process of natural erosion!

Contrary to critics, the DNA argument is not an illegitimate or false analogy. For there is a mathematically identical letter sequence in both

16. According to Richard Dawkins, "Some species of the unjustly called 'primitive' amoebas have as much information in their DNA as 1,000 *Encyclopedia Britannicas,*" each of which has 30 volumes (*Blind Watchmaker,* 116).

17. Uniformity is not the same as uniformitarianism, for the latter begs the question by assuming that all causes are natural causes.

DNA and written language. In both cases, the effects have the same basic characteristics, namely, the obvious signs of being the product of a mind, such as irreducible complexity (e.g., the human eye), specified complexity (as in the DNA), or anticipatory design (such as revealed in the anthropic principle, which states that the universe has been purposed for the emergence of life in general and human life in particular since its inception). To rule this out as legitimate signs of intelligent causality is to rule out such things as archaeology, cryptology, and the SETI program. In fact, it is to deny the scientific principle of uniformity by which alone we can know the past.

"CREATION THEORY MAKES NO PREDICTIONS AS SCIENTIFIC THEORIES DO"

One of the characteristics of a scientific theory is that it makes verifiable predictions. But evolutionists claim that creation theory makes no such verifiable predictions. Hence, they insist that creation is not scientific. However, this conclusion is faulty for several reasons. First of all, it applies only to *empirical* science, which can be empirically tested by observation and repetition. But as we have seen, both macroevolution and creation are not empirical sciences. Hence, we should not expect verifiable observation and repetition to confirm either theory. Second, both macroevolution and creationist views of origins are not *predictive* views as such but *retrodictive* views. That is, they are theories about the past origin of the universe and life, not theories about the present operation of the universe or life on which you can make predictions about the future. Rather than speaking about the operation of the current empirical world, they work like a forensic science, using evidence remaining in the present by means of the principles of causality and uniformity to retrodict (project backwards) and speculate on what kind of cause produced the unobserved and unrepeated events of origin.

Of course, there is a sense in which origin scientists use present regularities to determine what kind of cause (natural or intelligent) is regularly associated with what kind of effect.[18] So, regularity serves

18. Some creationists speak of predicting what should be the case if the theory of evolution were true, such as finding more missing links. However, scientific predictions about the

as the *basis* for their understanding of uniformity, but the *object* of the inquiry of origin science, unlike in the case of empirical science, is not a regularity in the present but a singularity in the past (like the origin of the universe or the origin of life). For example, if repeatedly in the present only intelligent causes are known to produce the kind of letter sequence found in the genetic code, then it is reasonable to postulate an intelligent cause for the genetic code in the first living cell. The same is true of pottery and arrowheads. Since no natural causes (only intelligent ones) are known by repeated observation to produce specified complexity and irreducible complexity,[19] then it is not reasonable to posit natural causes of the origin of life or of new life forms.

"Creation Is a 'God-of-the-Gaps' View"

Naturalistic scientists often appeal to what they call a "God-of-the gaps" fallacy in creationists' thinking. They argue that the mere fact that we cannot now explain the origin of the eye or of blood-clotting mechanisms in a strictly naturalistic, step-by-step fashion does not mean that we should invoke a God to fill in the gap with a miracle. They point to numerous things for which science once had no natural explanation but now does, including meteors, eclipses, earthquakes, and the flight of the bumblebee. Hence, they believe that, given enough time, they will eventually be able to explain the gaps between non-life and life and the missing links between lower forms of life and higher ones.

But here again there is a serious flaw in their thinking, for several reasons.

First of all, it is not the *absence* of evidence that is the occasion of creationists inferring an intelligent cause of first life. Rather, it is the

---

behavior of nature itself are possible only if there is a recurring pattern from which scientists can make projections.

19. See Michael J. Behe, *Darwin's Black Box: The Biochemical Challenge to Evolution* (New York: Free Press, 1996): "No one at Harvard University, no one at the National Institutes of Health, no member of the National Academy of Sciences, no Nobel prize winner—no one at all can give a detailed account of how the cilium, or vision, or blood clotting, or any complex biochemical process might have developed in a Darwinian fashion. But we are here. All these things got here somehow; if not in a Darwinian fashion, then how?" (187). He added, "Other examples of irreducible complexity abound, including aspects of DNA reduplication, electron transport, telomere synthesis, photosynthesis, transcription regulation, and more" (160).

presence of evidence—very strong evidence—that calls for an intelligent cause. To use an analogy, it is not the absence of evidence for a natural cause for the Lincoln Memorial that leads visitors to believe there was a sculptor who fashioned it, but the presence of clear evidence that it was sculpted by someone (which is based in turn on their uniform experience that only intelligent beings can produce that kind of effect). Likewise, even casual examination of the Mona Lisa leads one to believe there was an artist who painted it.

At this point it is important to note that David Hume's principle of uniformity (based on customary conjunction) is the grounds for Paley's argument for design. For only the repeated connection of certain kinds of causes with certain kinds of effects leads us to posit an intelligent cause for them. By this means we can know that this same kind of effect in the past must have had an intelligent cause. So, the principle of uniformity leads us by positive evidence to infer an intelligent cause for first life, since it is the only kind of cause known in the present to produce these kinds of effects.

Second, while naturalistic evolutionists wrongly criticize creationists of a "God-of-the- gaps" fallacy when positing a creator of the universe or of life, they are themselves guilty of a "Nature-of-the-gap" view. For even when there is more than sufficient evidence that something is designed by an intelligent being, they assume that a natural cause (like "a blind watchmaker") must have produced it.

Again, it is not the absence of evidence about an assumed natural cause that leads us to conclude that an arrowhead or a sculpture of Lincoln had an intelligent cause. Rather, it is the *presence of strong evidence* that they were designed that leads us to posit an intelligent cause. Likewise, it is not the absence of evidence that a living cell had a natural cause but the presence of strong evidence that its unique specified complexity points to a designer that leads us to posit an intelligent cause. When such evidence is present, such as it is in the irreducible complexity of the human eye and other highly complex systems in living things, it is not a "God-of the-gaps" fallacy to infer an intelligent cause. On the contrary, it is a "Nature-of-the-gaps" fallacy that stubbornly resists divine involvement in creation.

What about the clear cases of "God-of-the-gap" thinking among creationists of the past? Even the great Sir Isaac Newton made such an error when he assumed that certain elliptical orbits needed a direct supernatural intervention to account for them. Others assumed divine intervention to explain meteors, eclipses, and earthquakes. These indeed were errors because they dealt with regularly observable phenomena in the empirical world. As such, scientists have every right to continue to seek a natural cause for them because they are part of operational or empirical science, which is explainable only by natural law. So, in this empirical sense of science, both evolutionists and creationists agree that only natural causes apply. However, origin events are not part of empirical science. They are unobserved and unrepeated past events and, as such, are not the subject of empirical science, which is limited to natural laws. Just as when a detective investigates a gunshot wound (which no one observed and which cannot be repeated), unrepeated origin events call for a forensic scientific approach based on the principles of causality and uniformity. And if, based on these principles, the events show evidence of intelligent design, then it is an unreasonable "Nature-of-the-gap" fallacy to assume against the evidence that they must have had a natural cause.

The same is true of irregular and unrepeated events in the present such as skywriting, a sand castle, or a code. No empirical scientist has a right to claim for these kinds of events a natural cause, for at least two reasons. First, they are not regular, observable, repeatable events in the natural world. Second, they show evidence of an intelligent cause, not a natural one. The domain of empirical science deals only with observable, repeatable, and regular events in the present. These events have only natural causes. Into this sphere no supernatural or intelligent causes are permitted. Empirical science is king of this domain. But neither macroevolutionary speculation about unobserved and unrepeated events of origin nor creation is part of empirical science.

"Creation Places 'No Trespassing' Signs on Scientific Research"

This leads to the next charge that naturalistic evolutionists level against creation, namely, that positing an intelligent cause of any event in the natural world is in effect posting a "No Trespassing" sign warning scientists not to investigate that area. In other words, they claim that positing an intelligent cause is a "science-stopper." It is the enemy of science, in that it forbids science to investigate and analyze events such as the origin of the universe, the origin of life, and new life forms. Several important points must be made in response to this objection.

First, scientists are not being stopped from observing or analyzing anything. They can examine or analyze anything they wish. However, unless it is an observable, regular, and repeatable event, they have no right to consider it an object of empirical science. And if it is an unobserved, unrepeated event of the past, then it does not qualify as empirical science. In that case, it must be treated as forensic science—for which both macroevolution and creation qualify.

Second, scientists are absolutely right in insisting that all observable and repeatable events in the natural world are the proper object of empirical science, which posits only natural causes. Failure to observe this has resulted in embarrassing errors in the past. Creationists have no right to assume that regularly recurring but unexplained events have a supernatural cause. Indeed, scientists have every right to assume the contrary, namely, that they have an unknown natural cause. Empirical science is king of this natural domain. But neither macroevolutionary speculation about unobserved and unrepeated events of origin nor creation is part of empirical science. So positing an intelligent cause of past events of origin is not a science-stopper—for two reasons. First, empirical science deals only with observable events in the present, not unobservable events of the past. Second, empirical science deals only with repeatable events which form a pattern (law) and from which predictions can be made about the future. Singular events as such are not the object of empirical science. So, positing an intelligent cause for them is not a science-stopper.

Third, scientists, however, have no right to assume that every unrepeated singularity in nature, past or present, must have a natural cause. This is the error of methodological naturalism. Anomalies and singularities may or may not have a natural cause. In fact, an anomaly as such has no scientific standing. An event must recur (or be recurrable[20]) in order to be subject to natural explanation. Unrepeated events of the past may not be assumed *ipso facto* to have a natural explanation.

Fourth, if there is strong evidence of design (such as specified or irreducible complexity) in these unobserved past singularities, then they should not be assumed to have had a natural cause. For example, as we have noted, we observe that one primitive cell has enough genetic information to fill a thousand complete sets of encyclopedias, and therefore we can conclude that the very first one-celled organism was similarly complex and therefore, similarly, was designed and should not be assumed to have had a natural cause.[21] To disallow creation as a possible scientific explanation is contrary to the very nature of science. Science as a method should be open to all viable explanations. To refuse alternative explanations based on scientific evidence, simply because they represent a minority view, is to stultify the progress of science. Indeed, as we have noted, all great scientific discoveries were minority opinions when they first appeared. So to reject the possibility of creationist explanations of origins is contrary to the very openness to which science as a method is committed.

"Science Allows Only Natural Causes"

A more frank way to state the basic scientific objection to creation and ID is that science allows only natural causes. For example, in 1999 *Nature* magazine published a letter from Scott Todd, an immunologist at Kansas State University, who said, "even if all the data point to an intelligent designer, such an hypothesis is excluded from science because it is not naturalistic."[22] No one stated this naturalistic presumption of science more clearly than Harvard's Richard Lewontin when he wrote:

Our willingness to accept scientific claims that are against common sense is the key to understanding the real struggle between science and the

20. Some events, like eclipses, recur only after long periods of time, but they are predictable and recurrable no matter the length of the interval.

21. Microbiologists have shown a mathematically identical letter sequence in a human language (known to have an intelligent cause) to that in DNA which is, therefore, rightly assumed to have an intelligent cause. See Herbert Yockey, *Journal of Theoretical Biology* 91 (1981).

22. Scott Todd, letter to the editor, *Nature* 401/6752 (September 30, 1999): 423.

supernatural. We take the side of science in spite of the patent absurdity of some of its constructs, . . . because *we have a prior commitment . . . to materialism*. It is not that the methods and institutions of science somehow compel us to accept a materialistic explanation of the phenomenal world, but, on the contrary, *that we are forced by our a priori adherence to material causes . . . .* Moreover, that materialism is absolute, for *we cannot allow a Divine Foot in the door.*[23]

Of course, there is a sense in which this naturalistic criterion of science is correct. For empirical science, unlike origin science, is limited to only natural causes because it deals with the observable and repeatable in the present. However, neither creation nor macroevolution is an empirical science since both deal with unobserved and unrepeated events of the past. Hence, it is a serious methodological mistake to limit causes of the past to natural ones.[24] Archaeology is a clear example of a science about the past that posits an intelligent cause. But present events in the natural world that involve a regular pattern that is observable and repeatable always have natural causes. Hence, this objection that "science allows only natural causes" does not apply to origin events such as both creationists and evolutionists posit.

There are many reasons for rejecting this objection. First of all, it begs the question in favor of naturalistic evolution by assuming that every event must have a natural cause. This is precisely what is to be proven, and it cannot be assumed to be true up front. Second, if by the term "science" an intelligent cause is excluded, then, as we have seen, it is contrary to many accepted disciplines of science. For archaeology, cryptology, computer science, and the SETI program all allow intelligent causes as explanations. Third, if "science" is meant to exclude a supernatural

23. Richard Lewontin, "Billions and Billions of Demons," *New York Review of Books* (January 9, 1997), 28 (emphasis added).

24. Even events observed in the present that are not regular may not be naturally caused. For the domain of empirical science is only the observable and *regular* events in the present. A singular, unrepeated event of the present does not provide a pattern (being only one event) on which science can project a law or make predictions. It must remain an anomaly (no-law) until either the naturalist can show it is part of a broader pattern or the supernaturalist can provide evidence it has a supernatural cause. But it simply begs the question to assume either kind of cause without further evidence.

cause, then it is contrary to history, logic, and the scientific evidence. For to exclude supernatural causation is at best circular reasoning and at worst intellectual dogmatism.

(1) It is contrary to the history of science, since this is exactly what most of the founders of modern science did, namely, they held that a creator of the universe and first life was a reasonable inference from the scientific evidence. This includes men like Galileo (astronomy), Newton (physics), Andreas Vesalius (anatomy), William Harvey (physiology), Francesco Redi (microbiology), John Ray (botany), Anton van Leeuwenhoek (microbiology), Robert Hooke (microbiology), Carolus Linnaeus (systematics), Lazzaro Spallanzani (reproductive biology), Caspar Friedrich Wolff (embryology), Georges Cuvier (paleontology), Karl Ernst von Baer (embryology), Richard Owen (comparative biology), Louis Agassiz (zoology), and Gregor Mendel (genetics).

(2) It is contrary to sound logic, for there are only two basic kinds of explanation, natural or supernatural, and eliminating any reasonable possibility is unscientific by its very nature since scientists should be open to whatever explanation the evidence suggests.

(3) It is also contrary to the evidence of modern astrophysics, which affirms (in the Big Bang theory) that the universe had a beginning. This is based on multiple lines of evidence, such as the Second Law of Thermodynamics, an expanding universe, the radiation echo of the same wavelength of that expected from a gigantic explosion, and Einstein's general theory of relativity. All of these evidences point to a beginning of the entire material space-time universe at a definite moment in the past. If this is so, then the universe must have had a supernatural cause (since it was beyond the natural universe). The reasoning behind this conclusion is fundamental logic: (a) Every event has a cause. (b) The whole physical universe had a beginning. (c) Therefore, the whole physical universe had a cause. And this cause cannot be a natural cause, since it is the cause of the whole natural world and hence is beyond the natural and is therefore by definition supernatural. As agnostic astronomer Robert Jastrow put it:

Astronomers now find they have painted themselves into a corner because they have proven, by their own methods, that *the world began abruptly in an act of creation* to which you can trace the seeds of every star, every planet, every living thing in this cosmos and on the earth. And they have found that all this happened as *a product of forces they cannot hope to discover.*[25]

Indeed, Jastrow went on to say, "that there are what I or anyone would call supernatural forces at work is now, I think, a scientifically proven fact."[26]

To rule out a supernatural cause of the universe is contrary to what Jastrow called "a scientifically proven fact." Even granting for some hyperbole in Jastrow's statement, why should the courts refuse to allow this kind of evidence to be presented in public school science classes? The evidence for the supernatural origin of the natural world is strong enough and the inference from it reasonable enough that it clearly qualifies as the kind of evidence for creation that should be allowed in public schools. Remember, "science" as applied to origin events was defined by Arkansas Act 590 as "the scientific evidences for creation and inferences from those scientific evidences" (Section 4 [a]).

"To Posit a Cause Beyond the Natural World Is Not Science but Philosophy"

Still, some scientists on both sides of this debate insist that once one infers a cause beyond the natural world, he has left the realm of science and entered into the realm of philosophy. In response, we note several things.

First, he certainly has left the realm of empirical science, but as we have shown, neither creation nor macroevolution is an object of empirical science. If empirical science alone qualifies as science, then neither is macroevolution science.

Second, it is not unscientific to ask the causal question wherever it may lead, as long as it is about what caused the physical world and physical life. The principle of causality has been at the basis of science from the very beginning. Francis Bacon, often called the father of modern

---

25. Robert Jastrow, "A Scientist Caught Between Two Faiths," interview by Bill Durbin, in *Christianity Today* (August 6, 1982), 15 (emphasis added).
    26. Ibid.

science, declared that true knowledge is "knowledge by causes."[27] Pierre Laplace spoke of "the evident principle that a thing cannot occur without a cause which produces it."[28] Even the great British skeptic David Hume declared: "I never asserted so absurd a proposition as that a thing could arise without a cause."[29] So, there is nothing unscientific about pursuing the causal question as far as it will go. Indeed, as already noted, the founders of almost every area of modern science felt that positing a creator of the world involved no contradiction with their respective discipline.

Further, naturalistic scientists do not hesitate to speak of a natural cause of the whole universe. Hence, they cannot legitimately reject creationists speaking of a non-natural cause of it, if this is where the evidence points.

Third, if positing a supernatural cause of the universe goes beyond the realm of science, then so does naturalistic evolution when it insists there is no such supernatural cause, for that too is a statement that goes beyond the natural world. In short, if the affirmation of a supernatural cause is not science, then the denial of a supernatural cause is not science. If one view is philosophical, then so is the other. And if this is the case, naturalistic evolution would have to be taken from the science class and put in the philosophy class. If this is the case, then creationists would happily accompany the evolutionists down the hall to the philosophy class. In the final analysis, it is a moot question whether one should call this reasonable inference from the evidence "origin science" or "philosophy." Either conclusion—that there is a supernatural cause, or that there is none—is a legitimate inference if one has the evidence, and we should not be forbidden the right to draw legitimate inferences in science class. Whatever one wishes to call it—origin science or philosophy—creation is not religion and should not be forbidden a place in our public schools. Or, if it is religion, then so is macroevolution religion and, hence, it too should be eliminated.

27. Francis Bacon, *Novum Organum* (New York: Colonial, 1899), 121.
28. Pierre Laplace, *A Philosophical Essay on Probabilities*, trans. A. I. Dale (New York: Springer-Verlag, 1995), 4.
29. David Hume, *The Letters of David Hume*, 2 vols., ed. J. Y. T. Greig (New York: Garland, 1983), 1:187.

"Creation Has Unacceptable Theological and Moral Implications"

Few evolutionists do more than hint at this objection, but it may be the bottom line in the opposition against teaching creation in the public schools. The fact is that serious theological and ethical implications have been drawn from both views, however reluctant each side is willing to admit it. As I said forthrightly in my "Scopes II" trial testimony (see chapter 4), "creation implies a creator." To which the evolutionist judge replied in his ruling that "the concept of a Creator is an inherently religious concept."[30] While this is not true, it is true that the concept of a Creator is compatible with certain religions, and religious implications can be and have been drawn from it. Some evolutionists have been frank to admit this. To repeat the above quote from Harvard atheist Lewontin, "We cannot allow a Divine Foot in the door." Why not? Because if it is a supernatural God who created the world and all that is in it, then most people recognize this has both religious and ethical implications. This is why agnostic Robert Jastrow spoke of the strange reaction of scientists to the Big Bang evidence that points to a supernatural cause of the universe. "There is a kind of religion in science. . . . This religious faith of the scientist is violated by the discovery that the world had a beginning under conditions in which the known laws of physics are not valid, and as a product of forces or circumstances we cannot discover. When that happens, the scientist has lost control."[31] This same reaction is manifest in the illogical reaction of otherwise rational scientific minds when it comes to questions of origin. J. W. N. Sullivan notes that "it became an acceptable doctrine that life never arises except from life. So far as the actual evidence goes, this is still the only possible conclusion. . . . But since this is a conclusion that seems to lead back to some supernatural creative act, it is a conclusion that scientific men find very difficult to accept."[32]

---

30. *McLean v. Arkansas Board of Education,* 529 F. Supp. 1255 (E.D. Ark. 1982).
31. Robert Jastrow, *God and the Astronomers* (New York: Norton, 1978), 113-114.
32. J. W. N. Sullivan, *The Limitations of Science* (New York: New American Library, 1956), 94.

Some atheists acknowledge the theological implications of their view. Daniel Dennett calls Darwinism a "universe acid" that "eats through just about every traditional concept"—especially those of God. Richard Dawkins said "Darwin made it possible to be an intellectually fulfilled atheist." William Provine calls Darwinism "the greatest engine of atheism ever invented" because it shows "no gods worth having exist." Stephen Gould declared that "[evolutionary] Biology took away our status as paragons created in the image of God." Darwinian paleontologist George Gaylord Simpson wrote: "Man is the result of a purposeless and natural process that did not have him in mind. He was not planned." Jacques Monod said that because "the mechanism of Darwinism is at last securely founded. . . . Man has to understand that he is a mere accident."[33] Clearly, before Darwin most men of science believed in God. Indeed, as noted above, the pioneers of almost every area of modern science believed in God.

Moral implications have also been drawn from both creation and evolution, and neither side seems willing to be frank about their opposition to the other based on this for fear that it would hurt their cause to admit it. If there is a God who created life and is in control of it, then the inference may be drawn from this that we have a moral duty to him and to the life he created. Our founding fathers made such a connection. *The Declaration of Independence* speaks of "Nature's God" and "Nature's Laws" that provide "unalienable rights; and that among these are the right to life . . ." James Madison, the father of the Constitution, declared that "Before any man can be considered as a member of Civil Society, he must be considered as a subject of the Governor of the Universe."[34] But of course these are moral implications that naturalistic evolutionists are not willing to draw, nor willing to have our children draw either—at least from anything taught in a science class in public schools.

Clearly Hitler and others drew moral implications from evolution. He spoke of the moral "right" to eliminate inferior races of men based

33. All quotations in this paragraph cited by Wells, *Politically Incorrect Guide,* 95, 137, 172.

34. James Madison, *Memorial and Remonstrance Against Religious Assessments,* June 20, 1785, in Robert Rutland, ed., *The Papers of James Madison* (Chicago: University of Chicago Press, 1973), 8:299.

on Darwinian evolution.[35] A recent noteworthy work on Darwinism and Hitler by Richard Weikart states it well: "Darwinism by itself did not produce the Holocaust, but without Darwinism . . . neither Hitler nor his Nazi followers would have had the necessary scientific underpinnings to convince themselves and their collaborators that one of the world's greatest atrocities was really morally praiseworthy."[36]

What, then, should be our response to this argument against teaching creation in public school science classes? Several observations are relevant to this objection.

First, the objection applies equally well to teaching naturalistic evolution since it too is compatible with naturalistic religions and many have drawn religious and ethical implications from it. Hence, if creation should be eliminated on this ground, then so should evolution.

Second, neither scientific view as such is theological or ethical. Teaching what is compatible with a religion is not the same as teaching religion. If it were, then almost every ethical principle known to mankind would thereby be religious and thus out of bounds to teach in our schools. Hence, there is no reason to eliminate a strictly scientific presentation of either view.

Third, the mere fact that certain undesirable implications may be drawn from either view is neither here nor there in terms of the truth of the view. Truth is truth whatever the consequences are. If there is no scientific reason to conclude a creator exists, then so be it. Let the evidence speak for itself. On the other hand, if the evidence points to a creator, then there is no legitimate reason to exclude it from a science class. Scientists, of all people, should go where the evidence leads.

Fourth, as noted earlier, the concept of a first cause as such is not religious. The Greeks did not worship their first cause or ultimate being. However, calling on students to worship or make an ultimate commitment to such a cause is religious. As Tillich noted, one and the same object can be approached objectively as the result of a reasoned process or subjectively as an object of ultimate commitment. The latter has no place in a science class, but the former does—if the scientific evidence leads there.

35. Adolf Hitler, *Mein Kampf* (New York: Reynal & Hitchcock, 1940), 161-162.
36. Richard Weikart, cited in Wells, *Politically Incorrect Guide*, 164.

Finally, even if it is obvious to students that this "first cause" is the "God" normally associated with religion, it makes no difference. For creationists only propose that this is one of two views that should be presented—not the only one. And presenting both opposing views in no way is favoring or establishing one or the other. However, presenting only one view with religious implications, whether evolution or creation, is tantamount to establishing religion. And this is the de facto situation we now have in public schools, with evolution having a monopoly on the minds of our young people in science classes.

"TEACHING CREATION WOULD NECESSITATE TEACHING OTHER PSEUDOSCIENTIFIC VIEWS AS WELL"

First of all, this begs the question. Creationists could say the same about macroevolution. No debate is resolved by the fallacy of name-calling. Further, some evolutionists liken creation to the flat earth view and conclude that allowing creation into science classes would also demand that other outmoded and pseudoscientific views like flat earth and alchemy be allowed as well. However, this is not the case because these views are the subjects of empirical science, where observability and repeatability are the operating principles, and there is no observable and repeatable evidence to support these views. Hence, they fail the test as empirical science. Nor are they unobserved and unrepeated past phenomena like origin events in the physical universe.[37] Hence, creationists can agree that such views have no proper place in a public school science class except to be noted as nonscientific views that are not supported by empirical evidence,[38] which demands observable and repeatable events. And there is no such evidence for alchomy or the flat

---

37. As for other alleged supernormal or supernatural events, their identifiability would have to be determined on a basis other than natural laws, since they are not regular and repeatable events. For a discussion of these phenomena and how to determine their causes, see my *Miracles and the Modern Mind* (Grand Rapids, Mich.: Baker, 1992), especially chapters 4, 5, 9 and 11.

38. Of course, empirical science as such cannot deny the possibility of mental causes beyond the material world, since by its very nature empirical science is limited to observable and repeatable events. Making statements about the impossibility of such events is not science but scientism. It is in fact a metaphysical position, not one that sticks strictly to the observable and repeatable world (see ibid., chapters 1, 2, and 3). To deny that mind exists apart from matter involves the

earth view. In this sense they are properly called pseudoscience. Not so, however, with macroevolution or creation science, which are properly scientific in the forensic sense, as shown above.

"ALLOWING CREATION NECESSITATES ALLOWING OTHER VIEWS OF ORIGINS"

According to this objection, once the Judeo-Christian view of creation is allowed, then public schools would also have to make room for Buddhist, Hindu, Muslim, and numerous other religions' views of origin as well. However, this is clearly not the case, for two basic reasons.

First, the public schools should not allow any *religious* view as such into the science classroom. There are other classes, such as history, sociology, comparative religion, and literature, where one can legitimately teach *about* religion without engaging *in* the teaching of religion (see below). And the courts have ruled in favor of this. But science classes should stick to scientific evidences and reasonable inferences drawn from that evidence.

Second, elsewhere I elaborate on the point that there are only two scientific views on all the major points of origin (see appendix 6). Here, I note briefly that, concerning the origin of the universe, either there was a natural cause or there was a supernatural cause. There are no other possibilities. Also, with regards to the origin of life, either it had an intelligent cause or it had a non-intelligent, natural cause. This exhausts the logical possibilities. Likewise, concerning the origin of new life forms, including humans, either it was by natural causes or by intelligent intervention. Either we have a common ancestor by natural causes, or else we have a common creator (an intelligent cause) that intervened.

Of course, there are many combinations of and subviews within these categories,[39] but there are only two kinds of causes for each point of

---

reductionistic fallacy. It entails the self-defeating statement of a mind about all matter that only matter exists. If only matter exists, there is no mind to make this statement.

39. For example, one may believe there is a creator of the universe and even of first life but also believe that the creator designed natural laws to bring about new life forms. This is called theistic evolution. Such a person holds to a supernatural cause on the first and possibly second point of origin and a natural cause of the third point. Still, there are only two kinds of causes for each point of origin.

origin. So, it is proper to claim that there are really only two basic views on all points of origin (either an intelligent or a natural cause; either a natural or a supernatural cause).

One could also say that an intelligent cause of life and/or new life forms may be either within the universe (as in pantheism or panentheism), or beyond the universe (as in theism). But still, there are only two basic kinds of causes for each point of origin. If scientific evidence like the Big Bang or the anthropic principle can be used to show that the posited intelligent cause of first life (or new life forms) is beyond the universe, then the evidence would favor theism. But to exclude the use of such evidence and reasonable inferences from science class reveals a philosophical or religious bias by naturalistic evolutionists who falsely claim to be doing "pure" science when in fact they are violating the First Amendment by establishing their own religious point of view. It is neither scientific, fair, nor constitutional to allow only one view to be taught.

A Response to the Religious Arguments Against Teaching Creation

Two federal court decisions, *McLean* (1982) and *Edwards* (1987), ruled that teaching creation is a violation of the First Amendment forbidding the establishment of religion. But these are clearly flawed decisions for many reasons (see chapters 3 and 5). Let's consider the arguments used to pronounce creation a religious view and, thus, to outlaw it from public school science classes.

"A First Cause or Creator Is Inherently a Religious Object"

The courts objected that since creation implies a creator and since the creator is the object of religion, then to teach creation is to teach religion, which violates the First Amendment. However, this does not follow, for several reasons.

First of all, not every first cause or creator is necessarily an object of religion. As I testified in the Arkansas *McLean* case (see chapter 4), Aristotle's first cause or Unmoved Mover was not an object of religion; it was simply the result of a process of reasoning. He never worshiped his Unmoved Mover. Later, Justice Antonin Scalia made this same point in his dissent on the *Edwards* case (see chapter 6). The same is true of Plato's Creator (*Demiurgos*); he functioned as a world designer but not as the object of ultimate worth or commitment. Beyond this Creator was what Plato called the Good (the *Agathos*), but even the Good never functioned as God in Plato's system. Other religions, such as Gnosticism and many preliterate religions, did not worship the Creator of the universe either, even though they acknowledged there was one. So, the concept of a first cause or Creator need not be a religious one.

Second, one and the same Creator can be approached either in a scientific, *detached* way as the first cause of the universe, or as an object of ultimate *commitment* or worship.[40] Indeed, in the *Torcaso* case (1961), the high court accepted Paul Tillich's testimony that religion involved a commitment to an ultimate. There is nothing religious about positing a first cause of the world as an objective object of detached scientific or philosophical inquiry. A teacher would overstep his constitutional bounds only when he asks the students to consider this cause an object of ultimate commitment or worship.

Third, almost anything has been an object of religion at some time to some people. Some have worshiped rocks. For some New Agers, crystals have religious significance. Should we forbid students to study rocks or crystals in geology class simply because they can have religious meaning? Likewise, if the Court is right, then we must not present any historical evidence for the existence of either Buddha or Christ in history classes. For both are the object of religious devotion to millions, and presenting this evidence might have the effect of encouraging their followers to further religious devotion to them.

Fourth, our nation's founding legal document, *The Declaration of Independence,* speaks of a "Creator" and of human beings as "created," and yet our founding fathers never considered declaring the *Declaration* unconstitutional just because the First Amendment of the Constitution later forbade the official establishment of religion.[41] Indeed, as

40. See Paul Tillich, *Ultimate Concern* (New York: Harper & Row, 1965), 7–8, 12.
41. Furthermore, as Supreme Court Justice Antonin Scalia has pointed out, the simple belief that there is a God—which was common to almost all religions before modern

Blackstone's *Commentaries* show, the belief in the "higher law" or "the laws of nature and of nature's God" is the basic cornerstone of law and jurisprudence.[42] Indeed, even if reference to a "Creator" is religious, this does not mean it is excluded by the First Amendment. As long as it does not "establish" religion by coercing students to believe it, rather than merely exposing them to it along with the opposing view (evolution), then it does not favor one religion over another. What is more, as the courts have ruled, even religious premises can be presented, as long as they have a secular purpose.

So, reference to a Creator as the first cause of the universe or of life, or even as the giver of "nature's laws," does not thereby establish religion. It is simply the result of a reasoned process beginning with the scientific evidence and following the principles of origin science: the principle of causality and the principle of uniformity. To forbid this is to forbid scientific inquiry in the proper forensic and origin sense of the term.

Finally, there are naturalistic religions (like Hinduism, Taoism, and some forms of Buddhism) and non-naturalistic (i.e., supernatural) religions. Naturalistic evolution favors naturalistic religions. And creation favors supernatural religions. Hence, there are only two ways to avoid favoring one set of religions over another: (1) teach neither evolution nor creation; (2) teach both. One thing is certain: teaching only one view (e.g., evolution) does not avoid favoring one set of religious views over the opposing views. On the contrary, it establishes those views as favored.

"Creation from Nothing Is an Inherently Religious Belief"

The *McLean* decision declared: "Indeed, creation of the world 'out of nothing' is the ultimate religious statement because God is the only actor."[43] But this does not follow, for many reasons.

---

times—does not thereby violate the First Amendment by establishing one religion over others (see chapter 6).

42. See William Blackstone, *Commentaries on the Laws of England* (Chicago: University of Chicago Press, 2002).

43. *McLean v. Arkansas Board of Education,* 529 F. Supp. 1255 (E.D. Ark. 1982).

First, if the existence of a creator is a reasonable inference from the scientific evidence that the universe had a beginning, then how this reasonable inference from the scientific evidence violates the First Amendment is not at all clear, unless, of course, one begs the question by claiming that only natural causes are allowed in science. All proponents of creation wish to do is to draw the natural inference from the scientific evidence that Big Bang astrophysics has provided (see above), namely, that if the whole natural universe came into existence from nothing, then it is reasonable to posit a supernatural cause for it. To forbid this reasonable inference is to insist on the absurd conclusion that "nothing caused something." But no legal or reasonable principle demands that we be driven to absurdity in order to preserve constitutionality. For this reasoning violates the very principle of causality on which science was founded. It is more scientific to conclude that a supernatural cause beyond the world brought the world into existence from nothing. Otherwise, we are reduced to the absurdity of denying the principle of causality and agreeing with the British atheist Anthony Kenny, who said, "A proponent of [the Big Bang] theory, at least if he is an atheist, must believe that the matter of the universe came from nothing and by nothing."[44] Further, since atheists are now affirming the origin of the universe from nothing, then by this same reasoning atheism should be pronounced essentially religious!

Second, the Arkansas judge deliberately used the more loaded term "God," which the law at issue did not use and which term does have religious connotations to many people. The testimony was only that "creation" implies a "creator," as design implies a designer (see chapter 4). In fact, many creationists and particularly ID proponents prefer terms like "first cause" or "ultimate cause," which are even more neutral.

Third, even the term "God" need not be interpreted in a religious sense. *The Declaration of Independence* uses the term "God," and, as we have noted, our "national birth certificate" has never officially been declared by the courts to be unconstitutional! Nor have the mentions of God in the national anthem, on our coins, or on the front wall of the

44. Anthony Kenny, *Five Ways* (New York: Schocken, 1969), 66.

House of Representatives. As shown above, the same object (God) can be approached in an objective way as the ultimate cause of the world and life without calling on the students to make a religious commitment to or to worship this first cause.

Fourth, even *if* the use of the term "God" or "Creator" is considered religious, it does not mean that public school teachers cannot refer to it as one of two possible theories of origins, which some people believe. For allowing a view of origins, religious or not, which is only one of two possible views on the subject, to be taught along with its only alternative, does not thereby *prefer* (or establish) that view over the other. On the contrary, not to allow both possible views to be taught is to prefer one over the other.

Fifth, even if referring to a creator is held to be religious, it does not necessarily mean it is a violation of the Establishment Clause. One must claim that it is the true view in order to violate the First Amendment. For only the teaching *of* religion is a violation of the First Amendment, not merely teaching *about* religion (see *Abington,* 1963). One can teach *about* the theory that there is a creator of the world and of life, without engaging in the teaching *of* religion, for it would not be teaching that one view is the truth on the matter but simply offering the teaching of two views about origins. Further, as noted above, it is a twisted logic to claim that even the teaching *of* one religious view along with the only other view constitutes preferring one view over the other.

"Creation Comes from a Religious Source (the Bible)"

The essence of this argument, given by the judge in the *McLean* case, is that if the source of a theory is religious, then the theory is religious and cannot be allowed in public schools. However, this logic does not follow, for a number of reasons.

First, evolution is also found in religious books. Indeed, as we have seen, it is part of the "religion" of humanism.[45] Does that thereby dis-

45. Julian Huxley called it the religion of "Evolutionary Humanism" in his book, *Religion Without Revelation* (New York: Harper, 1957), 203ff.

qualify evolution from being taught as a scientific view in public schools? Certainly not.

Second, the Bible has been the source that prompted numerous archaeological findings in the Holy Land, but that does not make these findings unscientific or religious and thereby disqualify them as being part of the science of archaeology.

Third, many scientific and philosophical pursuits had a religious source. Socrates was inspired in his philosophical pursuits by the pagan Oracle of Delphi. The founder of modern rationalistic philosophy, René Descartes, began his philosophical pursuits when inspired by some dreams.[46] We would also have to reject Kekule's model of the benzene molecule, since he got it from a vision of a snake biting its tail![47] And we must also consider the alternating current motor unscientific because Nikola Tesla received the idea for it in a vision while reading a pantheistic poet.[48] Should all these scientific and philosophical views be rejected merely because their source was religious? Indeed, Herbert Spencer, whom Charles Darwin called "our great philosopher," came up with the idea of cosmic evolution while he was meditating on the ripples in a pond one Sunday morning.

Finally, it is widely acknowledged that belief in a supernatural cause played a vital role in the very origin of modern science.[49] Indeed, for the first two and a half centuries of modern science (1620–1860) most of the leading lights in science believed the universe and life gave evidence of a supernatural creator. One need only recall names like Bacon, Kepler, Newton, Boyle, Pascal, Mendel, Agassiz, Maxwell, and Kelvin—all of whom believed in a supernatural cause of the universe and life. This widespread belief of scientists even found its way into the very foundational document of American freedom—*The Declaration of Independence.* Indeed, it is widely acknowledged that the biblical doctrine of creation played a significant role in the origin of modern science. In a landmark

46. Jacques Maritain, *The Dream of Descartes,* trans. Mabelle L. Andison (London: Editions Poetry, 1946), 13–27.

47. Ian Barbour, *Issues in Science and Religion* (New York: Harper & Row, 1966), 158.

48. John O'Neill, *Prodigal Genius: The Life of Nikola Tesla* (New York: Washburn, 1944), 48–49.

49. Langdon Gilkey, *Maker of Heaven and Earth* (Garden City, N.Y.: Anchor, 1965), 35.

article on this point in the prestigious philosophy journal *Mind* (1934),
M. B. Foster stated that the Christian doctrine of creation is the source
of modern science.[50] It is strange, indeed, to hear scholars argue that the
foundation of science was based on belief in a supernatural cause, but
science today allows only natural causes of origin events.

"TEACHING CREATION IN SCHOOLS IS INSPIRED BY RELIGIOUS MOTIVES"

The above discussion (chapters 1–5) shows repeatedly that both
creation laws and the teaching of creation are inspired by religious motivation. On this ground such laws have been ruled unconstitutional.
But the fallacy of this can be seen by what has already been said.

First, as just noted, many scientific views were inspired by religious
motives, including evolutionary beliefs themselves. But no evolutionists would eliminate these views just because they are religiously
motivated.

Second, this confuses purpose and motive. It has become a given
in the courts that a law must have a secular purpose. But even religion
itself has a secular purpose, as our founding fathers believed. For religion
inspires good conduct, and good conduct makes for good government
and good citizens. Hence, even if teaching creation were religious, it
could have a secular purpose.

Third, the secular purposes for teaching both views of origins have
been repeatedly stated by creationists (see chapter 3). They include
enhancing student choice, encouraging critical thinking, providing a
balanced education, promoting scientific understanding, and prompting
scientific discovery. These secular purposes, as Supreme Court Justice
Antonin Scalia demonstrated (see chapter 6), are sufficient to justify
the laws proposed. So, when the Court goes beyond this and judges
these laws unconstitutional because those who proposed and/or voted
for them were religiously motivated, they go beyond the proper way
to judge a law. For most laws exist in part because people from various
religious backgrounds were religiously motivated to see them enacted.

50. See M. B. Foster, "The Christian Doctrine of Creation and the Rise of Modern Natural
Science," *Mind* 43/172 (1934), 448.

Certainly all laws dealing with moral actions—which includes most laws—were religiously motivated. But should we get rid of all those laws—including those against perjury, stealing, spouse abuse, child abuse, pedophilia, and murder—just because they are the result, in part or in whole, of religious motivation? One and the same law—including creation/evolution laws—can be religiously motivated and still have a good secular, non-sectarian, purpose. And what law promotes a non-sectarian secular purpose better than one that is open, fair, and balanced to both opposing points of view? And what law fits this description better than creation laws such as those at issue in *McLean* (1982) and *Edwards* (1987)?

Finally, the same courts that point to religiously motivated laws as unconstitutional sometimes argue that religious motivation is a good thing. For example, the *McCollum* decision (1948) praises the motives of Horace Mann, a primary forefather of current secular public school education. *McCollum* noted with pride that, "Horace Mann was a devout Christian, and the deep religious feelings of James Madison are stamped upon the Remonstrance. The secular public school did not imply indifference to the basic role of religion in the life of the people, nor rejection of religious education as a means of fostering it."[51] Apparently it is alright for secularists and evolutionists to be religiously motivated, but not for creationists.

"CREATION IS PART OF JUDEO-CHRISTIAN RELIGIONS"

The courts are fond of noting the religious beliefs and alleged motivations of those who want creation taught in public schools (see chapter 3). This they consider an evidence of its unconstitutionality. However, this is an unsound conclusion both logically and constitutionally.

First of all, if the courts pronounce a view religious simply because it is consistent with some religions, then most cosmological and ethical beliefs ever held by mankind, including evolution, are religious and thereby unconstitutional. For most of such beliefs and laws inspired by

51. *McCollum v. Board of Education,* 333 U.S. 203 (1948).

them have been part of some religion. Surely we do not want to forbid teaching school children that intolerance, rape, murder, and cruelty are wrong simply because many religions also prohibit these activities. Why, then, should one claim that creation is religious simply because some religions believe in it? Teaching what is compatible with certain religious beliefs or motivations does not necessarily constitute teaching that religion, let alone establishing its priority over other religions.

Macroevolution is compatible with the beliefs of religious humanists and other nontheists. But teaching the scientific evidence for biological macroevolution in origin science does not necessarily constitute teaching the religion of secular humanism or the like. Likewise, the mere fact that creationism is compatible with certain forms of Christian and non-Christian religions does not mean that to teach the scientific evidences for creation in origin science is to teach any of those religions.

What is more, it is not the reference to an object that some people worship that makes something religious but whether it is presented *as an object of worship or ultimate commitment.* We do not forbid the study of natural forces in science classes (such as rain, wind, and sun) just because some native religions have worshiped these forces. We simply insist that these forces be studied in an objective way, without attempting to evoke a religious response or commitment to them from the students. Indeed, as noted above, we don't forbid the teaching of scientific evidence for macroevolution simply because some have made evolution into a religion or religious object[52] or because some religions hold evolution as part of their beliefs.

Nor do we forbid the study of the cosmos simply because Carl Sagan made it an object of worship, saying, "Our ancestors worshiped the Sun, and they were far from foolish. And yet the Sun is an ordinary, even mediocre star. If we must worship a power greater than ourselves, does it not make sense to revere the Sun and stars?"[53] Hence, as long as a creator is posited as a causal explanation for origins, and not as an object of worship, there should be no religious objection to presenting

52. Henri Bergson, in *Creative Evolution,* trans. Arthur Mitchell (New York: Macmillan, 1911), saw evolution as a divine Life Force within nature.
53. Carl Sagan, *Cosmos* (New York: Random, 1980), 243.

creationist views in public school science classes. Likewise, Buddha and Christ can be studied from an objective historical vantage point without presenting them as objects for religious devotion. Indeed, as noted, the courts have never ruled that studies about religion or religious beings are unconstitutional. It is the teaching *of* religion which is considered illegal, not teaching *about* religion or religious objects (see *Abington,* 1963). Otherwise, it would be illegal even to study religious art, such as that of Michelangelo.

As we have noted, theologian Paul Tillich was consulted by the Supreme Court in its determination of the meaning of religion in the *Torcaso* case (1961). Tillich testified as to how a creator (or what he called an "Ultimate") may be approached in a nonreligious way. He noted that studying the ultimate from a *detached, objective point of view* is not religion; it is philosophy. However, when we approach the same ultimate from an *involved, committed perspective,* this is religious. Building on Tillich's distinction, as we have also noted, Langdon Gilkey (who testified for evolution in the *McLean* case) said that it is like two climbers scaling a mountain from different sides. They are not approaching two different peaks. There is only one summit. But there is more than one *way* that this ultimate can be approached.[54]

In view of this distinction, we would conclude that if one approaches a creator from the objective, detached vantage point of scientific inference, he has not thereby taught religion. But this is exactly what creationists propose should be done with regard to positing a creator as a possible scientific explanation of origins. But the proper domain for a creator is origin science. The idea of a cause or designer of the universe as such is religiously innocuous when presented as an explanation of origins in origin science. This is even more the case when creation must be presented as only *one* of two possible ways to explain the data. How can balanced teaching about *two* possible explanations in origin science be favoring or establishing only *one*? Indeed, it can be argued that allowing only evolution to be taught is establishing a religion of naturalistic evolution. For evolution is an essential part of

54. See Gilkey, *Maker of Heaven and Earth*, 35.

many naturalistic (nontheistic) religions, and by the courts' disallowing any opposing view to be taught, they have thereby established the naturalistic, nontheist religious view.

As Justice Scalia's dissent in *Edwards* (1987) noted, a decision respecting the subject matter to be taught in public schools does not violate the Establishment Clause "merely because the material to be taught 'happens to coincide or harmonize with the tenets of some or all religions.'"[55]

It is obviously wrong to reject a scientific model merely because of its source—even if the source is religious in nature. Scientists are not concerned about the *source* of a model but rather about its *adequacy* in explaining the data. As we have asked before, has any scholar ever rejected Socrates' philosophy simply because his inspiration for it came from a Greek prophetess? Or has any informed teacher ever refused to allow Descartes' rationalism into a public classroom simply because his inspiration came from three dreams on November 10, 1619?[56] Likewise, no fair-minded person should reject the idea of special creation simply because it comes from a religious source.

Summary and Conclusion

There are two main arguments leveled against allowing creationists' views of origins to be taught in public school science classes. It is argued that (1) it is not science, and (2) it is religious. The first of these objections against teaching creation is based on a failure to distinguish between operation science and origin science. The former is empirical science, but the latter is more like a forensic science. Operation science deals with observed regularities in the present. In this sense of the word, neither special creation nor macroevolution is science. Origin science, which includes both special creation and macroevolution, deals with unobserved singularities in the past. So while only natural (secondary) causes are to be allowed in operation science, a primary supernatural cause is possible in origin science.

55. He cited *Harris v. McRae* (1980) and *McGowan v. Maryland* (1961).
56. Maritain, *Dream of Descartes*, 13–27.

Second, to insist that to posit a primary cause of creation is religious because that view is compatible or congruent with certain religious beliefs about the supernatural (such as are found in traditional Judaism, Islam, and Christianity), is no more fair than claiming macroevolution is religious because it is compatible or congruent with certain naturalistic cause religions (such as Hinduism, Buddhism, and secular humanism). If we insist that the idea of creation should be rejected because it comes from a religious source (e.g., the Bible) we must, for consistency's sake, also reject the idea for the benzene molecule model or the alternating current motor because they too came from a religious source. If a primary cause of the origin of life is presented simply as one possible (or plausible) explanation of the origin of living things, then it has no more religious significance than would presenting natural forces or even "evolution," to which some people have given religious significance.

A Summary of Reasons Why the Teaching of Creation Should Be Allowed in Public Schools

Most of these reasons have been stated or implied in the above discussion. They will be spelled our here for simplicity and clarity.

(1) Creation as defined in the *McLean* (1982),[57] *Edwards* (1987), and *Dover* (2005) court cases is properly science in both a historical and contemporary sense. It was defined in *McLean* as "the scientific evidences for creation and inferences from those scientific evidences." Both the founders of modern science and contemporary scientists engage in science, particularly forensic-type sciences, in this same manner.

(2) Science in general has been and should always be open to minority views. In fact, if science had not been open to minority views among scientists, then evolution would never have gained its present predominance, since evolution was once a minority view. Indeed, minority views

---

57. For an excellent critique of the demarcation arguments used in *McLean,* see David DeWolf et al., "Teaching the Controversy: Is It Science, Religion, or Speech?" in *Darwinism, Design, and Public Education,* ed. John Angus Campbell and Stephen C. Meyer (Lansing: Michigan State University Press, 2003), 59–132.

are what make progress in science possible, since all new views are in the minority when they are first presented.

(3) Forbidding schools to teach the creation viewpoint, which is held by as many as 90 percent of Americans,[58] clearly amounts to a denial of the First Amendment right to freedom of speech to a majority of our citizens. Indeed, in the words of our founding fathers, "Taxation without representation is tyranny."

(4) Even an ACLU attorney at the 1925 *Scopes* trial claimed that both views should be taught. Here are his words from the trial transcript: "For God's sake let the children have their minds kept open—close no doors to their knowledge; shut no door from them. Make the distinction between theology and science. *Let them have both. Let them both be taught.*"[59]

This raises an important question: If the ACLU wanted both evolution and creation to be taught at "Scopes I" in 1925 when only creation was being taught, then why in 1981 at "Scopes II," at a time when only evolution was being taught, did the ACLU argue that only *that* one view should be taught? If it was "bigotry" (a word the ACLU used repeatedly of creationists at the *Scopes* trial) in 1925 when only creation was being taught, why was it not bigotry in 1981 (and today) when only evolution is being taught?

(5) John Scopes, the teacher found guilty of teaching evolution contrary to the laws of Tennessee in 1925, declared: "If you limit a teacher to only one side of anything, the whole country will eventually have

58. Multiple surveys and polls reveal that around 85–90 percent of Americans believe in some form of creation. See Jerry Bergman, "Teaching Creation and Evolution in Public Schools" (www.answersingenesis.org/docs/4178). Also, some 70 percent of attorneys believe that both views should be taught in schools. Wells, *Politically Incorrect Guide,* 250, cites these additional sources: Michael Foust, "Gallup Poll Latest to Show Americans Reject Secular Evolution." *Baptist Press* (October 19, 2005). Available online (June 2006) at http://www.bpnews. net/bpnews.asp?ID=21891. "Poll: Creationism Trumps Evolution," CBS News, November 22, 2004. Available online (June 2006) at http://www.cbsnews.com/stories/2004/11/22/ opinion/polls/main657083.shtml. Ontario Consultants on Religious Tolerance, "Religious Identification in the U.S." (2001). Available online (June 2006) at http://www.religioustoler-ance.org/chr_prac2.htm.

59. Dudley Field Malone, quoted in William Hilleary and Oren W. Metzger, eds., *The World's Most Famous Court Trial: Tennessee Evolution Case* (Cincinnati: National Book Company, 1925), 187. It matters not that the attorney called creation "theology." Whatever the name, he still wanted it taught in the public schools alongside evolution.

only one thought, be one individual."[60] But is this not precisely what is happening by the exclusion of creation from our classrooms today? Even *The Secular Humanist Declaration* (1980) affirmed that "A pluralistic, open, and democratic society allows all points of view to be heard."[61] Why then cannot our children hear about creation in their classes?

(6) If, as even many evolutionists admit, it is possible that creation is true, then by excluding creation are we not thereby declaring, in effect, that we do not want our children to be exposed to what may be true and what the vast majority of their tax-paying parents believe is true? With the exception of some vocal zealots for evolution,[62] most serious-minded scientists recognize that it is at least *possible* that creation may be true and evolution may be false. If this is so, then any court decision that forbids teaching creation will have the consequence of legislating the impossibility of teaching what admittedly may be true. It is difficult to believe that fair-minded scientists are willing to say in effect: "Creation may be true, but we will not allow it to be taught!" Certainly we should not want to legislate out of the science classroom the possibility of discovering the truth.

(7) Insisting that only natural causes count as a scientific explanation (which naturalistic evolutionists claim) is akin to demanding that science teachers not allow any explanation other than physical erosion for the faces on Mt. Rushmore. Or, forbidding the SETI program to proclaim that an intelligible message from outer space can be anything other than the result of natural laws. Or, that the writing on a newly discovered ancient manuscript must be explained by natural processes and cannot be considered to be the product of an intelligent mind.

8) Legally, to insist that *only* natural causes can be discussed in science classes dealing with origins is to unconstitutionally favor one religious point of view—the one embracing a naturalistic cause—over other religions that favor a supernatural cause of origins. That is to say, by denying a hearing for supernatural causes (such as Judaism,

---

60. John Scopes, quoted in P. William Davies and Eldra Pearl Solomon, *The World of Biology* (New York: McGraw Hill, 1974), 414.

61. Paul Kurtz, *The Secular Humanist Declaration* (Buffalo, N.Y.: Prometheus, 1980), 12.

62. See, e.g., Isaac Asimov, *Science Digest* (October 1981), 85.

Christianity, and Islam hold), the courts have favored (and thereby *established* the tenets of) nontheistic religions such as Hinduism, Buddhism, and secular humanism. By disallowing creation, the courts have established anti-Judeo-Christian beliefs. For example, as we have seen, in 1933 secular humanism declared itself a religion, and then, several years later, the Supreme Court noted that secular humanism is indeed a religion protected by the First Amendment (*Torcaso,* 1961). But three of the essential beliefs of the religion of secular humanism are: (1) there is no creator, (2) there was no creation, and (3) there are no supernaturally caused events.[63] Therefore, to insist that *only* these points of view can be taught in schools is to "establish" (that is, to prefer) these essential tenets of the religion of secular humanism in the public schools.

9) The founder of the evolutionary revolution in modern science called evolution only a "theory" alongside the "theory of creation."[64] But to allow only one view to be taught is to treat it like a fact, not merely as just one theory. Indeed, in his "Introduction" to his famous *On the Origin of Species* Darwin wrote words worth pondering:

> For I am well aware that scarcely a single point is discussed in this volume on which facts cannot be adduced, often apparently leading to conclusions directly opposite to those at which I have arrived. A fair result can be obtained only by fully stating and balancing the facts and arguments on both sides of each question; and this cannot possibly be here done.[65]

This is precisely what creationists have expressed in their attempt to have creation or intelligent design presented in our public school science classrooms!

In summation, the naturalistic arguments against allowing creationist views in science classes are baseless. They are in fact rooted in a meta-

63. Paul Kurtz, *Humanist Manifestos I and II* (Buffalo, N.Y.: Prometheus, 1973), 8.
64. Charles Darwin, *The Descent of Man,* in *On the Origin of Species and the Descent of Man,* vol. 49 of Great Books of the Western World (Chicago: University of Chicago Press, 1952), chapter 15.
65. Ibid., 6.

physically and/or methodologically naturalistic assumption. Thus, they beg the question in favor of naturalistic explanations and naturalistic religions. As such, they are opposed to the history of science and the nature of science as an open inquiry, they fail to distinguish empirical and forensic science, and they are contrary to strong scientific evidence to the contrary. Therefore, there is no basis in the history or nature of modern science to rule out creationist or intelligent design explanations of origins.

9

Lessons to Be Learned

A careful reading of the foregoing chapters on the creation/ evolution controversy yields many helpful lessons for the future. The battle is not yet over in the courts, and there is still a chance that we may win a hearing for teaching creation or intelligent design in public school science classes. However, the deck is stacked against us, and we must learn from past mistakes. Further, we must profit from a crucial previously unpublished bit of history from the arguments that were presented in the (1982) *McLean* case but were suppressed from the view of the Supreme Court for over five years (see chapters 3 and 4).

The Constitutional Issues

Several legal issues continue to plague the creationists' cause. These must be overcome before we can be victorious in the courts and reopen our schools to creationist views in science.

The Confusion of Motives and Purposes

Unfortunately the courts confuse religious motives and religious purposes. Thus, when they detect that some proponents of creation have religious motives for wanting it to be taught, they assume (wrongly) that the law allowing creation would amount to an establishment of religion. They overlook the fact that something can be religiously motivated, as most good laws are, and still have a secular purpose. Antonin Scalia made this point in his incisive dissent on the Ten Commandments *McCreary* (2005) ruling.

It has been common since the *Lemon* case (1971) for the courts to use that case's three-fold test for whether a law violates the First Amendment Establishment Clause: (1) Does it have a secular purpose? (2) Is its primary effect to advance or inhibit religion? (3) Does it foster excessive entanglement between government and religion? But Scalia points out in his *McCreary* dissent that these tests "have been manipulated to fit whatever result the Court aimed to achieve" (Section 2).[1] While all three tests have been misapplied, the combining of the first two tests into the notion of a "predominate" secular purpose has been particularly troublesome because the Court often moves from the stated purpose of the legislators to their alleged religious motivation. Ordinarily, stated purpose should be sufficient, absent compelling evidence to the contrary (see *Edwards,* 1987). In so doing, the Court wanders from stated purpose to unstated motives, making religious motives a new and unjustified test for constitutionality. But almost any law promoted by a devout person will have religious motivation, since he will see it as an attempt to bring honor to God and good to his fellow human beings. Religious motives, no more than a religious source (see chapter 7), do not disqualify a good law, otherwise we would have no laws against perjury, stealing, child abuse, rape, or murder—all of which laws religious people were motivated to enact. Indeed, in the *McCollum* (1948) case the Court praised the religious motives of James Madison, the father of the Constitution, and Horace Mann, the father of secular education, both of which helped promote court-accepted secular results. Why,

1. *McCreary County v. American Civil Liberties Union of Kentucky*, 545 U.S. (2005).

then, should religious motivation by creationists void the good secular purposes they have in bringing about a better, more balanced, more educationally beneficial scientific knowledge of our world?

The Neutrality Test

Some jurists insist that the state should be "neutral" when it comes to religion. This test has its roots in *Epperson* (1968), which insisted that "government . . . must be neutral in matters of religious theory, doctrine and practice. It may not be hostile to any religion or to the advocacy of nonreligion; and it may not aid, foster, or promote one religion or religious theory against another or even against the militant opposite."[2] But on this ground one can easily argue for balanced treatment of both evolution and creation. For to teach only one theory of origin (evolution) is to aid a view that is antithetical to religion in that it favors a controversial naturalistic metaphysics and epistemology. In teaching only a naturalistic view (evolution), the state is not merely promoting a view that is contrary to the views of some religious people, but it is promoting a point of view that "occupies in the life of its possessor a place parallel to that filled by [traditional belief in God]."[3]

The Misinterpretation of the First Amendment

Another serious problem that hinders the approval of creation laws by the courts is its constant misreading of the First Amendment as demanding "separation of church and state" (which it does not). This was applied (or misapplied) by the Supreme Court in *Everson* (1947) to include the establishing of religion by the state.[4]

2. *Epperson v. State of Arkansas,* 393 U.S. 97 (1968).
3. *United States v. Seeger,* 380 U.S. 163 (1965).
4. The original intent of the First Amendment was to keep the federal government ("Congress") from establishing one religion for the entire country. Of course, this was much later expanded in *Everson* (1947) by way of the Fourteenth Amendment to apply to all the States as well. Even so, this does not mean that states must outlaw any teaching that has religious origin, motivation, or implication. If it did mean that, then many good laws (including those against crimes) would also have to be eliminated.

Notwithstanding, the courts continue to misunderstand the prohibition of the Constitution against "establishing religion" as meaning it must maintain a total "separation of church and state." The *McLean* ruling is a case in point, where Judge William Overton said he would rule in accordance with "the separation of church and state guaranteed under the First Amendment."[5]

As the *McCollum* case (1948) noted, there is no need to erect "a wall of separation" between church and state. Indeed, the First Amendment was intended only to forbid government preference of one religion over another. And yet *Everson* (1947) insists that the wall "must be kept high and impregnable." Further, it declares that we must respect the "principle of eternal separation between Church and State."[6] Not only is this not the language of the Constitution, it is an unconstitutional reading of the Constitution. It is in fact an overzealous statement of secularist zealots who wish to change the meaning of the Constitution.

Of course, not all cases use this "separation" phrase, preferring to hide behind terms like "entanglement" imbedded in the so-called *Lemon* test. However, the effect is the same. They forget that the founders' intent was clearly not to create hostility to religion, as the very next "Free Exercise" clause states (see below).

There are numerous ways we know that the original intent of the First Amendment was not what the courts have often taken it to mean. First of all, five of the thirteen colonies that ratified the First Amendment had their own state religions, and these state churches were never forced by the federal government to disestablish.

Second, the U.S. Congress and three of the first four U.S. presidents signed laws passed by Congress to give money to missionaries doing evangelism among the Indians.

Third, the phrase "separation of church and state" does not come from a legal document but from a private letter of Thomas Jefferson.

---

5. From Judge Overton's closing statement, December 17, 1981, recorded in Norman L. Geisler with A. F. Brooke II and Mark J. Keough, *The Creator in the Courtroom: "Scopes II"* (Milford, Mich.: Mott Media, 1982), 156.

6. For a scholarly critique of separationist views see Daniel L. Dreisbach, *Thomas Jefferson and the Wall of Separation Between Church and State* (New York: New York University Press, 2002).

And even there it was a reference to building a wall between the federal government and the states' rights to administer their own affairs, including having their own state churches, if they so desired. Indeed, Jefferson was not even at the Constitutional Convention (1787) that ratified the First Amendment. He was in France at the time, as ambassador to that country.

Fourth, Congress has approved of the motto "in God we trust" on coins, in the national anthem ("In God is our trust . . ."), and on the front wall of the House of Representatives.

Fifth, Congress has given tax deductions to religious groups, and has had prayer before its sessions begin, as well as approving government paid chaplains for the military. Likewise, presidential oaths and Thanksgiving proclamations have been pronounced in God's name. Indeed, federal courts begin with the prayer "God bless the United States and this honorable Court"! So, there are numerous ways in which the government has shown that no such "separation" of God and government was intended by the First Amendment.

Sixth, the courts have upheld many laws that had religious motivation, such as those against polygamy, bigamy, theft, and murder.

THE ESTABLISHMENT CLAUSE FORBIDS TEACHING ONLY ONE VIEW OF ORIGINS

The Establishment Clause of the Constitution has long been used to exclude the teaching of creation in public schools. But the time is long overdue to turn the constitutional tables. If one view of origins can be excluded for this reason, then so can the other view. Both sides agree that creation and evolution are opposing views. Otherwise, there would be no reason for evolutionists to oppose the teaching of creation. But if teaching only creation is "establishing" one view, then so is teaching only evolution.

For several reasons, it will not do for evolutionists to argue that creation is a religious view and evolution is not. First, logically they are both opposing views on the same issues concerning origins (see appendix 6). Hence, whatever one is, so is the other. So, they are either both religious or else they are both not religious. Nor will it suffice to claim that one has an object of religious devotion (a creator) but the other does not. For some evolutionists have deified the evolution process. We have seen this to be the case with Alfred Wallace, who along with Darwin pioneered the theory of natural selection. We have seen it to be true of Henri Bergson in his *Creative Evolution,* of Julian Huxley, who in *Religion Without Revelation* spoke of "the religion of evolutionary humanism," and even of Darwin himself, who referred to "my deity 'Natural Selection.'"[7]

Further, the Supreme Court (in *Torcaso,* 1961) accepted Paul Tillich's definition of religion as an ultimate commitment, according to which even atheists can be religious. Likewise, one does not need to believe in a creator in order to make religious commitments to or statements about matters of origin. A natural law will suffice as an ultimate principle.

What is more, neither creation nor evolution is a religion as such, since neither calls for worship or an ultimate commitment to the posited cause of origin. Both are posited merely as a causal explanation of the scientific data and not as an object of devotion.

Finally, neither evolution nor creation is a religion or religious as such. Different views of origin are compatible with different religions. For example, creation is compatible with theistic religions, and evolution is compatible with nontheistic religions. But neither creation nor evolution itself is a religion. The mere fact that a view is compatible with a religion does not make it religious any more than the compatibility of certain moral principles with certain religions makes these moral principles religious. If it did, then laws against cheating, stealing, murder, racism, sexual abuse, genocide, and numerous other moral principles would all have to be declared unconstitutional.

According to the high court in *Planned Parenthood v. Casey* (1992), "at the heart of liberty is the right to define one's own concept of existence, of meaning, of the universe, and the mystery of human life."[8] When government schools, whose attendance is generally compulsory, delve into ultimate matters of origin, they in effect affirm an "orthodox"

7. Charles Darwin, in a letter to Asa Gray, June 5, 1861 (in Francis Darwin, ed., *The Life and Letters of Charles Darwin,* 2 vols. [New York: Basic Books, 1959], 2:165).
8. *Planned Parenthood v. Casey,* 505 U.S. 833 (1992).

position on such matters. This is particularly true of teaching evolution to the exclusion of its opposition. Indeed, in *Keyishian v. Board of Regents* (1967) the Court ruled that "the First Amendment does not tolerate laws that cast a pall of orthodoxy over the classroom."[9] But this is precisely what the Court has done by forbidding that creation be taught alongside evolution. It has in fact established one view as the "orthodox" view. And this is just as wrong now as it was when creation was established as the only allowable view in the schools.

Overlooking the Free Exercise Clause

Another problem at the base of the courts' unfavorable decisions on church/state issues is their isolating the Establishment Clause (that "Congress shall make no law respecting an establishment of religion, …") from the Free Exercise Clause which constitutes the rest of the sentence: "or prohibiting the free exercise thereof." Put positively, the Free Exercise Clause says Congress should encourage religion in general, while not establishing any one religion in particular. This is precisely what the government did in their early land grants to various denominations and in allowing tax deductions for all religious organizations. But by forbidding the teaching of creation, the courts are showing hostility to religions that hold to a belief in a creator. And by allowing only evolution, which is compatible with nontheistic religions, the courts are thereby establishing (i.e., preferring) these religions over theistic religions. Ironically, in their hostility to theistic religion, the courts have *established* religion—a religion of secularism. In view of this, there is a clear and present need to argue this point in the courts and public forums more effectively. Misdirected zeal for the Establishment Clause cannot negate the legitimate need to support the Free Exercise Clause of the First Amendment as well.

The Freedom of Speech Clause

To date the creationists' cause has not exploited the freedom of speech clause in the Constitution in their favor. On the other side, evolutionists

9. *Keyishian v. Board of Regents*, 385 U.S. 589 (1967).

have used it very effectively, beginning with the *Scopes* trial (1925). The initial statement of the defense at *Scopes* listed numerous reasons the Tennessee law forbidding evolution was not constitutional (see chapter 1). The last one cited Section 1 of the Fourteenth Amendment of the U.S. Constitution, which says, "No state shall make or enforce any laws which shall abridge the privileges or immunities of citizens of the United States."[10] This would include the First Amendment guarantee of freedom of speech. The *Scopes* defense also cited Section 19, Article I of the Tennessee constitution, which states: "That the printing presses shall be free to every person. . . . The free communication of thoughts and opinions is one of the invaluable rights of man, and every citizen may freely speak, write and print on any subject. . . ."[11] Defense attorney Hayes added, "I presume our teachers should be prepared to teach every theory on every subject. Not necessarily to teach the thing as a fact. . . . It should not be wrong to teach evolution, or certain phases of evolution, but not as a fact."[12]

But this is precisely what creationists are arguing today, namely, (1) not to teach one theory as a fact, but instead (2) to teach both theories in a balanced way. All one needs to do to get the point is to replace the word "evolution" in the above quote with the word "creation." It then reads, "I presume our teachers should be prepared to teach every theory on every subject. Not necessarily to teach the thing as a fact. . . . It should not be wrong to teach creation, or certain phases of creation, but not as fact."

Indeed, Clarence Darrow's anti-bigotry speech at the *Scopes* trial was permeated with the "freedom of speech" argument. He said, "Unless there is left enough of the spirit of freedom in the state of Tennessee, and in the United States, there is not a single line of any constitution that can withstand bigotry and ignorance when it seeks to destroy the rights of the individual; and bigotry and ignorance are ever active."[13] He added, "On no reading of 'the spirit of the law' concerning freedom of

10. See William Hilleary and Oren W. Metzger, eds., *The World's Most Famous Court Trial: Tennessee Evolution Case* (Cincinnati, Ohio: National Book Company, 1925), 50.
11. Ibid., 48–49.
12. Ibid., 56.
13. Ibid., 75.

religion should the truth about evolution be kept out of our schools."[14] By the same logic creationists should vociferously reply that "on no reading of 'the spirit of the law' concerning freedom of religion should the truth about *creation* be kept out of our schools."

The truth is that there is a direct parallel between what the evolutionists were arguing for in the *Scopes* trial (1925) and what creationists are arguing for today—freedom of speech in the public schools to teach their view on origins alongside the opposing view. *And if, as Darrow contended, it was "bigotry" to teach only one theory of origin when only creation was being taught, then it is still bigotry to teach only one theory of origin when only evolution is being taught!* It is a sad fact that there really is no actual freedom of speech in a public school science class for a creation view to be taught—a view that is held in one form or another by 85–90 percent of the American public.

To be more specific, the Court has ruled that teachers are engaged in protected speech under academic freedom and the First Amendment when they bring to the classroom relevant materials that supplement the curriculum and do not violate any law (see *Keyishian v. Board of Regents* [1967]). In *Epperson* (1968) "the Court ... acknowledges the state's power to prescribe the school curriculum, but it held [in *Meyer v. Nebraska* (1923)] that these were not adequate to support the restriction upon the liberty of teacher and pupil."[15] On these grounds, there is no constitutional basis for not allowing creation to be taught alongside evolution, with or without a school board policy or state law mandating it.

The Misuse of Stare Decisis

Stare decisis is defined legally as a decision that has been made on a certain set of facts that becomes a precedent to be applied to all subsequent cases which have the same facts. There are several problems with the application of this principle. First, it is not found in the Constitution. It comes from the English common law tradition. Hence, it should not

14. Ibid., 82.
15. *Epperson v. State of Arkansas,* 393 U.S. 97 (1968).

be given sacred legal status. At best, it is only a guideline to be considered. It is not a Constitutional principle to be mandated.

Second, it is not infallible. There are numerous times in our history when the Supreme Court was wrong and had to be overturned. The classic case was the *Dred Scott* (1857) decision which declared that African-Americans were not "persons" with certain constitutional rights. Fortunately, this was overturned eight years later by the Thirteenth Amendment (1865). (Unfortunately, the *Roe v. Wade* decision [1973], which declared the unborn are not persons whose life is protected by the Constitution, has not yet been overturned.)

Third, the facts are not really the same in all the creation cases, yet the courts have used *stare decisis* in deciding subsequent cases with different facts. For example, clearly the *Scopes* law (1925) that forbade teaching any view that contradicted the biblical view is not at all the same as the "creation science" laws, as in *McLean* (1982) and *Edwards* (1987), or the *Dover* (2005) school mandate relating to teaching intelligent design. Yet the subsequent courts used the precedents of the preceding courts to decide their cases as though they were based on the same set of facts when clearly they were not. Certainly there is a difference between laws that want only creation taught *instead of* evolution if either is taught (*Scopes*, 1925) and those that want creation taught *alongside* evolution (*Epperson* [1968], *McLean* [1982], *Edwards* [1987], and *Dover* [2005]). In such cases the principle of precedent does not apply.

Fourth, each situation has its own unique characteristics and, hence, a precedent does not always apply. For example, in some precedent cases no constitutional or moral right is being violated by applying the precedent. In others, the right to life is at stake and, hence, a precedent not involving a right to life does not apply. Likewise, the right to freedom of speech to teach creation as science cannot be denied for creationists simply because a precedent case with different circumstances found that creation was taught as a religion.

Finally, being fallible, the Supreme Court has not always interpreted and applied the Constitution accurately. Judges are known to have ideological and political biases. If the first decision misinterprets the Constitution when applying it to these facts, then there is no obligation on future courts to make the same mistake. The Supreme Court has been seriously wrong many times in other cases, and there is no reason to assume they are not wrong in these creation cases. In fact, we have shown (in chapter 8) many good reasons to indicate they were wrong in these cases. Hence, future courts should look afresh at these decisions and not blindly follow them because of a fallible, extra-constitutional principle that has had numerous misapplications in the past. Since *McLean, Edwards,* and *Dover* are seriously flawed (see chapters 3, 4, 5, and 7), any new creation/evolution case presented to the Court should have a fresh look in the light of the Constitution itself. Otherwise, the Court is not finding constitutional truth, it is merely compounding traditional errors. *Stare decisis* must be reexamined and reapplied or it will completely undermine the meaning of the Constitution with decisions based on bad precedent. We need attorneys dedicated to the Constitution who will comprehensively and exhaustively rethink the erroneous understanding and application of precedent to decide the constitutionality of laws.

The Civil Tolerance Argument

Creationists have not yet exploited the civil tolerance issue in the courts. In the *Mozert v. Hawkins County Board of Education* (1987) case, students and parents had claimed that it was a violation of their First Amendment religious rights of free exercise for the school board to be "forcing student-plaintiffs to read school books which teach or inculcate values in violation of their religious beliefs and convictions." Evolution was one such view to which they objected. Their wishes were upheld by the district court but overruled by the Sixth Circuit Court. The latter court argued that even though students were offended, there was no evidence that one was "ever required to affirm his or her belief or disbelief in any idea or practice" taught in the text or class. The court insisted that there was a difference between "exposure" and being "co-erced" to accept the ideas. They noted that the only way to avoid all offense was not to teach anything. They insisted that: "The lesson is clear: governmental actions that merely offend or cast doubt on religious beliefs do not on that account violate free exercise." They insisted that this exposure to offensive views was simply a matter of "civil tolerance" of other views and did not compel anyone to a "religious tolerance" of other views whereby they were compelled to give equal status to other religious views. "It merely requires a recognition that in a pluralistic society we must 'live and let live.'"[16]

If this was a sound decision, then why can't the sword cut both ways? Why cannot creationists argue that the presentation of their views, even if considered religious and offensive by others, is not thereby coercing the students to believe in but simply to be exposed to them? Why cannot evolutionists learn to "live and let live" too? The courts seem to have two sets of rules—one set by which evolution is allowed and another by which creation is excluded from the public school classrooms. Creationists need to insist that all players in the game follow the same rules. By a fair reading of the civil tolerance rule, creation should be allowed alongside evolution. After all, creationists are not insisting that their view be taught as true to the exclusion of all other views. They simply desire that it be allowed as one view among others to which young people should be exposed. This is certainly the most tolerant thing to do in a civil society.

Forgetting Why We're Here: Taxation Without Representation

Serious citizens need to consider the little regard given by the courts, particularly in the creation issue, to the venerable principle on which our federal republic was founded: "Taxation without representation is tyranny." Surveys show that some three-fourths to 90 percent of tax-paying Americans do not have their creationist view represented in public schools.[17] Were the founding fathers to return to contemporary America and see how citizens are being forced to pay taxes to public schools to teach their

16. *Mozert v. Hawkins County Board of Education*, 827 F. 2d 1058 (1987).
17. A recent Pew Forum on Religion poll (August 30, 2005) found that 78 percent of Americans believe God was involved in the creation of "life on earth." Another five percent believe life was created by a "higher power" or "universal spirit"—which are just other words for God. Still more (up to 90 percent) believe God created the universe. And 95 percent believe in God. Only one-fourth believe that human life arose by "natural selection" (evolution) not guided by a Supreme Being (http://pewforum.org/surveys/origins/).

children contrary to their cherished beliefs, they would be scandalized. Indeed, were Thomas Jefferson to reappear on the scene, he would discover that he was being forced to pay taxes without representation of his views on a "Creator" and that "all men are created equal." Indeed, he would find that these very views immortalized in *The Declaration of Independence* had been so scandalized by the courts that they had in effect declared our national birth certificate unconstitutional! While I am not advocating it, I have no doubt that Jefferson would start a second American Revolution!

Avoid Laws and Policies That Appear to Mandate Creation

The courts are almost paranoid about laws that mandate the teaching of creation in any way, even if only alongside evolution and not instead of evolution. And they are almost blind to the fact that, in effect, they have mandated a situation where only evolution can be taught, unchallenged by any real competing view. The *Epperson* (1968) decision struck down any law forbidding the teaching of evolution. And this, with the subsequent *Edwards* (1987) decision, gives evolution a de facto monopoly on the market.

Creationists must understand this tendency of the courts to establish evolution, and they should avoid the temptation to gain back ground by mandating creation alongside evolution. As noble as such efforts have been, they have not worked and probably should be laid aside until there is a more sweeping change in the Supreme Court. On the last creation vote in the Supreme Court there were only two votes for creation (Rehnquist and Scalia), and Scalia is the only sure vote left, although one or more of the newer members (like Thomas, Roberts, or Alito) may vote for creation. This still leaves us short of the needed five for a favorable majority vote for creation.

One thing is worth noting about court decisions on the mandated balanced treatment laws; namely, they misinterpreted the statutes. Neither Arkansas nor Louisiana actually mandated teaching creation. They left open the option that neither view could be taught. All they mandated was that, *if* either view is taught, then the other view must be presented in a balanced way. This is significantly different from mandating that creation be taught, and it is totally removed from mandating a favored position to creation. No such law has ever been proposed by creationists, let alone passed by a state legislature. So, the courts have ruled against a straw man! Nonetheless, given the track record of the courts, it seems advisable to avoid mandating teaching creation in any form.

An Important Distinction: Government Endorsement vs. Private Expression

In a number of cases, some Supreme Court justices have made a legitimate distinction between the unconstitutionality of government endorsed religious views and the right of private expression of the same views. In short, the former are unconstitutional and the latter is not. Private religious speech has the same right as secular speech. Indeed, this seems to be a principle behind the Supreme Court forbidding school endorsed prayer but not disallowing student led prayers (see *Lee v. Weisman,* 1992). If this were not permissible, then the right of students to freedom of speech would be violated. In fact, if student initiated and controlled prayer were not possible, then secular free speech would be given a higher status than religious free speech. But the free speech clause of the First Amendment makes no such distinction. Thus, even if creationists' views are considered religious, they should be allowed under the equal status of free speech concept.

The same distinction is now widely accepted with regard to other beliefs. There is no prohibition by the courts against the expression of other beliefs that are religious. For example, one can believe that Confucius lived and taught certain moral principles. And these principles could even be taught as part of a course in values. Confucius taught, for example, that we should not do to others what we do not want them to do to us (the so-called "negative" Golden Rule). This would not be considered unconstitutional by the courts merely because it was part of the religion of Confucianism. Likewise, the Supreme Court could rule (and has ruled) in favor of monogamy. When it did so it explicitly referred to its basis in the "Christian" religions (see *Davis v. Beason,* 1890). This it did, not because it was legislating the truth of the

Christian religion above other religions but because it acknowledged a secular purpose and a social value to this principle that happened to come from the Christian religion. There is no reason the Court cannot do the same for the teaching of creation. Since creation has educational value (to teach both sides of an issue) and since the positing of an intelligent designer has value in itself as a scientific concept (being used in archaeology, cryptology, information theory, and the SETI program), then why cannot it be taught despite the fact that it is a part of certain Abrahamic religions (such as Judaism, Christianity, and Islam)?

Appointing Non-Activist Judges

Perhaps the most vexing problem facing the courts is that so often judges fail in their constitutional duty to merely *interpret* the law and instead, in effect, they *make* the law. By doing so, the people's short-term and recall-able elected representatives (the legislatures) are replaced with lifetime appointed (not elected) and virtually non-recallable members of the high courts. This destroys the constitutional separation of powers and renders void the will of the people (Article 3, Section 2 of the Constitution). They forget that the Constitution begins, "We the people. . ." and not "We the Supreme Court." Until this situation is rectified, we should not expect any significant change in the Court's First Amendment decisions.[18]

Currently, the best way to make changes in the system is to elect conservative presidents who will elect judges who will interpret the law instead of making the law. Along with this kind of president, the people must elect conservative legislators who will support Court nominees who will strictly interpret the Constitution.

In theory, Supreme Court justices can be impeached, but it is practically impossible to do so. As even the late conservative Chief Justice Rehnquist emphasizes in his history of the Supreme Court, it has been viewed as a settled practice since the impeachment trial of Justice Samuel Chase in the early 1800s that disagreement with a justice's decisions or judicial actions is not an appropriate basis for impeachment and

18. See Mark R. Levin, *Men in Black: How the Supreme Court Is Destroying America* (Washington, D.C.: Regnery, 2005).

removal. There is another, constitutionally sanctioned way to challenge the power of the Supreme Court, but it has not been utilized by the Congress in recent times.

The Use of Article Three, Section 2 of the Constitution

According to this section of the Constitution, "in all the other cases before mentioned, the Supreme Court shall have appellate jurisdiction, both as to law and fact, *with such exception and under such regulations as the Congress shall make*" (emphasis added). In effect, the Congress could limit the Supreme Court's jurisdiction and power, if it wished to do so. This would curb the authority of a runaway judiciary. It is constitutional, but it takes courage to do it. The people's elected representatives could pass laws to negate the high court's illegitimate legislating from the bench. Some fear this may precipitate a constitutional "crisis," but maybe this would be a good thing. After all, it is the Constitution itself that allows doing this. Any alleged crisis that such an action might engender couldn't be much worse than what we have now, and it may be much better if it turns out that it "clips the wings" of a Court which in recent history has had no real checks on it.

A Constitutional Amendment to Curb the Supreme Court's Power

Yet another way to put the brakes on the high court is a constitutional amendment curbing its power. But it is questionable that there are enough votes to do this, since it takes ratification by three-fourths of the states. Then there is the fact that, once the amendment would be put into effect, the Supreme Court would be the supreme interpreter (or misinterpreter) of this new part of the Constitution. And we would be right back where we are now.

Train More and Better First Amendment Attorneys

Two-thirds of the attorneys in the world are said to be in the United States—way too many! And a good percentage of these are conservative, many of them in spite of the liberal law schools they have attended. An evidence of this, related to the issue under discussion, is that some 70 percent of attorneys believe that both creation and evolution should be taught in the public schools.[19] At least three evangelical universities have law schools: Liberty University, Regent University, and Trinity University. Unfortunately, however, most Christian law students do not major in First Amendment issues. Frankly, there is no money in it. This situation has to be reversed if we are ever going to win these First Amendment battles. The activist, broad constructionist interpretation of the First Amendment has dominated the courts for so long that it is often taken as normative. Being a First Amendment attorney must become a priority for bright, conservative young minds. The reason for this is not only to argue court cases, but to enter the legislative arena as well. Most politicians have a law degree, and they pass the laws. And most judges, from local courts to the Supreme Court, are chosen from among attorneys. Penetrating this virtual liberal monopoly must become a number one priority if we are ever to restore the teaching of creation in our public schools.

There are, of course, some notable exceptions to this bleak picture—people like Antonin Scalia and Clarence Thomas. Hopefully, newly appointed Chief Justice John Roberts and Justice Samuel Alito will fall into the same category. But even if all of these would vote favorably (and it is not known whether they would), it is still not enough votes to get creation through the Supreme Court. And with the recent shift to a liberal majority in Congress there are no immediate prospects for getting another conservative Supreme Court justice.

The Philosophical Issues

I am not a scientist by formal training, though I have some training in science and have done a lot of reading in the area. My doctorate is in philosophy. But one of the reasons I got involved in the creation/evolution debate is that I discovered that at root it is a philosophical issue, and that is my area of expertise, especially as it bears on religion. When

19. See chapter 8, note 58.

I was called as an expert witness in the "Scopes II" trial (*McLean,* 1982),
I discovered that the debate needed philosophers to help clarify the issues and make important distinctions. The most fundamental of these
distinctions is that between origin science and operation science.

Failure to Distinguish Origin and Operation Science

I soon discovered that evolutionists and creationists were like ships
passing in the night. Evolutionists charged that creation was not science,
and many creationists dubbed evolution a religion. While there is some
truth in both assertions, there is a desperate need to make a fundamental
distinction between science about the past and science about the present.
Both are called science, but they are different kinds of science with different objects and different principles. Once the differences are known,
then it is clear to see that neither creation nor evolution is an empirical
science about the present. Rather, both are like a forensic science about
the past. This distinction was made in my suppressed testimony in Arkansas (see chapter 4) and spelled out in *Origin Science* (1987).[20]

OPERATION SCIENCE

Science in the strict sense is about the operation of the universe.
This is based on the principles of observation and repetition. Thus,
any theory about nature must match the repeated patterns observable
in nature.[21] On the basis of these observed repetitions, empirical (or

20. Norman L. Geisler and J. Kerby Anderson, *Origin Science* (Grand Rapids, Mich.: Baker,
1987). It was also outlined as early as 1983 in my book *Is Man the Measure? An Evaluation of
Contemporary Humanism* (Grand Rapids, Mich.: Baker, 1983), chapter 11. The roots of the
distinction go back to early scientists who spoke of the difference between cosmogony (about
origins) and cosmology (about the operation of the cosmos). See Norman Geisler, "A Scientific
Basis for Creation: The Principle of Uniformity," *Creation Evolution Journal* 4/3 (Summer 1984).
The same distinction was made between biogeny and biology and anthrogeny and anthropology.
Even one evolutionist witness at the *Scopes* trial (1925) made a similar distinction (see chapter
1). Currently, scientists still distinguish between a scientific understanding of the past, which
uses a forensic type method and is found in astrophysics, paleontology, and archaeology, and
sciences in the present, which are not forensic but empirical.

21. It would be unfruitful, for many reasons, for evolutionists to argue against this on the
basis of the alleged randomness in the subatomic world. First, this alleged randomness may
result from investigator interference, since one has to bombard the subatomic world with an
electron microscope in order to see it. So, the scientist may be observing the result of his own

operation) science can make testable predictions and the theory can be either confirmed or denied. Clearly origin events do not fall into this category, since they are neither presently observable nor repeatable. In this strict sense of empirical, observable, and repeatable events, neither macroevolution nor creation is a science.

ORIGIN SCIENCE

We learned, however, and testified in Arkansas (see chapter 3) that there is a broader sense of "science" that can deal with the past. Archaeologists, paleontologists, astrophysicists, and forensic scientists have been doing origin science for centuries. But like the examination of a homicide with no witnesses or recordings, origin events were not observed and they are not being repeated regularly in the present. Hence, origin science, like forensic science, must depend on principles other than observability and repeatability. We discovered that from the very beginning the two basic principles being used were causality (every event has an adequate cause) and uniformity (the present is the key to the past). Since the search for causality has been at the foundation of science from the beginning, the principle of uniformity translates into a causal principle which can be formulated thus: The kinds of causes known (by repetition) to produce certain kinds of effects in the present are the kinds of causes that produced these kinds of events in the past. And since causes fall into two basic categories, natural and intelligent, it is necessary to determine which kind of effects call for which kind of cause. From a commonsense point of view it is not difficult to see how repeated observation in the present informs us that round rocks in a

---

disturbing. Second, even great minds like Albert Einstein rejected this view, saying "God doesn't play dice with the universe" (in a letter to Max Born, December 4, 1926, quoted in Elizabeth Knowles, ed., *The Oxford Dictionary of Quotations* [Oxford: Oxford University Press, 1999], 290). Third, despite the alleged randomness, the final result is a regular and well-patterned natural world which alone is the basis for natural law. Fourth, both evolutionists and the courts have committed themselves to the belief that only such observable, repeatable, natural laws are the basis for science. Finally, once evolutionists and the courts allow for spontaneous eruptions in nature, not subject to observable and repeatable patterns, they have opened a wide door to creationist views, which argue that not every event in the natural world calls for a natural cause. And this would be fatal to the monopoly the evolutionary establishment now holds on the schools and courts.

stream are produced by natural forces and arrowheads are created by intelligent causes. The sciences of cryptology and information theory have both confirmed the difference between intelligent and natural causes.

In applying these principles to the origin of life and new life forms in the creation/evolution debate, we must ask, What are the distinguishing characteristics of a living organism? Two of these characteristics turn out to be specified complexity and irreducible complexity. Another is anticipatory design, which is manifest in nature as well as in the "anthropic principle," the fine-tuning of the initial conditions of the universe that makes life possible. All of these characteristics we know from repeated observation and experimentation are evidence of intelligent causes. Indeed, Claude E. Shannon in 1948 developed the revolutionary information theory that is used to demonstrate that the letter sequence in DNA is mathematically the same as that in a human language. Thus, it is scientific to posit an intelligent cause for both. Thus, the scientific creationism or intelligent design approaches are just as scientific in this sense of the term "science" as is evolution. Both involve knowing that the kind of causes seen in repeated observation (and experimentation) in the present produce certain kinds of effects—whether natural or intelligent (as in archaeology and cryptology). Thus, evolutionists have every right to show how natural causes can produce changes, as they can be shown to have done in microevolution. The debate has nothing to do with religion as such. It is simply a matter of demonstrating from repeated observation and experimentation which kind of cause—natural or intelligent—can produce life to begin with and new life forms after that. The failure of the courts to understand this distinction has led them to throw out the creationist "baby" with the "bathwater" of bad empirical science. Of course, creation is not an empirical science, but neither is macroevolution. Both deal with past unobserved and unrepeated events. Neither is an empirical science. Both are forensic type sciences, and forensic type sciences utilize the principles of causality and uniformity for unobserved and unrepeated past events such as the origin of the universe, first life, and new life forms.

Failure to Distinguish Objective Study and Religious Commitment

Another issue calling for philosophical insight was that no clear distinction was being made between the objective approach of philosophy/science on the one hand and the commitment called for in a religious experience. In fact one of Paul Tillich's students, Langdon Gilkey, was a witness for evolution at the "Scopes II" trial because both he and his mentor made this kind of distinction.[22] That is to say, one and the same object (say, a first cause or creator) can be approached from an objective scientific/philosophical perspective or from a committed religious point of view. In traditional terminology, it is simply a matter of whether a "creator" is being posited as a result of a reasonable inference from the scientific evidence (which is science, not religion) or whether the creator is presented as an object of worship and religious devotion. Since Langdon Gilkey, the main witness on this topic for evolution, had already made this distinction, it seemed fitting that I should use it as well. The judge saw fit to ignore the argument, however, and the authorities saw fit not to print my testimony until after the Supreme Court had called creation inherently religious. But creation science certainly is not, just as Aristotle's Unmoved Mover was not, an object of religion or ultimate devotion. Nor was Plato's Creator (*Demiurgos*) the object of devotion or worship. This distinction was brushed aside by the judge and was never really addressed or refuted. But it is at the heart of whether a public school science teacher can refer to a first cause or creator as the source of the universe, first life, and new life forms.

The Religious Issues

The definition of religion has been a crucial point in First Amendment decisions. Traditionally in America, religion was defined as the worship of God or a Supreme Being.[23] This was due largely to the Judeo-Christian

22. See Paul Tillich. *Systematic Theology,* 3 vols. (Chicago: University of Chicago Press, 1951–1959), 1:18–28; and Langdon Gilkey, *Maker of Heaven and Earth* (Garden City, N.Y.: Anchor, 1965), 35.

23. For an excellent review of this issue, see the article by John W. Whitehead and John Conlan on "The Establishment of the Religion of Secular Humanism and Its First Amendment Implications," in *Texas Tech Law Review* 10 (Winter 1978): 19.

influence on our system. Indeed, belief in God was a condition for holding public office in many states. Later, however, John Dewey and other humanists called their beliefs a religion and signed *Humanist Manifesto I* (1933), proclaiming their new nontheistic religious beliefs to the world. In 1934 Dewey had broadened the definition of "religious" to include "any activity pursued in behalf of an ideal end against obstacles and in spite of threats of personal loss."[24] Later, in the 1940s, nontheistic conscientious objectors who were denied draft exemptions because they did not believe in God won cases which in effect said you can have your First Amendment religious rights without believing in God. This was a significant turning point, since in effect the Court had redefined religion in a nontheistic way. By 1961 in *Torcaso v. Watkins* the courts had shifted their definition with the more pluralistic culture, and with the help of Harvard theologian Paul Tillich had begun to define religion in broader terms that included atheist and agnostic, Buddhist, Taoist, and humanist by name. Tillich claimed that anyone with an ultimate concern about anything was religious.[25] At first this seemed to be a complete disadvantage for conservatives and creationists. However, it turns out to be a double-edged sword that can be used to our advantage. In my testimony (see chapter 4) in Arkansas (1981)[26] I pointed out that humanism is a self-labeled religion that believes in evolution. Indeed, some evolutionists like Julian Huxley even referred to it as "the religion of evolutionary Humanism."[27] I went on in my testimony to note that if creation is considered religious because it is attached to a theistic religion, then evolution can be considered religious because it is attached to nontheistic religions. And, if evolution can be considered nonreligious because one can extract evolution from its religious source and context and treat it purely scientifically, then the same is true of creation. The truth is that the courts have argued out of both sides of their mouth on this issue. The

24. John Dewey, *A Common Faith* (New Haven, Conn.: Yale University Press, 1934), 27.

25. For a more detailed legal history of the meaning of religion in the courts, see Whitehead and Conlan, "Establishment of the Religion of Secular Humanism," 13–14.

26. The testimonies were given in December of 1981, but the Court's decision was not rendered until January 5, 1982.

27. See Julian Huxley, *Religion Without Revelation* (New York: Harper, 1957), 203ff.

time is long overdue to press the courts for consistency. For by forbidding creation they have in effect established beliefs of the religion of humanism and other nontheistic religions. Of course, the courts *have* ruled that it is wrong to establish a religion of secularism. The *Abington* court (1963) declared: "We agree of course that the State may not establish a 'religion of secularism' in the sense of affirmatively opposing or showing hostility to religion, thus 'preferring those who believe in no religion over those who do believe'"[28] (cf. *Zorach v. Clauson,* 1952). And even though it is understandable that in the *Peloza* case (1994) the Supreme Court by refusal to hear upheld the lower court decision that forcing a teacher to teach evolution did not require him to teach a religion of humanism,[29] nonetheless, in the *Washington Ethical Society* case (1957) a federal appeals court ruled that secular humanism is a nontheistic religion which deserves a tax-exempt status. But if secular humanism is a religion by its own self-designations and Court recognition (cf. *Torcaso, Zorach,* etc.), then this argument needs to be exploited more by those contending for balanced treatment of both creation and evolution.

Public Relations and a Biased Media

As documented below, there is a serious media bias against creation. (See also appendix 1.) This is understandable in view of the high percentage of persons in the mainstream media who are evolutionist and secularists. Various polls show a consistently high number of secularists and anti-creationists in the media. About the time of "Scopes II" (1981), statistics showed that the predominant mainline media held liberal views and some 92 percent did not attend religious services regularly. It is frightening to realize that in a quarter of a century we have not made any significant progress on this issue. This too must change.

28. *Abington School District v. Schempp,* 374 U.S. 203 (1963).

29. This decision is understandable, even justifiable, for the same reason that teaching the scientific evidence for creation does not, as such, establish theistic religions. This, however, does not mean that court decisions favoring evolution to the exclusion of creation, do not favor tenets compatible with one set of religious beliefs over other religions that do not share these beliefs. And this is precisely what the court decisions favoring the exclusive teaching of evolution have done.

My experience at the Arkansas trial taught me that no matter how many good arguments, scientifically and philosophically, creationists put forward—and there were many, as Wayne Frair noted (see the preface to this book)—nonetheless, when filtered through a biased court and media, creationists were made to look bad. Two examples make the point. Donald Chittick flatly denied agreement with a statement made by a member of the Bible Science organization (to which Chittick also belonged) that he wanted to get the Bible and Christ back into public school science classes. Nevertheless, Chittick was associated with that statement in the news report on his testimony at the trial (see appendix 1).

Bernard Goldberg, who served for nearly thirty years as a reporter and producer for CBS News, states in his *New York Times* bestseller *Bias,* "In 1985 the *Los Angeles Times* conducted a nationwide survey of about three thousand journalists and the same number of people in the general public to see how each group felt about the major issues of the day . . . :

- 23 percent of the public said they were liberal; 55 percent of the journalists described themselves as liberal.
- 56 percent of the public favored Ronald Reagan; 30 percent of the journalists favored Ronald Reagan.
- 49 percent of the public was for a woman's right to have an abortion; 82 percent of the journalists were pro-choice.
- 74 percent of the public was for prayer in public schools; 25 percent of the journalists surveyed were for prayer in the public schools.
- 56 percent of the non-journalists were for affirmative action; 81 percent of the journalists were for affirmative action.
- 75 percent of the public was for the death penalty in murder cases; 47 percent of journalists were for the death penalty.
- Half the public was for stricter handgun controls; 78 percent of the journalists were for tougher gun controls.[30]

My own testimony (see chapter 4), which was to the heart of the issue, was almost totally ignored by the mainstream media—and unfortunately

30. Bernard Goldberg, *Bias* (Washington, D.C.: Regnery, 2002), 126.

even the Christian media, who were absent from the trial, used second-hand reports for their stories (see appendix 2). Instead, in a very successful diversionary tactic, the ACLU decided to take advantage of the judge's bias by allowing testimony about witnesses' religious beliefs about the devil and demonic deception in the world. This made great headlines, but it totally distorted the real issue (Can creation be taught from a scientific point of view in schools?). These diversion and distortion tactics totally buried my testimony which, according to eyewitnesses present, had destroyed the ACLU case (see the foreword to this book).

Further, there is the mysterious episode of the court stenographer's refusal to transcribe my testimony until after the Supreme Court had ruled on this issue some five years later (in 1987)—this in spite of my repeated efforts to get the testimony transcribed. Once I met with an Arkansas attorney who worked regularly with that court, and he assured me that he could get the testimony transcribed. He was shocked when the person who did that job refused to transcribe it, without explanation. When he asked why, she would only smile at him. Then, stranger than fiction, within weeks after the Supreme Court ruled against creation in *Edwards* (1987), the Arkansas court began transcribing my testimony, and eventually I was given a copy by the attorney general's office. Now, I am not a supporter of conspiracy theories in general, but given the facts of this situation, I can only conclude that someone did not want my testimony available for later legal appeals, including the appeal to the Supreme Court. Interestingly enough, without a court-transcribed record of my testimony, Supreme Court Justice Antonin Scalia used a similar argument in his strong dissent on the *Edwards* case (see chapter 6). One can only speculate as to what the Court would have ruled had they seen the fuller argument and taken it into consideration in their decision. However, my experience with a biased judiciary on these matters does not leave me with a lot of optimism about the hypothetical outcome.

This is the problem, but what is the solution? It is easier to smell a rotten egg than to lay a better one. Further, I am painfully reminded of how long it took evolutionists to gain dominant cultural recognition of their view. Darwin wrote *On the Origin of Species* in 1859, and it was not until over a hundred years later (in *Epperson*, 1968) that the first Supreme Court decision came down in their favor. Yes, they gained a moral and media victory in 1925, but even this was two generations after Darwin's book. It took over a century for Darwin's idea to become law in the United States. And as disappointed as I am to say it, we are not going to win this battle tomorrow, this year, next year, or probably for many decades to come.

Meanwhile, it is better to light a candle than to curse the darkness. Here are some candles to light:

1) Vote for conservative candidates for political office. Make sure they are judicially conservative, not just economically, socially, or militarily conservative.

2) Become a journalist and do something about media bias yourself.

3) Run for public office, starting with your local school board. It is an easier election to win (I did twice), and you can be an influence on school policies and textbooks, including creationist material.

4) Become a scientist and learn how to defend creation scientifically.

5) Attend a good seminary (like Southern Evangelical Seminary in Charlotte, N.C.) that teaches how to defend the truth. A recent poll shows that less than 10 percent of Christians understand what it means to have a Christian worldview, and even fewer know how to defend their faith.

6) Get a Ph.D. in science and/or philosophy. The root issues in the creation/evolution debate are philosophical, and the battle must be won on an ideological level.

7) Send your children to a good Christian school or teach them at home, where they can be educated in a Christian worldview.

8) Send your children to a good Christian camp (like Summit Ministries in Manitou Springs, Colo.) where they will be educated in worldview issues, not just entertained.

9) If your children go to a secular school, make sure they get involved in a good Christian group on campus; and read J. Budziszewski's book on *How to Stay Christian in College;* Phillip Johnson's book on *Defeating Darwinism;* and *I Don't Have Enough Faith to Be an Atheist,* which I coauthored with Frank Turek.[31]

31. J. Budziszewski, *How to Stay Christian in College* (Colorado Springs: NavPress, 1999); Phillip Johnson, *Defeating Darwinism* (Downers Grove, Ill.: InterVarsity Press, 1997); Nor-

10) Become a public school teacher. There are many things that can be done legally, and the Supreme Court has not yet forbidden the presentation of scientific evidence for intelligent design as a matter of private freedom of speech; it has only ruled on a case that mandated teaching creation along with evolution in public schools. Further, the courts have ruled many things in our favor, including:

a) The released time program, whereby students can be released to go off campus to study a topic considered religious by the courts (in *McCollum,* 1948).

b) The Bible can be taught *as literature,* without claiming it is true. Students are smart enough to make up their own minds or ask questions.

c) Teachers can share their own beliefs on creation (or other topics), if asked by students.

d) The courts allow teaching *about* religion, but not the teaching *of* religion (*Abington,* 1961). This can be used to teach *about* creation and not the teaching *of* creation.

e) Your life will be an influence in and of itself, and can lead to legitimate student-initiated in-class discussion or after-school opportunities.

The Educational Issue

Before concluding, two more issues need to be briefly discussed. First, the educational issue. There is great educational value in teaching both sides of issues. By weighing the arguments pro and con, students not only learn a lot more, but they are in a better position to make up their own minds. And even if their minds are pretty well set on one view before they study the other, it will enable them to see why others believe what they believe and, if nothing else, better enable them to defend their own view. A curriculum expert, Larry Parker of Georgia State University, gave eloquent testimony to the value of teaching opposing views such as creation and evolution. After describing five major principles as the

---

man Geisler and Frank Turek, *I Don't Have Enough Faith to Be an Atheist* (Wheaton, Ill.: Crossway, 2004).

basis of a good curriculum, he affirmed that "teaching two sides of a controversy like this is consistent with all those principles."[32]

It is amazing how many pro-evolutionists have made statements that favor in principle teaching creation alongside evolution. Consider John Scopes himself, the defendant at the *Scopes* trial (1925). He said: "If you limit a teacher to only one side of anything, the whole country will eventually have only one thought, be one individual."[33] On December 3, 1976, just a few years before *McLean*, the ACLU Academic Freedom Committee wrote: "One of the objectives of universal free education is to develop in children the intellectual capacities required for the effective exercise of the rights and duties of citizenship. Experience demonstrates that this is best accomplished in an atmosphere of free inquiry and discussion." Even the Supreme Court itself (in *Edwards*), when ruling on creation, said "all scientific theories about the origins of humankind" can be taught or "any scientific theory that is based on established fact."[34] And, as we saw in chapter 1, the ACLU itself at the *Scopes* trial declared: "For God's sake let the children have their minds kept open—close no doors to their knowledge; shut no door from them. . . . Let them have both. Let them both be taught."[35]

The Value of a Free Market of Ideas

In a free market country like ours, it should be a point of pride to allow all views to be presented. The market of ideas should be free as well. Squelching ideas is the worst form of government control. It frustrates creativity and productivity in both the ideological and eco-

32. Cited from a news reporter's detailed account of Parker's testimony at the *McLean* (1981–1982) trial. See Geisler, *Creator in the Courtroom*, 119.

33. John Scopes, quoted in P. William Davies and Eldra Pearl Solomon, *The World of Biology* (New York: McGraw Hill, 1974), 414.

34. *Edwards v. Aguillard*, 482 U.S. 578 (1987). It is true that this can be read two ways: (1) "all" or "any" view can mean any view including creation, or (2) "any" and "all" naturalistic views. Nonetheless, it expresses openness, and creationists have every right to test what it means by encouraging teachers to voluntarily teach creation alongside evolution.

35. Dudley Field Malone, quoted in William Hilleary and Oren W. Metzger, eds., *The World's Most Famous Court Trial: Tennessee Evolution Case* (Cincinnati: National Book Company, 1925), 187.

nomic markets. It is strange indeed that a country that prides itself in First Amendment "freedom of speech" will not allow this freedom to public school teachers in science classes. The fact is that there are two well-known and opposing views on origins, evolution and creation, and we are not allowing teachers to teach both. What a disgrace to our cherished ideals.

The Argument for Minority Rights

Minority rights have been a strong political issue for generations. We mobilize, protest, and march when they are violated—and we should. Even our own national birth certificate, *The Declaration of Independence,* speaks of the "inalienable rights" granted us by the "Creator," who is called "Nature's God." But the right to express what is seen as a minority view of origins has been suppressed time and again by the courts. This is an intolerable form of ideological tyranny. It is the stuff of which revolutions are made. The question is how long a frustrated minority will tolerate this intolerable condition. Not only are "minority rights" in this area being frustrated, but this "minority" is being forced to pay taxes to have the courts and schools violate its rights. This is a classic example of "taxation without representation."

Furthermore, the issue is not even minority rights, since a majority (up to 90 percent) of Americans believe a creator was involved in producing the universe. So, it is really a suppression of *majority* rights by a tyranny of the minority. This must be brought to a speedy resolution or else our nation's cherished belief in free speech is a mere sham. Far from being a beacon to the nations, it is an example of hypocrisy and inconsistency.

The Tactical Issues

Before concluding, a couple of tactical issues should be touched upon. The first is judicial idealism, and the second is courtroom theatrics.

Idealism About Our Judicial System

One of the things I came away with from the Arkansas trial (*McLean,* 1981–1982) was what a poor forum the courtroom is for discovering truth. I went in with a kind of idealistic vision of both sides presenting their arguments objectively and clearly, and the case being decided impartially. I was in for a real shock. In actual fact, deception and distraction dominated. The judge was biased (see chapter 3 and appendix 1). Logical fallacy pervaded presentations and the final decision. One example of this was the evolutionist Michael Ruse's claim that evolution was a fact, even though the evolutionist brief said that it was a scientific theory that could be falsified. When the cross-examining attorney asked how a fact could be falsified, the witness was caught in an inextricable trap.[36] Also, the first witness for the evolutionist side was the judge's Methodist bishop, who said only evolution should be taught! Just imagine a case where Jerry Falwell is the first witness for teaching only creation and the judge is one of his deacons! The media would have shouted bias from the rooftops! Further, the judge called creation "Sunday school" stuff during the hearing. What is more, his ruling was filled with logical fallacies (see chapter 3). Needless to say, the almost two weeks at the trial was an education in reality.

Courtroom Theatrics

One of the distinct impressions I came away with was that a trial is theatrics and the best actors win. Not only did the ACLU have more actors (nearly three times as many lawyers), but they also trained their witnesses in theatrics. One witness, Langdon Gilkey, later admitted this in his book on the trial.[37] Knowing he was going into Arkansas, the heart of the Bible Belt, Gilkey cut his hair and took a ring out of his ear to make a better impression on the judge. I also noted a distraction tactic being used by the ACLU during the court proceedings. When there

---

36. See a reporter's account of this in *Creator in the Courtroom,* 72.
37. See Langdon Gilkey, *Creationism on Trial: Evolution and God at Little Rock* (Minneapolis: Winston, 1985), 16.

were effective creation witnesses, the ACLU attorneys were shuffling back and forth in the front of the courtroom. When evolution witnesses were on the stand, the creationist attorney sat in quiet respect.

Also, the ACLU attorneys used diversion tactics. When the creation witnesses were being effective, they would change to another subject and ask irrelevant questions about the witness's religious beliefs (see appendix 4). They knew this would attract the attention of the media to the sensational and divert their attention from the essential. And the truth is that it worked. They won! The courtroom turned out to be not a forum for truth but a stage for theatrics. So, the best actors won, and the truth lost![38] Most people who watched the O. J. Simpson trial came to this same conclusion.

A Reversed Scopes Strategy

Many have felt, even before the Arkansas trial, that a better strategy for creationists would be a "reverse" *Scopes* trial. That is, find a public school science teacher who on his own, apart from state or school board mandate, teaches both evolution and creation from a strictly scientific point of view. Then, let a lawsuit be leveled against him. Of course, what he is teaching must be clear of religious connotations, and he must be free of actual statements of or implications about religious motivation. Ideally, he should be a highly respected, award-winning, and well-liked teacher. Let this case go to court and let us find out once and for all how biased the court will be about anything that smacks of an intelligent cause. At least then we will know for sure whether our tactics must shift to arenas other than the courts. Of course, many of these things are goals of the intelligent design movement. Unfortunately, in the *Dover* case, the "baby" of intelligent design was thrown out with the "bathwater" of an unfortunate law mandating the students be exposed to intelligent design, by a biased court. Let's hope this issue can be revisited in a better form in a higher court. Other cases have failed using a similar approach.

38. For an excellent book on the ACLU's agenda to redefine moral values, see Alan Sears and Craig Osten, *The ACLU v. America* (Nashville: Broadman & Holman, 2005).

These include *Webster* (1990), *Peloza* (1994), and *LeVake* (2000).[39] While none of these are as much of a reverse *Scopes* trial as we may like, they failed because of the bias of the court. This leaves us with the necessity of overcoming the objections addressed above.

In Conclusion

We can learn many lessons from the history of the creation/evolution controversy in the courts. Indeed, if we are to be successful in the future, we must learn lessons from the past. We have listed constitutional, legal, political, philosophical, religious, public relations, educational, and tactical lessons. In order to implement these lessons, we need a whole army of trained and dedicated attorneys, judges, legislators, teachers, scientists, philosophers, and informed citizens to undertake this momentous task. We did not lose this battle overnight, and it will not be re-won overnight. We must be in it for the long haul. It must be won on the ideological, political, legal, and educational levels. It will not just happen on its own. It is a war, and successful wars take good planning, trained soldiers with good weapons, and a well thought out and executed game plan. It will take cooperation between various creationist groups, citizens, activists, politicians, lawyers, and judges. Most of all, it will take persuasive communication on the part of our moral leaders as to the value of the enterprise. We must not grow weary in well doing. We must agree with the famous American patriot Edward Everett Hale (1822–1909), when he declared:

> *I am only one,*
> *But still I am one.*
> *I cannot do everything,*
> *But still I can do something.*
> *And because I cannot do everything*
> *I will not refuse to do*
> *The something that I can do.*

39. See the introduction to this book.

Secular Media Coverage of the *McLean* Trial

C omparing eyewitness and later court records of the *McLean* trial (see chapter 4) with mainstream media reports reveals a strong media bias against creation and in favor of evolution (see chapter 3). The following samples from the secular media illustrate the bias in terms of both the way they reported and what details of the trial they chose to report on.

What the Media Reported—And How It Was Biased Against Creation

In these representative selections from the mainline media I will print their headlines and what they actually reported, then briefly comment on the bias reflected. At the end I'll offer some general comments about media bias.

Jacksonville Journal, Friday, December 11, 1981:

Evolution Key Word, Textbook Official Says

LITTLE ROCK, ARK. (AP) Creationists began lobbying for their point of view to be taught in public schools after a leading biology textbook organization decided to use the word evolution in its books, the group's director testified in federal court.

The word is a red flag to fundamentalists, William V. Mayer testified yesterday in the trial of an Arkansas law that requires balanced treatment of creationist thought and evolution if the latter is taught in schools. Mayer is the director of the Biological Science Curriculum Study in Boulder, Colo.

Bias noted: When evolutionists testified, they were not said to be "lobbying" for their view. Also, while creationists were referred to as "fundamentalists," a word with generally negative connotations to the broader public, the evolutionists at the trial, many of whom were either atheists or Marxists, were not referred to by either of those terms.

Newsweek, December 21, 1981:

Creation Goes to Court

Perhaps Charles Darwin was wrong. The more things evolve, the more they seem to remain the same. Fifty-six years after the famous *Scopes* trial, ten lawyers stood in an Arkansas courtroom last week debating once again the competing—and occasionally complementary—truths of science and religion. Instead of a traditional assault on Darwin's ideas, the case displayed a new mutant of the attack on evolution. At issue was the constitutionality of an Arkansas law which requires that whenever evolution is taught, teachers must give equal time to creation science, a set of theories that look a great deal like the Biblical account of Creation dressed in a lab coat. Supporters of the law, mainly fundamentalist Christians, say they are merely seeking a fair hearing in the secular schools. Opponents argue that the law is not only poor science, but bad law, in that it violates the First Amendment ban against the official establishment of religion.

Bias noted: Once again, supporters of creation were called "fundamentalists." They were compared to the 1925 *Scopes* group, when the 1981 case involved an entirely different law—one supporting teaching evolution too—and an entirely different set of witnesses, namely credible, educated experts in science and philosophy.

The Washington Post, Wednesday, December 9, 1981:

ACLU Opens Attack on Creation-Science

By Philip J. Hilts
Washington Post Staff Writer

LITTLE ROCK, ARK., Dec. 8. One witness characterized the methods of so-called "creation scientists" as "sleazy" and another said he knew of no creation-scientist who had ever submitted a paper to a scientific journal for publication, as the plaintiffs in the Arkansas creation trial got its [*sic*] argument under way here. The plaintiffs, represented by the American Civil Liberties Union, are seeking to show that what is called creation-science is no science at all, but merely religious apologetics for the word-for-word literal reading of the Bible.

Bias noted: The report refers to "so-called 'creation scientists'" and depicts creationists as "sleazy" and as not being real scholars. It depicts creation as a religious view because it comes from the Bible. To a large degree, the bias in this report is shown by what details the media selects for its reporting.

The following items also show this "bias of selection." Obviously, the reporters are simply reporting what the witnesses said. And yet, they just as easily could have chosen to report the words of witnesses more favorable to creationism:

Arkansas Gazette, Little Rock, Wednesday, December 9, 1981:

Creationism Premises False, Twist Science, Trial on Act 590 Told
2nd Try Fails to Get Limit on Testimony

By GEORGE WELLS
Gazette Staff

Creation-science is not science, its main premises are false, and its writers frequently twist the work of accepted scientists to meet preconceived notions, a series of witnesses said Tuesday in federal court.

Saint Louis Post-Dispatch, **Wednesday, December 9, 1981:**

Creation-Science Law Assailed

LITTLE ROCK, ARK. (UPI) Requiring teachers to teach creation-science along with evolution would be dreadfully wrong, a geneticist testified Tuesday as scientists continue to criticize the Arkansas creation-science law word by word.

Creation science is not science, said Francisco Ayala, a genetics professor at the University of California at Davis, and no evidence exists to back up the theory as explained in the Arkansas statute.

Jacksonville Journal (Jacksonville, Florida), **Wednesday, December 9, 1981:**

Creation-science Is Absurd, Geologist Tells Arkansas Court

LITTLE ROCK, ARK. (AP) The creation-science which Arkansas law says should be taught alongside evolution in its public schools is as absurd as the theory that the Earth is flat, according to a geologist. G. Brent Dalrymple of the U.S. Geological Survey was one of four witnesses called yesterday by American Civil Liberties Union lawyers as they attacked the state law as an unconstitutional establishment of religion.

Dallas Times Herald, **Wednesday, December 9, 1981:**

Scientists Ridicule Evidence of Creationists

United Press International

LITTLE ROCK, ARK. Scientists testifying against Arkansas' creation-science law Tuesday said evidence intended to back up the concept is based on outdated or discredited research, errors, and misleading statements.

The creation-scientists' claim that the Earth is no more than 20,000 years old, for example, ranks with the flat Earth hypothesis and the hypothesis that the sun goes around the Earth, said Brent Dalrymple of the U.S. Geological Survey.

Jacksonville Journal, Thursday, December 10, 1981:

Creationism Bad for Classes, Official Says

LITTLE ROCK, ARK. (AP) Enforcement of Arkansas' creation statute would turn classrooms into circuses, with students trying to catch
teachers disobeying it, says a school official who opposed the law. If you
implement the law, students would have ample opportunity to catch
the teacher doing wrong, Dennis Glasgow, science director for Little
Rock schools, testified yesterday in the federal court trial of a lawsuit
challenging the statute's constitutionality.

Dallas Times Herald, Thursday, December 10, 1981:

School Official Cites Conflict in Teaching Creation-Science Under New Arkansas Law

United Press International

LITTLE ROCK, ARK. Teachers could not possibly tell their students about creation-science under Arkansas' new law without discussing religion, the science supervisor for Little Rock schools testified
Wednesday.

Testifying in Arkansas' version of the Scopes monkey trial, Dennis
Glasgow said: The first time I came across any of these ideas was in my
Sunday School class.

Bias noted: In addition to the "anti-creationist selectivity" we are
seeing in these news reports, note the pejorative reference to the Scopes
"monkey trial."

The Most Sensational and Distorted Media Reporting of All

The reporting on my own testimony (chapter 4) and cross-examination
(appendix 4) was the most distorted part of the entire trial. It was selec-
tive, twisted, and grossly misleading, as the following typical selections
from the mainline media will demonstrate.

First of all, the entire court transcript of my time on the stand is seventy-seven pages. Of this, the media largely reported on only *two and a half lines!*

Secondly, the media almost entirely ignored my prepared testimony (see chapter 4), which not only was to the heart of the issue but represented some two-thirds of my time on the stand. Instead, they reported only a couple of lines of cross-examination on an entirely irrelevant matter—my personal religious beliefs about demonic deception—which the biased judge should have disallowed.

Third, the entire thrust of the media blitz on my testimony had the effect of discrediting creationism by associating it with the occult, the demonic, and UFOs. This would not have been possible, since the defense attorneys repeatedly objected to it, unless the biased judge (see chapter 3) had allowed it and a biased media had exploited it:

Washington Post, **Friday, December 11, 1981:**

Creationist Tells of Belief in UFOs, Satan, Occult

LITTLE ROCK, Dec. 11. The defense of the Arkansas creation law opened today with a *spectacular courtroom fireworks display* as the opening creationist witness described, under cross-examination his belief in unidentified flying objects, demon possession and the occult, which he said he sees as actual satanic attacks in the world [emphasis added].

Bias noted: First of all, no such thing happened—even figuratively. This was a gross exaggeration. There simply was no "spectacular courtroom fireworks display." This statement is more like a spectacular *media* fireworks display. Second, to ignore the entire testimony—which was at the heart of the controversy—and concentrate on things the ACLU attorneys had no right asking about is a total distortion of objectivity.

The *Post*'s baseless report of courtroom "fireworks" and their focus on UFOs was then picked up by many other newspapers all around the world:

Dallas Times Herald, Saturday, December 12, 1981:

Theologian Testifies UFOs Work of Satan

LITTLE ROCK, ARK. A theology professor testifying Friday in a court test of how creation should be taught in public schools said he believes UFOs exist and are the work of Satan.

St. Petersburg Times, Saturday, December 12, 1981:

Defense in Arkansas Creation Trial Opens With Fiery Cross-Examination

LITTLE ROCK, ARK. The defense of the Arkansas creation law opened Friday with a spectacular courtroom fireworks display as the first witness described under cross-examination his belief in unidentified flying objects, demon possession, and the occult, which he sees as actual satanic attacks in the world.

The Saturday Herald and Leader, Lexington, Ky., December 12, 1981:

Theology Teacher Says He Believes UFOs Satan's Work

LITTLE ROCK, ARK. A theology professor testifying yesterday in a court test of how creation should be taught in public schools said he believes UFOs exist and are the work of Satan.

Norman Geisler, professor of theology and philosophy at Dallas Theological Seminary in Dallas, who testified as the state's first witness, said unidentified flying objects are a satanic manifestation in the world for the purpose of deception.

Jackson Clarion Ledger, Jackson, Miss., December 12, 1981:

Creationism Defense Witness Describes Belief in UFOs, Occult

LITTLE ROCK, ARKANSAS. The defense of the Arkansas creation law opened Friday with a spectacular courtroom fireworks display as the opening creationist witness described under cross-examination his belief in unidentified flying objects, demon possession, and the occult, which he sees as actual satanic attacks in the world.

Arkansas Gazette, Little Rock, Saturday, December 12, 1981:

Theologian Contends UFOs Work of Satan

The final witness for the plaintiffs and the first witness for the state agreed Friday that Act 590 of 1981, the state creation-science law, was inspired by Genesis, but disagreed on whether the law should stand.

In his testimony, Dr. Norman Geisler, a professor of theology and philosophy at Dallas Theological Seminary, who was the first witness called by the state in the trial of the law's constitutionality, also said, "I believe in UFOs—I believe they are a satanic manifestation in the world for the purpose of deception."

Los Angeles Herald Examiner, Saturday, December 12, 1981:

Witness in Creation Trial Links UFOs to Satan

LITTLE ROCK, ARK. (AP) A theology professor testifying yesterday in a court test of how creation should be taught in public schools said he believes UFOs exist and are the work of Satan.

Norman Geisler, professor of theology and philosophy at Dallas Theological Seminary in Dallas, who testified as the state's first witness, said unidentified flying objects are a satanic manifestation in the world for the purpose of deception.

Arkansas Gazette, Little Rock, Saturday, December 12, 1981:

Highlights of Trial

A Dallas theologian, the first witness for the state in the creation-science trial, said Friday that he believed UFOs exist: "I believe they are a satanic manifestation in the world for the purpose of deception."

The witness was Dr. Norman Geisler, professor of theology and philosophy at Dallas Theological Seminary, who also said that he believed that Act 590 reflected the book of Genesis, but that the Bible served as the inspiration for many legitimate scientific inquiries.

Detroit News, Saturday, December 12, 1981:

Creationist Takes Stand, Calls UFOs Work of Devil

LITTLE ROCK, ARK. UFOs are the work of the devil, says the first witness called to defend an Arkansas law that allows teaching creationism in public schools.

They're a satanic manifestation in the world for the purposes of deception, said Norman Geisler, a professor of theology called to help defend the law against a federal suit by the American Civil Liberties Union. Geisler, who said he believes everything in the Bible is true, made his comments under a grueling cross-examination by Anthony Siano, a New York attorney, who with Little Rock attorney Robert Cearley Jr., is assisting the ACLU in the case.

Bias noted: First, the media sensationalized two and a half lines of my seventy-seven-page testimony and largely ignored the heart of the arguments given in favor of teaching creation. Further, not only did the media report it on the day it happened (Dec. 11), but they continued to report it on the 12th, 13th, 14th, and 15th (see below), even though it was old news and new witnesses had taken the stand and given significant testimony.

The Tampa Tribune-Times, Sunday, December 13, 1981:

Creative Testimony at Creationism Trial

LITTLE ROCK, ARK. (AP) Testimony in the trial of a state law requiring balanced presentations of evolution and creation-science has so far encompassed UFOs, the devil and fears about student vigilantes.

Bias noted: Far more relevant testimony as to why creation was science and should be taught alongside evolution was almost totally neglected by the media in favor of the irrelevant, distorted, and exaggerated comments engendered by ACLU attorneys' questions on religious belief which would have been ruled out of order had the judge not been biased against creationism.

The Miami Herald, **Sunday, December 13, 1981:**

UFOs Are Caused by Satan, Witness at Creation Trial Says

LITTLE ROCK, ARK. (AP) A witness who supports teaching creationism in Arkansas public schools says he finds evidence in the Bible for UFOs, which he called a satanic manifestation in the world for the purpose of deception. "I believe everything the Bible affirms is true," Norman Geisler of Dallas Theological Seminary in Dallas testified Friday.

Bias noted: Here again, they make it look as if it was just Bible-thumping theologians who supported the biblical view of creation, when in fact it was a philosopher with a Ph.D., and noted scientists with doctorates in their fields who were only asking that the court be fair and allow both of the only two possible views on origins, rather than just one. The mainline media never presented a fair picture of what really happened. Even my friends reading the reports ended up with a totally lopsided view. And the days following yielded more of the same:

The Daily Democrat, **Woodland-Davis, Calif., Sunday, December 14, 1981 (caption):**

Key ACLU attorney Philip Kaplan catches up on his phone messages during a break in the creation science trial in Little Rock, Ark. this week. Dr. Norman L. Geisler, a professor at Dallas Theological Seminary led off the defense by saying UFOs are a satanic manifestation.

Arkansas Gazette, **Little Rock, Monday, December 14, 1981:**

Satan's UFOs

Considering all the testimony that had preceded creationism's first witness, it could hardly be surprising that Satan has now been introduced in the constitutional test before Federal Judge William R. Overton of Arkansas' creation-science law, Act 590 of 1981. Introducing this fresh element into the trial on Friday was Dr. Norman Geisler, a professor of theology and philosophy at Dallas Theological Seminary, as he began the testimony of defense witnesses called by Attorney General Steve Clark. It was interesting testimony, not only on direct examination but also on cross examination by the attorneys for the American Civil Liberties Union, which represents the plaintiffs, half of them religious leaders themselves.

Bias noted: Neither the law itself, nor the defense attorneys, nor the creation witness had "introduced" "Satan" into the trial. It was the ACLU who introduced him, with the approval of the judge, in order to discredit creation and its witnesses.

The West Australian, Tuesday, December 15, 1981:

Fiery Start to Trial on Creation Law

LITTLE ROCK, Mon: The defense of the Arkansas creation law has opened with a *spectacular courtroom fireworks display* as the opening creationist witness said he believed in unidentified flying objects, demon possession and the occult, which he sees as satanic attacks in the world [emphasis added].

Bias noted: It is noteworthy that not only did media halfway around the world pick up the same bias but they plagiarized the very words from the *Washington Post* report (above). Even some Christian media (see appendix 2) did this same kind of secondhand distorted reporting. The same sensationalized reporting continued after the trial and into the next month, as the next selections indicate:

Chemical and Engineering News, December 21, 1981:

Creationists Expected to Lose Arkansas Fight

There have been some strange moments as the trial has unfolded. For instance, in cross-examination, Norman Geisler, of the Dallas Theological Seminary in Texas, testified that unidentified flying objects are Satanic manifestations in the world for the purpose of deception.

Discover, **February 1982:**

Judgment Day for Creationism

Siano pounced on the Satan reference, pressing Geisler to recall any personal experience that confirmed his belief in the Devil. Geisler declared, "I believe UFOs exist." He explained that they are a satanic manifestation in this world for the purposes of deception.

Bias noted: The ACLU attorney had not "pounced" on the reference to Satan; it was he who, during cross-examination, pried this irrelevant information out of a reluctant witness because a biased judge, overruling the repeated objections of the defense attorneys, allowed him to do so to the discredit of the presumed innocent defendant for whom he was supposed to be providing a fair trial. An unbiased reading of the actual court transcript suppressed for five years (see appendix 4) will verify this analysis.

Other Reports, Some Fair, Many Biased

The following three excerpts are rare examples of good reporting:

The New York Times, **Tuesday, December 15, 1981:**

Professor Defends Teaching of Creation as Stimulating

LITTLE ROCK, ARK., Dec. 14 (AP) Teaching evolution in the public schools without also teaching creationism is tantamount to indoctrination, an educator testified today in defense of Arkansas' new creation science law. Larry Parker, a professor of education at Georgia State University in Atlanta, also said that teaching creationism as well as evolution in public schools would make classes stimulating and thought-provoking.

Arkansas Gazette, **Little Rock, Tuesday, December 15, 1981:**

Perceives Benefits

The other witness Monday was Dr. Larry Parker of Dunwoody, Ga., a professor of education at Georgia State College, who said that students would benefit from being taught both concepts. He said educational psychologists had established that children who were given divergent questions showed an increased divergence of ideas.

Commercial Appeal, Memphis, Tuesday, December 15, 1981:

Creationism Defenders Trip Over Question from Judge

The first witness to testify Monday cited local and national polls that indicate most people want both theories taught in public schools. Students should learn how to think in schools, not what to think, said Dr. Larry E. Parker, associate professor in the department of curriculum and instruction at Georgia State University.

But most reports were biased, as these last few examples show (the first of these also comes from the *Commercial Appeal* article):

Commercial Appeal, Memphis, Tuesday, December 15, 1981:

Creationism Defenders Trip Over Questions from Judge

Another scientist who testified Monday referred to Charles Darwin, the father of evolutionary theory, and said, "I feel if Darwin were alive today he'd be a creation scientist." Dr. Wayne Frair, professor of biology at The King's College in New York, said Arkansas was on the cutting edge of a progressive movement that is cutting through decades of ignorance to let students consider creationism in public schools.

Bias noted: This is a fair but severely truncated statement of one of the most credible witnesses for creation, who is a world-renowned expert on turtles and a member of the American Academy for the Advancement of Science.

Arkansas Democrat, December 16, 1981:

Educators Say Plant Ancestry Proves Creation

Scientific evidence on the ancestries of plants and minerals challenges accepted principles of evolution, creation scientists said Tuesday in defense of Arkansas' creation science law. But one witness confirmed he was a member of the Bible Science Association, which says putting Christ and the Bible and the power of the Holy Spirit back into science is one of the most powerful methods of witnessing in the church today.

Bias noted: This was one of the worst distortions of what a witness actually said. Donald Chittick had just told the ACLU attorney that he did *not* agree with that very statement by another member of the Bible Science Association. Yet the reporter, using guilt by association, lumped Chittick with the very statement he denied, as though he wanted to try to get "Christ and the Bible and the power of the Holy Spirit back into science."

Dallas Times Herald, Wednesday, December 16, 1981:

Zoologist Bases Belief of Origins on Bible

Donald Chittick of Newberg, Ore., explained one way creation-scientists had arrived at the 10,000 year figure for the Earth's age. He said uranium releases helium as it turns into lead, and the amount of helium now in the earth's atmosphere could have been reached in about 10,000 years. Chittick, a Quaker, is a member of the Bible Science Association, Inc. of Minneapolis, Minn., which refers in its creed to evolution as a pagan religion.

Bias noted: More bias against a very credible scientist and witness is expressed here through "guilt by association," giving his religious background and association with a group with "Bible" in their name. All this adds to the impression that creation is just a religious view.

Discover, February 1982:

Judgment Day for Creationism

Little scientific research to support creation had been done by the state's witnesses. Frair's testimony, for example, was essentially negative. He explained that, according to evolutionists' predictions, red blood cells should be smaller in advanced vertebrates. But he had found that some amphibians, although higher on the evolutionary scale than fish, had larger blood cells.

Bias noted: Frair speaks of the bias against him, particularly by *Discover* magazine, in the preface to this book. Having heard his testimony and read his book *The Case for Creation*,[1] I can testify that his testimony was not "essentially negative." He gave numerous positive evidences for creation.

Dallas Times Herald, **Wednesday, December 16, 1981:**

Zoologist Bases Belief of Origins on Bible

Little Rock, Ark. A zoologist testifying in support of Arkansas' creation-science law admitted some of his ideas about the beginning of life *are based on biblical scripture.* Harold Coffin of Loma Linda University, a Seventh-day Adventist school in California, said Tuesday the earth was only about 5,000 years old—contrary to most scientists' opinions—and that life was once wiped out by a massive flood. His belief, he testified, was *based mostly on scripture.* Coffin said the fossils found from the Cambrian period are fully formed, complex creatures much like animals that exist today. Most geologists say the Cambrian period, when the first organisms appeared, was about 500 million years ago. But Coffin said it was 5,000 to 7,000 years ago—not long before a worldwide flood wiped out most animals and left their fossils.

"My data for that is *religious and not really scientific,*" Coffin said. He said the genealogical record in Genesis is one basis for his belief in a young Earth. Based on the scientific evidence alone, Coffin said, he could not argue with evolutionists [emphasis added].

Bias noted: As the emphasized words indicate, three times in this short text reference is made to the creation witness's belief as based on the Bible and not science. This leaves a totally false impression that the Arkansas law he was supporting would be teaching a biblical view, but this is exactly what the law forbade. Coffin was only referring to where he got his view, not the kind of evidence that could be presented for it in a public school.

1. Wayne Frair, *The Case for Creation* (Chicago: Moody, 1976).

Chemical and Engineering News, December 21, 1981:

Creationists Expected to Lose Arkansas Fight

Robert Cearley, a Little Rock lawyer working with the ACLU summed up the state's case for creationism in a post-trial press conference. "I think you saw in the courtroom," he said, "the best effort that could be made on the part of the creation movement to demonstrate the legitimacy of their science and there is no legitimacy."

Bias noted: Why choose an opponent of creation to sum up the creationists' testimony? The media did not use creationists to sum up the evolutionists' view.

Arkansas Gazette, Little Rock, Thursday, December 17, 1981:

Life Brought to Earth from Space, Witness for Defense Testifies

Life arose on earth as a result of organic molecules brought from space by comets, an astronomer testified Wednesday in federal court during the eighth day of the creationism trial. Dr. N. C. Wickramasinghe, head of the applied mathematics and astronomy department of University College of Wales University at Cardiff, said that terrestrial life had its origins in the dust clouds of space. He also said that his theory [was] developed in collaboration with Sir Fred Hoyle, a noted British astronomer.

Bias noted: The media did not mention that the witness believed that life had an intelligent creator. Nor did it mention that he did not identify this creator as being supernatural—both of which were opposite the stereotype the media wished to generate about creationism. The judge also ignored this in his decision that creation involved the idea of a supernatural creator and thus was essentially religious.

Arkansas Gazette, Little Rock, Thursday, December 17, 1981:

Highlights of Trial

Robert Gentry of Oak Ridge, Tenn., testified that radiation damage to rocks indicated the earth might be only a few thousand years old, rather than the 4.5 billion years usually accepted by geologists.

Bias noted: This report is accurate as far as it goes, but does not give the whole story. Gentry presented unrefuted testimony for a view that, if true, would totally destroy the case for evolution. This deserved at least a mention in the report, since the whole case for the only view the court allowed in school (evolution) is entirely dependent on Gentry being wrong. (No science witness for evolution even attempted to respond to Gentry, and the judge dismissed his testimony as a "tiny mystery.")

Chemical and Engineering News, December 21, 1981:

Creationists Expected to Lose Arkansas Fight

The scientists who testified on behalf of creationism maintain that it and evolution are mutually exclusive. Therefore, any evidence against evolution counts as evidence for creationism. The research they testified about, *much of it done in a library,* is directed at showing that what they call evolution cannot have happened and that, therefore, creation must have happened. Much of the rest of their testimony concerned theories purporting to prove that the Earth is only 10,000 years old and that the Earth's geology can be explained by Noah's flood [emphasis added].

Bias noted: The writer said of creationist research that "much of it [was] done in a library," as though this were less than scholarly. The truth is that only a very small fraction of what *any* scientist knows comes from firsthand experimentation; the greater part of *any* scientist's knowledge comes from books in a library.

Judge Overton's Closing Statements

At the close of the trial Judge William R. Overton said, "I will not undertake to decide the validity of the Biblical version of creation nor the theory of evolution." He said, rather, that he would decide whether Act 590 itself is constitutional—in other words, whether it violates the separation of church and state guaranteed under the First Amendment, whether it violated academic freedom, and whether it is unconstitutionally vague.

Bias noted: This is hollow-sounding judicial rhetoric in view of the above noted bias the judge revealed against creation science and the Bible view of creation. He obviously favored "science," which he defined as excluding creation (see chapter 3). He clearly snapped at a witness, saying creation was what you learn in "Sunday school" and is not "science" (see chapter 3).

Discover Magazine (March 1982)

Typical of the secular media, the widely read *Discover* magazine did a major write-up on the trial, photos and all, but it was so biased that it provoked the following letter from me:

Dear Editor:

Your article on the Arkansas Creation-Evolution trial gave me new insights into how evolution has maintained itself in the absence of substantial evidence for over a century.

First, you *emphasized the irrelevant.* The judge said the court would never criticize or discredit any person's testimony based on his or her religious beliefs. Yet you made sure that the irrelevant personal religious beliefs of the creationist witnesses were clearly noted. There was, on the other hand, a conspicuous absence of the radical liberal, agnostic, and atheistic and even Marxistic beliefs of the evolution witnesses.

Second, *you omitted the essential.* Creationism was judged wrong because of its religious source. Yet you omitted all of the crucial testimony that source has nothing to do with the scientific justifiability (as evolution witness Dr. Ruse said). You also failed to inform your readers of my testimony about the source of Kekule's model for the Benzene molecule—

a vision of a snake biting its tail. Or of Tesla (whom you heralded in the same issue) whose source for the alternating current motor was a vision while reading a pantheistic poet (Goethe). What about Socrates, whose inspiration for philosophy came from a religious prophetess, the Oracle of Delphi? Has anyone ever rejected their scientific theories simply because of their odd religious-like source?

Finally, have you told your readers what the ACLU lawyer, Clarence Darrow, said in effect at the Scopes trial (1925), that it is bigotry for public schools to teach only one theory of origins?[2] Oh yes, my insight into evolution. When you emphasize the irrelevant, omit the essential, and forbid the opposing view a hearing, it is easy for a theory to long outlive its evidence. Myths die hard.

Sincerely,
Norman L. Geisler

Conclusion

The media bias at "Scopes II" was sometimes blatant, as seen here, but often more subtle. It was reflected in headlines, pejorative words, guilt by association, and in the very selection of what to cover and what not to cover. Nowhere was this more evident than in my testimony. The best way for readers to verify this for themselves is to read the above news reports of my testimony and then read the word-for-word report of it from the court stenographer, revealed for the first time in this book (in chapter 4 and appendix 4).

The main stereotype of creation perpetrated by the press was that it is a religious view of fundamentalists that is found in the Bible. The courts themselves have bought into this same myth, describing genuine attempts to teach only the scientific evidence both for and against creation/evolution as thinly veiled attempts to establish a fundamentalist religion in the public schools. Nothing could be farther from the facts.

The real tragedy is that the general public is dependent on the media for their impression of what really transpired at this historic and precedent setting trial. And that general impression was seriously distorted.

2. This entire sentence was omitted by *Discover* magazine, with no indication of an omission, when they published my letter.

Christian Media Coverage of the *McLean* Trial

The evangelical Christian media coverage of the trial was generally scant, poor, and secondhand. No major Christian magazine or newspaper assigned anyone to attend the trial daily.

The Moral Majority and the *700 Club* (Pat Robertson) concentrated on unjustly criticizing the attorney general. They gave little substantive reporting on the actual trial proceedings. *The Moral Majority Reports* (February 2, 1982) did publish one eyewitness evaluation of the trial (on page 15).

Eternity magazine (May 1982) published a strongly negative article on the trial by someone who didn't attend. They gave only limited space to an article by a trial eyewitness. But this was granted only after the eyewitness had requested space to try to balance the picture.

Moody Monthly (May 1982) strongly supported the creationists' cause but strangely enough attacked the creation witnesses and defense of the trial. In an article titled, "Arkansas: Where Creationism Lost Its Shirt," they asked: Why did creationism lose? They answered in large bold print:

Its defenders simply would not fight science with science (11). But this is totally false, since the substance of the creationists' case was to present numerous credible scientists who testified to the scientific evidence for creation. *Moody,* not being present at the trial, had bought into the same myth widely circulated by the secular media that it was a "religion vs. science" issue. Like many others, they joined the chorus of criticism of the defense handling of the trial, especially on the matter of question-ing the witnesses' religious beliefs. *Moody Monthly* reported: "Geisler stood behind the state and explained that Clark's staff had objected to this type of question earlier in the trial to no avail and that it would have been futile to have done so again. But Clark's spokesman did not agree with Geisler, and he told *Moody Monthly,* 'It was just part of our strategy not to. We didn't plan to win the case on cross-examination. We planned to win it under direct testimony.'" *Moody's* statement was false since both approaches were true.

Letter from Attorney General's Office to *Moody Monthly*

These false criticisms were apparently due to some misquotes and mis-implications drawn by a freelance reporter *Moody* hired to give his account of the trial. The *Moody* article drew the following response:

Dear Editor:
    The article entitled "Arkansas: Where Creationism Lost Its Shirt," which appeared in the May, 1982 issue of your magazine, suffers from numerous and substantial inaccuracies. While space would not allow an exhaustive cataloging of all errors which the author, Mr. Martin Mawyer, made, it is important that your readers be informed of some of the more serious errors, lest they be lulled into accepting Mawyer's comments as a fair and accurate representation of the trial that actually occurred in Little Rock. Please permit us to bring to your attention the following inaccuracies:
    1. Paul Ellwanger did not help Arkansas legislators and attorneys construct Act 590, as your article states. (page 10.) Ellwanger and other individuals (including Wendell Bird) were solely responsible for draft-ing the bill which eventually became Act 590. No changes were made

in his draft by the Arkansas Legislature, nor was the Attorney General's Office ever consulted prior to passage of the legislation. If we had been consulted prior to the bill becoming law, the result would have been a sounder, more defensible act.

2. Act 590 did not require teachers to spend as much time on creation-science as they spend teaching evolution science. (page 10.) The bill mandated balanced treatment, not equal time. Throughout our defense of the Act, we stressed that balanced treatment did not necessarily mean equal time. Our reading of balanced treatment (and the testimony of defense witnesses) was to the effect that giving balanced treatment would require spending a sufficient amount of time on both creation-science and evolution science so that students could fully understand both theories. The amount of time devoted to each would necessarily vary, depending upon the perceptiveness of the students, the ability of the teachers, and the available scientific evidence for both theories.

3. Mr. Mawyer's characterization of the attempted participation by attorneys Wendell Bird and John Whitehead similarly is inaccurate in several respects. First, Mawyer labeled Bird and White [*sic*] as constitutional attorneys and as experienced creationist attorneys. To the degree that either attorney is called a constitutional expert, they are only self-appointed experts. Since graduation from law school, most of Bird's employment has been as a law clerk to 7 federal judges, a job which consists of reading trial transcripts and doing research. As a law clerk, there is no opportunity to try cases. The difference between reading trial transcripts and actually trying cases is analogous to the difference between reading medical textbooks on the human heart and performing open heart surgery.

The second error by Mawyer lies in his editorializing that we offered Bird only a minor role. In fact, Bird was offered the opportunity to participate in all aspects of the case, but as one member of a team. (This is the same role which expert attorneys have had in other cases with our office in the past.) Not content to merely serve as an integral part of a team, Bird stated in no uncertain terms that if he could not run the team, he would not play at all. It need only be pointed out that it is Steve Clark—not Wendell Bird—who is elected by the people of Arkansas as the State's chief legal officer. Steve Clark never has nor will he ever abdicate the duties and responsibilities entrusted to him by the people of Arkansas.

4. The article states that the Attorney General became extremely upset when, out of 16 witnesses scheduled to witness, only 8 appeared. One, a

Dr. Dean Kenyon, flew into Little Rock and left the next morning. (Page 11.) It is correct that Kenyon left Little Rock abruptly. (We accept as accurate the statement in Mawyer's article that Kenyon left at the urging of Bird. Tampering with witnesses is not looked upon with favor in the legal profession.) Beyond the departure of Kenyon, it is a falsehood to say that the Attorney General was extremely upset when only eight witnesses appeared. The fact is that we made a conscious decision not to call several witnesses whom we had previously listed as potential witnesses. The individuals were not called because we did not need their testimony or they presented various strategic problems for the defense which would have hurt our case more than it could have helped.

5. Perhaps the most serious of Mawyer's many errors is found on page 12, where he states: "Virtually all defendants [witnesses] admitted that they were only familiar with creation in the context of the Bible, not scientific study. This admission laid bare the essential weakness of the entire defense." First, this statement is patently false. The defense expert witnesses said that in their opinion the scientific evidence fit the creation-science model better than that of evolution. All of the defense expert witnesses had done work which in their professional opinion supported creation science. Almost all of the defense science witnesses have had articles published in scientific journals. Thus, there is no basis in fact for the author's quoted statement. Perhaps Mawyer was attempting—in his own inarticulate, imprecise way—to allude to another aspect of our defense. Some (but not all) of our witnesses did admit that their initial interest into [sic] delving into the scientific evidence for creation had been spurred by their study of Genesis. The testimony at trial was uniform that this fact was not relevant to the scientific validity of creation science. The source of a scientific theory is absolutely irrelevant if the facts justify or support the theory. Witnesses for both the plaintiffs and defendants agreed on this point. (For example, Dr. Michael Ruse, one of the plaintiffs' experts in the philosophy of science, testified under cross examination that Marxism is a religion, and that Harvard Professor Stephen J. Gould is motivated by Marxism in espousing a variant on evolution known as punctuated equilibrium. Nonetheless, Ruse said, the fact that Gould's source is religion does not require dismissal of the theory.)

6. Illustrative of Mawyer's slanted postmortem is the slight mention of Dr. Robert Gentry of Oak Ridge, Tennessee, who testified on behalf

of the defendants. Gentry's work is the most compelling evidence within the scientific community for a relatively recent age of the earth. His work, which centers on the age of the granites which underlie the continents, strongly indicates that these granites had to have cooled in a matter of minutes, rather than over millions of years as evolutionary theory presupposes. Mawyer neglected to point out that Gentry is acknowledged as the leading expert in the world on this theory and has provided a test to falsify his theory. To date, his theory has not been falsified.

7. Another glaring error was the statement attributed to a spokesman for the Arkansas Attorney General concerning the testimony of Dr. Norman L. Geisler, a Professor of Theology at Dallas Theological Seminary. (Page 13.) In the context of the article, Mawyer quotes a spokesman for the Attorney General's Office as disagreeing with Dr. Geisler's statement on the reasons why no objection was made to Geisler's testimony on UFOs. Quite the contrary is, in fact, true. Dr. Geisler was the State's leading expert witness on philosophy and religion. The substance of his testimony was never challenged by attorneys for the ACLU on cross examination. Rather, they chose to question Dr. Geisler about a totally unrelated matter, i.e., his belief in the existence of Satan.

Throughout the first several days of the trial the Attorney General strenuously objected to all questions concerning the religious beliefs of witnesses. These objections were consistently overruled by the Court. Indeed, we told the Judge that we had a continuing objection to any question concerning a witness'[s] religious beliefs, and this objection was noted in the official court record. Inasmuch as Dr. Geisler testified on the fifth day of trial (and after the entry of our continuing objection), it would have been mere folly to again object to this line of questioning.

The article further implies that we did not object to the cross examination of Dr. Geisler because it was just a part of our strategy not to. "We didn't plan to win the case on cross examination. We planned to win it under direct testimony." (Page 13.) In actuality, what Mr. Mawyer has done is construct what lawyers term a classic non sequitur (i.e., an inference that does not follow from the premises). The quoted statement deals solely with our cross-examination of ACLU witnesses, not the ACLU's cross examination of our witnesses. The decision not to object to the cross-examination of our own witness (Dr. Geisler) had nothing whatsoever to do with our plan not to win the case on cross examination of the witnesses for the ACLU. In other words, we felt that witnesses for the State could, on direct examination, offer convincing evidence in support of the creation model of origins. We certainly never expected witnesses for the ACLU, who were irrevocably committed to the evolution model of origins, to offer any evidence favorable to our position during cross-examination. Thus, in view of the Court's previous rulings on the admissibility of witnesses' religious beliefs, absolutely no useful purpose would have been served by again objecting during Dr. Geisler's cross examination. To have done so would have only served to emphasize an inconsequential detail.

In conclusion, Mawyer's article is a misleading and inaccurate attempt to utilize the Office of Attorney General and the defense witnesses as convenient scapegoats for the failure of Act 590. The issue of creation science and evolution-science is a complex one, and will continue to be debated for years to come. Mr. Mawyer's article hurts, rather than helps, that debate. But, perhaps we expected too much of him. On page 12 of the article, Mawyer identified Dr. Ariel Roth as a woman (referring to "her deposition"). In all our meetings with Dr. Roth both before and during the trial, he was a man. Someone who cannot accurately report the sex of one individual should not be entrusted with the responsibility of reporting the origin of all mankind.

Yours truly,
STEVE CLARK Attorney General
DAVID L. WILLIAMS RICK CAMPBELL
Deputy Attorney General Assistant Attorney General[1]

The Coverage by *Christianity Today*

Christianity Today hired a freelance reporter who attended only a short time on one day, even though he was living in the Little Rock area. When we asked him why he didn't attend the trial daily, he told us he was going to write a contemporary historical account based largely on the newspaper reports. It was no surprise that the *Christianity Today* report on the trial (January 22, 1982) reflected the same stereotypical

1. This letter, written May 10, 1982, was published by *Moody*. Unfortunately, I am unable to provide the publication date.

irrelevant, sensational, and distorted picture presented in the secular press. I wrote the following letter in response to their coverage:

Dear Editor:

Your article on the Arkansas creation trial was a colossal disappointment and a gross distortion of the truth. By mimicking the secular media's focus on the out-of-context, irrelevant, and sensational, you held up the creation witnesses and defense attorneys to public scorn. You also misrepresented a spokesman for the Attorney General, thereby casting aspersions on the credibility of another witness. Further, you distorted the testimony of the valiant science witnesses, many of whom risked their professional reputations to testify.[2] And contrary to your uninformed claim that they did not fight science with science, these scientists gave three solid days of scientific evidence for creationism. If your reporter had attended the trial he would have known this. Duane Gish, Cal Beisner, Mark Keough, and myself were all evangelical writers present for the whole science testimony, and we all disagree with your gross misrepresentation. Why didn't you get someone who knew what they were talking about? Why did you hire an absentee, free-lance writer from Washington, D.C.? And why did you refuse to print a firsthand account offered you by an evangelical writer [Cal Beisner] who did attend the trial? Why didn't your reporter even telephone any of the above mentioned eye-witness writers to get the facts? And why didn't he use the firsthand material of the prepublication manuscript on the trial (The Creator in the Courtroom, Mott Media) sent to him?

To cap it all off, you printed an interview with Dr. W. T. Brown in which you proudly paraded the scientific evidence you believe should have been given at the trial. Well, a little firsthand knowledge would have told you that this very same scientific evidence was presented at the trial. In brief, your report was woefully ignorant, grossly distorted, and potentially libelous. This is the kind of thing we expect from the world, but not from fellow Christians.

Sincerely,
Norman L. Geisler

2. Robert Gentry was informed after the trial that his contract at the Oak Ridge National Laboratory (Tenn.) would not be renewed. I learned later from an inside source that his boss was not happy that he had testified at the trial.

Institute for Creation Research (ICR) Article

The Institute for Creation Research (ICR) had an accurate but brief (2-page) report in their *Impact* (March, 1982, No. 105) on the trial by Duane Gish, who was an observer at the trial. He spoke of the defense testimony as brilliant and excellent, and concluded: "From his decision it is obvious that Judge Overton (as well as most of the news media) completely ignored the scientific evidence presented by the defense witnesses while accepting without question evidence offered by the plaintiffs' witnesses. Many remarks made by Judge Overton during the trial revealed his bias against the creationist side."

Cornerstone Magazine article (March–April, 1982)

A few other evangelicals took time to talk to eyewitnesses of the trial. Their reports were more insightful. The national magazine of Jesus People USA, *Cornerstone* (March–April, 1982) is an example. The article concludes: "The religion of humanism has such a stranglehold on the courts and on the public school system that if we're going to survive with our religious liberty, we're going to have to stand up and be counted."

Unfortunately however, most of the good reports were brief and/or did not represent the main fountainheads of evangelical public opinion. Secondhand reports, taken largely from secular sources, were the dominant influence on the Christian media.

My *Christianity Today* Article on the *McLean* Trial

After the fact and after its distorted coverage of the Arkansas *McLean* trial (see appendix 2), *Christianity Today* did allow two counterpoint articles on the topic. One article was written by a theistic evolutionist, George Marsden, then of Calvin College, who defended teaching only evolution in the schools. Strangely, Marsden was a confessed evangelical, yet he supported the law which allowed only evolution to be taught and not the view most evangelicals hold, namely, creation. The other article was by myself, defending the right to teach the scientific evidence for both evolution and creation in public school science classes. The article gives what the trial was all about and why I supported the law and was willing to testify for it. The following is a copy of the article, which appeared on March 19, 1982:

Creationism: A Case for Equal Time[1]

By Norman L. Geisler

Between December 7 and 17 of last year [1981], a historic trial took place in Little Rock, Arkansas. The American Civil Liberties Union charged that the recently enacted Arkansas Act 590 (of 1981), which mandated a balanced treatment of creation-science and evolution-science, was a violation of First Amendment guarantees of the separation of church and state. I was asked to be a religious witness for the state in defense of the constitutionality of the law.

The Essence of Act 590

The preamble to the Act states well its purposes:

An Act to require balanced treatment of creation-science and evolution-science in public schools; to protect academic freedom by providing student choice; to ensure freedom of religious exercise; to guarantee freedom of belief and speech; to prevent establishment of religion; to prohibit religious instruction concerning origins; to bar discrimination on the basis of creationist or evolutionist belief; to provide definitions and clarifications. . . .

The crucial section of Act 590 is the fourth, which defines the meaning of "creation science" and "evolution science":

Section 4. Definitions. As used in this act:
(a) "Creation-science" means the scientific evidences for creation and inferences from those scientific evidences. Creation-science includes the scientific evidences and related inferences that indicate: (1) Sudden creation of the universe, energy, and life from nothing; (2) The insufficiency of mutation and natural selection in bringing about development of all living kinds from a single organism; (3) Changes only within fixed limits of originally created kinds of plants and animals; (4) Separate ancestry for man and apes; (5) Explanation of the earth's geology by catastrophism,

1. They should have said "balanced treatment," rather than "equal time."

including the occurrence of a worldwide flood; and (6) A relatively recent inception of the earth and living kinds.

(b) "Evolution-science" means the scientific evidences for evolution and inferences from those scientific evidences. Evolution-science includes the scientific evidences and related inferences that indicate: (1) Emergence by naturalistic processes of the universe from disordered matter and emergence of life from nonlife; (2) The sufficiency of mutation and natural selection in bringing about development of present living kinds from simple earlier kinds; (3) Emergence by mutation and natural selection of present living kinds from simple earlier kinds; (4) Emergence of man from a common ancestor with apes; (5) Explanation of the earth's geology and the evolutionary sequence by uniformitarianism; and (6) An inception several billion years ago of the earth and somewhat later of life.

(c) "Public schools" means public secondary and elementary schools.

Several things should be noted about these "definitions." First, the lists are parallel and opposing views, point by point. Second, the lists are suggestive, not exhaustive. The key word is "includes," which does not mean "limited to." Third, not only are these series of six factors opposing, they are in fact logically opposite.

For example, the universe and life either arose spontaneously, or they were created; there is no third alternative. Also, all living things either have one common ancestry, or they have separate ancestries. The same is true of man (4). Further, either there are changes between fixed kinds or there are not. And the world is either billions of years old, or it is more recent (6). The same contrast is true between "uniformitarianism" and "catastrophism" as explanations of earth's geology (5). Both cannot be true, since one involves millions of years and the other a very short worldwide flood.

It should also be noted that the Act does *not* imply that no combinations of choices can be taught. For example, someone holding to points 1 through 4 of "creation-science" might also opt for 5 and 6 of "evolution-science," or many other combinations. (In fact, I testified in defense of the Act even though for years I have been inclined against catastrophism and a recent earth. These are viable views, held by credible people who have a right to be heard even if I don't believe them.) What the Act does insure is that both sides of *each* issue will be presented.

Another important point is brought out in Section 5:

This Act does not require each individual classroom lecture in a course to give such balanced treatment, but simply requires the lectures as a whole to give balanced treatment; it permits some lectures to present evolution-science and other lectures to present creation-science.

One final point is important (from Section 5):

This Act does not require any instruction in the subject of origins, but simply requires instruction in both scientific models . . . if public schools choose to teach either.

There is thus always the option of avoiding either evolution or creation and sticking to the observable and repeatable areas of science.

Some Misconceptions About Act 590

An informed reader of Act 590 can see that many of the popular misconceptions of what the Act intends are obviously false. Among these false ideas are beliefs that:

1. It mandates teaching of the biblical account of creation. (It actually forbids that.)

2. It is opposed to teaching of evolution. (It actually mandates teaching evolution alongside creation.)

3. It refers to God or religious concepts. (There is no reference to God and it opposes teaching religion.)

4. It forces teachers who are opposed to creation to teach it anyway. (Actually, teachers do not have to teach anything about origins, and/or they can have someone else teach and give the lectures they do not want to give.)

5. It is a "fundamentalist" act. (Actually, the "fundamentalists" of the 1920s were categorically opposed to teaching evolution and wanted only the Genesis account of Creation taught. This Act is contrary to both attitudes.)

Why I Supported Act 590

My first reason for supporting Act 590 is one uttered by Clarence Darrow, the famous ACLU lawyer for the 1925 Scopes trial. He called it "bigotry for public schools to teach only one theory of origins." I found it a strange irony to hear the same ACLU 56 years later argue that, in effect, it would be religious bigotry to allow two models of origins to be taught.

This same inconsistency can be seen in the most recent statement of "A Secular Humanist Declaration" (Winter 1980/81, *Free Inquiry*). It declares admirably:

"The lessons of history are clear: wherever one religion or ideology is established and given a dominant position in the state, minority opinions are in jeopardy. A pluralistic, open democratic society allows all points of view to be heard. Any effort to impose an exclusive conception of Truth, Piety, Virtue, or Justice upon the whole of society is a violation of free inquiry" (p. 4).

And yet only two pages later, in an inconceivable inconsistency, the same declaration says:

"We deplore the efforts by fundamentalists (especially in the United States) to invade the science classroom, requiring that creationist theory be taught to students and requiring that it be included in biology textbooks. This is a serious threat both to academic freedom and to the integrity of the educational process" (p. 6).

For the same reason therefore that I regret the narrow-mindedness of some Christian religionists in the 1920s who opposed the teaching of evolution as a scientific theory, I now deplore a similar narrowness on the part of those holding a humanistic religious perspective (and their sympathizers), who would exclude the teaching of creation as a scientific theory in public schools.

Second, I favor Act 590 in the interest of openness of scientific inquiry. As anyone who has studied the history of Copernicus and Galileo knows, minority scientific opinions are often the cutting edge of progress. Suppression of the "loyal opposition" is seldom if ever good politically, and never scientifically. Academic freedom entails hearing opposing points of view. Many times during the trial I was reminded of the value of the adversary relationship of the courtroom. When only one side of an issue is presented (without cross-examination or rebuttal), a judge or jury would often come to an invalid conclusion.

The same is true when only one view is presented in the classroom: it is a trial without opposing witnesses. Since there are serious religious implications when origins are taught from only one perspective—one that favors humanistic religion—it is necessary as a guarantee to religious neutrality that the opposing view also be taught.

Third, teaching creation is no more teaching religion than is teaching evolution. Creation and evolution are both beliefs that belong to religions, but teaching creationism is no more teaching the Christian religion than is teaching evolution teaching the humanist religion. If teaching a part of a religion is automatically teaching that religion, then teaching values (such as freedom and tolerance) are also teaching religion. But the courts have ruled that values can be taught apart from religion, which may hold the same values. Likewise, creationism can be taught apart from the religious systems of which it may be a part.

The fact that "creation" may imply a Creator while "evolution" does not is no proof that the former is religious and the latter is not. Believing that there is no God can be just as religious as believing that there is a God. Humanists hold, and the Supreme Court has ruled, that belief in God is not essential to religion (*U.S.* v. *Seeger,* 1964).

Fourth, scientific progress depends on teaching alternative models. There would be little progress in science if it were not for minority scientific opinions. Copernicus's view that the earth revolves around the sun was once a minority scientific view. So was the view that the earth is spherical, not flat. If no alternative models to Newton's law of gravitation were allowed, then Einstein's insights (and space travel) would have been rejected and scientific progress retarded.

That creationism may be a minority view among scientists today does not make it wrong, and certainly does not mean it should not be heard in science classes. (Arguing that it should be taught only in social studies classes is like telling someone running for the Senate that he can present his views only to sociologists' groups, but not to political gatherings.) One of the most despicable examples of intellectual prejudice I have ever witnessed was when evolution scientists at the Arkansas trial claimed that creationism was not science and that creationists were not scientists. It reminded me of Voltaire's famous satire in which he described ants on one anthill looking at different colored ants on another anthill and declaring that they were not really ants and that what they were on was not really an anthill.

John Scopes summed up well when he said, "If you limit a teacher to only one side of anything the whole country will eventually have only one thought, be one individual." I believe it would be (is) a gross injustice for the court to rule it unconstitutional to teach both sides of any issue. Although I would not go as far as some in these matters, one can understand why Francis Schaeffer in his recent book, *A Christian Manifesto* (Crossway, 1981), has called upon Christians to engage in civil disobedience and even use force to overcome the tyranny he sees implied in a negative decision in the Arkansas creation-evolution issue.[2]

2. Reprinted by permission.

ACLU Mockery
of Creationist Beliefs

The Cross-Examination
They Refused to Transcribe

Introduction

Very little of the substance of my courtroom testimony was published in the mainline media. The court refused to transcribe it for five years, until after the Supreme Court had ruled on the issue it addressed (in *Edwards,* 1987). Instead, the media chose to stress irrelevant personal religious beliefs of the witness (see appendix 1) which were more sensational and put creationists in a bad light. This kind of questioning was irrelevant and should have been ruled out of order by the judge. Objective reporting should have mentioned that the judge refused to overrule this irrelevant questioning about a witness's personal religious beliefs and that no such questioning took place concerning the liberals, agnostics, atheists, and Marxists who testified for the evolutionists (see also chapter 3).

Defense Protest of ACLU Question About Personal Religious Beliefs of Creationists Overruled by the Judge

The defense attorneys protested on several occasions when the ACLU raised questions about religious beliefs of the witness, but it was to no avail. First, it was objected to in the pretrial depositions. For example, the record reads: "Mr. Campbell: For the record, I object to these questions on the occult, as to their relevance." Second, the defense attorneys made the same objection to the judge during a pretrial discovery on November 16, 1981, but the judge overruled it. Third, at least twice during the trial, defense attorney David Williams objected to using personal religious beliefs of creationists in their testimonies, citing rule of evidence 610, but the judge overruled it again. Finally, our attorney asked for a continued objection to be recorded for the rest of the trial, instead of our having to bring it up every time, and this objection was noted in the official court record. So, it was futile to bring it up again when the ACLU basically ignored the heart of my testimony and decided to divert attention from it by bringing up the more sensational questions about demons, the occult, and the UFO phenomena. This was an obvious attempt to discredit creationists and creationism. With the willing assistance of a biased media, it worked very well. The following is the court record of the rest of my time on the witness stand, namely, the cross-examination:

ACLU Cross-Examination of Norman L. Geisler (December 11, 1981)

CROSS EXAMINATION
BY MR. SIANO: [of the ACLU]
Q Good afternoon, Dr. Geisler.
A Good afternoon.

Q Dr. Geisler, we spoke before on November 14th, didn't we?

A We spoke before, and I'll trust your memory for the 14th.

Q In fact, you gave a deposition that day, isn't that true?

A That's correct.

Q Have you had occasion to read that deposition since that time?

A Yes, I have.

Q Have you made any corrections to it?

A I made about three pages. There were over 100 corrections.

Q All right.

MR. SIANO: Your Honor, as yet I have not received those. I would ask the state for those now.

BY MR. SIANO:

Q Did you give those to the Attorney General's office?

A I think I mailed them back with the deposition.

MR. SIANO: For the record, your Honor, plaintiff has not received these.

MR. WILLIAMS [defense attorney]: Your Honor, I want to state for the record also this is the first time we've been given notice of that. It was my understanding that we had given that to them, and I would have appreciated it if they had let me know before this time. We certainly will get those. I think we have them. Perhaps in all of the documents going back and forth we have not given those.

THE COURT: Do you have them here in court?

MR. WILLIAMS: I do not think—I don't think we have them here, your Honor. We have to check in our office.

THE COURT: Maybe you ought to have somebody do that.

MR WILLIAMS: I'll be glad to do that, your Honor.

BY MR. SIANO:

Q Dr. Geisler, did you make substantive changes in your answers, or did you just correct typographical errors?

A I would say the vast majority of them were typographical. There were a few that commas and periods changed the meaning that might qualify as substantive, depending on how you interpret it. And I can't recall what they were from memory, but I know that if you put a period instead of a comma, something like this, or run two sentences together instead of a period and a capital, that it changed the meaning. There were a couple of those but I can't recall.

Q There were a couple substantive changes?

A Well, it might be considered substantive, because it did change the meaning. Where you put the comma or period changed the meaning.

MR. SIANO: Your Honor, I would ask for a brief recess to see if the state could find their changes. I don't feel appropriate to attempt to use the deposition at this point in time in light of the comment that the witness has made.

THE COURT: Well, I mean—

MR. SIANO: I can state for the record that my cross examination is very brief, and I'm just—there's an appropriate use of a transcript to be made in certain circumstances, but I find myself in an impossible situation. The witness has said he's made corrections. I haven't seen them.

MR. WILLIAMS: Your Honor, I point out for the record, if Mr. Siano had asked this morning, or anytime prior to this, pointed out that perhaps he had not gotten those, we could have had these here and could have avoided the problem and delay.

THE COURT: Well, it may be that the points you're going to ask him about aren't even covered in the corrections. So why don't we go along and if you run into a problem like that we'll take it up.

MR. SIANO: Fine, your Honor.

BY MR. SIANO:

Q Dr. Geisler, you described this taxonomy of transcendence in the various set of descriptions of God. Which of those various descriptions of God is God in the active tense, God active?

A I didn't directly discuss that issue in my typology or categorization of those.

Q Is the theistic God the active God?

A That's certainly one, but it's not the only one, for example—

Q Is that the God of the Bible?

A May I finish?

Q I ask you, sir, is that the God of the Bible?

A No, could I finish my first answer? I wasn't finished.

Q All right, sir, go ahead.

A The theistic God is one; the pantheistic God is also active and the deistic God is also active in the initial creation, and the escatalogical [eschatological] or forward moving God is active; the God up there is active, and coming down. The only one that might not be active of that initial one would be the God who is the ground underneath. But, yeah, about four or five of them are active.

Q Is the theistic God the God of the Bible?

A Theistic God is a God that is the God of the Moslems, historic Judaism and historic Christianity, and there are also some other forms of theism in certain forms of Hinduism. So a theistic God is quite a broad category.

Q Is the God of the Bible a theistic God?

A The God of the Bible is a theistic God, but not all theistic concepts of God are the God of the Bible.

Q In your opinion, Dr. Geisler, could you state what the phrase macro-evolution means to you?

A *I'm not a scientist* [all emphasis added in this appendix].[1]

Q Do you have any understanding at all of the meaning of the phrase macro-evolution?

A Macro means large and micro means small.

Q That's your only understanding of that term?

---

1. As the emphasized words show, I repeatedly denied being a scientist or claiming that my views about the occult were scientific, so as not to lend credibility to the charge I knew they would make that creationists hold weird scientific views.

A I wouldn't say that, but I certainly would say at least that. I don't—*I am not a trained scientist,* and so I wouldn't know how a trained scientist would use that word, but I would say *that in my layman's understanding,* macro means large jumps and micro means small jumps.

Q Doctor, do you recall being asked the following question and giving the following answer in your disposition [deposition] on November 14th?

"Question: That's right. Now, is there any other characteristic of macro-evolution or anything else other than evolution between various kinds of animal life?" Page 145.

A Could I have a copy of that so I could see it?

Q Certainly.

A Thank you very much.

Q Page 145, Doctor, line 18.

MR. WILLIAMS: Excuse me, your Honor, I've been informed by my office that the corrected original was given Ms. Joan Leggett who works for the plaintiffs in this case, and I want that noted for the record, please.

THE COURT: So noted.

MR. SIANO: Thank you, your Honor.

BY MR. SIANO:

Q Do you have that in front of you now?

A Yes, I do.

Q "Question: That's right. Now, is there any other character—

A Which line? I'm sorry.

Q 18.

A Uh-huh.

Q "[Question:] Now, is there any other characteristic of macro-evolution or of anything else other than evolution between various kinds of animal life?"

A "[Answer:] Well, as I understand macro-evolution it is the belief that all living forms are the result of a process of development from previous animal life and that this is ultimately derivable [derivable] from non-living things so that you move from a process of non-living things to living things through the whole philogenetic [phylogenetic] tree up to all the existing families and genera and species that we have today.["]

[Q] Do you recall being asked that question and giving that answer?

A I recall being asked that question and giving that answer but—

Q Thank you, Doctor, that was all my question was.

A Well, I didn't finish my answer. Could I finish it?

Q That was all my question.

A Well, I didn't finish it.

Q Go right ahead, Doctor.

A That was immediately following line 17 where I said *I'm not a scientist,* where you agreed that *I was not a scientist* and that I had accepted that. So, that's my *non-scientific definition.*

Q Doctor, on what line does that answer end?

A Which answer?

Q The answer I just read to you.

A It's on the next page, about line 3 on page 146.

Q And you said it was immediately following your saying—

A No.

Q —you are not a scientist?

A —I said that immediately follows your acknowledgement to my answer that *I am not a scientist* on line 17 of page 145.

Q So you testified as a philosopher that was your understanding of macro-evolution?

A *I testified as a non-scientist* that that was my definition of macro-evolution.

Q And as a non-scientist is it your view that theistic evolution is a macro-evolution model?

A Well, theistic evolution can be understood two ways. It's macro-evolution in the sense that it is macro leaps from the creation of the original life up to the top. It's not macro-evolution in the broader sense that it includes, namely, spontaneous generation instead of the creation. So you can take macro-evolution in two ways.

Q Is it your view that theistic evolution is a macro-evolution model?

A I believe I just answered that.

Q I would ask you to answer me again.

A My answer is that if you understand macro-evolution as the enlarged leaps that it's a macro-evolution model; if you understand macro-evolution to include everything including the original inception of life and man, it's not a macro-evolutionary model.

Q Doctor, I direct your attention to page 178 of the deposition, line 25, and I ask you do you recall being asked the following question and giving the following answer?

["]Question: So you are suggesting that evolution science as it is defined here, forecloses the existence of God?"

"Answer: Well, it does not foreclose it entirely but it implies it, and apart from the theistic evolution model, you know, we're back to our old question about two aspects now. It doesn't foreclose the theistic evolution but it certainly—theistic evolution is a macro-evolution model. Once the first life is created between that and the creation of man's soul, it is macro-evolution in the middle."

Is that a fair statement?

A Yeah, that's just what I said a moment ago.

Q Now, in your opinion does section 4 [b] of Act 590 permit the teaching of theistic evolution?

A Well, let me take a look at that if I may. I think I have a copy here. Would you repeat that reference for me?

Q In your opinion does section 4(b) of Act 590 permit the teaching of theistic evolution?

A Seems to me that if you look at this Act 4(b), which is obviously a subdivision of 4, which includes (a), that as a whole, yes.[2]

Q Section 4(b) permits the existence of God in the context of what you define as macro-evolution.

A That wasn't my answer. My answer is that since (a) and (b) are sub points of 4, you have to take them both together. Taken both together, they surely do.

Q Does section 4(b) permit the existence of God in the context of what you define as macro-evolution?

A Yes, it does, because 4(b), remember, is only one Model. 4(b) is not the total thing that can be taught.

Q So, section 4(b) permits the existence of God in the context of what you describe as the macro-evolution.

A That's correct. 4(b) permits that because it's part of the total Act which permits that to be taught. It's only one part that's being taught.

Q Is it correct that you don't see anything in section 4(b) which directly implies or negates the existence of God?

A 4(b), it seems to means the evolution science means, if that's what you're talking about, evolution science as a theory, a total theory of macro-evolution in the broader sense I defined it earlier, not the God created original life, in the total sense, that theory as a theory eliminates God. There may be a God, but the theory as a theory does not lead to him.

Q Doctor, is it correct to say that you do not see anything in section 4(b) which directly implies or negates the existence of God?

A 4(b) I do see some things that directly imply as the result of that theory, the non-intervention of God into the world, yes.[3]

2. I testified that nothing in the law forbade teachers or students from believing some things from one model and some from another. Thus, it allowed for the teaching of theistic evolution. I also pointed out in my testimony that I did not hold everything in the creation model myself, since I believed in an old universe of billions of years, not a young one of thousands of years as the creation model did.

3. In this section I refused to admit what the ACLU wished to show, namely, that there are more than two views on each point of origin of the universe, first life, and new life forms.

Q Doctor, do you recall being asked the following question and giving the following answer in your deposition?

"Question:" Page 179, line 13, Doctor.

A Let me get it. 179, line 13.

Q "Question: Would theistic evolution in your view come within this description in 4(b) in this statute?"

"Answer: Uh-huh."

"Question: It would?"

"Answer: Uh-huh. Because—let me look at it again. I don't see anything in there with respect—I don't see anything in there with respect to the existence of God directly implied or directly negated. I would have to look at it more closely. Let me look at it. The only thing that would be problematic is point 4, the emergence of man. It all depends on how you define man. If you define man there just in a biological sense, if you define man in a theological sense as having a soul and that was created, then that would be subsequent. Other than that I don't see anything in there that rules out a theistic model, which is part of the good feature. See, it include [*sic*] both. It includes—doesn't eliminate the teaching of the theistic evolutionary model either right along with the other models.

"Question: That's in 4(b)?"

"Answer: Uh-huh."

Q Do you recall being asked those questions and giving those answers?

A Yeah, I agree a hundred percent with what I'd said there, because 4(b) is part of the total act that includes 4(a), and because secondly, the theory as such does not necessarily mean that because a biblical implication of the theory is that no God is needed to originate life, that you have eliminated that possibility of there being a God built on some other grounds, religious experience or what have you.

Each event had either a natural cause or an intelligent cause but not both. Thus there are only two basic models (see appendix 5).

Q Dr. Geisler, is it your view that creation implies a creator?

A Yes, it is.

Q Is it your view, sir, that creation assumes a creator?

A I don't know what you mean by assumes.

Q Doctor, I ask you to direct your attention to page 180 of the transcript, and I ask you if you recall being asked this question and giving this answer.

"Question: 4(a) assumes the existence of a creator you testified."

"Answer: Yeah, that's right."

Do you recall being asked that question and giving that answer?

A Uh-huh.

Q Is it your view that creation assumes a creator, Doctor?

A Well, in the context in which I understood the word assume at that time, I certainly agree.

Q And, Dr. Geisler, does section 4(a) of Act 590 set forth a model for creation science?

A I don't know. Let's look at it. 4(a)? A model for creation science. Yes. Yes, it does.

Q And is it a fact, sir, that you would find it absurd to talk about a creation science model with no God?

A Oh, I think that that's a logical implication. As I testified earlier, when you talk about creation to me, you must logically infer a creator.

Q So you would find it absurd to talk about a creation science model without a God? [4]

A I find it absurd to think of Webster's unabridged dictionary resulting from explosion in a printing shop.

Q Dr. Geisler, I asked you—

A Yes is the answer to that question.

---

4. The ACLU wanted us to admit that creation implied a creator (which it does), but they also wanted us to use the word "God," since they knew it was loaded with religious connotations to many people. Hence, I preferred to use the term "creator" or "designer."

Q Thank you.

A That's my illustration.

Q Now, do you acknowledge Mr. Henry Morris as an authority on creation science?

A I acknowledge that I was not an authority on science, but in my non-scientific understanding I understood that he was a scientist, a hydrologist who had a Ph. D. and who wrote on this topic, and in that sense was an authority, yes.

Q Do you acknowledge him today as an authority on creation science?[5]

A In that same sense, yes.

Q And do you acknowledge Mr. Morris's book "Scientific Creationism" as an authoritative work in the field of creation science?

A I think—I didn't read the larger book. You may recall my deposition. I only read that smaller one which had a slightly different title. So, I can't really tell you.

Unless the larger one was a lot better than the smaller one, I would say he's not one of the better authorities on it.

Q So, you don't recognize his book: "Scientific Creationism"?

A I recognize him as a scientist who has a Ph.D. and in that sense is an authority and who wrote on this topic, but I don't think that his book that I read, the smaller one, which is the case, I think it's called "The Case for Scientific Creationism," and I did not read the larger one as I told you in the deposition, I don't consider that little one to be one of the better cases I've seen.

Q Doctor, I ask you to look at your deposition and I ask you if you recall being asked the following question and giving the following answer. Page 87, line 18, Doctor.

"Question: This gentleman Morris that you—is that Henry Morris?"

5. Throughout this section I refused to call many of these people experts because I knew the ACLU would use that to imply that I approved of things these people may have said in their books that would make creation science look like a religious view.

"Answer: Yeah, Henry Morris."

"Question: Is he in your mind an authority on creation?"

"Answer: He's one of the authorities on scientific creationism, yeah."

And on the next page, Doctor, being asked the following question.

"Question:" Line 9. "I'm just trying to get if you recognize him as an authority of scientific creation."

"Answer: Yes. Yes, I do recognize him as an authority and so—Gish also."

Do you recall being asked those questions?

A I agree with that.

Q And giving those answers?

A Yes. That's what I just said.

Q And on page 125. "Do you recognize Mr. Morris's book "The Scientific Case for Creation" as a recognized work in the area of scientific creationism?"

A You may recall at this time there was some ambiguity in my mind as to whether that was the little one or the large one or he had two, and I recognize that he had written one by a similar title. It turned out in the end that we clarified when you brought out the books that it was the smaller one I had read.

Q And that's the one you recognize?

A That's the one I recognize, yes.

Q Doctor, I would ask you if you would agree with the following statement from what has been marked—

A Could I ask for a copy of that so I can see it in context?

Q Certainly.

A Thank you.

Q The last page of the preface, Doctor, and I ask you if you agree with this statement. "The scientific model of origin that best fits all the available scientific data is that of recent supernatural creation of the universe and all its basic components by a transcendent creator."

Do you agree or disagree with that statement?

A I disagree.

Q Now, Doctor, is R. L. Wysong an authority on creation science?

A I think I should state why I disagree.

Q Well, I didn't ask you a question about that, Doctor, and if Mr. Campbell wants to, he can ask you one.

Now, is Mr. Wysong an authority on creation science?

A I don't know Mr. Wysona [*sic*]. I know one book he has written which he compares the two models which I have read, and I thought it was an excellent comparison. But to tell you the truth, I don't recall what his degrees were. I think he was a doctor, he had some kind of doctor's degree, but he may have been a medical doctor for all I recall.

Q And acknowledge Mr. Wysong's book: "The Creation Evolution Controversy" as an authoritative work in the field of creation science?

A I recognize it as a book in that field written by somebody who I think had a doctor's degree, and that as I read the book, and I did read that book, it had an excellent comparison between the two models, and in that sense an authority, yeah.

Q You consider it an excellent book don't you?

A An excellent comparison of the two models, yes. It's brief, it is a summary but it's a good comparison of the two models.

Q Did you not describe to me, sir, the book as an excellent one?

A Yes, that's just what I said. It's an excellent comparison of the two.

Q Did you use the word comparison in your answer to me?

A I think I told you that I thought the book was balanced because it compared both models and it came to no explicit conclusions at the end. It more or less said here are the two models, draw your own conclusions.

Q Doctor, I ask you to direct your attention to page 88 of your deposition, and I ask you, sir, if you recall being asked the following question and giving the following answer.

"Question: All right. Have you had occasion to examine any other books in the area of scientific creationism?"

"Answer: Yes. One of the things I brought and I think I gave you is a bibliography on evolution. It's called "Select Bibliography on evolution." And there are a number of books on there that I have examined. A good one on this topic is by Wilder Smith, the second one from the last, called "Man's Origin, Man's Destiny." Another excellent one is by Wysong, W-y-s-o-n-g, entitled "The Creation Evolution Controversy," Inquiry Press, 1978. I've also looked at a number of other books on this list, but they are two that I would recommend as creditable books from that point of view."

Do you recall being asked that question and giving that answer?

A Yes, I agree with that answer.

Q I direct your attention, sir, to page 7 of that book and I ask you do you agree or disagree with the following statement in the middle of the page there. "Many have drawn conclusions from evolution and made applications to various facets of life (i.e. they have followed through from origins to world view to behavior). Social evolution provided in part the basis for fascism and its oppressive racist actions. Evolution pervaded Mussolini's thinking to the point that he justified war as did Nietzsche on the basis that it provided["]—what's the next word, Doctor, there?

A The.

Q "The reason for evolutionary progress."

A You read that incorrectly.

Q What's the word I missed?

A You missed means.

Q —"means for evolutionary progress." Do you agree or disagree with that statement?

A I certainly agree with that statement, because it says many have drawn these conclusions and surely many have.

Q Doctor, I direct your attention to page 10 of that book, and I ask you do you agree or disagree with the following statement. "There are two possible explanations for the origin of life."

A Excuse me, I don't see where you—

Q Excuse me, page 10 below figure 1 possible roots. "There are two possible explanations for the origin of life. If we owe our existence to change, then our approach to life could be amoral, i.e., it could take any direction and be justified. On the other hand, if we were created, we are responsible to that Creator. We must then seek his will, the correct religion." Do you agree with that statement?

A I think some people have drawn that implication from that statement. Nietzsche himself did when he said If [sic] God is dead all values die with him.

Q Do you agree or disagree with that statement?

A I have to have great admiration for the atheist Nietzsche. I think he had some profound insights, and I think that's one—

THE COURT: Excuse me, that's a yes or no answer.

THE WITNESS: I think that's one of them, yes.

BY MR. SIANO:

Q I'd like to read you another statement from that page, sir. "Without regard for whether particular actions are correct relative to the true will of the Creator, let's examine the far reaching effects creation has had. Belief in a supernatural Creator or religion as it is commonly termed, is or has been part of every human society. Religion has held sway from the African witch doctor menacing his tribe under an iron hand to modern political church-state marriages. Religion up to the present century ruled practically absolute on all aspects of human activity. Not only was a moral code dictated, but in premature [imprimatur] was required for scientific inquiry and even philosophical thought."

   Do you agree or disagree with that statement?

A I'd have to look at the context. Is this what he is saying or is this what he is describing someone else believes?

Q You have the book, Doctor.

A Well, if you'll give me time to read the chapter, I'll be glad to answer it. If you know now, you'll facilitate my time.

Q Doctor, when you recommended this book to me, had you read it?

A Yes, I have, uh-huh.

Q And would you like to examine it again now?

A If you would like me to answer that question, I'd like to see the context.

Q I would like to ask you, sir, do you—can you now, sitting on the witness stand, agree or disagree with that statement?

A If I, knew what the statement meant, I could. You can't agree or disagree until you know what it means.

Q And I believe, sir, you acknowledge Mr. Dwavne [Duane] Gish as an authority on creation science?

A That's correct.

Q And you acknowledge Mr. Gish's book "Evolution, the Fossils say No," as a recognized work in the area of creation science?

A I haven't read that book.

Q Do you acknowledge it, sir, as a recognized work in the area of creation science?

A If you recognize what I said, that I'm a non-scientist and that I haven't read it and would you like to have a comment from a non-scientist who hasn't read the book, I can give you an ignorant comment, too.

Q Do you rec—

A Namely, I don't—I would guess that it might be.

Q Is that a yes, sir?

A That's the best I can do having not read the book.

Q You are a theologian, sir?

A Philosopher and theologian, that's correct.

Q And in fact, sir, you believe that the Bible is factually inerrant?

A I believe that everything the Bible affirms is true, is true.

Q Is it your opinion, sir, that the Bible is factually inerrant?

A That's what I mean by inerrancy. Inerrancy has classically been defined that same way from time immemorial from Augustin[e], Aquinas, B. B. Warfield, and I believe the same way. Whatever the Bible teaches is true, is true.

Q Doctor, could you turn your transcript to page 74.

A Yes, I will.

Q Do you recall being asked the following question and giving the following answer?

"Question: Could you, not to test your memory beyond the realm of reason, but could you identify for me as many of those points as you recall?"

"Answer: Well, I'll simplify the matter. I'll identify the points that relate directly to this. We believe that the Bible is inerrant, that it is without error in everything it teaches on every topic that it teaches anything on, including science and creation in the book of Genesis."

Do you recall being asked that question and giving that answer?

A That's exactly what I just told you a moment ago.

Q And is it your opinion, sir, that strict factual inerrancy is the orthodox Christian view of the Bible?

A If you could tell me what strict means I could answer.

Q Doctor, I'd like to direct your attention to page 118 of the deposition. Line 19, sir. Do you recall being asked this question and giving this answer?

"Question: But you were quite clear in answer to my question that strict factual inerrancy was not sectarian."

"Answer: That's right. Because strict factual inerrancy is the historic, fundamental, orthodox position and I would define sectarian as that which is broken away from the orthodox position."

A If that's what strict means, then I accept strict, because if strict means everything the Bible teaches is true, I believe everything the Bible teaches is true.

Q So you believe, sir, that the strict factual inerrancy of the Bible is the orthodox Christian view of the Bible?

A I believe that it's the orthodox view that whatever the Bible teaches is true is true, and if that is what you mean by strict factual inerrancy, that's been believed by all orthodox down through the years up to modern times.

Q Doctor, as an expert, do you have an understanding of the meaning of the word Satan?

A As a theologian I do: yes.

Q What is your understanding, sir, as a theologian of the meaning of the word Satan?

A I don't really have anything to add to my original definition I gave earlier. If you'd like me to repeat it, I'd be glad to.

Q I would like you to tell me, sir, what your understanding of the word Satan is.

A My understanding is, as I said earlier, that there is a supreme God who created good spiritual beings called angels and that some of these good spiritual beings rebelled against God. The leader of the group, whose name was Lucifer, was then turned into Satan, an adversary of God and that he is in the world deceiving people and doing things to distort and destroy the program of God in the world, and he was the one who tempted Jesus and that Jesus talked to and resisted in his temptation in the Gospels.

Q Doctor, do you recall being asked the following question and giving the following answer in your deposition? "Question:"—

A What page, sir?

Q 133, line 7.

A 133, line 7. Thank you.

Q "Question: In this quote I read to you from one of the quotes I read to you from Mr. Morris in connection with evolutionary philosophy, he used the term Satan. As an expert, do you have a view of the meaning of that word?"

"Answer: Yes, uh-huh, I do. I believe that the word Satan as described in the Bible and as held by orthodox Christians down through the years refers to an intelligent, personal superhuman being who rebelled against God and with him a whole host of other beings called angels who are now demons."

Do you recall being asked that question and giving that answer?

A That's just what I said a moment ago.

Q And do you believe that Satan exists?

A I believe the Bible and the Bible teaches that Satan exists. I believe Jesus; he taught Satan exists, so, yes, I do.

Q Has your belief in the existence of Satan been confirmed by any experiences?

A Since I believe that the Bible is true, I try to make correspondence between my views and the world in which I live so that the Bible says that certain things happen like Hesekiah [Hezekiah] had a tunnel and I think it's worthwhile for archeologists to do, and if the Bible says that Satan can perform certain acts of deception in this world, that he can move physical objects, for example, then I believe that it's perfectly legitimate for me to use that model to help interpret the data I see in the world, like the occult.

Q Has your belief been confirmed by any experience, Doctor?

A I think that if you want to call that confirmation, that is, correspondent occult observation in the world to what the Bible model teaches, that I think that the answer would be yes.

Q Doctor, what other experiences have confirmed to you as an expert the existence of Satan?

A If by expert you mean as a theologian who takes the Bible as true on every topic, and who looks for that as it's applied to the world, I would say a number of them. Demon possession, exorcism, number of things that one could think—occult activities such as I described earlier, that it occurs in contact with the force so that you can move physical objects, that type of thing.

Q Anything else, Doctor?

A I don't know how long you want to take.

Q Doctor, do you recall on page 134 of your deposition being asked the following and giving the following answer. "Question: What experiences have confirmed to you, sir, as an expert the existence of Satan?"

"Answer: Dealing with demon possessed people, exorcism, the study of UFO phenomena and the study of the occult."

Do you recall being asked that question and giving that answer?

A That's correct, I agree with that.

Q Doctor, what do the letters UFO stand for?

A Unidentified flying object.

Q And have you read books on UFO's?

A Yes, I have.

Q And have you seen films on UFO's?

A Yes. Yes I have.

Q And have you talked to people who claim to have had UFO experiences?

A Yes, I have.

Q And is it your professional opinion that UFO's exist?

A My professional opinion that the Bible is true and the Bible teaches such phenomena exist in the world, and I would identify the UFO as one of those phenomena, and I would draw your attention to the fact that credible scientists such as Carl Sagan believes [*sic*] in extraterrestial [extraterrestrial] intelligence with not nearly as much evidence and that people believe in parapsychology on the same kind of basis, and I would identify on the basis of a "Science Digest" article, 1981 which says that scientists have observed UFO's, that many scientists themselves have confirmed it, and Dr.

Heinich [Hynek][6] of Northwest [*sic*] University and University in Chicago area [*sic*] has, and on the basis of that evidence and the Biblical model, I think that confirms what I understand by Satanic deception.

Q Doctor, do you have a professional opinion about the existence of UFO's?

A I think I just answered you. My professional opinion as a theologian is the Bible is true and the Bible teaches this kind of thing can and does occur in the world, and this seems to me to be an example of it.

Q Doctor, do you recall me asking you this question in a deposition?

A I'm looking at it right here.

Q Do you recall me asking you the question in the deposition?

A Yes, I do.

Q Do you recall the question being asked and the following answer given? "Question: Do you have any professional opinion as to the existence"—

MR. CAMPBELL: What page?

MR. SIANO: 136, line 24.

BY MR. SIANO:

Q "Question: Do you have any professional opinion as to the existence of UFO's?" "Answer: Yes. I believe that UFO's exist." Do you recall being asked that question and giving that answer?

A I recall already answering it three times today.

Q And I ask you, sir, how are UFO's connected with Satan?

A And I think I've already said that I think that they are a Satanic manifestation in the world for the purpose of deception.

MR. SIANO: No further questions, your Honor.

THE COURT: Anything else, Mr. Campbell?

MR. CAMPBELL: No, your Honor.

6. J. Allen Hynek, one-time professor at Northwestern University and coauthor of *The Edge of Reality* (Chicago: Regnery, 1975).

THE COURT: You can step down, Dr. Geisler.

MR. CEARLEY: Your Honor, I would like to note for the record on Mr. Williams' behalf that those corrections were delivered to my office and in the tumult surrounding getting ready for this case, they were overlooked.

THE COURT: Okay, well, you're fully off the hook. It's on the record, Mr. Williams .

MR. WILLIAMS: Thank you, your Honor.

THE COURT: We'll take a recess until 2:30.

(Recess.)

The *Webster* Case

Introduction

The case known as *Webster v. New Lenox School District* (1990) was argued February, 1990, and decided on November 6, 1990. Ray Webster had sued the New Lenox school district, where he taught, claiming his First and Fourteenth Amendment rights were violated when New Lenox prohibited him from teaching a nonevolutionary theory of creation in the classroom. The district court denied his claims, as did the appeals court, whose decision follows:

BACKGROUND

The district court dismissed Mr. Webster's suit for failure to state a claim upon which relief can be granted. . . . It is well settled that, when reviewing the grant of a motion to dismiss, we must assume the truth of all well-pleaded factual allegations and make all possible inferences in favor of the plaintiff. . . .[1]

1. Ellipses denote places where technical legal references have been eliminated.

A complaint should not be dismissed "unless it appears beyond doubt that the plaintiff can prove no set of facts in support of his claim which would entitle him to relief." . . . This obligation is especially serious when, as here, we deal with allegations involving the freedom of expression protected by the first amendment. . . . ("where government action is challenged on first amendment grounds, a court should be especially 'unwilling to decide the legal questions posed by the parties without a more thoroughly developed record of proceedings in which the parties have an opportunity to prove those disputed factual assertions upon which they rely'") (quoting *City of Los Angeles v. Preferred Communications* . . . (1986)). Courts may, however, consider exhibits attached to the complaint as part of the pleadings. . . . (1988). With these constraints in mind, we set forth the pertinent facts.

A. *Facts*

Ray Webster teaches social studies at the Oster-Oakview Junior High School in New Lenox, Illinois. In the Spring of 1987, a student in Mr. Webster's social studies class complained that Mr. Webster's teaching methods violated principles of separation between church and state. In addition to the student, both the American Civil Liberties Union and the Americans United for the Separation of Church and State objected to Mr. Webster's teaching practices. Mr. Webster denied the allegations. On July 31, 1987, the New Lenox school board (school board), through its superintendent, advised Mr. Webster by letter that he should restrict his classroom instruction to the curriculum and refrain from advocating a particular religious viewpoint.

Believing the superintendent's letter vague, Mr. Webster asked for further clarification in a letter dated September 4, 1987. In this letter, Mr. Webster also set forth his teaching methods and philosophy. Mr. Webster stated that the discussion of religious issues in his class was only for the purpose of developing an open mind in his students. For example, Mr. Webster explained that he taught nonevolutionary theories of creation to rebut a statement in the social studies textbook indicating that the world is over four billion years old. Therefore, his teaching methods in no way violated the doctrine of separation between church and state. Mr. Webster contended that, at most, he encouraged students to explore alternative viewpoints.

The superintendent responded to Mr. Webster's letter on October 13, 1987. The superintendent reiterated that advocacy of a Christian viewpoint was prohibited, although Mr. Webster could discuss objectively the historical relationship between church and state when such discussions were an appropriate part of the curriculum. Mr. Webster was specifically instructed not to teach creation science, because the teaching of this theory had been held by the federal courts to be religious advocacy.

[This paragraph was a footnote in the actual court record.] *Edwards v. Aguillard* . . . (1987), the Supreme Court determined that creation science, as defined in the Louisiana act in question, was a nonevolutionary theory of origin that "embodies the religious belief that a supernatural creator was responsible for the creation of humankind."

Mr. Webster brought suit, principally arguing that the school board's prohibitions constituted censorship in violation of the first and fourteenth amendments. In particular, Mr. Webster argued that the school board should permit him to teach a nonevolutionary theory of creation in his social studies class.

B. *The District Court*

The district court concluded that Mr. Webster did not have a first amendment right to teach creation science in a public school. The district court began by noting that, in deciding whether to grant the school district's motion to dismiss, the court was entitled to consider the letters between the superintendent and Mr. Webster because Mr. Webster had attached these letters to his complaint as exhibits. In particular, the district court determined that the October 13, 1987 letter was critical; this letter clearly indicated exactly what conduct the school district sought to proscribe. Specifically, the October 13 letter directed that Mr. Webster was prohibited from teaching creation science and was admonished not to engage in religious advocacy. Furthermore, the superintendent's letter explicitly stated that Mr. Webster could discuss objectively the historical relationship between church and state.

The district court noted that a school board generally has wide latitude in setting the curriculum, provided the school board remains within the boundaries established by the constitution. Because the establishment clause prohibits the enactment of any law "respecting an establishment of religion," the school board could not enact a curriculum that would inject religion into the public schools. U.S. Const. amend. I. Moreover, the district court determined that the school board had the responsibility to ensure that the establishment clause was not violated.

The district court then framed the issue as whether Mr. Webster had the right to teach creation science. Relying on *Edwards* ... (1987), the district court determined that teaching creation science would constitute religious advocacy in violation of the first amendment and that the school board correctly prohibited Mr. Webster from teaching such material. The court further noted: Webster has not been prohibited from teaching any nonevolutionary theories or from teaching anything regarding the historical relationship between church and state. Martino's [the superintendent] letter of October 13, 1987 makes it clear that the religious advocacy of Webster's teaching is prohibited and nothing else. Since no other constraints were placed on Webster's teaching, he has no basis for his complaint and it must fail.

Webster v. New Lenox School Dist., Mem. op. at 4-5 (N.D. Ill. May 25, 1989). Accordingly, the district court dismissed the complaint.

[This paragraph was a footnote in the actual court record.] The district court also addressed the claims of another plaintiff, Matthew Dunne. Mr. Dunne was apparently a student in Mr. Webster's social studies class. The district court determined that Mr. Dunne failed to state a cognizable first amendment claim because his desire to obtain information about creation science was outweighed by the school district's compelling interest in avoiding establishment clause violations and in protecting the first amendment rights of other students. Mr. Dunne is not a party to this appeal.

Analysis

At the outset, we note that a narrow issue confronts us: Mr. Webster asserts that he has a first amendment right to determine the curriculum content of his junior high school class. He does not, however, contest the general authority of the school board, acting through its executive agent, the superintendent, to set the curriculum.

This case does not present a novel issue. We have already confirmed the right of those authorities charged by state law with curriculum development to require the obedience of subordinate employees, including the classroom teacher. Judge Wood expressed the controlling principle succinctly in *Palmer v. Board of Educ* .... 1979. ... when he wrote:

"Parents have a vital interest in what their children are taught. Their representatives have in general prescribed a curriculum. There is a compelling state interest in the choice and adherence to a suitable curriculum for the benefit of our young citizens and society. It cannot be left to individual teachers to teach what they please." Yet Mr. Webster, in effect, argues that the school board must permit him to teach what he pleases. The first amendment is "not a teacher license for uncontrolled expression at variance with established curricular content." . . . (holding that individual teacher has no constitutional prerogative to override the judgment of his superiors as to proper course content) . . . (1973). Clearly, the school board had the authority and the responsibility to ensure that Mr. Webster did not stray from the established curriculum by injecting religious advocacy into the classroom. "Families entrust public schools with the education of their children, but condition their trust on the understanding that the classroom will not purposely be used to advance religious views that may conflict with the private beliefs of the student and his or her family." *Edwards* . . . (1987).

A junior high school student's immature stage of intellectual development imposes a heightened responsibility upon the school board to control the curriculum. See *Zykan v. Warsaw Community School Corp.* . . . (1980). We have noted that secondary school teachers occupy a unique position for influencing secondary school students, thus creating a concomitant power in school authorities to choose the teachers and regulate their pedagogical methods. *Id.* "The State exerts great authority and coercive power through mandatory attendance requirements, and because of the students' emulation of teachers as role models and the children's susceptibility to peer pressure." *Edwards.* . . . (1987)

It is true that the discretion lodged in school boards is not completely unfettered. For example, school boards may not fire teachers for random classroom comments. *Zykan.* . . . Moreover, school boards may not require instruction in a religiously inspired dogma to the exclusion of other points of view. *Epperson v. Arkansas* . . . (1968). This complaint contains no allegation that school authorities have imposed "a pall of orthodoxy" on the offerings of the entire public school curriculum, *Keyishian v. Board of Regents* . . . (1967), "which might either implicate the state in the propagation of an identifiable religious creed or otherwise impair permanently the student's ability to investigate matters that arise in the natural course of intellectual inquiry." *Zykan* . . . . Therefore, this case does not present the issue of whether, or under what circumstances, a school board may completely eliminate material from the curriculum. *Cf. Zykan....* (school may not flatly prohibit teachers from mentioning relevant material). Rather, the principle that an individual teacher has no right to ignore the directives of duly appointed education authorities is dispositive of this case. Today, we decide only that, given the allegations of the complaint, the school board has successfully navigated the narrow channel between impairing intellectual inquiry and propagating a religious creed.

Here, the superintendent concluded that the subject matter taught by Mr. Webster created serious establishment clause concerns. *Cf. Edwards* . . . ("The Court has been particularly vigilant in monitoring compliance with the Establishment Clause in elementary and secondary schools."); *Epperson* . . . (schools may not adopt programs that aid or oppose any religion). As the district court noted, the superintendent's letter is directed to this concern. "Educators do not offend the First Amendment . . . so long as their actions are reasonably related to legitimate pedagogical concerns." *Hazelwood School Dist. v. Kuhlmeier* . . . (1988). Given the school board's important pedagogical interest in establishing the curriculum and legitimate concern with possible establishment clause violations, the school board's prohibition on the teaching of creation science to junior high students was appropriate. See *Palmer v. Board of Educ....* (1979) (school board has "compelling" interest in setting the curriculum). Accordingly, the district court properly dismissed Mr. Webster's complaint.[2]

Conclusion

The same biases of the court are evident here as in *McLean* (1982), *Edwards* (1987), and *Dover* (2005). Our comments on those cases will not be repeated here (see chapters 3, 5, 7, and 8).

2. *Webster v. New Lenox School District,* 917 F. 2d. 1004 (7th Cir. 1990).

Only Two Views
of Origin Events

A common objection evolutionists level at creationists is that their belief that there are only two views of origin—creation and evolution—leads to a false dualism. Creationists disagree, of course, but the courts have agreed with evolutionists. We will now look at two wrong conclusions that both evolutionists and the courts often draw because of their belief in this false dualism on the part of creationists.

First Wrong Conclusion: "If Creation Is Taught, Many Other Views Should Also Be Taught"

Creationists often argue that only evolution is taught in schools, and creation is the only other view, and therefore, creation should also be taught. Evolutionists often respond by noting that there are many other views of origin, and if creation is taught, then all these other religious views (e.g., Buddhist, Hindu, Polytheist, etc.) would have to be taught too. Creationists respond as follows:

First, creation science or intelligent design are not religious views (see chapter 8). In all the major court cases since *Scopes* (1925) creationists have proposed to teach origins only from a scientific point of view and have proposed laws explicitly forbidding the use of any religious sources as a basis for teaching creation. So, the evolutionists' objection is a straw man.

Of course there is truth in the objection that there is more than one view of creation. Some creationists want young earth and catastrophism (flood geology) taught as well (see *McLean,* 1982). Others, as in the *Edwards* case (1987) left this out of their law. Further, there are creationists who believe that the intelligent designer is within the universe (such as Fred Hoyle, Chandra Wickramasinghe, and Francis Crick). Most other creationists arguing in the U.S. courts have believed that the schools should be open to hearing evidence for a supernatural creator outside the universe. Evolutionists ask: Which creation view should be taught? If we allow one, then will we not have to allow all?

However, creationists point out that the same problem exists with evolution, which includes more than one view. There are Darwinists and neo-Darwinists. There are gradualism and punctuated equilibriumism. Which one should be taught? The answer is both. Any evolutionary view that has scientific evidence to offer should be allowed to offer it. Likewise, any creationist view that has evidence to offer should not be refused the opportunity to offer it.

Second Wrong Conclusion: "Evidence Against Evolution Is Not Evidence for Creation"

Even more important to the debate is the evolutionists' contention that what argues *against* evolution does not necessarily argue *for* creation. The absence of evidence for a natural cause does not automatically mean that there must have been a supernatural cause. The *absence of evidence* is not *evidence for absence* of a natural cause. There may be an unknown natural cause, and scientists should not give up looking for it. In response to this argument, it is important to remember several things.

First, when we break down the origin dispute into its three main issues—the origin of the universe, the origin of first life, and the origin of new life forms—we can see that, logically, there can be only one of two possible views on each issue.

On the origin of the universe, it has either a natural cause or a supernatural one. There are no other logical alternatives. So, if it was not a natural cause, then it must have been a supernatural cause. This is precisely why even agnostic proponents of the Big Bang theory, like Robert Jastrow, are willing to say: "That there are what I or anyone would call supernatural forces at work is now, I think, a scientifically proven fact."[1] For if, as the Big Bang theory concludes, the universe had a beginning, then the cause of it would have to be beyond the natural world and would, then, by definition be a supernatural cause.

On the origin of first life, even evolutionists agree that there are only two possible causes: natural and intelligent. Famous evolutionist George Wald affirmed: "The reasonable viewpoint was to believe in spontaneous generation; the only alternative, to believe in a single, primary act of supernatural creation. There is no third possibility."[2] Even Charles Darwin speaks of the two opposing views as "the theory of creation" and "the theory of evolution."[3] Jastrow agreed, saying: "Either life was created on the earth by the will of a being outside the grasp of scientific understanding, or it evolved on our planet spontaneously, through chemical reactions occurring in non living matter lying on the surface of the planet [or some other place]."[4] There are no other alternatives.

On the origin of new life forms, there are only two possible views: common ancestry or a common creator. Either new life forms emerged by natural processes (like natural selection) without any direct intelligent

1. Robert Jastrow, "A Scientist Caught Between Two Faiths," interview by Bill Durbin, in *Christianity Today* (August 6, 1982), 15.

2. George Wald, *Scientific America* (August 1954).

3. Charles Darwin, *The Descent of Man,* in *On the Origin of Species and the Descent of Man,* vol. 49 of Great Books of the Western World (Chicago: University of Chicago Press, 1952), 234, 235.

4. Robert Jastrow, *When the Sun Dies* (New York: Norton, 1977), 62.

intervention, or they were caused by special acts of an intelligent creator. There are only two possible views.

Second, of course there are subviews within both evolution and creation, but this should not eliminate either view being taught in schools. Evolutionists do not agree on the means of evolution. And creationists do not agree on the time or precise nature of creation. But this is beside the point, which is that there are only two basic views on all disputed points of origin. Hence, allowing creation does not open the door for any views other than evolution, nor does allowing evolution open the door for any view other than creation.

Third, this also answers the objection often put forward by evolutionists that the creation/evolution dichotomy does not allow for theistic evolution. It does, for it allows for any combination of the two and only two views on every point of origin (as shown above). So, for example, one could believe in a supernatural cause of the universe or of the universe and first life, and still believe in evolution (natural causes) of new life forms.

Fourth, when there are only two views, then what argues *against* one is an argument *for* the other. Many evolutionists recognize this; Darwin did. He knew that missing links argued against his view. He also knew that immediate appearance of new forms of life argued against his view.[5] Hence, when creationists argue from the sudden appearance of fully formed, fully functioning new life forms in the fossil record, it is not just an argument against evolution; it is also an argument for creation.

Fifth, the evolutionist claim that the creationist view is built simply on the absence of evidence for evolution is completely wrong. It is not the absence of evidence that leads to creationists' conclusions. For example, it is not the absence of evidence for a natural cause of the beginning of the universe that leads to positing a supernatural cause. Rather, it is the presence of multiple evidences that the universe had a beginning.

The presence of evidence for a cause of the universe. Astronomers point to many lines of evidence that converge to demonstrate that the entire material universe came into existence some finite amount of time ago.

5. See Charles Darwin, *On the Origin of Species* (6th ed., 1872; New York University Press, 1988), 154.

This includes 1) the second law of thermodynamics, 2) the expanding universe, 3) the radiation echo, 4) Einstein's general relativity,[6] and 5) the large mass of energy discovered by the COBE space telescope in 1992.

The presence of evidence for an intelligent cause of first life. Likewise, it is not the absence but the *presence* of evidence that leads creationists to posit an intelligent cause of first life. And it is evidence based on two well-established scientific principles: the principle of causality and the principle of uniformity. Respectively, 1) every event has an adequate cause; 2) the kind of causes known by constant conjunction in the present to cause certain kinds of events are assumed to be the kind of causes that produced like events in the past. And it is known by repeated experience in the present that only an intelligent cause produces specified complexity, irreducible complexity, and anticipatory design (such as life has). Hence, it is reasonable to posit an intelligent cause for the beginning of life in the past. The scientific evidence for this is the evidence for the principle of uniformity, namely, this is the kind of cause we regularly and repeatedly see connected with these kinds of events in the present. So, it is not the lack of evidence for a natural cause but the *presence* of evidence for an intelligent cause that leads creationists to posit an intelligent cause for first life. To illustrate, when we come upon an old book in the attic, we naturally assume that someone wrote it; we don't assume that it came to be by mere chance. The assumption that someone wrote the book does not come about because of any *lack* of evidence that it came to be by *chance.* Rather, our assumption of a human author is based on the evidence of specified complexity (in this case, written language) that the book exhibits.

The presence of evidence for an intelligent cause of new life forms. Space does not permit exhaustive elaboration on this final point, but the same logic applies as in regard to first life. We have either a common ancestry or a common creator. And since, other than creation, there are only natural causes to account for the appearance of new life forms, then what argues against one view argues for the other view. Further, positive evidence based on the principle of uniformity that argues for an intelligent cause

6. See Robert Jastrow, *God and the Astronomers* (New York: Norton, 1978); and Hugh Ross, *The Creator and the Cosmos* (Colorado Springs: NavPress, 1995).

of new life forms is further proof for creation. Creationists believe this is not based merely on the absence of a particular means for explaining evolution (because there may be other unknown natural explanations), but it is the presence of positive evidence (based on uniform experience) that leads us to posit an intelligent cause for new life forms.

Evolutionists have every right to continue to find natural causes for whatever they can, based in uniform experience. But in the absence of all known natural causes and in the presence of known causal connections between new life forms and intelligent causes, creationists have every right to present their evidence for an intelligent cause of new life forms. When this is applied consistently, creationists believe the result is fair for both sides. For it turns out that microevolution is based on repeated observational evidence in the present, but macroevolution is not, for two reasons. First, macroevolution involves not current events but past, unobserved events. Second, there are no known forces regularly producing the specified and irreducible complexity in a living form. And in the light of fossil evidence for the sudden, fully formed appearance of new life forms, it is reasonable to posit an intelligent cause of them. Other evidence from the nature of complex systems, interdependence of basic forms of life, anticipatory design in nature, and the like also point to an intelligent cause. And there is no reason this should not be presented as one view, along with the opposing view, in high school science classes.

Conclusion

There is a valid basic dualism between creation and evolution. There are only two views on each point of origin. And whatever argues against one is thereby an argument for the other. But more than that, it is not the mere lack of known natural causes that leads creationists to posit an intelligent cause of life. It is the presence of evidence that points to an intelligent cause.

Of course, it is also true that what argues against one means (mechanism) for evolution does not thereby refute evolution. Other natural causes may be possible, but it is up to the evolutionist to find them. But when there are no known mechanisms, then maybe there are no natural causes. And maybe creationists are right. And where there are no known natural mechanisms and there *are* known positive evidences for intelligent design, then evolutionists (and courts) have no right to disallow the presentation of a creationist's explanation for origins.

One final point. While there may be other natural explanations for the means (mechanism) of evolution, there is only one alternative to natural explanations—and that is an intelligent cause. And what argues against there being any natural cause (since there is only one other kind of cause), is an argument for creation. And what argues positively for an intelligent cause is also thereby an argument against any natural cause. A basic dualism cannot be avoided, and what argues for one argues against the other, since they are mutually exclusive. For either new life forms appeared by purely natural forces, or they did not. And if they did not, then the cause must have been an intelligent one, there being no other kind of cause.

Bibliography

Books

Bacon, Francis. *Novum Organum*. New York: Colonial Press, 1899.

Barbour, Ian. *Issues in Science and Religion*. New York: Harper & Row, 1966.

Beckwith, Francis. *Law, Darwinism, and Public Education*. New York: Rowman & Littlefield, 2003.

Behe, Michael. *Darwin's Black Box*. New York: Free Press, 1996.

Bergman, Jerry, and George Howe. *"Vestigial Organs" Are Fully Functional: A History and Evaluation of the Vestigial Organ Origins Concept*. Kansas City: Creation Research Society Books, 1993.

Bergson, Henri. *Creative Evolution*. Translated by Arthur Mitchell. New York: Macmillan, 1911.

Blackstone, William. *Commentaries on the Laws of England*. Chicago: University of Chicago Press, 2002.

Budziszewski, J. *How to Stay Christian in College*. Colorado Springs: NavPress, 1999.

Campbell, John Angus, and Stephen C. Meyer, eds. *Darwinism, Design, and Public Education*. East Lansing, Mich.: Michigan State University Press, 2003.

Conkin, Paul K. *When All the Gods Trembled: Darwinism, Scopes, and American Intellectuals*. New York: Rowman & Littlefield, 1998.

Darwin, Charles. *On the Origin of Species*. 6th Edition, 1872. New York: New York University Press, 1988.

———. *On the Origin of Species and the Descent of Man*. Great Books of the Western World. Vol. 49. Chicago: University of Chicago Press, 1952.

Davis, Percival, Dean Kenyon, and Charles B. Thaxton. *Of Pandas and People: The Central Question of Biological Origins.* Dallas: Haughton, 1993.

Dawkins, Richard. *The Blind Watchmaker.* New York: Norton, 1987.

Dembski, William. *The Design Revolution: Answering the Toughest Questions About Intelligent Design.* Downers Grove, Ill.: InterVarsity Press, 2004.

Dembski, William, ed. *Mere Creation: Science, Faith, and Intelligent Design.* Downers Grove, Ill.: InterVarsity Press, 1998.

Dembski, William, and Michael Ruse, eds. *Debating Design: From Darwin to DNA.* New York: Cambridge University Press, 2004.

Dewey, John. *A Common Faith.* New Haven, Conn.: Yale University Press, 1960.

DeWolf, David, John West, Carey Luskin, and Jonathan Witt. *Traipsing into Evolution: Intelligent Design and the Kitzmiller vs. Dover Decision.* Seattle: Discovery Institute Press, 2006.

DeWolf, David, et al. "Teaching the Controversy: Is It Science, Religion, or Speech?" In *Darwinism, Design, and Public Education.* Edited by John A. Campbell and Stephen C. Meyer. East Lansing, Mich.: Michigan State University Press, 2003.

Dreisbach, Daniel L. *Thomas Jefferson and the Wall of Separation Between Church and State.* New York: New York University Press, 2002.

Frair, Wayne. *Biology and Creation: An Introduction Regarding Life and Its Origins.* Chino Valley, Ariz.: Creation Research Society Books, 2002.

——. *The Case for Creation.* Chicago; Moody, 1976.

——. *Science and Creation: An Introduction to Some Tough Issues.* Chino Valley, Ariz.: Creation Research Society Books, 2002.

Geisler, Norman. *Is Man the Measure? An Evaluation of Contemporary Humanism.* Grand Rapids, Mich.: Baker, 1983.

——. *Knowing the Truth About Creation.* Eugene, Ore.: Wipf & Stock, 2003.

——. *Miracles and the Modern Mind.* Grand Rapids, Mich.: Baker, 1992.

Geisler, Norman, and Kerby Anderson. *Origin Science: A Proposal for the Creation-Evolution Controversy.* Grand Rapids, Mich.: Baker, 1987.

Geisler, Norman, and William Nix. *A General Introduction to the Bible.* Chicago: Moody, 1986.

Geisler, Norman, and Frank Turek. *I Don't Have Enough Faith to Be an Atheist.* Wheaton, Ill.: Crossway, 2004.

Geisler, Norman, with A. F. Brooke II, and Mark Keough. *The Creator in the Courtroom.* Milford, Mich.: Mott Media, 1982.

Gentry, Robert. *Creation's Tiny Mystery.* Knoxville: Earth Science Association, 1988.

Getting the Facts Straight: A Viewer's Guide to PBS's Evolution. Seattle: Discovery Institute Press, 2001.

Gilkey, Langdon. *Creationism on Trial: Evolution and God at Little Rock*. Charlottesville: University of Virginia Press, 1998.

———. *Maker of Heaven and Earth*. Garden City, N.J.: Anchor, 1965. Reprint, Lanham, Md.: University Press of America, 1985.

Gish, Duane. *Evolution: The Fossils Say No!* San Diego: Creation-Life, 1973.

Goldberg, Bernard. *Bias*. Washington, D.C.: Regnery, 2002.

Haeckel, Ernst. *The Riddle of the Universe at the Close of the Nineteenth Century*. New York: Harper & Brothers, 1900.

Hilleary, William, and Oren W. Metzger. *The World's Most Famous Court Trial: Tennessee Evolution Case*. Cincinnati: National Book Company, 1925.

Hitchcock, James. *The Supreme Court and Religion in American Life*. Vol. 1. Princeton, N.J.: Princeton University Press, 2004.

Hitler, Adolf. *Mein Kampf*. New York: Reynal & Hitchcock, 1940.

Hodge, Charles. "What Is Darwinism?" In *What Is Darwinism? And Other Writings on Science and Religion*. Ed. Mark A. Noll and David N. Livingstone. Grand Rapids, Mich.: Baker, 1994.

Hume, David. *The Letters of David Hume*. 2 Vols. Ed. J. Y. T. Greig. New York: Garland, 1983.

———. *New Letters of David Hume*. Ed. Raymond Klibansky and Ernest Campbell Mossner. Oxford: Clarendon Press, 1954.

Hunter, Cornelius G. *Darwin's God: Evolution and the Problem of Evil*. Grand Rapids, Mich.: Brazos Press, 2001.

Hunter, George William. *A Civic Biology*. New York: American Book Company, 1914.

Huxley, Julian. *Religion Without Revelation*. New York: Harper, 1957.

Hynek, J. Allen. *The Edge of Reality*. Chicago: Regnery, 1975.

Jastrow, Robert. *God and the Astronomers*. New York: Norton, 1978.

———. *When the Sun Dies*. New York: W. W. Norton, 1977.

Johnson, Phillip. *Darwin on Trial*. Washington, D.C.: Regnery, 1991.

———. *Defeating Darwinism*. Downers Grove, Ill.: InterVarsity Press, 1997.

———. *The Wedge of Truth: Splitting the Foundations of Naturalism*. Downers Grove, Ill.: InterVarsity Press, 2002.

Kenny, Anthony. *The Five Ways: St. Thomas Aquinas' Proofs of God's Existence*. New York: Schocken, 1969.

Kolenda, Konstantin. *Religion Without God*. Buffalo, N.Y.: Prometheus, 1976.

Kurtz, Paul, ed. *Humanist Manifestos I and II*. Buffalo, N.Y.: Prometheus, 1973.

Laplace, Pierre. *A Philosophical Essay on Probabilities*. Translated by A. I. Dale. New York: Springer-Verlag, 1995.

Larson, Edward J. *Summer for the Gods: The Scopes Trial and America's Continuing Debate over Science and Religion*. New York: Basic Books, 1997.

———. *Trial and Error: The American Controversy over Creation and Evolution*. New York: Oxford University Press, 2003.

Laudan, Larry. "Science at the Bar—Causes for Concern." in *But Is It Science?* Ed. Michael Ruse. Buffalo, N.Y.: Prometheus, 1996.

Levin, Mark R. *Men in Black: How the Supreme Court Is Destroying America*. Washington, D.C.: Regnery, 2005.

Limbaugh, David. *Persecution*. Washington, D.C.: Regnery, 2004.

Livingston, David. *Darwin's Forgotten Defenders*. Grand Rapids, Mich.: Eerdmans, 1987.

Lubenow, Marvin L. *From Fish to Gish*. San Diego: Creation-Life, 1983.

Maritain, Jacques. *The Dream of Descartes*. Translated by Mabelle L. Andison. London: Editions Poetry, 1946.

Marx, Karl, and Friedrich Engels. *Marx and Engels On Religion*. Moscow: Progress, 1957. Reprint, New York: Schocken, 1964.

Meyer, Stephen C. "The Methodological Equivalence of Design and Descent." In *The Creation Hypothesis*. Ed. J. P. Moreland, Downers Grove, Ill.: InterVarsity Press, 1994.

Montgomery, John Warwick. *The Law Above the Law: Why the Law Needs Biblical Foundations, How Legal Thought Supports Christian Truth, Including Greenleaf's Testimony of the Evangelists*. Minneapolis: Bethany, 1975.

Moore, James R. *The Post-Darwinian Controversies*. New York: Cambridge University Press, 1979.

Moore, John N., and Harold Schultz Slusher, eds. *Biology: A Search for Order in Complexity*. Grand Rapids, Mich.: Zondervan, 1974.

Morris, Henry. *Studies in the Bible and Science*. Grand Rapids, Mich.: Baker, 1966.

Morris, Henry, ed. *Scientific Creationism*. El Cajon, Calif.: Creation-Life, 1974.

O'Leary, Denyse. *Design or By Chance? The Growing Controversy on the Origins of Life in the Universe*. Minneapolis: Augsburg, 2004.

O'Neill, John Jacob. *Prodigal Genius: The Life of Nikola Tesla*. New York: Washburn, 1944. Reprint, Blue Ridge Summit, Pa.: Brotherhood of Life, 1994.

Roberts, Jon H. *Darwinism and the Divine in America: Protestant Intellectuals and Organic Evolution, 1839–1900*. Madison: University of Wisconsin Press, 1988. Reprint, Notre Dame, Ind.: University of Notre Dame Press, 2001.

Ross, Hugh. *The Creator and the Cosmos*. Colorado Springs: NavPress, 1995.

Russell, Jeffrey Burton. *Inventing the Flat Earth: Columbus and Modern Historians.* Westport, Conn.: Praeger, 1997.

Schaeffer, Francis. *A Christian Manifesto.* Westchester, Ill.: Crossway, 1982.

Sears, Alan, and Craig Osten. *The ACLU v. America.* Nashville: Broadman & Holman, 2005.

Tillich, Paul. *Systematic Theology.* 3 Vols. Chicago: University of Chicago Press, 1973–1976.

———. *Ultimate Concern.* New York: Harper & Row, 1965.

Torrey, R. A., ed. *The Fundamentals.* Los Angeles: Bible Institute of Los Angeles, 1917.

Wells, Jonathan. *The Politically Incorrect Guide to Darwinism and Intelligent Design.* Washington, D.C.: Regnery, 2006.

Whitcomb, John C., and Henry Morris. *The Genesis Flood: The Biblical Record and Its Scientific Implications.* Phillipsburg, N.J.: Presbyterian & Reformed, 1961.

Whitehead, John W. *The Separation Illusion.* Milford, Mich.: Mott Media, 1982.

Wiker, Benjamin, and Jonathan Witt. *A Meaningful World: How the Arts and Sciences Reveal the Genius of Nature.* Downers Grove, Ill.: InterVarsity Press, 2006.

Woodward, Thomas. *Doubts About Darwin: A History of Intelligent Design.* Grand Rapids, Mich.: Baker, 2004.

Articles

Agassiz, Louis. "Professor Agassiz on the Origin of Species." *American Journal of Science* 30 (June 1860):143–147.

Asimov, Isaac. "Asimov on Science Fiction." *Science Digest* (October 1981).

Asimov, Isaac, and Duane Gish. "The Genesis War." *Science Digest* (October 1981).

Beckwith, Francis. "Public Education, Religious Establishment, and the Challenge of Intelligent Design." *Notre Dame Journal of Law, Ethics, and Public Policy* 17/2 (2003): 461–519.

Bird, Wendell R. "Freedom from Establishment and Unneutrality in Public School Instruction and Religion School Regulation." *Harvard Journal of Law and Public Policy* (June 1979).

———. "Freedom of Religion and Science Instruction in Public Schools." *Yale Law Journal* 87 (January 1978): 515–570.

Cheng, Andrew. "The Inherent Hostility of Secular Public Education Toward Religion: Why Parental Choice Best Serves the Core Values of the Religion Clauses." *University of Hawaii Law Review* 19 (1997).

Cornelius, Richard M. "The Trial That Made Monkeys Out of the World." *USA Today Magazine* (November 1988).

De Wolf, David K. "Academic Freedom After Edwards." *Regent University Law Review* 13 (2000–2001).

Foster, M. B. "The Christian Doctrine of Creation and the Rise of Modern Natural Science." *Mind* 43/172 (1934).

Frair, Wayne. "Effects of the 1981 Arkansas Trial on the Creationist Movement." In *Proceedings of the Fourth International Conference on Creationism*, August 3–8, 1998. Technical Symposium Sessions. Ed. R. E. Walsh. Pittsburgh: Creation Science Fellowship, 1998. 229–239.

Geisler, Norman. "A Scientific Basis for Creation: The Principle of Uniformity." *Creation Evolution Journal* 4/3 (Summer 1984).

House, H. Wayne. "Darwinism and the Law: Can Non-Naturalistic Scientific Theories Survive Constitutional Challenge?" *Regent University Law Review* 355 (Spring 2001).

Jastrow, Robert. "A Scientist Caught Between Two Faiths." *Christianity Today* (August 8, 1982).

Lewin, Roger. "Where Is the Science in Creation Science?" *Science* 215 (January 8, 1982): 141–146.

Lewontin, Richard. "Billions and Billions of Demons." *New York Review of Books* (January 9, 1996).

O'Neill, Michael R. "Government's Denigration of Religion: Is God the Victim of Discrimination in Our Public Schools?" Pepperdine Law Review 21 (1994).

Wald, George. "The Origin of Life." *Scientific America* 191 (August 1954).

"Wallace, Alfred." In *The Encyclopedia of Philosophy*. Vol. 8. Ed. Paul Edwards. New York: Macmillan, 1967.

Whitehead, John, and John Conlan. "The Establishment of the Religion of Secular Humanism and Its First Amendment Implications." *Texas Tech Law Review* 1 (1978–1979).

Yockey, Herbert. "Self-Organization Origin of Life Scenarios and Information Theory." *Journal of Theoretical Biology* 91 (1981): 13–31.

Legal Cases

Abington School District v. Schempp, 374 U.S. 203 (1963).

Aguillard v. Treen, 440 So. 2d (1983); 720 F.2d (CA5 1983); 634 F. Supp. (ED La. 1985).

Bartels v. State of Iowa, 262 U.S. 404 (1923).

Bethel School Dist. No. 403 v. Fraser, 478 U.S. 675 (1986).

Bishop v. Aronov, 926 F. 2d 1066 (11th Cir. 1991).

Board of Education v. Allen, 392 U.S. 236 (1968).

Brandon v. Board of Education, 487 F. Supp. 1219, 1230 (N.D. N.Y.), affd., 635 F. 2d 971 (2nd Cir. 1980).

Cantwell v. Connecticut, 310 U.S. 296 (1940).

Celotex Corp. v. Catrett, 477 U.S. 317 (1986).

Chrysler Corp. v. Brown, 441 U.S. 281 (1979).

Clements v. Fashing, 457 U.S. 957 (1982).

Committee for Public Education & Religious Liberty v. Nyquist, 413 U.S. 756 (1973).

Committee for Public Education & Religious Liberty v. Reagan, 444 U.S. 646 (1980).

Davis v. Beason, 133 U.S. 333 (1890).

Dred Scott v. Sanford, 60 U.S. 393 (1857).

Edwards v. Aguillard, 482 U.S. 578 (1987).

Engel v. Vitale, 370 U.S. 421 (1962).

Epperson v. State of Arkansas, 393 U.S. 97 (1968).

Everson v. Board of Education of Ewing, 330 U.S. 1 (1947).

Fed. Energy Admin. v. Algonquin SNG, Inc., 426 U.S. 548, 564 (1976).

Fletcher v. Peck, 6 Cranch 87 (1810).

Freiler v. Tangipahoa Board of Education, No. 94-3577 (1997).

Grand Rapids School District v. Ball, 473 U.S. 373 (1985).

Harris v. McRae, 448 U.S. 297 (1980).

Hazelwood School District v. Kuhlmeier, 484 U.S. 260 (1988).

Hobbie v. Unemployment Appeals Comm'n of Florida, 480 U.S. 136 (1987).

Illinois v. Krull, 480 U.S. 340 (1987).

Jay v. Boyd, 351 U.S. 345 (1956).

Joseph Burstyn, Inc. v. Wilson, 343 U.S. 495 (1952).

Keith v. Louisiana Department of Education, 553 F. Supp. 295 (MD La. 1982).

Keyishian v. Board of Regents, 385 U.S. 589 (1967).

Kitzmiller v. Dover Area School District, 400 F. Supp. 2d 707 (M.D. Pa. 2005).

Larkin v. Grendel's Den, Inc., 459 U.S. 116 (1982).

Lee v. Weisman, 505 U.S. 577 (1992).

LeVake v. Independent School District, 656, CX-99-793 (D.Minn. 2000).

Lemon v. Kurtzman, 403 U.S. 602 (1971).

Levitt v. Committee for Public Education & Religious Liberty, 413 U.S. 472 (1973).

Los Angeles [City of] v. Preferred Communications, 476 U.S. 488 (1986).

Lynch v. Donnelly, 465 U.S. 668 (1984).

Marsh v. Chambers, 463 U.S. 783 (1983).

McCollum v. Board of Education, 333 U.S. 203 (1948).

McCreary County v. American Civil Liberties Union of Kentucky, 545 U.S. 844 (2005).

McDonald v. Board of Election Comm'rs of Chicago, 394 U.S. 802 (1969).

McGowan v. State of Maryland, 366 U.S. 420 (1961).

McLean v. Arkansas Board of Education, 529 F. Supp. 1255 (E.D. Ark. 1982).

Meek v. Pittenger, 421 U.S. 349 (1975).

Meyer v. State of Nebraska, 262 U.S. 390 (1923).

Modrovich v. Allegheny County, 385 F.3d 397 (2004).

Moore v. Gaston County Board of Education, 357 F. Supp. 1037 (W. D. N. C. 1973).

Mozert v. Hawkins County Board of Education, 827 F. 2d 1058 (1987).

Mueller v. Allen, 463 U.S. 388 (1983).

NLRB v. Jones & Laughlin Steel Corp., 301 U.S. 1 (1937).

Palmer v. Board of Education of the City of Chicago, 603 F. 2d 1271 (7th Cir. 1979).

Palmer v. Thompson, 403 U.S. 217 (1971).

Peloza v. Capistrano Unified School District, 917 F. 2d 1004 (1994).

Pierce v. Society of Sisters, 268 U.S. 510 (1925).

Planned Parenthood v. Casey, 505 U.S. 833 (1992).

Reed v. Van Hoven, 237 F. Supp. 48 (W. D. MI 1965).

Richards v. United States, 369 U.S. 1 (1962).

Roe v. Wade, 410 U.S. 113 (1973).

Rostker v. Goldberg, 453 U.S. 57 (1981).

Scopes v. State of Tennessee, 105, I20, 289 S.W. 363, 367 (1927).

Segraves v. State of California, Ca. Super. Ct. 278978U (1981).

Shelton v. Tucker, 364 U.S. 479 (1960).

Sherbert v. Verner, 374 U.S. 398 (1963).

Smith v. State of Mississippi, 242 So. 2d (1970).

State of Tennessee v. John Scopes, 5232 (1925).

Steele v. Waters, 527 S.W. 2d 72 (1975).

Stone v. Graham, 449 U.S. 39 (1980).

Texas Education Agency v. Leeper, 893 S. W. 2d 432 (Tex. 1994).

Thomas v. Review Board, Indiana Employment Security Division, 450 U.S. 707 (1981).

Tilton v. Richardson, 403 U.S. 672 (1971).

Tinker v. Des Moines Independent Community School District, 393 U.S. 503 (1969).

Torcaso v. Watkins, 367 U.S. 488 (1961).

United States v. Emmons, 410 U.S. 396 (1973).

United States v. O'Brien, 391 U.S. 367 (1968).

United States v. Seeger, 380 U.S. 163 (1965).

Van Orden v. Perry, 545 U.S. 677 (2005).

Village of Arlington Heights v. Metropolitan Housing Corp., 429 U.S. 252 (1977).

Wallace v. Jaffree, 472 U.S. 38 (1985).

Walz v. Tax Comm'n of New York City, 397 U.S. 664 (1970).

Washington Ethical Society v. District of Columbia, 101 U.S. App. D.C. 371, 249 F. 2d. 127 (1957).

Watson v. Jones, 80 U.S. (13 Wall.) 679, 728 (1872).

Webster v. New Lenox School District, 917 F. 2d. 1004 (7th Cir. 1990).

Widmar v. Vincent, 454 U.S. 263 (1981).

Willoughby v. Stever, No. 15574-75 (D. D. C. May 18, 1973); affd. 504 F. 2d 271 (D. C. Cir. 1974), cert. denied, 420 U.S. (1975).

Wisconsin v. Yoder, 406 U.S. 205 (1972).

Witters v. Washington Department of Services for Blind, 474 U.S. 481 (1986).

Wolman v. Walter, 433 U.S. 229 (1977).

Wright v. Houston Independent School District, 366 F. Supp. 1208 (S.D. 1972).

Zorach v. Clauson, 343 U.S. 306 (1952).

Zykan v. Warsaw (Indiana) Community School Corporation and Warsaw School Board of Trustees, 631 F. 2d. 1300 (7th Cir. 1980).

Index